# Kwanzaa

Since 1966, Kwanzaa has been celebrated as a black holiday tradition—an annual recognition of cultural pride in the African-American community. But how did this holiday originate, and what is its broader cultural significance?

*Kwanzaa: Black Power and the Making of the African-American Holiday Tradition* explores the political beginning and later expansion of Kwanzaa, from its start as a Black Power holiday, to its current place as one of the most mainstream of the black holiday traditions. For those wanting to learn more about this alternative observance practiced by countless African-Americans and how Kwanzaa fits into the larger black holiday tradition, Keith Mayes gives an accessible and definitive account of the movements and individuals that pushed to make this annual celebration a reality, and shows how African-Americans brought the black freedom struggle to the American calendar.

Clear and thoughtful, *Kwanzaa: Black Power and the Making of the African-American Holiday Tradition* is the perfect introduction to what is now the quintessential African-American holiday.

**Keith A. Mayes** is Assistant Professor of History and African American & African Studies at the University of Minnesota, Twin Cities.

# Kwanzaa

Black Power and the Making of the
African-American Holiday Tradition

**Keith A. Mayes**

Routledge
Taylor & Francis Group

NEW YORK AND LONDON

First published 2009
by Routledge
270 Madison Ave, New York, NY 10016

Simultaneously published in the UK
by Routledge
2 Park Square, Milton Park, Abingdon, Oxon OX14 4RN

*Routledge is an imprint of the Taylor & Francis Group, an informa business*

© 2009 Taylor & Francis

Typeset in ITC Legacy Serif by
RefineCatch Limited, Bungay, Suffolk
Printed and bound in the United States of America on acid-free paper by
Walsworth Publishing Company, Marceline, MO

*Library of Congress Cataloging in Publication Data*
Mayes, Keith A., 1967-
    Kwanzaa : black power and the making of the African-American holiday
tradition / Keith A. Mayes.
        p. cm.
    Includes bibliographical references and index.
    1. Kwanzaa – United States – History.  2. African Americans – Social life
and customs.  3. Black power – United States. I. Title.
    GT4403.M39 2009
    394.26120973 – dc22                                     2009001049

ISBN 10: 0–415–99854–9 (hbk)
ISBN 10: 0–415–99855–7 (pbk)
ISBN 10: 0–203–87486–2 (ebk)

ISBN 13: 978–0–415–99854–3 (hbk)
ISBN 13: 978–0–415–99855–0 (pbk)
ISBN 13: 978–0–203–87486–8 (ebk)

For

DENISE
MYLES
MARCUS

# Contents

## Chapter 5

# Illustrations

Every effort has been made to cite completely and fairly the original source for each work included in this book. In the event that something has been inadvertently used or cited incorrectly, every effort will be made in subsequent editions to rectify the error. We offer our sincere thanks to all of the sources that were courteous enough to help us reproduce the images in this volume.

## CHAPTER 2

**Figure 1:** Maulana Karenga teaching Swahili in Los Angeles, 1965. Courtesy of Library of Congress, Prints & Photographs Division, Look Magazine Photograph Collection, LC-L9-66-2755-W

## CHAPTER 3

**Figure 2:** Children's Kwanzaa celebration in school. Courtesy of Library of Congress, Prints & Photographs Division, Look Magazine Photograph Collection, LC-L9-695396-II

**Figure 3:** Karamu Ya Imani held in Chicago—one of the largest public Kwanzaa celebrations during the 1970s. Courtesy of Mansong Kulubally

**Figure 4:** Some Positive Party Organization promoting pre-Kwanzaa Workshop in 1980 in Jacksonville, Florida. Courtesy of Mansong Kulubally

# Acknowledgments

Writing a book is never a sole endeavor. I have incurred many debts over the years as this enterprise has passed through the various stages. First and foremost, I would like to thank my dissertation advisor, former Edwards Professor of History, Nell Irvin Painter of Princeton University, now retired from teaching but whose graduate seminar, "Social History" led me to choose the topic Kwanzaa. Not only did Nell allow me to engage my seminar colleagues about Kwanzaa and other ways African-Americans remembered the past, but dared me to take the subject up as a dissertation topic. I would also like to thank current and former members in Princeton's History Department who helped shape the project in its infancy, notably the dissertation committee Dan Rodgers, Colin Palmer, William Van Deburg (outside reader) from the University of Wisconsin–Madison. A special thanks to Bill Jordan for teaching the Mellon summer dissertation seminar and for the laughs on the softball field about my continuous overstatement of Kwanzaa celebrants. Thank you to Stan Katz of Princeton University's Woodrow Wilson School and Director of the Center for Arts and Cultural Policy Studies, also Liz Lunbeck, Dirk Hartog, Tera Hunter, Kevin Kruse, Sheldon Garon, and Christine Stansell. Thank you to the Princeton Center for African American Studies and its faculty, Noliwe Rooks, Al Raboteau, Eddie Glaude and Cornel West. I also would like to thank my graduate student colleagues for six years of fun and commiseration: Cheryl Hicks, Sam Roberts, Nicole Sackley, Jesse Hoffnuff-Goskoff, Todd Stevens, Crystal Feimster, Barbara Krauthamer,

Ken Mack, David Silverman, James Wilson, Jarbel Rodriguez, Chad Williams, Anastasia Curwood, Madeline Lopez, Sara Igo, Tammy Brown, and Eric Love. Equally important were colleagues in other departments that evolved into lasting friendships: Andrea Morris (molecular biology), Tariq al-Jamil (religion), Kevin Jones (Woodrow Wilson School of Public Policy), Elaine Bonner-Tompkins (Woodrow Wilson School) and her husband and very dear friend of mine from Columbia University's School of Social Work, Dr. Willie Tompkins, who keeps me laughing on a weekly basis about our New York upbringing and the twist and turns of our lives (or I should say mine).

My colleagues at the University of Minnesota, Twin Cities have been tremendously supportive, ensuring that the book gets published. I want to especially thank my department, African American & African Studies, including Rose Brewer, John Wright, Alexs Pate, Walt Jacobs, Njeri Githire, Yuichiro Onishi, Keletso Atkins, Vicky Coifman, Pearl Barner, Hisham Khalek, Angaluki Muaka, Ben Pike, Pam Fletcher, Yolanda Williams, Tade Okediji, Sidow Mohammad, Agnes Mrutu-Maliaka, and Charlene Hayes. From the Department of History I would like to thank various faculty writing circles that read portions of the manuscript: Malinda Lindquist, David Chang, Tracey Deutsch, Kevin Murphy, Hiromi Mizuno, Christopher Isett, Patrick McNamara, J.B. Shank, and Tom Wolfe. I would also like to thank from the History Department: Allen Issacman, Erika Lee, Tamara Giles-Vernick, M.J. Maynes, Sarah-Jane Mathieu, Lisa Norling, Michelle Wagner, Kirsten Fischer, and Eric Weitz. A very special thanks goes to Rod Ferguson from the Department of American Studies who read and commented on much of the manuscript. Thank you also to American Studies faculty: Jeannie O'Brien, Jennifer Pierce, Elaine May, Trica Keaton, and Riv-Ellen Prell. Thank you to faculty in other departments: August Nimtz (political science), Karen Ho (anthropology), Douglas Hartmann and Enid Logan (sociology), and Kirt Wilson (communications). Out of all of the names above I need to isolate my tenure committee who kept me on track each year: Rose Brewer, Rod Ferguson, and Jeannie O'Brien. Thank you to both the University of Minnesota and Princeton University for research grants and time away from regular duties to write.

I would like to thank the family of colleagues in the book's two main fields. These scholars have either read parts of the manuscript, included chapters in their anthologies, used parts of it in their classes, or shared a conference dais with me. Thank you to both my Black Power colleagues, including Scot Brown, Peniel Joseph, Komozi Woodard, Rhonda Williams, William Van Deburg, Hasan Jeffries, Stephen Ward, Jeffrey O.G. Ogbar, and Fanon Che Wilkins, and to my American holiday colleagues, Len Travers, Matthew Dennis, Ellen Litwicki, Mitch Katchun, Jack Santino, and Leigh Eric Schmidt. A special thank you to filmmaker and documentarian extraordinaire M.K. Asante, Jr. for including me in the making of the Kwanzaa documentary, *The Black Candle: A Kwanzaa Celebration*, narrated by Maya Angelou.

I would also like to thank the scores of individuals associated with the history of Kwanzaa and other black holidays that granted me interviews, particularly Maulana Karenga, and former members of the US Organization, namely Clyde Halisi and Ngoma Ali. Also, Maisha Ongoza from the Kwanzaa Cooperative not only was a very special interviewee but shared documents and many stories about the development of Kwanzaa in Philadelphia. Likewise, I would like to thank Ayo Handy-Kendi for sharing stories about Kwanzaa in Washington, DC and her own history in the creation of other black holidays. In addition, a big thank you to the libraries at Princeton University, particularly Emily Belcher, the Schomburg Center for Research in Black Culture, the Library of Congress, UCLA, especially the Center for African American Studies library under the direction of Itibari Zulu, Howard University's Moorland-Spingarn Library, the University of Chicago, the University of Minnesota, the University of California, Berkeley, the University of Illinois at Urbana-Champaign, and the University of Wisconsin-Madison. Without the staff support and cooperation in locating materials this book could not have been written.

Thank you to my current and former students at the University of Minnesota. Not only have they endured my lectures and ruminations on civil rights and black power, they have helped me with some aspect of the manuscript, especially my two graduate student advisees now PhDs, Andrea Burns (Department of History) and Nalo Johnson (Department of American Studies). Six other students deserve honorable mention: Joyce Bell (now Assistant Professor of Sociology at the University of Georgia), Anne Mitchell (former graduate student in Educational Psychology and currently a doctoral candidate in Women's Studies at the Ohio State University), Alisha Volante (current graduate student in the History Department), Nneka Onyilofor (Masters in Liberal Studies and bibliography compiler),

Matthew Stofflet (former student in African American & African Studies, currently a graduate student at the University of Massachusetts, Amherst), and Jennifer Jones (an undergraduate from the University of Michigan who spent a summer with me at the University of Minnesota in an undergraduate research program and traveled with me to the Library of Congress), current graduate student in Princeton's Department of History.

During the last writing phase of this project with all of the exigencies of teaching and advising, I escaped to three locations that were critical in completing the manuscript. I learned some time ago that to get any writing and thinking accomplished I had to leave my campus office and the university grounds to find other places to work. I found those places in Caribou Coffee in Apple Valley and St. Louis Park, Minnesota as well as inside the library of the University of St. Thomas Law School in downtown Minneapolis. Not only did the employees and students wonder about the man who came with stacks of books and documents seemingly taking up all available space, eventually they could not help asking me a panoply of questions about who I was and what I was working on. After a few months in the Caribou locations, I was receiving free drinks from the employee staff, and was adopted by the law school's class of 2010 as a regular member of their study groups. As they worked on legal briefs and memos, I sat with them revising manuscript chapters.

A very large thank you must go to my editor at Routledge Kimberly Guinta, her assistant Matthew Kopel, and the entire production team in New York and the UK, particularly Siân Findlay, Sophie Cox, and Heidi Cormode. I was introduced to Kim through Peniel Joseph's anthology on Black Power. Kim embraced my project from the very beginning, seeing the potential in the history of Kwanzaa and Black Power in ways I could not. Kim has been enthusiastically gracious and kind as much as she has been thorough and exacting in every step of the anonymous review and subsequent revision process. Kim, by the time *Kwanzaa: Black Power and the Making of the African-American Holiday Tradition* comes out in 2009, the second book currently in progress will go to press. I promise.

Finally, I must thank my family, close friends, and people there with me from the very beginning for their unwavering support throughout this entire process, especially Rose Marie Judkins and the entire Judkins family, sons Myles Mayes and Marcus Mayes, Keith Mayes, Sr., Marion Mayes, Michael and Edith Mayes along with the rest of the Los Angeles Mayes contingent, Daphne Hinkson-Moxam, Karen Spearman and family, Mikiesha Terrell and family, my childhood buddy from New York City, Eric "one day I'll move to North Carolina" Stewart, Wynfred Russell, and the City University of New York (CUNY) faculty who dared me to make the leap into the life of the mind: Louis P. Masur, Darren Staloff, David Jaffee, Robert Twombly, Robert Viscusi, Saul Brody, and Gail Smith.

This book is dedicated to my mother, Denise Mayes, who passed away in 1999, neither witnessing her son from Harlem obtain that PhD from Princeton, nor seeing her two grandchildren, Myles and Marcus. Your voice, laughter, and wisdom lives with me daily.

# Introduction

*Kwanzaa: Black Power and the Making of the African-American Holiday Tradition* examines the creation and development of Kwanzaa as a response to racial oppression that manifested in black cultural and holiday invisibility in the twentieth century. As black civil rights organizations and white policymakers focused on changing Jim Crow laws, Black Power cultural workers provided black America with new ways of celebrating and observing. For Black Power activists, Kwanzaa was just as important as the Civil Rights Act of 1964 or the Voting Rights Act of 1965. Kwanzaa was their answer to what they understood as the ubiquity of white cultural practices that oppressed them as thoroughly as had Jim Crow laws. This book explores how Kwanzaa fits into the larger black holiday tradition, bridging older black observances that preceded it with those that came after its creation in 1966. *Kwanzaa* also examines the process of holiday appropriation. The appropriation of Kwanzaa by American corporate and cultural institutions in the 1980s and 1990s captures the holiday's development and yields how Kwanzaa served the needs of institutions outside black America. By the last decade of the twentieth century, Kwanzaa ceased being the sole property of the Black Power community; it had been embraced by a broader segment of African-Americans, corporate and religious bodies, cultural and media institutions, and the federal government. By looking at the holiday over time, the book will explore two different Kwanzaas, or two moments in Kwanzaa's history: the Black Power Kwanzaa created by Maulana Karenga and promoted by black cultural nationalists, and secondly, the "multicultural" Kwanzaa—the holiday of corporations and mainstream cultural institutions. By investigating Kwanzaa's trajectory, this book addresses how the Civil Rights and Black Power movement changed course, re-envisioning itself by making "holiday" civil rights a central concern before being co-opted by American public culture.

The changing discourse on race and the repositioning of people of color in the post-Civil Rights and Black Power era is historically unique considering what Kwanzaa initially represented and ultimately where it ended up. The holiday was engendered during the oppositional climate of the Black Power period, specifically cultural Black Power—that stratum of the movement that privileged African language, clothing, and holiday rituals. However, by the late 1980s and early 1990s, Kwanzaa had become part of mainstream American culture, no longer the exclusive property of black cultural nationalists or the wider African-American population. The Civil Rights and Black Power movement's ability to open up American society and the acceleration of consumer capitalism in the second half of the twentieth century meant that cultural militancy of Kwanzaa's sort would not remain free of market and mainstream institutions. It would not take long before Kwanzaa, which included an invented Africa, essentialized notions of race, and rabid critiques of Christmas to be transformed by corporate America to sell mass-produced consumer goods and services in its name.

Corporate America and white cultural institutions did not come to Kwanzaa empty-handed or headed. They sized up Kwanzaa and approached the holiday using the discourse of multiculturalism. The politics of identity and the multicultural mood that swept the nation in the 1980s and 1990s greatly contributed to the holiday's appeal in American public culture. The multicultural milieu of the last two decades of the twentieth century contributed mightily to Kwanzaa's shift from a provincial Black Power cultural holiday to a recognizable black celebration. The nationalist language of the early Kwanzaa centered profoundly on concepts of power, liberation, and revolution. One generation later, cultural institutions like museums, religious bodies, educational institutions, as well as the media and the federal government advanced Kwanzaa in the name of diversity, recognition, inclusion, and goodwill. As a racial cultural holiday associated uniquely with

African-Americans, Kwanzaa fit snugly into the new discourse on corporate and institutional multiculturalism.

Chapter 1 sketches out the black holiday tradition, bridging modern-day black holiday observances with earlier ones. While Kwanzaa represents one of many holidays in the tradition, the history of Kwanzaa cannot be understood apart from it. When holiday critic Basir Mchawi uttered the words in 1974, "it is time for we as black people to put down crazy cracker celebrations," his declaration tied directly into Frederick Douglass' statement expressed in 1852 about Fourth of July celebrations. One hundred and twenty-two years may have separated the statements, but a century or more of American holiday criticism and black holiday-making forever linked them in history. Kwanzaa is part of a long tradition in African-American holiday-making that serves as an index for certain historical junctures in black oppression. I begin the book with this acknowledgment. The black holiday tradition never existed on its own; it needed the American holiday tradition and its accompanied calendar to do its work of exclusion and marginalization. Douglass' and Mchawi's remarks were conceived by a kind of Jim Crow reality on the American calendar that rendered black participation in mainstream holiday observances minimal to nonexistent. What emerged was the black protest calendar, providing African-Americans temporal space for their holidays and commemorations. The black protest calendar was also a perennial reminder of what events and issues were important in black America. Though the black holiday tradition is long, Chapter 1's contribution is to explain the growth of Black Power holidays and their attempt to challenge the hegemony of dominant American holiday traditions: Kwanzaa (December 26–January 1) versus Christmas (December 25); Umoja Karamu—the black Thanksgiving (fourth Sunday in November) versus Thanksgiving's Day (fourth Thursday in November); and Black Solidarity Day (first Monday in November) versus Election Day. Not only were these novel observances part of the twentieth-century phenomenon of creating a distinctly black protest calendar, these new observances also underscored a certain logic in black holiday placement. Though the preoccupation of placing black holidays next to dominant American ones began with July Fifth celebrations in the nineteenth century, Kwanzaa re-makes this tradition in the late twentieth century.

Chapter 2 will examine Kwanzaa's beginnings in black invention politics, capturing the process of Kwanzaa's "making" and Maulana Karenga—

the holiday founder's "remaking." Kwanzaa's making at the level of holiday and Karenga's re-making at the level of the individual speaks profoundly to a convergence of black social movements in the United States and new thinking about the continent of Africa. This chapter will explore Ronald Everett's transformation—from student at Los Angeles City College and UCLA—into Maulana Karenga—social activist, ascertaining the impact of African independence movements, civil rights, and Black Power on Karenga's thinking and his subsequent creation of Kwanzaa. For Karenga, the rise of Africa meant a veritable cultural return to continental roots and codifying this return into a form of US-based black cultural nationalism for the purposes of black cultural and holiday liberation. But Karenga did not import an "original" Africa; he imagined one after an existential crisis with Christmas in December 1965. Chapter 2 will examine this imagined return by looking at the dilemma Christmas posed and the multiple discourses on Africa that Karenga drew from to create Kwanzaa. The chapter will also examine Kwanzaa's constituent parts: borrowed syncretic African agricultural rituals from different parts of the continent. This chapter will not only introduce the man and the organization that created Kwanzaa, but ask what kind of Africa did they offer black Americans. After mapping Kwanzaa and its ceremonial procedures, I will deconstruct the holiday's African and black American components and demonstrate how Kwanzaa fits into a larger pattern of US-based black nationalist performance. The Black Power Movement enshrined black nationalist performance in the form of Afros, raised fists, and African dashikis. To partake in Kwanzaa was to perform "Africa" by speaking and greeting in Swahili, lighting candles, pouring libations, calling on the name of the ancestors, as well as feasting during the last week in December.

Chapter 3 explores Kwanzaa's promotion during the Black Power period. If Kwanzaa was about a certain kind of cultural performance, it would then need a safe political space to operate effectively. Using the literature of the public sphere as a point of departure, I posit the notion of secondary and tertiary black nationalist publics—spheres that existed outside the bourgeois and mainstream black public sphere of mainline denominational churches and civil rights organizations. Most often, the mainstream black public sphere was not a safe political space for Kwanzaa to evolve and mature, particularly in the early years of the holiday's history.

The need for alternative spaces arose. This chapter takes up the question of Kwanzaa promotion within the Black Power public—the secondary black counter-public of black independent schools, community-based organizations, community centers, and to some extent, the major arteries of a neighborhood. The apparatuses of Kwanzaa promotion within what I call urban networks of Black Power used large public feasts, parades, and pre-Kwanzaa celebrations in unique institutional spaces to educate African-Americans about this new holiday. This chapter will show how black media, black nationalist churches, black museums, and predominantly black public schools played a pivotal role in introducing the holiday to the larger African-American community. By centering activist men and women as well as apolitical blacks, this chapter underscores Kwanzaa's emergence as a Black Power holiday in black neighborhoods across the United States prior to transcending its boundaries into the American mainstream.

Chapter 4 explores the theme of appropriation, but first within the context of economic partnership between black producer and black consumer. Kwanzaa's fourth principle, Ujamaa (cooperative economics), set the terms for commercial activity around the holiday and provided a blue-print for black economic uplift, only to be met with competition from white corporate interests. The presence of white-owned corporations in racial and ethnic markets like Kwanzaa underscored the confluence of multiculturalism and corporate culture in the last two decades of the twentieth century. Using the theory of "corporations of culture," Chapter 4 examines the politics of Kwanzaa's appropriation by corporations as well as museums and churches. Despite their different functions, these institutions partake in a similar appropriative politic. The fact that the end result is not profit for museums, churches, and schools does not hide the absence of marketplace intent. So Kwanzaa with seemingly no monetary exchange value in the cultural institutional context equally became a fetishized and reified commodity in the name of holiday multiculturalism. Thus, Kwanzaa's growing visibility and acceptance in the late twentieth century appeared endemically tied to the marketplace decision-making and appropriation of corporate, cultural, and media institutions, with the result of legitimizing the holiday in American public culture.

Chapter 5 assesses Kwanzaa's impact on the black holiday tradition and surveys black holiday development in the 1970s, 1980s, and 1990s.

Kwanzaa's mainstream appearance and success has generated additional black holidays: an alternative Valentine's Day—Black Love Day; an alternative Memorial Day—Ancestor Honor Day; an alternative Easter—A Day of Praise; and an alternative Columbus Day—African Holocaust Day. Indeed, these black holidays represent Kwanzaa's competitors in American public culture, with their creators hoping for a similar growth pattern within black communities as well as recognition beyond the boundaries of black America. But in the last twenty years Kwanzaa's greatest holiday competitors have not been those above, but more Martin Luther King, Jr. Day, Black History Month, and to a lesser extent, Malcolm X Day and Juneteenth. If Chapter 1 through Chapter 4 establishes the historical fact that there is indeed something called a black holiday tradition, then Chapter 5 will ask and answer the question of what is the state of that tradition in the late twentieth and early twenty-first centuries. Do any of these holidays have what I call calendar legitimacy? Calendar legitimacy in American culture can come in different forms, but the form that is most recognized is federal and state acknowledgment of some sort. If black holidays have not achieved a certain kind of calendar legitimacy, I argue that these holidays have instead remained part of the black protest calendar, doing the critical work they have always done.

The critical work black holidays engage in are annual conversations about black identity, the African-American past, and black America's access to the larger American public. As a recognizable public holiday, Kwanzaa commences a conversation about social justice, black advancement and retrogression, as well as the importance of cultural memory that continues with the arrival of Martin Luther King, Jr. Day in January and Black History Month in February. Thus, inasmuch as *Kwanzaa: Black Power and the Making of the African-American Holiday Tradition* is about Kwanzaa, the book is also about how Kwanzaa fits simultaneously into the black holiday tradition and its American counterpart. But no matter how much Kwanzaa is appropriated by American institutions, Kwanzaa was and still is about taking aim at the American calendar. Taking aim at the American calendar by developing separate observances was to simultaneously develop a black protest calendar and bring the black freedom struggle to the American calendar.

# CHAPTER 1

# *The Black Protest Calendar and the African-American Holiday Tradition*

On July 4, 1852, the black abolitionist Frederick Douglass provided one of the first scathing criticisms of black participation in American holidays:

> What have I or those I represent to do with your national independence? I am not included within the pale of this glorious anniversary! Your high independence only reveals the immeasurable distance between us. The blessings in which you this day rejoice are not enjoyed in common. The rich inheritance of justice, liberty, prosperity, and independence bequeathed by your fathers is shared by you, not by me. This Fourth of July is *yours*, not mine. *You* may rejoice, *I* must mourn.[1]

Nearly one hundred and twenty-two years later, another calendar critic named Basir Mchawi similarly appraised American holidays, but called the entire American holiday tradition into question: "It's time that we as Black People with Black families put down *crazy cracker* celebrations for something that is for us. Think about it: Easter, Thanksgiving, Passover, Chanukah, X-Mas, Columbus, George Washington, Independence Day, on and on . . . Zillions of white holidays and lily white images—but nothing for us. Think about all of the negative effects of these so-called holidays."[2] On the surface, the criticisms rendered by Douglass and Mchawi explore the theme of black exclusion and omission from mainstream holiday celebrations, Douglass at the level of citizenship highlighting the contradiction between slavery and liberty, Mchawi at the level of race asking about their celebratory value for African-Americans. To say that the statements above allow us to understand the problems blacks faced in participating in American holiday fetes is to be correct, but the appraisals given by Douglass and Mchawi do so much more.

Douglass and Mchawi's commentary lets us know that holidays and the calendar that annually present them are not solely times of leisure and celebration, of gaiety and frivolity. Holidays are political and the calendar represents a site of struggle, contestation and defeat, sometimes victory and triumph. Hence, the American calendar is worth exploring. Deconstructing the calendar allows us to enlarge our understanding of the spatial arrangements of social movements, to take our eye off of the street, the legislature, and the judiciary for a moment and to discover other "places" of political activity. If we understand the calendar not as a series of days but as spaces to be filled up and occupied by groups in society, the calendar takes on new meaning. Days on the calendar are manifestations of power and in many ways they represent a form of property. Claimants to the calendar have historically been both dominant and subordinate groups who have "filled up," or to use a more apt term, "politicized" the calendar through the creation of their holidays. Matthew Dennis has aptly discerned that "... holiday rites have functioned as barometers of the political situation."[3] Though the holidays of subordinate groups are political and have been initiated, developed and sustained over long periods of time, Douglass and Mchawi's consensus remarks speak to who really owns and controls calendar space in American life and culture. The metaphor of "filling up" or "occupying" spaces on the American calendar is what I will unravel in this chapter. First, I will offer some thoughts on the spatial arrangements of American holidays, then open up and examine a new area of Black Power inquiry: the black protest calendar and the logic of holiday placement. By doing so, my goal is to show the depth of the black holiday tradition and its proclivity in the late twentieth century to operate as an alternative tradition with a penchant to de-legitimize mainstream American holidays. Indeed, the entire black holiday tradition can be seen as an alternative tradition to mainstream American observances, but some black holidays in the nineteenth century have been more about black incorporation onto the mainstream American calendar and bringing African-Americans as a people into the fold of American citizenship. Other black holidays have sought to move African-Americans away from mainstream American observances. If the black freedom struggle has exhibited this propensity: oftentimes wanting in, sometimes desiring to be out, then the black holiday tradition, at least in its Black Power phase, was no different. To speak of a black protest calendar is not only to acknowledge and take seriously what Douglass and Mchawi had to say about American mainstream holidays, but to deeply understand how African-Americans used the calendar to perennialize their struggle and annually politicize themselves into existence.

## THE POLITICS OF CALENDAR SPACE IN AMERICAN CULTURE

Calendars are living entities, forever changing and always in process. Clearly, calendars reveal more than holidays; they represent space and time, things astrological, daylight savings, solstices—which keep us all in a day-to-day, week-to-week, month-to-month, and season-to-season rhythm. But to talk specifically about a black protest calendar is to simultaneously examine the evolving American holiday calendar, specifically, how the American calendar coalesced around white commemorative interests to the exclusion of people of color. Ellen M. Litwicki has rightly maintained that by 1865, Americans "had a long tradition of group celebrations of public holidays."[4] Sponsored by a variety of civic, voluntary, and labor organizations, holiday and public celebrations in the United States reflected interest-group politics. Individual American holidays appeared and prospered because they had advocates that believed in their importance every year. Due to recent scholarship, we now know what holidays won out by their continued endurance. But if we now know more about major holidays in American culture, does that equally mean we know as much about the American calendar? I would argue no. The drive to nationalize and "federalize" holidays is just as much about the politics and history of the calendar as it is about the politics and history of individual holidays. Holidays need calendars to represent them, not only to validate them but to sustain them. One author noticed the importance of the calendar as a legislator of holidays, perhaps requiring a separate area of inquiry altogether:

> Julius Caesar's calendar, called in his honor the Julian Calendar, was revised in A.D. 1582 by Pope Gregory XIII. This calendar, the Gregorian, adopted by

England and the American colonies in 1752, is the one we use today. The way these calendars, each one improving on the one before, have brought the year to its present exact monthly divisions would be an interesting study itself. You might also like to discover the difference between our 'solar calendar' and the 'lunar calendar' still used in some countries . . . If we tried to go further with these investigations here, this might become a Book of Calendars instead of Holidays! That book we will leave for one of you to write someday.[5]

I have only taken McSpadden up on part of his offer to write that book. I would like to acknowledge the presence of the black holiday tradition and its accompanied calendar. In doing so, we need to examine the extent to which the American calendar reflected diverse white America: its colonial celebratory past, its handed-down European rituals, and its own homegrown holiday traditions emanating from different white ethnic and class constituencies. Antebellum holiday variegations and divisions among whites gave way to post-bellum holiday standards that led to an agreed-upon American calendar. African-Americans were indeed part of American calendar development and the country's preoccupation with nationalizing red-letter days; however, blacks were unable to get on the official American calendar and have it represent them in any meaningful way.

The official American calendar is the ontological center that not only represents dominant white interests but has historically dictated how Americans observe. Many US holidays have existed for quite some time in some form or fashion. It was not until these public celebrations were codified by calendar officialdom—municipalities, states, and the federal government—that annual holiday consensus by the majority of Americans was adhered to. Indemnified in the late nineteenth century, the American holiday calendar had become a coalition of the willing, quieting old disputes and erasing sectional, white ethnic, religious and class rifts. The American holiday calendar, despite historical frictions, proved elastic, having incorporated the Irish with St. Patrick's Day, Italians and the Irish again with Columbus Day, the labor movement with Labor Day, and fallen soldiers as well as self-sacrificing patriots with Memorial and Veterans' Day, respectively. True to its colonial past and Western heritage, the American holiday calendar imported Easter, Christmas, New Year's Day and Valentine's Day, with American celebrants placing their own unique stamp on them. Inherited holidays notwithstanding, the central aspect of the American holiday calendar was its commemorative narrative of America becoming—from George Washington's Day, Independence Day, and Lincoln's Birthday—providing the holiday ritual frame to its Gregorian foundational base. Though a seamless flow of these observances punctuated the American holiday calendar almost every single month of the year, white calendar consensus and legitimacy was not an easy accomplishment in the United States.

The politics of calendar space in American culture is most observable with Columbus Day, St. Patrick's Day, Memorial Day, Veterans' Day, and Labor Day. When casually examining the holiday calendar, what gets lost, or is not easily discernable, are the politics: what groups or organizations advocated for their particular holidays and why? And what days on the calendar did certain groups want over others? An explorer, a saint, the memory of sacrifice, and a grand appreciation to the plight of workers is as polyglot as a set of concerns to be commemorated as you can get. But more than just a remembrance of the past, these different sets of commemorative interests became a way for white ethnic groups to gain entrance into American nationality. If Columbus "discovered" the Americas, then certainly there can be agreement on his importance. And if Columbus is indeed central to the American narrative of discovery promulgated by Anglos, perhaps his ethnicity—Italian, and his religion—Catholicism, could be elevated over time. With waves of Italian and Irish immigrants pouring into the United States in the nineteenth and early twentieth centuries and claiming Columbus as one of their own, Irish and Italians would use Columbus as a weapon against discrimination and nativism. The Irish and the Italians would also use Columbus as a case for American acceptance. Indeed, they attempted to similarly with St. Patrick; the patron saint, however, was tied too closely with the old world of Ireland and manifested more as a form of ethnic nationalism in Irish-American communities in the United States. Columbus, on the other hand, evolved as a true American hero for white Americans. Assuming more of the annual Columbus Day responsibilities and logistics from groups like Tammany, as well as establishing their own organizations like the Knights of Columbus, immigrant Irish and Italian Catholics would control the ritual public-scape and offer new interpretations of American identity. As historian Matthew Dennis describes,

Uniting with other Catholics in the now more ethnically diverse city—including immigrant communities from Lithuania, Poland, and Italy, as well as French Canada—Irish Americans adopted a broader, more inclusive self-definition as patriotic American Catholics. . . . Through 'St. Columbus,' Irish Americans not only built a larger and more powerful ethnic coalition among co-religionists, but they found a potent champion who could represent them locally and nationally as legitimately American, because, not in spite, of their Catholicism.[6]

The American holiday calendar not only contained battles over ethnicity and religion, but also internal struggles around "appropriate" historical narration and calendar legitimacy. Memorial and Labor Day holiday interests fought for whose observance would represent the dominant and mainstream memory of events. Both holidays revealed factional and sectional politics, holiday-naming disputes, different interpretations of history, and different days of official observance. While northern states like New York officially recognized the last Monday in May as Memorial Day in the 1870s, southern states initiated their observance in the 1860s on April 26 as Decoration Day and on June 3 as Jefferson Davis Day. Similarly in the 1880s, some in the labor movement deemed Labor Day an important recognition for the struggle for workers' rights, while other labor groups and trade unions instituted May Day (May 1) to commemorate working-class solidarity and international class consciousness. Though the nineteenth century tolerated these calendar skirmishes, the twentieth century demanded holiday consensus. Factions who promoted mainstream American values won out, lining up their holiday under conceptions of American citizenship. Increasingly, holiday choices had to be made between Memorial Day interpretations of the Civil War on the last Monday of May as a day of national reconciliation or April 26/June 3 as a day to honor the lost cause. Confederate memory indeed lost calendar space, which in the end mirrored the elimination of May Day. May Day's Communist boosters would eventually concede defeat from mainstream labor interests, leaving September's first Monday as the only official day for Labor on the American calendar. Thus, in many ways, American holidays paralleled American politics in the twentieth century with its ongoing search for a vital center and its preoccupation with consensus.[7]

This drive toward holiday acceptance and consensus in American culture had many objectives. One aim, however, proved most intrinsic for purposes of legitimacy and long-term sustainability: federal holiday recognition. Federal holiday status is not easy to come by. Most observances take years to achieve congressional status. Public commemorations of annual events usually exist at the level of community. Many popular commemorations received municipal recognition in the form of city hall proclamations from mayors and/or city councils. If the political winds are blowing in a favorable direction, then state recognition, either from governors or legislatures, is the next level of attainment. Many holidays are able to obtain presidential proclamations that have the effect of providing national recognition to long-standing public commemorations. But in order to cement a holiday on the calendar, congressional lawmakers must push it through committees and bring it up for a vote like other pieces of legislation. Historian Matthew Dennis neatly outlines how this process worked for Columbus Day:

> In 1905, Colorado observed the first official state Columbus Day in a Noncentenary year; two years later, after the persistent lobbying of Italian American Angelo Noce, new legislation made Columbus Day an annual state holiday in Colorado. Throughout the United States, Italian Americans, led by the Knights of Columbus, which had grown from eight men in 1882 to a membership of some forty thousand men by the end of the century, pressed for such official endorsement of Columbus Day. By 1910, it was an annual holiday in fifteen states, and the inaugural state observances were commemorated with huge parades in Boston and Providence. By 1938, thirty-four states celebrated Columbus Day officially, when President Franklin Roosevelt's proclamation made it a national holiday, but it was not until 1971 that it became an official federal holiday, set annually for the second Monday in October.[8]

Federal calendar recognition, indeed, is a tremendous achievement born out of years of struggle. But achieving federal status, however, does not remove politics from holidays, their boosters, the holidays' audiences, or even Congress. What federal status suggests is that holidays have garnered mainstream acceptability and are widely acknowledged by the groups and communities that originally promoted them and by the majority of American citizens. Only calendar legitimacy through the United States Congress or something that approximates this process of political legitimation allows long-term recognition to be even remotely possible.

The process of calendar legitimacy by Congress also demonstrates the degree to which grassroots holiday movements can be co-opted for purposes different from the original holiday activists and boosters. The May 1968 *Congressional Record* reveals the finer details of the debate in the House of Representatives to make Columbus Day a federal holiday. The *Record* also reveals the effort to standardize other Monday observances on the basis of non-historical circumstances. Representative Byron Rogers of Colorado reiterated to the House that as of 1968, the United States had eight national holidays with Columbus Day pending as the ninth. "In addition," Rogers added, "we propose to make Washington's Birthday, Memorial Day, Columbus Day, and Veterans Day fall on a Monday." Though the motives for local holiday promoters varied for each of these observances, none of the grassroots local holiday movements would have provided the reason Congress gave for commemorating the country's first president, the memory of soldiers, and the man who "discovered" the Americas. Representative Rogers argued for the institutionalization of Monday holidays based on the benefits of American families spending more time together:

> We have witnessed a growing tendency for families to become separated. Sons and daughters often venture great distances from the homes of their parents. ... Grandparents in many families rarely have the opportunity to enjoy the company of their grandchildren. ... One of the principal advantages of the observance of holidays on Monday is the increased enrichment which such observance will bring to the family life of our Nation.

What Representative Rogers' remarks show is that the politics of calendar space in American history and placing days on the calendar does occur at the grassroots level, but can, and does re-occur at the national level. The basis of federal calendar politics are one, selectivity: "the 90th Congress has ... seen the introduction of almost 500 bills calling for the new observance of additional holidays and other commemorative events. ... Obviously, if any new holidays are to be created, we in the Congress are faced with the difficult task of being selective"; two, calendar placement: "We are not changing George Washington's Birthday. . . . But we are changing the date when his birthday will be observed to the third Monday in February"; and three, following state precedent: "Thirty-four states of the Nation now observe Columbus Day. So we are not making a great change insofar as making this a national holiday."[9]

With holiday politics still in effect but now better managed by a growing federal calendar, the American holiday calendar has become a national institution with police-like power to surveillance the boundaries of acceptable observances. This institutionalized calendar has not only naturalized American holidays, but has emerged logo-centric and the sole arbiter of American observances. This "logo" or "phonocentric" calendar, to use Jacques Derrida's terminology, intentionally represses holiday difference, is impermeable, and in many respects, indifferent to observances outside of the sphere of white America.[10] To monitor difference is to recognize the existence of binaries where one part of the binary inhabits the other. The binary here is the American holiday calendar and the black protest calendar, seemingly locked in an opposing relationship with the latter fully aware of its position as an insurgent undertaking, and former thoroughly oblivious to its political enterprise of marginalization. So naturalized is the binary, the hegemony of the American calendar and its accompanying national holidays can rationalize places for oppressed groups in mainstream observances as this Congressional testimony did by tying blacks to Columbus Day: "So, in effect, by designating Columbus Day as a national holiday, we honor the Irish, the Spanish, Portuguese, Negroes, and others, who came to this continent in the earliest days of its discovery and settlement."[11] In spite of black holiday observances, the American holiday calendar has remained suspect to the celebratory practices of black Americans, and when challenged by African-Americans for calendar space, the American holiday calendar proved elusive and paternal at best, intolerant and silent at worse. Thus, what has manifested in black holiday America over time were both the drive for American holiday acceptance and the simultaneous appearance of a black holiday calendar. The two historical manifestations—holiday acceptance and holiday separation—were accompanied by a third preoccupation by blacks: American holiday criticism.

## CRITICIZING AMERICAN HOLIDAYS

"Our remembrance cannot possibly be the same as that of whites who will celebrate Columbus," writes historian Molefi Asante, "Our history is different."[12] Asante's criticism of Columbus Day in 1991 occurring on the eve of Columbus' Quincentenary was both a critique of mainstream observances as well as a critique of the American historical narrative. Indeed, by the latter three decades of the twentieth century, African-Americans identified the American calendar as fair game for the black freedom struggle. The Black Power decades of the 1960s and 1970s issued a clarion call to blacks to turn their sights on the American calendar. The net effect of Black Power's clarion call was a holiday named Kwanzaa. From sheer inspiration, Kwanzaa mega-phoned other black holidays into existence. The Black Power era and the decades that followed can be recast and thoroughly understood as upping the holiday ante. The 1960s, 1970s, 1980s, and 1990s played host to an onslaught, an attempted holiday massacre, perhaps even a calendar coup that was part of the rise of Black Power, Afrocentricity, curriculum and canon debates, and the period's great culture wars. So imagine Carter G. Woodson, one of the foremost black holiday-makers, calling for the elimination of Abraham Lincoln's birthday in 1926. Not only would Woodson have thought such a thing absurd, his holiday times called for consensus-building for the purposes of African-American acceptance. Instead of criticizing Lincoln with the effect of de-legitimizing Lincoln's legacy, Woodson embraced Lincoln's birthday and welded it with Frederick Douglass' to create the observance Negro History Week. But blacks were a long way from the 1920s. The second half of the twentieth century were, indeed, different times in the history of American holiday criticism and black holiday-making.

Black criticism of American holidays was not solely a feature of the Black Power and post-Black Power era as witnessed by Frederick Douglass' July 4, 1852 speech in Rochester, New York. Because of what the Fourth of July represented—liberty and equality—the chasm of freedom talk opened and re-opened every year, hastening a black critique of Independence Day. The Fourth of July represented something the United States could not deliver to its black citizens, making the holiday an easy target for criticism. What appeared new about American holiday criticism in the latter decades of the twentieth century were two things: more American holidays were criticized, and everybody seemed to be a holiday critic. Criticizing American holidays and advancing black ones by African-Americans indicates a major shift in the black freedom struggle.

Molefi Asante joined other scholar-activist and cultural workers in the late 1980s and early 1990s—such as Marta Moreno Vega, Executive Director of New York's Caribbean Cultural Center, John Henrik Clarke, professor of Black Studies at Hunter College-CUNY, and Ayo Handy, founder of the African American Holiday Association—in putting black Americans on notice about the dangers of partaking in white American celebrations. Partaking in white holidays obviously could have multiple meanings. For blacks to either celebrate, accept, revel, or tacitly acknowledge white holidays was not only to be culturally off-guard and uprooted, but perhaps something more dangerous: to have ingested the dominant historical narrative that holidays carry with them. For Irish and Italian Catholics in the United States, Columbus represented cultural affinity, pride in ethnicity, American acceptance, coherence in religion, and the beginning of America's becoming; for African-Americans, Columbus was a symbol of physical and cultural genocide, slavery, European greed, and a gross misinterpretation of history. Raising these contradictions on the days leading up to popular American holidays was common for black critics. Asante argued: "We have been completely dislocated by Columbus. No single year in our history so disrupted the harmony of the physical, political, cultural, economic, and spiritual environment as the great 1492. Nothing was to be as dramatic in African or American history as the vile tearing apart of the cultural fabrics of two great peoples: Africans and Native Americans." To convince his audience of blacks that Columbus Day was a dangerous holiday as the country approached the 500-year anniversary of Columbus' "discovery," Asante couched his remarks within the context of Douglass' critique of the Fourth: "I think of Frederick Douglass's words when he gave a speech on the Fourth of July. He asked the question: 'What, to the American slave, is your Fourth of July?' I echo that question: 'What can Columbus mean to us?'" Asante provides three primary answers that mirror most black critical thinking on American holidays, which are: 1) stand in the shoes of African-Americans: "I must ask those who wish to celebrate Columbus to stand for one moment in my history, to ask the questions I ask, to see through my eyes the horror of the past 500 years"; 2) develop multiple activities and interpretations that can sit alongside one another: "make . . . the quecentennial [sic] a period of purification, confirmation and rededication to harmony"; and 3) create a more honest interpretation of history: "Mr. Columbus should be placed in the proper perspective. He was neither the discoverer of the American continent nor the most enlightened person of the period. He was the advance guard of white cultural and economic imperialism."[13] If Asante saw fit to call Columbus Day into question by reinterpreting the dominant Columbus narrative, then other African-Americans, like historian John Henrik Clarke, felt a day of mourning in black churches should govern black behavior with "all flags in our communities flying at half mast." Other Columbus Day critics called for more drastic measures, such as fasting, abolishing Columbus Day, and even renaming the holiday Indigenous People's Day or creating an alternative observance on the day after Columbus called African Holocaust Day.[14]

St. Patrick's Day, the Fourth of July, and other "white" holidays equally sat in the black holiday crossfire. "How well do we really understand the holidays we celebrate?" asked one black publication in 2003.[15] According to the vast majority of black critics, reveling in white holiday traditions was a zero-sum game. Partaking in mainstream holidays at the slightest level meant that blacks had long lost their identity: "What does all of this have to do with Africans living in America?" asked Ayo Handy, an American holiday critic and a black holiday-maker (who is covered more extensively in Chapter 5). "Very little. . . . St. Patrick's Day becomes another opportunity for us to forget who we are as we try to imitate Europeans and their customs," says Ayo Handy. Columbus proved a convenient target due to the explorer's pervasiveness in America's public culture—schools, textbooks, memorialization, etc. Because St. Patrick was a lesser known figure to black Americans, it should follow that St. Patrick's Day was less of a target for black holiday critics. Not so. For Ayo Handy, celebrating St. Patrick's Day was no less of an incongruity than celebrating Columbus: "Africans wearing green and falling out of pubs drunk trying to out drink their Irish compatriots and office-workers is as incongruent as our celebrating the so-called exploratory exploits of Columbus as a holiday." For many critics of white holidays, the United States, despite the progress of the Civil Rights Movement, still proved elusive to black demands for full inclusion, equality, and institutional access. Turning against America's holidays was akin to addressing larger questions about black political,

social, and economic stagnation, or worse, retrogression. Holiday participation for blacks should only focus on where blacks are as a people. "But
what is most important," writes Jill Nelson in reference to the Fourth of
July, "is that we look at ourselves," and understand the Revolutionary
battlefield that pitted Patriot against Tory in the eighteenth century has
now pitted white against black, and black against black in the late twentieth as Nelson further explains: "for it is within each of us and within our
minds that the battlefields of the present, and the future, lie. . . . We are, as
a people, betwixt and between: neither part of the American way nor at one
with ourselves and one another. We are floundering as a people," Nelson
resolved. Ultimately, holidays were about taking stock, inventorying both
the larger society's commitment to ideals of democracy, and the internal
black community's present rate of survival in the United States. How
could holidays be anything other than barometers of a community's
survival, said Ron Daniels, Director of the National Rainbow Coalition,
and past Deputy Director of Jesse Jackson's Presidential Campaign '88?
"Hence our celebration of holidays should reflect our need to survive and
develop as a people." "The way we celebrate," Daniels concluded, "therefore will either be part of the solution or part of the problem." For black
critics, African-American participation in Columbus Day, St. Patrick's Day,
and even the Fourth of July was to take stock of someone else's predicament, not their own.[16]

## US HOLIDAYS AND HISTORIOGRAPHY

But to render a series of critiques against American holidays and black
participation in them is to acknowledge the existence of an American
holiday tradition. If queried about what is the American holiday tradition
many people on first thought would inevitably name popular holidays
celebrated in the United States as evidence of the existence of the tradition,
such as Christmas, Easter, Thanksgiving, Fourth of July, etc. The phrase
"American holiday tradition" is tricky to pin down. For one, there are many
American holiday "traditions" that exist independently of one another,
such as *famous personality days*: the birthdays of P.T. Barnum, Lucy Stone,
and Boone Day; *statehood and territory days*: Statehood Day in Tennessee,
Kentucky Union Day, Delaware Statehood Day; *religious holidays*: Feast of
St. Clare of Assisi, All Saints' Day, Ascension Day; *event days*: Custer's Last

Stand Day, Bunker Hill Day, V-J Day; and *federal holidays*: New Year's Day, Fourth of July, Martin Luther King, Jr. Day. Within the federal holiday tradition there exists an additional tradition: the *Monday holidays* of George Washington and Abraham Lincoln known as Presidents' Day, Memorial Day, Labor Day, and most recently, Martin Luther King, Jr. Day. Secondly, American holiday traditions overlap regionally, thematically, and also in the audiences in who they cater to. American holiday traditions are independently and co-dependently communal—neighborhood based; local—city-based; state—observed only by those who live within its boundaries; or national—recognized and/or observed by most Americans. To discern one single American holiday tradition then is to pick and choose certain holidays over others, to set aside and demarcate holidays, to understand how holidays slip and slide out of communal, local, state, and national parlance, and to take note of the process of holiday selection by someone or something.

Holiday tradition building involves everyone who creates, promotes, catalogues, writes, and intellectualizes about it. Those who create, promote, research, catalogue, write, and invest significant amounts of time are holiday selectionists of sorts and contribute to the making of a tradition. Over time, the making of a holiday tradition bares the stamp of local communities, states, the national government, scholars, historians, and commentators. Two tendencies have historically been at play—an endogamous preoccupation on the part of holiday-makers, boosters, sponsors, and participants to create, perpetuate, and sustain their traditions, and secondly, the external and more distant community of scholars, intellectuals, cataloguers, examiners, and external commentators identifying a holiday tradition during different moments in history. The second tendency codifies holiday tradition in policy as well as research and publication.

Holiday-makers initiate and create holidays. Local communities develop and sustain them. Municipalities and states recognize, perpetuate, and codify a few of them in law. Presidents proclamize and nationalize holidays, thereby coalescing their citizenry around them. Congress chooses a few from the many and legalizes them. Cataloguers follow and index them. Commentators both revere and/or condemn them. And credentialed intellectuals and scholars, such as historians, research, analyze, interpret and create additional knowledge about them. All persons above more or less participate in what Susan Davis calls, borrowing a phrase from Raymond Williams, "selective traditionalizing," and what I deem the cornerstone of making a holiday tradition.[17]

Though holiday-makers create holidays and local communities grow and sustain them, a tendency exists to privilege some observances over others. School districts move at the behest of their employees and boards of directors when creating and observing school holidays, but many districts carve their calendars differently from the city or state. Municipalities and states move at the direction of local sponsors and boosters, recognizing the will of communities by issuing proclamations and legalizing some holidays while rejecting others. Some holidays are fortunate enough to get into the regular rotation of annual presidential proclamations and public announcements, but most do not. The United States Congress treats the federalizing of holidays like any other piece of legislation that is debated in committee and makes it to the floor, but never has Congress accommodated every holiday request brought by boosters, and giving most holidays a tacit recognition on the floor at best. The cataloguer, indexing exhaustively, brings to the public's attention popular and lesser-known holidays, but encyclopedic inventorying, however, still involves a process of selection. Scholars can never research and write about every single holiday, so they will cover those observances with similarities of theme, ultimately deciding what holidays can make their arguments more cogent and provide the most interpretive power.

Though not scholarly in their attempts, three books that catalogued American holidays in the twentieth century are J. Walker McSpadden's *The Book of Holidays* published in 1917, and expanded and reissued in 1940 and 1958, respectively, Jane M. Hatch's *The American Book of Days* published in 1937, 1948, and 1978, and Robert J. Myers' *Celebrations: The Complete Book of American Holidays* published in 1972. McSpadden and Myers focused their attention on major US observances along with several "minor" holidays emerging close to the time of publication while Hatch's work was much more encyclopedic in its calendar coverage, identifying multiple holiday observances for every day of the year. All three authors struggled over what holidays to include and exclude from their respective texts, and all agree to be captive of a growing festive calendar. McSpadden indirectly argued that the passage of time dictated selectivity: "Holidays never grow old, but books about them do. New holidays keep coming along; old holidays sometimes take on a new and added significance. To keep abreast of these changes we have prepared this completely new edition . . . " Hatch placed the onus of what holidays to include and exclude in her survey squarely on the American people when she said "many of the ways in which Americans note holidays and anniversaries have ... changed, with some special days and observances receiving more attention than before . . . " Thus, some holidays receive more attention, some less, some disappear altogether, some linked together, some deemed more important than others, and some identified more with a national American identity.[18]

Professional historians have picked and chosen similarly. Historian Matthew Dennis avoided using the phrase "American holiday tradition," but framed it as such when he discerned that the American public calendar "thickened" over time. Though mushrooming at a rate faster than most observers can follow, scholars have made choices as in the case with Dennis whose book *Red, White, and Blue Letter Days* included the Fourth of July, Thanksgiving, Columbus Day, Presidents' Day, Memorial and Labor Days, and Martin Luther King, Jr. Day. Ellen M. Litwicki, whose book *America's Public Holidays*, published two years prior to Dennis', similarly focused on Memorial and Labor Days, but added a mixture of ethnic holidays to her corpus. Jack Santino chose to research and write about holidays whose ties with American popular culture are deep seated and profound, as did Leigh Eric Schmidt's *Consumer Rites* whose holiday focus zeroed in on observances wreaked with commercialization. Len Travers' two-volume anthology entitled *Encyclopedia of American Holidays and National Days* is as exhaustive as it is ambitious, but when trying to decide what holidays to include and exclude he too confessed to strict limitations and hard choices:

> In order to treat the holidays in this volume in appropriate depth, the editors have had to impose restraints in breadth. This collection is not and cannot be exhaustive; we have for example excluded the nearly innumerable state and local holidays that now make up (or once did) so much of Americans' cultural experience. To determine the entries for this book, we first looked for rites and holidays with significant regional or national scope, eschewing those of strictly local consequence. We determined to include local treatments of both civic and major religious holidays, rather than impose distinctions, on the understanding that Christmas and Easter as practiced in the United States

might be as American as Memorial Day. The editors also desired to address festive and ceremonial occasions derived from major ethnic and cultural groups within the present United States. Hence the reader will find in this book treatments of Kwanzaa, Native American Powwow, and Passover, as well as the more universally familiar Mother's Day, Thanksgiving, and Independence Day. Last, we sought out scholars whose work has focused on the holidays and festive occasions meeting the above criteria. Thus, while not comprehensive, our collection comprises most of America's premier holidays, while hinting at the rich variety of commemorative activity that exists beyond this volume's bounds.[19]

The appearance and reappearance of "selected" American holidays with new angles of analysis and insight by researchers, historians, and editors contributed to the making of an American holiday tradition in scholarship and general knowledge.

As the American holiday tradition takes shape, so too does the African-American holiday tradition. US historiography on black holidays has slowly evolved, beginning with journal articles and culminating with recent monograph treatments. In the last three decades of the twentieth century, several articles appeared that broke new ground on the celebratory history of black Americans, most exclusively on slave commemorations and freedom holidays. The first generation of journal scholarship, such as Leonard Sweet, "The Fourth of July and Black Americans in the Nineteenth Century: Northern Leadership Opinion Within the Context of the Black Experience," and William B. Gravely, "The Dialectic of Double-Consciousness in Black American Freedom Celebrations, 1808–63," contextualize black holiday-making within the trouble waters of nineteenth-century black civic engagement and crowd public behavior toward black celebrations. Historians Shane White in "'It Was a Proud Day': African Americans, Festivals, and Parades in the North, 1741–1834," and Geneviève Fabre in "African-American Commemorative Celebrations in the Nineteenth Century," returned to the early years of black holiday formation in the second generation of journal scholarship, addressing issues of historical memory and commemoration as part of an emerging black expressive culture. Other recent essayists have written on black emancipation holidays with the effect of providing greater theoretical analysis on why public celebrations were important to nineteenth-century blacks. Full monograph studies of black holidays began with the work of William H. Wiggins' *O Freedom!: Afro-American Emancipation Celebrations* (1987). Trained as a folklorist, Wiggins' *O Freedom!* takes the reader through a range of experiences associated with emancipation celebrations in the distant past and the recent present. While Wiggins' *O Freedom!* assumed an anthropological cast of participant–observer, Mitch Kachun's *Festivals of Freedom* (2003) and Kathleen Ann Clark's *Defining Moments* (2005) truncated their studies, providing a tight temporal, regional, and historical window into the most significant freedom day celebrations in the long nineteenth century. Hence, by privileging some celebrations over others, by zoning in on specific regions of the United States, and by identifying the role of various black institutions in promoting black holidays, the scholars above collectively contributed to the making of the black holiday tradition.

## FREEDOM CELEBRATIONS AS BLACK HOLIDAY FOUNDATION

Freedom Day observances are longstanding and the most recognizable part of the black commemorative and holiday tradition. Freedom Day celebrations emerged in association with the abolition of the slave trade on January 1, 1808, British Emancipation in the West Indies on August 1, 1834, the signing of the Emancipation Proclamation, and the day it went into effect on September 22, 1862 and January 1, 1863, respectively, and east Texas slaves learning of their freedom on June 19, 1865, known as Juneteenth. In addition, a number of state emancipation holidays were initiated and well observed, such as the abolition of slavery in New York State on July 4, 1827. The Civil War as a transition from slavery to freedom did not abate the making of more freedom celebrations in the twentieth century as witnessed by the creation of National Freedom Day in 1948. During this 140-year period, author William J. Wiggins, Jr. observed that "divergent historical circumstances have given rise to at least fifteen different Emancipation celebrations," dotting the black protest calendar in order of event occurrence.[20]

It was easy to see why African-Americans would begin to construct a distinctly black calendar out of momentous historical events. The idea of freedom not only permeated larger black communities—both slave and free, but "freedom" as an abstract notion needed to be materialized and made palatable to blacks. Perennially recognizing watershed emancipation events, no matter how large, small, close or distant, proved effective in raising the consciousness of African-Americans and sustaining an alternative holiday tradition. Some emancipation events came suddenly; others were pre-planned. When the US Constitution was adopted in 1787, outlining the abolishment of the slave trade on January 1, 1808, the framers had no idea that African-Americans would construct an alternative holiday vision based on freedom. As Absalom Jones, a black Episcopal clergyman, said with the coming of black America's first freedom holiday, "Let the first of January, the day of abolition of the slave trade in our country, be set apart in every year, as a day of public thanksgiving for that mercy." Black Freedom holidays as part of a growing alternative tradition in the early nineteenth century would also be fed by other holiday streams in the United States: the first was black America's own slave ritual tradition, the second, American Independence Day celebrations.

One of the most striking features of the black protest calendar from the late eighteenth century to the late twentieth century has been its holiday alternativity. Late twentieth-century black holidays upped the oppositional ante, making alternativity a strident enterprise and a calendar way of life. The deliberate attempts by the makers of Kwanzaa (alternative Christmas), Umoja Karamu (alternative Thanksgiving) and Black Solidarity Day (alternative Election Day) to take blacks away from their dominant calendar neighbors fit comfortably with the politics and approach of Black Power. But the Black Power Movement did not have a monopoly on making black alternative holidays and counter-observances. Creating alternative observances was just as much a feature of Election Week/Negro Election Day and July 4/July 5 observances in the eighteenth and nineteenth centuries. Election Week, beginning in the late 1600s, was a fixture of the New England calendar during the latter part of May. As a time during the year where whites held their annual meetings, chose officers, and received commissions from the royal Governor, Election Week was a special occasion for white New England stakeholders who were charged with making major decisions for the colony of Massachusetts. Blacks took note of this ritual in New England politics, which manifested in a form of holiday mimesis that gave birth to a black alternative festival known as Negro Election Day. As a people with no political power, enslaved Africans still desired to acknowledge and validate power in their own communities by electing and coronating their own leaders on a day during Election Week designated strictly for them. Enslaved Africans in Massachusetts did not create a holiday alternative called Negro Election Day as much as it was forced upon them by whites who initially refused to have slaves partake in the main attractions of Election Week. Over the course of time, Negro Election Day became a featured attraction for whites. Though initially an act of exclusion, blacks were able to use Negro Election Day to negotiate the use of public space in order to sustain a festival that was distinctly African and a holiday of their own.[21]

If carving Negro Election Day out of New England Election Week proved difficult, then laying claim to Independence Day celebrations was nearly impossible. With a growing black community in seaport cities like Philadelphia, Boston, and New York, many free blacks attempted to claim the Fourth of July as their holiday after Independence Day observances grew in significance post-1812. In some cities, blacks celebrated the Fourth unmolested by whites. But in some celebrations, joyous participation could quickly turn to consternation when black celebrants became the victims of marauding white mobs. Physical attacks coupled with the incongruity of what the Fourth of July meant to African-Americans forced them to think of creative alternatives. For some blacks, July Fifth emerged as an alternative black holiday for Independence. Other blacks used January 1, the day many northern state emancipation statutes took effect, to acknowledge American independence as they celebrated their own freedom. Clearly, there existed among many a begrudging sense of disrespect from being excluded from July Fourth celebrations. Black America's first newspaper, *Freedom's Journal*, was clearly fed up with July 4 holiday talk, making it abundantly clear in 1827 that black America needed to look for an alternative. Peter Osborne reiterated as much to groups of blacks gathered at the African Church in New Haven, Connecticut in 1832, but maintained some semblance of hope when he said: "Fellow Citizens—on account of the misfortune of color, our fourth of July comes on the fifth; but I hope and trust that when the Declaration of Independence is finally executed, which declares that all men without respect to person, were born free and equal, we may then have our fourth of July on the fourth."[22] After the Civil War, blacks indeed had their fourth on the fourth as the black alternative of July 5 faded. But little did Osborne know, observing dominant holiday traditions on the day before or after a major white observance would come to represent the cornerstone of the black protest calendar. No matter how much African-Americans tried, black Independence Day observances on July 5 or January 1 were not the same as commemorating the nation's founding on July 4. For nineteenth-century blacks, holiday alternativity of this kind was a necessary evil. For late twentieth-century African-Americans, alternative holidays, like July 5, were a "positive good."[23]

Late twentieth-century blacks who lived and struggled in the 1960s and 1970s did not possess a monopoly on commemorating their past. In fact, nineteenth-century freedom celebrations made perennial memorializing a staple of the black community and its black protest calendar. In fact, every single historical breakthrough, whether it was various state emancipations, the abolition of the slave trade, the Emancipation Proclamation or the efforts of men like Crispus Attucks and Nat Turner, demanded immediate celebration and subsequent reception, with the objective of fixing these dates on the black protest calendar.[24] The dates that became ensconced on the black protest calendar are the holidays associated with freedom in one vein or another: January 1 as the observance of the abolition of the slave trade in 1808 and the Emancipation Proclamation in 1863; February 1 as the observance of the signing of the 13th Amendment to the Constitution in 1865; August 1 as the observance of British Emancipation in the West Indies in 1834; and probably, the most widely observed freedom holiday in the United States: June 19 as the observance of Juneteenth in 1865 with southwestern blacks becoming the last to know about their newly won emancipation. Arguably, when blacks instituted the variety of freedom celebrations, they in essence created the foundation for the black holiday tradition.[25] More than dominant American holidays, freedom celebrations dotted the black protest calendar and took on epic proportions in black churches, schools, and in big cities' public squares during the immediate post-bellum period. So strong was the desire to observe the memory of freedom in one incarnation or another, jubilee and centennial observances remained strong some fifty to one hundred years later. W.E.B. Du Bois wrote in 1915, "The jubilee of Emancipation has been celebrated already by expositions in New York, New Jersey and Pennsylvania. Further celebrations are planned in Illinois and Virginia."[26] Unlike whites in the nineteenth century who developed an infinity for one holiday or another based on ethnic and religious affiliations, blacks on the other hand left nothing to chance, placing as many freedom days on the black protest calendar as author Geneviève Fabre noted:

> While Baltimore preferred to commemorate Toussaint L'Ouverture and the Haitian Revolution, Cleveland recommended the downfall of slavery in Haiti or Nat Turner's birthday. [James] McCune Smith suggested Turner's rebellion of 1831 or [Denmark] Vesey's death in South Carolina in 1822. In the late 1850s, Massachusetts began to honor Crispus Attucks on March 15, in protest against the Dred Scott decision. The Commemoration Festival, held in Faneuil Hall in Boston, celebrated, together with Attucks, Peter Salem, Prince Whipple, the 'Colored Patriots,' the Sons of Freedom, and the black soldiers who had fought in the American wars (the revolutionary war and the War of 1812), and famous places like Lexington, Bunker Hill, or King Street. . . . In Syracuse, New York, another significant celebration, begun in 1851, was directly connected with immediate history: Jerry Rescue Day, in memory of a fugitive slave and in protest against the 1850 [Fugitive Slave] law.[27]

Jubilees and centennials of certain freedom celebrations spoke to the enduring nature of black holidays in the twentieth century. As fixtures on the black protest calendar, many believed one freedom holiday out of the panoply would rise to the level of a major US observance and become America's first recognized black public holiday. In the late 1940s with the backdrop of Jackie Robinson's entrance into major league baseball, Senator Wiley in 1947 and Representative Reed in 1948 requested of President Harry Truman to declare February 1 as National Freedom Day. Senator Wiley explained the purpose of the bill was "to authorize the President of the United States to designate the 1st of February of each year as National Freedom Day to commemorate the signing by President Abraham Lincoln, on February 1, 1865, of the joint resolution proposing the Thirteenth Amendment to the Constitution of the United States of America. . . . " Bridging the constitutional amendment abolishing slavery with Jackie Robinson's color-barrier breakthrough, National Freedom Day as a black emancipation observance could exist nationally for the good of the entire country. Senator Wiley remarked: "The Committee feels that the enactment of this resolution will go far toward the spreading of good will and the promotion of a better understanding between and harmonious cooperation among the white and colored citizens of the United States."[28]

Freedom jubilees and centennials came and went. Though National Freedom Day is still recognized today, the observance never took hold in black communities or in American culture. One holiday alternative African-Americans accepted, promoted, and believed would greatly help better relations with whites was Negro History Week. Carter G. Woodson is one of the most important black holiday-makers in the United States. Led by a passion to write the history of black Americans into the larger narrative of United States history, Woodson opened up intellectual and calendar spaces where none previously existed. As a scholar in American history, Woodson created the Association for the Study of Negro Life and History; the *Journal of Negro History* and the *Negro History Bulletin*; a publishing company named Associated Publishers; and a new black observance commemorating the birthdays of Frederick Douglass and Abraham Lincoln he called "Negro History Week."[29]

Black personality days, such as Nat Turner or Crispus Attucks, were part of the freedom holiday tradition. To celebrate the role played by Turner in initiating an 1831 slave rebellion, and Attucks in standing up to British soldiers in 1770 is to acknowledge the struggles waged by African-Americans to gain state emancipation, the abolishment of the slave trade, and freedom from the entire institution of slavery. Commemorating the lives of black heroic figures or white ones, such as John Brown, was to remember their role in making freedom a reality, no matter how provincial or large the enterprise. For Woodson to reference personalities, a "freedom" president in Lincoln and an important "freedom" fighter in Douglass, was to build on the existing freedom holiday tradition of January 1 and February 1. By fusing the birthdays of Lincoln and Douglass, February 12 and February 14, respectively, Woodson acknowledged the existing white presidential holiday tradition by memorializing the "Great Emancipator." Bringing Douglass into the celebratory fold was part of Woodson's grand project of promoting harmony "between the races." Calculated to use the legacy and example of these two men and begin a campaign to promote a "biracial" version of black history in the United States, Woodson's Negro History Week can be understood as a twentieth-century black freedom holiday.

Inaugurated in February 1926, Negro History Week was marketed directly to state departments of education, local school districts, individual schools, churches, civic associations, city councils and other municipal, state and federal institutions. In order to popularize and cement the holiday in the consciousness of the American public, Woodson issued clearly defined instructions before the first observance: "Call a meeting of the outstanding citizens of your community. . . . Secure the interest and cooperation of a number of professional men, businessmen, teachers, and ministers . . . Persuade your pastor to deliver an address on the Sunday beginning the celebration. . . . Appeal to the board of education of your local school system and the head of your school."[30] Unlike his later twentieth-century Black Power counterparts, Woodson's commemoration immediately sought mainstream recognition, official backing, and geographical ubiquity by ensuring Negro History Week was "observed everywhere in the United States."[31] Clearly, one sees in Woodson's marketing approach a politics of inclusivity, never allowing Negro History Week to be claimed by one audience or constituency, and never allowing Negro History Week to remain an isolated observance among blacks. "The purposes of the celebration," Woodson writes, "are to popularize the study of Negro History and to secure more support for its promotion."[32]

Negro History Week was a time on the calendar to set the historical record straight and capture days on the calendar. Like his late twentieth-century black nationalist counterparts, Woodson, a trained historian and academic, wanted to use the holiday to underscore the African-American contribution to US history in the areas of science, labor, art, the military, business, and education. Underscoring the black contribution in these key areas was not to fashion a subfield called "Negro History," but to speak of the "Negro in history"; was not to show up or divide white America from black America, but to build consensus and demonstrate commonalties between groups of people. Woodson wrote:

> This celebration, therefore, is not so much a Negro History Week as it is History Week. There is no such thing as Negro History or Jewish History or Chinese History in the sense of isolated contributions. The relations and interrelations of races, the close communication of peoples, and the widespread diffusion of ideas have made it necessary for one group so to depend upon the other and so to profit by the achievements of the other that it is difficult to have any particular culture ear-marked. History, then, is a record of the progress of mankind rather than of racial or national achievement.[33]

Like Karenga, Asante, Handy, Daniels, and other black holiday boosters in the late twentieth century, Woodson used Negro History Week to elevate black Americans. Woodson similarly believed that blacks should choose their holiday observances carefully. But unlike his latter-century holiday activists, Woodson would have never promoted the idea of black cultural genocide due to black participation in white holidays; or advanced the idea that blacks were misguided, perhaps misdirected or, to use a famous Woodson term from another context, "miseducated" about the deleterious effects of white observances. Instead, Woodson argued to America that Negro History Week was not designed for blacks to "learn less of George Washington," or not "to appreciate the unusual contribution of Thomas Jefferson to freedom and democracy," but to place the likes of Phyllis Wheatley and Benjamin Banneker alongside Washington and Jefferson. "A man can love his own race," Woodson surmised, "without hating others."[34] Woodson's efforts would pay dividends in the 1940s and 1950s with local and state Negro History Week proclamations, and an elongation of Negro History Week to Black History Month during America's bicentennial celebration in 1976.[35] Though Woodson's holiday achievement proved monumental, opening up twenty-eight days of calendar space for African-Americans, the elongated observance produced some criticism, with some like John Hope Franklin arguing that Black History Month had become too commercialized and was nothing more than a calendar version of affirmative action. Some blacks not only criticized but challenged Woodson's observance by attempting to rename February "Afrikan History Month" in 1981, which proved to be impossible. If breaking the hegemony of Black History Month proved difficult, other black critics thought that the month of August had more celebratory offerings for blacks, and deemed August "African Heritage Month" in 1980.[36]

What makes the Freedom Day tradition an enduring one like Negro History Week/Black History Month is the way black communities used public spaces to commemorate. To be a public people was to exercise subjectivity, to wrest control of parks, town streets and the city's thoroughfares from whites who controlled them. Black uses of public space were manifold—parading, speech-making, proselytizing, showcasing, etc. For example, parading in Emancipation Day and Negro History Week celebrations were acts of grandiosity, a kind of controlled pageantry where the naked eye of the bystander met columns of processioners who were ministers, abolitionists, free blacks, former slaves, teachers, civic leaders, and apolitical individuals. The file-past or march-past is where the parade's power laid—its unavoidability and its intrusivity to the casual or unsuspecting onlooker. Freedom Day parades and Negro History Week pageantries communicated messages of emancipation, remembrance and history to all in their wake, from and through their ability to street showcase as well as through the act of oratory and speech-making. For a people that lacked financial resources, parades were the most inexpensive forms of communication in that the procession itself cost very little; it was the motorcade-like accouterments that accompanied parades that made them very expensive, which black holiday promoters tried to avoid. Arguably, black holidays and commemorations made African-Americans a public people—a people who not only wanted to showcase their cultural traditions, but who cherished opportunities to communicate their reality in the widest possible forum. This is a powerful link between nineteenth- and twentieth-century black observances.

Even more so than the use of the public, Freedom Day traditions and Negro History Week used various commemorative occasions to engage in historical re-narration. Commemorative occasions afforded African-Americans the opportunity to re-write and re-set American history. In the nineteenth century, proslavery thinkers and other apologists of white racism wrote histories, developed theories, and scientifically rationalized African-American inferiority and the place of blacks in society. Blacks worked at every turn to combat historical misrepresentations, and along with the black press and independent black institutions used perennial occasions like commemorations and holidays to tie blacks to a larger diaspora history, underscoring and emphasizing black achievements in the United States and in the world as evidence of black humanity. Freedom holidays and Negro History Week set the historical record straight and provided a re-narration of history that was African centered. The major difference between the "African centeredness" endemic in Freedom Day/Negro History Week observances and the later "Black Power" holidays was tone and appearance. One would find large numbers of whites in Freedom Day and Negro History Week festivities that provided these observances with an interracial tenor. In addition, though Freedom Day and Negro History Week celebrations remained strident about projecting an African-centered black historical narrative into the public sphere, the tradition was always careful to promote a distinctive black American citizen–subject coalescing around a larger understanding of what it meant to be American. But Black Power holidays were not interested in promoting ideas about citizenship and democracy uncritically. Many black holiday-makers in the late twentieth century moved in a different direction and closed ranks around a more militant black protest calendar. Black Power holidays operated under other assumptions: African-Americans were not free, and observances that spoke to this notion missed the historical mark.

## BEYOND FREEDOM DAYS: BLACK POWER AND THE BLACK HOLIDAY TRADITION

The black holiday tradition has been primarily a tradition of commemorations, not holidays. Freedom Days were/are calendrical moments of remembering major historical events—like the abolishment of the slave trade, emancipation in the British Caribbean, or slaves in east Texas learning of their freedom on June 19, 1865—Juneteenth. Though they have much in common, twentieth-century black holidays are different from nineteenth-century commemorations in that they are not centrally rooted in a historical moment, but instead born of American calendar invisibility, mainstream holiday criticism and strategic calendar placement. Many black twentieth-century holidays were creatures of their creators, not necessarily of time and events. What produced Kwanzaa was its creator, Maulana Karenga. What produced Emancipation Day was the Battle of Antietam on September 17, 1862 that led to a presidential proclamation on September 22. The effective date of Lincoln's Emancipation Proclamation was January 1, 1863. Freedom Days were born of physical oppression and emancipation; Kwanzaa was born of American calendar exclusion and lock-out.

Kwanzaa did not begin the black holiday tradition; it both elaborated on and diverged from the pre-existing nineteenth-century Freedom Day traditions. Inasmuch as Kwanzaa and other twentieth-century black holidays elongated the nineteenth-century freedom day tradition, the newer "Black Power" holidays also overlapped with emancipation observances on the black protest calendar, as with the last day of Kwanzaa and Emancipation Proclamation Day (both January 1). The greatest contribution made by many twentieth-century black holidays is their radicalization of the black holiday tradition. Kwanzaa and other Black Power holidays diverge from their foundational freedom commemorations in that they deliberately sought to challenge observances on the mainstream American calendar. This challenge to American holidays by creating alternative observances and placing them next to mainstream celebrations not only took the black holiday tradition to another commemorative level, but also the black freedom struggle for civil rights. Movement and holiday scholars have not discovered a black holiday tradition in the post-1965 period or even identified one beyond Freedom celebrations. But if one wishes to examine the black holiday tradition at a deeper level, it is important to understand how the Black Power Movement bequeathed a black holiday and celebratory legacy. Black Power staked out other areas for movement concern, moving beyond the traditional areas of social and economic justice. When one understands the range and the political tenor of the Black Power Movement, it is not hard to discern how and why calendar politics took center stage and why blacks insisted on creating holidays more radical than Freedom Days.

One of the more fascinating aspects of late twentieth-century black holiday-making is that African-American critics of American observances constantly called for the creation of a new black holiday tradition as if none previously existed. In 1968, an African-American holiday celebrant spoke about the need for "black-letter" days when he unabashedly said, "We need our days ... At the time Washington was very busy being the father of our country, we were very busy being slaves. He doesn't have much relevance for us. We hope to celebrate other days that are relevant—Nat Turner Day or Marcus Garvey Day."[37] When these words were written in 1968 the context had long existed to call for such black holidays. But what is increasingly clear is although Freedom celebrations established a black tradition, many of these observances no longer held court on the black protest calendar, and by the late twentieth century lost import for many African-Americans. A new set of events and concerns would serve as evidence and references in the black holiday year: the traumatic assassinations of Malcolm X and Martin Luther King, Jr.; continental discontent and independence in Africa; and seemingly those nagging mainstream holidays like Thanksgiving, Election Day, Columbus, and Christmas that served as a constant reminder of black cultural misrepresentation. These ongoing critiques of American holidays, forgetting or eschewing old black observances, and creating new holidays, were not mere exercises; they were part of movement business.

From Kwanzaa's beginning in 1966 to as recently as 2002, the black holiday tradition had increased significantly and expanded the black protest calendar. The expansion of the black protest calendar was due to the Black Power Movement's emphasis on culture in the late 1960s and early 1970s; the rise of Afrocentricity as both a philosophical position and an epistemological questioning of mainstream American and Western culture in the 1980s; the return of black nationalist thinking in the early 1990s; and the increasing reality of social service regression in the Republican-dominated post-civil rights period. But Black Power served as the primary catalyst for new black holiday formations, taking the 1960s and early 1970s black freedom struggle beyond traditional areas of protest. Not only would African-Americans march on Washington and in the South, file legal cases in district courts, test Supreme Court rulings by riding on local or interstate busses, or even stop the building process on urban construction sites. Blacks would also take direct aim at the American calendar as observed by one writer in the context of new Malcolm X observances.

> Impatient at the rate of change within the Republic toward full implementa-
> tion of the black man's constitutional rights, they have decided, rightly or
> wrongly, that pressure on the white man's conscience has proven inadequate
> to overcome the obduracy and prejudice of centuries. Their only resort now
> seems, to them, shock tactics. Next Thursday will be celebrated as the
> anniversary of George Washington's birthday: It's a national holiday. In many
> parts of the country, Negroes have chosen the eve of that birthday to mark
> another anniversary: that of the shooting and killing in 1965 of Malcolm X.
> In some cities—Boston is one of them—Negro institutions will be seeking to
> honor Malcolm's memory by closing for the day, just as institutions across
> the land will be closed for the national holiday 24 hours later. To the extent
> that these coincidences are happenstance, there is piquancy in them. To the
> extent that they are being exploited deliberately by those blacks determined
> to assert their identity as blacks, much of society will be part puzzled, part
> shocked—even outraged. The fact is, however, that this is precisely the intent
> of many black activists.[38]

The fact that a significant segment of black America wanted to honor Malcolm X with an annual observance was neither a resort to "shock tactics" nor any intent on the part of black activists to "outrage" the country. For many black Americans in 1965, Malcolm X personified courage in the face of white hostility, exhibited inflexibility in his stance to see the United States racially evolve, and remained dedicated in staying the course toward a more just society. Malcolm X also represented living "black manhood" as eulogized by famed actor Ossie Davis during Malcolm's funeral, individual transformation from "Detroit Red" to Minister Malcolm X, religious integrity in the Islamic faith, and flexibility in social thought. Above all, many blacks believed Malcolm was a national black leader, on par with Marcus Garvey, Booker T. Washington, Ida B. Wells, Frederick Douglass, and Nat Turner, all who became commemorative subjects after their passing.

It was more than a convenient befitting to honor Malcolm with a commemoration. In some ways, Malcolm X observances were instinctually and reflexively grassroots as witnessed at Ferncliffe Cemetery in Westchester County, New York. When Malcolm was being laid in his final resting place on February 27, 1965, black mourners took the opportunity to begin the process of memorialization by wresting control of Malcolm's body from Ferncliffe Cemetery officials. When white grave-diggers attempted to place Malcolm in the ground as their job description directed them to do, the cemetery was turned into a site of struggle, prompting an individual to yell out to the media nearby, "They won't let the white man bury him."[39] The explanation about proper protocol and procedure given to African-Americans by cemetery officials would not be sufficient. Malcolm eulogist Ossie Davis and members of Malcolm's group, the Organization of Afro-American Unity reiterated their position to cemetery officials: "we'll bury him first man."[40] This scene at Ferncliffe Cemetery makes clear that although federal recognition and congressional creation of holidays from a person's life's work could perhaps represent the ultimate mainstream distinction, the black commemorative process and the making of black holidays was almost always a grassroots endeavor and could potentially begin at the grave. Pilgrimages to Ferncliffe Cemetery became annual occurrences led by Black Power activists and organizations, with inaugural visits occurring on Malcolm's birthday on May 19, 1965.[41] Malcolm X's organization, The Organization of Afro-American Unity, headed by his sister, Ella Collins, led annual community-wide delegations to Ferncliffe Cemetery, expressing her "deepest appreciation to the many friends of Malcolm X for their dedicated efforts in making this day possible."

Early commemorations of Malcolm X either on his day of assassination, February 21, or on his birthday, May 19, would prove strong in major US cities across the country. In addition to black nationalist organizations, public schools held some of the largest Malcolm X Day celebrations. Sixteen hundred students were excused early from school to attend a Malcolm memorial at the Apollo Theater in 1969.[42] James Fenimore Cooper High School in Brooklyn, New York did not excuse its students but instead invited the general public to their own Malcolm X Day celebration where Betty Shabazz, Malcolm's widow, was one of the featured speakers. In Minneapolis, Minnesota, it was reported that a thousand or so students remained home on May 19, 1968, with many gathering at the local community center called "The Way" to celebrate Malcolm's legacy. Institutions of higher education, particularly Black Student Unions like the Organization of African and Afro-American Students at American University amassed a broad array of students to hear speeches and poetry that paid "homage to the memory of Malcolm X."[43] Fordham University, Long Island University, and The City College of New York held Malcolm commemoration exercises in 1969. In 1971, the Brooklyn League of Afro-American Collegians of Brooklyn College paid a tribute to Malcolm in February. The evolution of Malcolm X Day coincided with the demand for Black Studies at some white universities like Brooklyn College, City College, and Princeton University. Black Brooklyn College students assembled for a Malcolm X memorial vigil, and then boycotted classes on February 21 demanding a relevant Black Studies curriculum. Black college students made no distinction between fighting for a black-centered curriculum and ushering in new black holidays. For them, calendar politics were just as important as Black Studies: "whether you're black, white, or Puerto Rican, Malcolm X and other freedom fighters that died for justice and equality for all mankind should be remembered on the anniversary of their births and deaths."[44] The Black Student Union at Howard University concurred with their counterparts at Brooklyn College, issuing a call to make Malcolm X a legal holiday in Washington, DC as reported in the *Congressional Record*: "A Black Student Union request that next

Monday, the birthday of the late Malcolm X be declared a legal black holiday has been relayed to the District Board of Education by Superintendent William R. Manning."[45]

Though the Black Power Movement made early commemorations of Malcolm X and another slain leader, Martin Luther King, Jr., extremely popular, black holidays were promoted by a diverse constituency of black nationalists, black politicians, civil rights organizations, and ordinary African-Americans. When Martin Luther King, Jr. was assassinated on April 4, 1968, it immediately set off urban rebellions across the United States. Though many people in the country, both black and white, were furious that a man who talked and practiced peace would be silenced by a lethal dose of racism, the ensuing violence in black urban America only captured part of the story. Within the violence stood the black attempt to memorialize, commemorate and create permanent black holidays from the legacy of Martin Luther King, Jr. Only four days removed from King's assassination, Congressman John Conyers from Michigan introduced House bill HR 16510 to "designate the birthday of Martin Luther King, Jr. [on January 15] as a legal public holiday."[46] Senator Edward Brooke of Massachusetts joined Conyers' proposal by issuing Senate Joint Resolution 159 on the same day, which

> Resolved, that, in honor of the Reverend Doctor Martin Luther King, Junior, who was born on January 15, 1929, January 15 of each year is hearby designated as 'Martin Luther King Day.' The President is authorized and requested to issue a proclamation each year calling upon the people of the United States to commemorate the life and service to his country and its citizens of the Reverend Doctor Martin Luther King, Junior, and to observe that day with appropriate honors, ceremonies, and prayers.[47]

Brooke understood the magnitude of what he was asking his fellow senators by calling for a national King observance: not merely to forestall the violence in the streets precipitated by an assassin's bullet, not merely to assuage the rest of black America; but to place King alongside the handful of notable Americans who have been honored with a place on the calendar. "No Negro American," said Brooke "has yet been added to that small company of distinguished patriots who have received such a tribute."[48] Though it may have appeared easy to the inside world of black politics that two African-American congressmen introduced legislation attempting to make January 15 a legal holiday, convincing their white colleagues, however, in 1968 and for the next twenty years would prove much more difficult. Despite congressional fault lines that revealed themselves every time the subject of creating an observance for King came up, black holiday-making on behalf of King and Malcolm continued unabatedly at the local level.

In the first few years after Congressman Conyers and Senator Brooke introduced their respective resolutions, Washington, DC became a showdown city for black holiday-making. With the congressional bills as backdrops, merchants were persuaded to close their stores to recognize both Malcolm X and Martin Luther King, Jr. Days. Additionally, the DC City Council argued over whether to officially make King a local holiday. As the month of May approached in 1968, the Malcolm X Memorial Committee sent flyers and leaflets to businesses in the District urging them to recognize May 19 by closing their stores for at least part of the day. The merchants approached about shutting down for part of the day were both black and white, but some merchants felt threatened by the call to cease commercial operations in honor of the two fallen black leaders. So forceful were the calls to commemorate Malcolm, the Washington, DC police and the Board of Trade were summoned by local merchants to investigate what they interpreted as pressure tactics by black groups. The *Washington Post* reported on May 17, 1968 that "merchants are being urged to describe the persons soliciting their cooperation and to report on the manner in which the requests are made. ... Len Kolodny, manager of the Retail Bureau of the Board of Trade, is drawing up a list of merchants approached and is conferring with Deputy Mayor Thomas W. Fletcher on the matter." In April 1969, the business community in DC felt similarly pressured to close for the growing recognition of Martin Luther King, Jr. Day. White businesses were especially appalled by the call from black civil rights groups that all of them should "come out in the open and specify their intentions" to shut down operations on King's birthday. Many merchants felt that holding them to a holiday litmus test was misguided politics and misplaced rage, and that perhaps a more fitting tribute should come from the City Council and not directly from the business community. Little did city merchants know, the City Council was already steeped in black holiday politics as public hearings on a public recognition of

Martin Luther King continued throughout 1968 and 1969, forcing the law-making body to consider making April 4 a local holiday for city employees.[49]

While the grassroots Malcolm X and Martin Luther King, Jr. Day movements proved strong, black holiday promoters and constituencies varied. Though one can locate a cross-over section of black support for both holidays, Malcolm X holiday boosters tended to be more black nationalist in orientation than their King holiday counterparts. For example, Malcolm X Day celebrations brought out appearances by black student unions, the Black Panther Party, cultural nationalists like the US Organization, the poet and activist Amiri Baraka, Stokely Carmichael, black united fronts, and others who were nationalist oriented in their thinking and teaching, such as historians Dr. Chancellor Williams, Dr. John Henrik Clarke, and Dr. Yosef Ben Jochannon. In addition, Malcolm X holiday gatherings brought the audience closer to Africa in the form of African dancing and drumming performances, such as in the May 18 and May 19 gatherings at Washington, DC's Lincoln Park (12th & Massachusetts NE) and Malcolm X Memorial Park (15th & Euclid NW), respectively.[50] Though the call for a national King holiday began during the Black Power Movement, the drive to make King's legacy a holiday reality would come primarily from elected officials, mainstream civil rights leaders and organizations. A King memorial service at the Los Angeles Coliseum on April 11, 1968, attended by black politicians like Tom Bradley and religious figures like Dr. Ben Herbster of the National Council of Churches, was revealing of who would, and eventually did, support the effort to annually observe Martin's memory.[51] Although each broad holiday constituent group supported their respective cause to observe King and Malcolm, there was certainly not always agreement among blacks as to who was more worthy of a public holiday. J.W. Haywood, Jr. captured this sentiment in the *Washington Post*:

> The intention of the D.C. Board of Education to make the birthdays of Martin Luther King, Jr. and Malcolm X school holidays is half-baked, to say the best. Few would dispute MLK's merit to that distinction. Malcolm, however, operated in a narrow context of Muslimism in the USA. Secondly, he was almost psychotically anti-white during most of his public life. Thirdly, he did not come anywhere near MLK's national or global stature in fastening

. . . himself [to] . . . the civil rights cause. There are many more adequate ways to give a place of honor to Malcolm X, for he does deserve a measure of honor.[52]

Even as the momentum for a public and legal King holiday grew over the 1970s and into the 1980s, few would dare dispute Malcolm's national and international commitment to black advancement. By the late 1970s and early 1980s, however, many blacks realized that King, the patron saint of civil rights protest and struggle, would also have a hard time finding his place onto the American calendar. As we shall see in Chapter 5, King would eventually make it on the American calendar, but at great cost. But if King struggled mightily to make it on the official American calendar, Malcolm, then, had no real chance, remaining relegated instead to the black protest calendar.

With Malcolm X Day commemorations growing in popularity and with Kwanzaa's emergence as a viable alternative to Christmas, African-Americans unleashed a fury of new holidays during the Black Power period. Two of the new holidays were Black Solidarity Day and Umoja Karamu, both created in 1969. Like Kwanzaa, Black Solidarity Day and Umoja Karamu marked a departure from "personality" holidays. Black Solidarity Day cared less about remembrance of the past. Black Solidarity Day sought to forestall the effects of national policies advanced by the Nixon Administration while dealing with some of the local ramifications of public policies in city municipalities, trade unions, work sites, and in the public service sector. Carlos Russell, an adjunct professor at Medgar Evers College at the City University of New York (CUNY) focused his attention on public policy and its implications on the lives of black folk. Russell, the holiday's founder, assembled a cross-section of New York politicians, activists and professionals in October of 1969 under an umbrella group called the Black Solidarity Day Committee. Sponsored by Dr. Eugene Chandler and the New York Urban Coalition and Lloyd Johnson of Columbia University's Urban Center, the Black Solidarity Day Committee was made up of both grassroots activists and the city's black elite. Though Black Solidarity Day's committee membership varied from the likes of professors, black grassroots activists, and the likes of Assemblyman Charles Rangel, State Senator Basil Patterson, and Manhattan Borough President Percy Sutton, the committee still reflected a Black Power ethos and assumed a black nationalist posture. The committee's main charge was to determine how to bring pressure to bear on the City of New York through the objective of a one-day boycott. The goal was to change racist practices manifested against the city's African-American population. Calling his holiday Black Solidarity Day, or "A Day of Absence"—which was inspired by a drama of the same name by black arts playwright Douglas Turner Ward in which black residents of a southern town disappeared for the day—Russell placed the holiday on the Monday before Election Day. Since Election Day occurs annually on the first Tuesday in November, Russell believed blacks could capitalize on the publicity Election Day provided. Russell thought if blacks stayed home from work and school, they could spotlight the issues that not only plague black New Yorkers but also black America. For Russell, the vehicle of protest would be the holiday; the tactic would be the one-day boycott; the messengers would be African-Americans, the local media, and the coming of Election Day; the messages of Black Solidarity Day were loud and clear: stay home from work and school, bring the city to its economic knees, and force white elected officials to deal with black material realities.[53]

In the context of 1968, creating a holiday like Black Solidarity Day would have great appeal if the central tactic remained the boycott. Like Malcolm X days and Martin Luther King observances, Black Solidarity Day demonstrated the power of the boycott—to change policies, yes—but if nothing else, to use the power of the boycott and the media to make demands for change. On the inaugural Black Solidarity Day observance in New York City, thousands of black residents stayed home from work and attended rallies throughout the city. Some New York City schools in black neighborhoods closed when a large majority of their students did not report. Many black hospital workers observed the day by not going into work, as did black college students who did not attend classes. Many African-Americans also refrained from purchasing durable goods in downtown stores. Some businesses reported a drop in sales. African-Americans who participated in Black Solidarity Day activities followed some of the recommended procedures by the holiday committee: non-attendance of classes; a refusal to work and shop in stores; a commitment to wear red, black, and green armbands; and a request to drive with headlights on. While the first Black Solidarity Day failed to cripple the city economically as it was intended, the holiday was able to raise the consciousness of black

New Yorkers and represent another observance on the calendar perennially used for black advancement. With New York's black population at close to three-quarters of a million, certainly not all blacks participated in Black Solidarity Day and not all whites even knew a black holiday was observed the day before Election Day. The news media overplayed this fact, on the one hand reporting high rates of black participation and the holiday's intended effect, but on the other, calling the observance a failure by using the barometer of total black population participation. The media also covered individual stories of black workers who lost their jobs due to their insistence on staying out of work and observing the holiday. Carlos Russell, the holiday's founder, used another barometer of measuring Black Solidarity Day's success: the spirit of a growing closing ranks philosophy associated with the Black Power Movement:

> Black people don't need the approval of the white community to celebrate our holidays, be they Dr. King's or Malcolm X's. Black Solidarity Day was our day, and even if those black people who did not participate this time will think long and hard about not participating on future days. Black people have tremendous power when we act in unison, and we hope that the momentum and the spirit of Black Solidarity Day will continue during the many days of solidarity we must plan for the future.[54]

Russell was right. Black Solidarity Day did not need the support of whites. It continued to grow through the 1970s, spreading to other cities like Boston and Philadelphia. Like New York, the Boston Black Solidarity Day was held on the first Monday in November. Sometimes black Boston merged their Black Solidarity Day with Malcolm X Day on May 19— Malcolm X's birthday. It was befitting, many in the Boston black community thought, to sometimes merge the new Black Solidarity Day with the memory of a man whose service to African-Americans and blacks in the diaspora often focused on the concept of solidarity. In support of Malcolm X Day on May 19, 1970, a Black Solidarity Day parade in the South End section of Boston was organized by local community activist Calvin Hicks and the Boston Black United Front. The parade route traveled up Warren Avenue to Blue Hill Avenue, proceeding across Seaver Street and terminating at Franklin Park.[55] The parade procession played some of Malcolm's famous speeches that underscored the theme of solidarity. Whether on the first Monday in November or on Malcolm X's birthday, the Black Solidarity Day remained a fixture of the northeast black protest calendar, giving African-Americans a chance to be heard, if not on Election Day with their vote, then certainly with their voice a day before.

Two years after Black Solidarity Day was created, Philadelphia blacks inaugurated another November observance, again taking direct aim at a long-standing American holiday tradition: Thanksgiving. In 1971, community activist Edward Sims, Jr. created a holiday called Umoja Karamu—a Swahili-named observance meaning unity feast. Umoja Karamu occurred on the fourth Sunday in November as a day for members in the black community to share in a feast of thanksgiving, or as early promoters believed, a feast to reverse the "misgiving" of Thanksgiving. Modeled directly on its December holiday predecessor Kwanzaa, Umoja Karamu was meant to be both a private family holiday as well as black public gathering and feast. Edward Sims and other Black Power activists in North Philadelphia like the Reverend Ishakamusa Barashango heavily promoted Umoja Karamu throughout the months of October and November. Black radio in Philadelphia suggested to African-Americans to forego Thanksgiving's Day in November 1971 and instead plan their family gathering on the Sunday, rather than the Thursday. Segments of the black community in Philadelphia gathered close to a thousand persons in 1971, and annually thereafter in community centers, churches and in public parks to promote Umoja Karamu. By 1972, Washington, DC blacks held corresponding public Umoja Karamu celebrations, eventually drawing bigger crowds than Philadelphia. Umoja Karamu not only brought black people together in food and feast, the new holiday directly challenged the hegemony of Thanksgiving. One of Umoja Karamu's boosters hoped it would replace Thanksgiving's Day in black America. "It is our hope," Barashango wrote, "that many Black Families will be persuaded to institute this ritual as a meaningful alternative to the American traditional Thanksgiving Day celebration." Sims and Barashango believed that a black celebration of Thanksgiving's Day or "Misgiving's Day," as Barashango dubbed it, was tantamount to an American celebration of Pearl Harbor or Jews honoring the Third Reich. Identifying what they understood as the absurdity of a black recognition of Thanksgiving, Sims and Barashango urged African-Americans to "examine all such American celebrations with a critical eye, apply logic, and consider alternatives."[56]

Like Kwanzaa, Umoja Karamu was steeped in ritual activity and historical symbolism. The "black" Thanksgiving consisted of five historical phases, with the first recalling the black family's past in Africa, the second, the family's destruction under slavery, the third, the era of emancipation, the fourth, the liberation struggles of the 1960s, and finally, the black family's future potential. Correspondingly, five distinct colors—black, red, green, orange, and gold—representing the five historical periods décored homes, community centers, and churches where the Umoja Karamu celebration was held. An elder in the community usually reads a narrative that speaks to each historical time period. Bowls of food are passed around at each period. This continues until all five eras have been covered and five different courses of food consumed. The eating and the retelling of history is accompanied by prayers, the pouring of libations, candle lighting, and the Umoja Karamu song:

> Umoja Karamu, a unity feast of Thanksgiving for the Black Family. Walking in Our own sacred ways. Celebrating Our Holy Days. O, come Sun People of Our Motherland. Arise and take your destiny in hand. For you are destined to have power again. Yes, We are destined to be free again. Umoja Karamu, We are New Afrikan people, whose hour of power has come. Throughout all eternity forever will Blackness be. Coming together, We unite as one. Transcending our differences We face the sun. Receiving unto Us its energy, recreating life for what it was meant to be. Umo-Umoja Karamu.[57]

African-Americans also initiated pan-African holidays or made popular commemorations that sprang from the context of African liberation struggles. African Liberation Day was arguably one of the most (if not the most) popular black holiday in the United States during the early 1970s. Developed in the context of African anticolonial struggles, Kwame Nkrumah created African Freedom Day on April 15, 1958 to celebrate the advance of liberation movements on the continent of Africa. After assuming pan-African proportions, the holiday was moved to May 25 in 1963 where millions of blacks paused and took stock of African continental concerns. In the United States, African-Americans partook in African Liberation Day on May 27 of each year. Promoted by the likes of Kwame Ture (formerly Stokely Carmichael) and his All African Peoples Revolutionary Party as well as Owusu Sadauki (formerly Howard Fuller) the African Liberation

Support Committee based in the United States, African Liberation Day was able to marshal a broad-based network of people: members of the Congressional Black Caucus like Charles Diggs and Walter Fauntroy, the Black Panther Party and other political black nationalists, Amiri Baraka and the community of black cultural nationalists, Assemblyman Willie Brown from California, Mayors Richard Hatcher (Gary) and Maynard Jackson (Atlanta)—all organized under various local African Liberation Day Committees. Twenty cities played host to the inaugural African Liberation Day in the United States, including New York, Washington, DC, San Francisco, Chicago, Atlanta and Houston. African-Americans joined thousands of other blacks in London, Accra, Kingston, and Toronto to observe the success of past decolonization efforts and encourage present African struggles in progress. With African Liberation Day positioned next to Memorial Day, blacks in the United States were able to support their brethren living under repressive regimes in places like Angola, Mozambique, and South Africa while reflecting on what it means to be a global black person facing similar conditions in the United States. Not only were repressive colonial governments called into question, so was the United States for engaging in commercial trade with counties that oppressed Africans. Parades throughout the streets of the United States told the stories of individual Africans who suffered mightily, and grassroots leaders imprisoned and killed for standing up.[58]

### THE BLACK PROTEST CALENDAR

"Filling up" or "occupying" spaces on the American calendar are indeed apt metaphors for what black holiday-makers achieved. Throughout the eighteenth and nineteenth centuries, most groups in the United States engaged in holiday creation but did so to the rhythms of their own community. Perennial recognition of events were not only provincially contrived celebrations but controlled by the power brokers inside those communities, be they politicians, civic associations, and the like. Many of our most cherished annual celebrations began in this manner (i.e. Columbus, Labor, Memorial Day, etc.). But holiday creation was relatively slow in the nineteenth century. As white ethnics, labor, and other groups ascended to power, the pace quickened with the need to "establish a unifying national culture at the turn of the century." Between 1865 and 1920, according to Ellen M. Litwicki, Americans created more than two dozen holidays. "The most important function of holidays was to reconstruct America," and broadly redefine a new American identity.[59] If the American calendar solidified itself, creating a unifying national culture by reconstructing the nation and broadening the definitions of who was an American via celebration, then the American calendar could not represent the wishes, desires, and aspirations of an oppressed people, specifically African-Americans. Jim Crow ordered the lives of African-Americans, and despite the annual occurrence of freedom holidays, Jim Crow became implicated in the making of the American calendar.

The presence of freedom holidays on the calendar does not demonstrate African-American inclusivity as Litwicki suggests, but quite the opposite. If the American calendar were truly on the road to representativeness during the turn-of-the-century period of nationalizing celebrations, one black freedom holiday out of several in existence (January 1, June 19, August 1, February 1, etc.) could have been used to prove America's great leap from slavery to freedom. The country, however, was not ready to hear black demands for inclusion, and certainly the official American calendar was not in a position to represent them. Thus, in this context of talking about occupying space on the calendar, I would like to argue for a black protest calendar, a calendar that has been historically oppositional and an alternative to the dominant Gregorian and its American offspring. The black protest calendar provided visibility and a public voice to African-Americans. It also perennialized their struggle, annually affirmed their history, and assessed yearly where they were as a people. Although the black protest calendar was oppositional in nature, it could not exist on its own. Since it was and still is a counter-calendar, by necessity, it needs the dominant American Gregorian to do its work of exclusion—the work of dictating who and what gets honored and affirmed annually.

But all protest calendars need their dominant counterparts to exist. In some instances, what was once a dominant calendar tradition may have been greatly altered by revolution, such as in the case with the French Revolution and its concomitant French Republican calendar, as well as with the American and Russian Revolutions and their respective calendars. Similarly to the French, Russian, and American, the English Revolution produced similar upheavals. In Britain, one can discern the tension between the standard ecclesiastical calendar and the dynastic calendar worked out over time. The dynastic calendar started as the insurgent undertaking, and with the growth of royal influence, the monarchical calendar began to order the celebratory lives of its citizens. Due to the Glorious Revolution, Parliament's influence eventually trumped royal calendar prerogatives but never completely eliminated monarchical observances. With powerful entities vying for calendar space, compromises were reached in time that allowed for the simultaneous existence of all three as author David Cressy explained: "A new set of national anniversaries flourished in the seventeenth century as distinctive reference points in the English Protestant year, tying together God's calendar, the king's calendar, and the calendar of the Protestant nation."[60] Similarly, Irish, Welsh, and African "nationalisms" criticized the English Protestant calendar for religious, cultural, and racial invisibility. These nationalist impulses added "local" holidays to their provincial calendars that coalesced with their respective historical, local and regional traditions. In post-Independence Africa, countries like Tanzania and Kenya kept to the calendrical rhythms of the English calendar but added holidays such as Independence Day, Zanzibar Revolution Day, Union Day, Farmers' Day and Presidents' Day (Kenyatta and Moi Day in Kenya; Nyerere Day in Tanzania). With the growing influence of Islam in African countries, Muslims in both Kenya and Tanzania have captured official calendar space, elongating the original English Protestant calendar and the British holiday tradition with observances such as Iddi El Fitry (end of Ramadan) and Iddi El Haji (feast of sacrifice). What is unique about the English calendar tradition in Britain and in many of Britain's former colonies is tacit recognition and respect at the very least. By the second half of the twentieth century in some countries it appeared that oppositional calendar politics was a thing of the past; but not so in the United States.

To show how beholden the black protest calendar was and still is to its American counterpart, one only has to look at black holiday placement and the evolution of this calendar. Black holiday placement has been historically dictated by five primary motivations: one, exclusion from dominant celebrations such as on July 4; two, the recognition of important historical moments as in the banning of the slave trade and the signing of the Emancipation Proclamation; three, the memory and ongoing memorializing of historical personalities, that is, Malcolm X and Martin Luther

King, Jr.; four, the black contribution to the American historical narrative, that is, Negro History Week/Black History Month; and lastly, a desire to de-emphasize holidays from mainstream white America as with the Christmas/Kwanzaa nexus (December 25 and 26). I argue that it is the last proclivity that has defined the black protest calendar of which Kwanzaa as an alternative to Christmas has returned us to. Exclusion, indeed, led blacks on their journey of holiday-making. Frederick Douglass' critique of Independence Day celebrations during the early nineteenth century partly describes the history of black exclusion from July 4 celebrations. The act of forbidding black participation led to the alternative July 5 as a day to share in the moment of national independence. African-Americans reinstated themselves in the memorial of Independence as if to say the new nation also belonged to them as well.

But sharing in the cause of independence or other fetes is only one way to look at the black protest calendar and holiday placement. By creating alternative observances next to dominant holidays, African-Americans equally sought to delegitimize and make mockery of them. They also attempted to partially redefine dominant holidays. Black July 5 celebrations served as a reminder of how incomplete the drive for independence remained, and sermons from black pulpits annually underscored the blatant hypocrisy. If July 4 represented freedom for whites—a boisterous memorial for liberty against British tyranny, then July 5 was a loud, thunderous roar from the nearly 4 million blacks still held in bondage. We can discern similar critiques of American celebrations in Kwanzaa (December 26), Umoja Karamu (Thanksgiving weekend), Black Solidarity Day (the day before Election Day), and Black Love Day on February 13 (the alternative to Valentine's Day discussed in greater detail in Chapter 5). While historical circumstances in the nineteenth century dictated when and where a black holiday appeared on the calendar, twentieth-century black holiday formations stood in the tradition of July 5 where black holiday-makers sought to delegitimize and redefine dominant American days by placing black days next to traditional American celebrations. More than just a black Christmas, Kwanzaa's appearance on the calendar one day after December 25 was meant to attack one of Christmas' basic manifestations—a crass commercialism that had come to embody Christ's birth. Instead Kwanzaa called for hand-made gifts to be at the center of any exchange, and for blacks not to fall prey to overconsumption. Likewise,

Umoja Karamu, the so-called black Thanksgiving, was indeed about feasting but in the context of remembering four hundred years of enslavement and Jim Crow. Black Solidarity Day, one day before Election Day, was both a political and economic critique of the nation: a call for blacks on the one hand to use their vote wisely, and on the other, to engage in a national day of absence from schools and the workplace. And the black alternative to Valentine's Day on February 13 represented a chance for African-Americans to expand the definition of romantic love, especially when urban black America in the 1980s was paralyzed by a viscous black-on-black violence.[61] Thus, the black protest calendar would not solely rely on the day-to-day unfolding of history to dictate how and when blacks celebrated, such as a momentous event or the death of a leader, but would understand the freedom struggle in strict calendrical and spatial terms, using dominant American holiday traditions as points of departure to establish their own black holidays.

Placing black holidays next to dominant American ones may speak to a concern and a need for what I call "calendar legitimacy" for black holidays, a topic I will cover in more detail in Chapter 5. Calendar legitimacy is achieved either from official federal government recognition or non-official recognition from the private sector, cultural institutions, schools, the media, etc. Not all black holidays have procured an official calendar stamp of approval. In fact, out of all the black holidays, only one, Martin Luther King, Jr. Day, has achieved such status. But others, like Kwanzaa, have at least earned non-official recognition from museums, schools, and the media. Calendar legitimacy in many ways means capitalizing off of mainstream celebrations, to use the holiday locations of the dominant culture, pulling and collecting energy from a mainstream neighbor. Calendar legitimacy for black holidays may also mean running the risk of being redefined by the dominant culture, particularly as the "black" Christmas (Kwanzaa) or the "black" Thanksgiving (Umoja Karamu), even when the original intent by black holiday-makers was to avoid such a connection despite the holiday's placement there. Most black holidays are struggling for legitimation from within—not all African-Americans have embraced all black holidays or even know about them—and from without—in order for black holidays to gain wider acceptance they must possess some import for the larger American culture. The fact is most black holidays do not have mainstream appeal, save for King, Black History Month, and Kwanzaa. But as black holidays increased, serving notice to the public about a different kind of spatial politics on the calendar, their rejection or acceptance gave greater meaning to the evolution of a black protest calendar and the making of the black holiday tradition. There can be no doubt about Kwanzaa's role in all of this. In many ways Kwanzaa was the precipitator of new holidays and the glue that held the tradition together. Kwanzaa is most often the frame of reference when black holidays are discussed. It is Kwanzaa's history we now focus on in the next three chapters.

# CHAPTER 2

# *Maulana Karenga, the US Organization, and the Making of Kwanzaa*

The theme of invention will sit front and center in this chapter. Invention informs and captures the process of Kwanzaa's "making," and Maulana Karenga—the holiday's founder's "remaking." Kwanzaa's making at the level of holiday and Karenga's re-making at the level of the individual speaks profoundly to a transformation in civil rights politics and new thinking about the continent of Africa. African continental politics manifested in the 1950s and 1960s. Africa's rise was real—independence struggles that informed the American Civil Rights and Black Power Movements —as well as metaphorical and imagined—the creation of new holiday rituals like Kwanzaa. For black Americans, the rise of Africa meant a veritable cultural return to continental roots and codifying this return in a form of a US-based black cultural nationalism that focused on black cultural liberation. But black cultural nationalism did not import an "original" Africa; it imagined one after an existential crisis with Christmas in December 1965 and two centuries of white holiday representations. Chapter 2 will examine this imagined return by looking at the dilemma Christmas posed, and the multiple discourses that Karenga used to create Kwanzaa. The chapter will closely examine Kwanzaa's constituent parts: borrowed syncretic African agricultural rituals from different parts of the continent. This chapter will not only introduce the man and the organization that created Kwanzaa, but ask what kind of Africa they offered black Americans. After mapping Kwanzaa and its ceremonial procedures, I will deconstruct and separate the holiday's African and black American components and demonstrate how Kwanzaa fit into a larger pattern of US-based black nationalist performance. The Black Power Movement enshrined black nationalist performance in the form of Afros, raised fists, and African dashikis. To partake in Kwanzaa during the last week of December was to perform Africa by speaking and greeting in Swahili, lighting candles, pouring libations, calling on the name of the ancestors, as well as feasting. More than remembering an African past, Kwanzaa insisted that African-Americans maintain a deep visceral connection with the continent and its "history"—one that involved visible activity even outside of the official Kwanzaa period.

## INVENTING AFRICAN DISCOURSES AND BLACK POWER RITUALS

In 1973, anthropologist Clifford Geertz wrote that "in ritual, the world as lived and the world as imagined, fused under the agency of a single set of symbolic forms turns out to be the same world."[1] Seven years removed from the birth of Kwanzaa, Geertz's remarks speak to the politics of Kwanzaa's making and black American ritual invention in general. Invention, style, expression, and improvisation are key words in African-American discourse, at the level of both structured meaning and social experience. But more than discourse, these words not only inform black life in the United States, they serve as identifiable markers shaping most, if not all, of black life and culture in the diaspora. Invention as a form of improvisational necessity occurred on slave ships, in the American colonies, and on nineteenth-century plantations, helping form what we understand as black America. The terms "black" "America," though in many ways a contradiction in terms, speak directly to a form of identity contrivance that was all at once historically based, oppression driven, and politically dictated. Black churches, fraternal, and other social organizations were forms of institutional invention, combating racist oppression and serving many black communities over time. In a similar fashion, the black holiday tradition is not only an example of black invention politics, but perhaps one of its greatest manifestations.

Beyond Eric Hobsbawm's concept of "invented tradition" which speaks to ritual creation in historical European contexts, and of which I am thoroughly indebted and shall return to later in this chapter, the idea of inventing and re-inventing is encoded in the making of Kwanzaa in a number of respects: Kwanzaa and black holidays as invented traditions; the creator of Kwanzaa and the makers of other black holidays as re-invented peoples; the continent of Africa as a geographical invention; and new ideological and political inventions like novel conceptions of black cultural nationalism quite distinct from previous forms of black national-ism. The "making" of Kwanzaa—the black American synthetic invention of African cultural practices, of African languages, of African history, and of African peoples—represents more than an expansion of black calendar politics, or a growing African-American holiday tradition, but an attempt to create new knowledge through old ritual practices, using African cultural formations as sites of black protest.

But before the invention of Kwanzaa, the social movement known as Black Power had to take hold. Black Power politics—radical and national-istic forms of black protest, preceded the Black Power period. Prior to Peniel Joseph's study, *Waiting 'Til the Midnight Hour*, 1966 has served as a convenient marker to delineate the Civil Rights phase of the black freedom struggle from its black consciousness and Black Power phase. But as Joseph pointed out, 1966 belies our understanding of black radical protest. What we've come to know as Black Power—strident comments against white oppression, organizational vibrancy at the local level, and closing ranks around ideas of blackness—assumed its political character at least one decade prior to 1966. Though Kwanzaa was first celebrated in December 1966, the genealogy of the holiday in the form of radical African culture and politics actually begins in the late 1950s and early 1960s, underscoring Joseph's claim of the existence of Black Power before Black Power.[2] But if Black Power protest preceded the Black Power period, then what was different post-1966? I would argue that the post-1966 period in black protest is defined primarily by "ritual." What will characterize and represent a defining feature of black radical activity post-1966 will be some aspect of ritualized behavior and performance. That to think, act, talk, look and be black would mean to perform it, to display it, to visualize it, to manifest and actualize "blackness" and "African-ness" in some capacity. Believability and the process of convincing one of a converted blackness would lie in ritual creation and performance which would come to thor-oughly define the decade of 1966 to 1976 in black protest.

Black Power ritual was a variegated cultural and political enterprise with Kwanzaa being one of several incarnations. Communicative styles and speech vernaculars dominated everyday discourse among younger African-Americans. Terms of endearment, such as "brother," "sister," "blood," "black" were internal greetings between individual African-Americans as well as lines of social demarcation between blacks and whites. Black Power speech was often accompanied by Black Power bodily gestures, especially within the repertoire of black male handshakes. But 1960s black vernaculars and gestures inform only part of the ritual narrative of Black Power. Ritualized speech and bodily acts encompassed geographical appropriations and approximate understandings of Africa and African cultural practices. Arguably, doing it the "African" way played a major role in authenticating blackness. Manifesting "African-ness" was a ritualized performance designed to recapture a previously lost way of being and acting "black" or "African" in the world. Thus, the mere fact that "African-ness" had to be recaptured, re-donned, re-inculcated, and re-received meant that "Africa" at the level of geography, identity and consciousness had to be invented or re-invented by black Americans for black Americans. Kwanzaa as both ritual and holiday speaks profoundly to this quest for cultural recovery.[3]

In his two works on the "invention" and the "idea" of Africa, V.Y. Mudimbe charts the development of the continent at the level of discourse and has uncovered what he termed "genres of African knowledge." *The Invention of Africa* is Mudimbe's methodological pursuit of an African epistemology—a project in how do we know what we know about Africa—that serves as the basis of his intellectual task as well as an outline he is looking to sketch: "The question I am dealing with is one which would account for the possibility of anthropological knowledge and its meaning for the foundation of both Africanist knowledge and African gnosis." For Mudimbe, the well-spring of African knowledge runs deep and wide, encompassing religious missionary discourses, which Mudimbe defines as a "language of derision"; applied anthropology—which both uses missionary texts as well as dismisses them; and finally, African anticolonial responses such as Negritude. For Mudimbe, these Africanist discourses, or genres of African knowledge represented in travel literature, ethnology, applied anthropology, and anticolonial texts are the "locus" of Africa's discovery, invention, and projection. Inasmuch as these discourses are important, black Americans developed discourses about Africa that are very much connected to Mudimbe's genealogy of African knowledge. Mudimbe rightly places the work of Edward Wilmot Blyden in the order of African knowledge but confines the black American contribution to the genres of African knowledge to this one major thinker. I would like to argue, however, that the genealogy of African knowledge is very much tied to the genealogy of Kwanzaa, of which Maulana Karenga, as a important African diaspora thinker, as ritual importer, as holiday-maker, as social activist, is signatory.[4]

Historically, black American thinking about Africa falls into the intellectual pattern of civilizationist discourses—knowledge promulgated by elite and educated blacks that centered on the Christian and Western redemption of Africa. Black American thought about Africa mirrored European and Christian missionary thought, both of which metaphorically emphasized the bringing of European light to African darkness. Despite various commercial enterprises, religious projects, and intellectual musing beginning with Paul Cuffe in 1815 up until the first half of the twentieth century, there was little variation in the thinking about Africa, its people, its culture, and its future. The majority of knowledge about Africa centered on what black Americans could bring to help Africans, never the converse, as Paul Cuffe profoundly acknowledges: "I have for these many years past felt a lively interest in their behalf, wishing that the inhabitants of the colony might become established in the truth, and thereby be instrumental in its promotion amongst our African brethren. It was these sentiments that first influenced me to visit my friends in this colony . . . having found many who are inclined to listen and attend to the precepts of our holy religion."[5] Even as late as the twentieth century, conceptions about what Africa could provide black Americans were not only absent, but perhaps inconceivable. Despite a few signs of African political and social development in the eyes of Western blacks, the continent was understood to be culturally compromised at best, and because of the absence of Christianity in many parts of the continent, culturally wayward and suspect at worse. Indeed, the notion of Africa as a repository of knowledge and a source of cultural reality that black Americans can learn and personally prosper from can be discerned in the writings of Edward Blyden and Marcus Garvey, despite their redemptionist leanings. However, Africa having something to offer in the way of knowledge was not a commonly shared belief by black American thinkers, even as late as the twentieth century. The shift begins with the emergence of Negritude as a cultural movement; the influence of its offshoot in the United States, the American Society of African Culture; the writings of Paul Robeson and his wife Eslanda Robeson; the African scholarship of Carter G. Woodson; and the emergence of an academic sub-field known as cultural anthropology. Even with forward momentum in the mid-twentieth century, Negritude turned out to be an intellectual movement of black diaspora elites, the American Society of African Culture was red-baited out of existence along with the Robesons, Carter G. Woodson was more known for his scholarship on African-Americans than Africans, and despite "going native" on the African continent, cultural anthropology remained the purview of professors and their graduate students. I would like to argue that the major shift would come in the mid-1960s with Maulana Karenga's attempt to raise the cultural IQ of black Americans, insisting on how the continent of Africa was a source of cultural knowledge and the key to political liberation.

## MAULANA KARENGA AND AUTOBIOGRAPHICAL (RE)-INVENTION

Ronald McKinley Everett was born in 1941. Maulana Karenga was born sometime in 1963. Thus, Maulana Karenga created Kwanzaa; Ronald McKinley Everett did not. To make this distinction is to underscore the importance of "body" politics through self-invention; to recognize, borrowing a phrase from the women's movement, that the "personal" is indeed always "political," and that Kwanzaa's emergence could not have come if it were not for a profound autobiographical act. To also say that Karenga created Kwanzaa and Everett did not is to equally argue that his autobiographical belligerence manifesting in a kind of narrative suicide in one context, and his "African" rebirth in another is inseparable from his conception of Africa, his political activism, and his creation of the holiday Kwanzaa. Everett's autobiographical belligerence, which was for him the first political maneuver from which all else followed, including the creation of Kwanzaa, is a thorough self-realization of where power lies and how it is manifested, a kind of Foucauldian understanding of the world. It was indeed Foucault who said that "we all have power in our bodies," and that "individuals are the vehicles of power. ... they are always ... the elements of its articulation."[6] African independence movements and African Studies at the University of California at Los Angeles (UCLA) not only made global power discernable to Everett, but also brought him to a Foucauldian moment pre-Foucault, of recognizing the "circulations" of power in the body, mind, thinking, name, and clothing of Ronald McKinley Everett, of seeing himself personally and individually as a European subject, of needing to experience, to use sociologist Orlando Patterson's phrase, a certain kind of "social death" to live freely again in the world as an "African."[7]

For Everett, it is geography initially that makes re-invention possible. Reclaiming "Africa" as part of Everett's personal identity began in earnest after he relocated from rural Maryland to southern California in the late 1950s. Everett eschewed his family's rural home, farm upbringing, and his father's Baptist teachings on the eastern shore of Maryland. When military dictates and individual desires had already propelled two of the three Everett brothers to California in the early 1950s—Matthew, the oldest, a US merchant marine stationed in southern California, and Chestyn, a public school teacher and part-time actor, writer, and visual artist—Ron likewise decided to relocate. Ron, the youngest, would follow his brothers to southern California but chart a very different path—a path that included the life of the mind and social activism. At the same time Everett moved west during the late 1950s, anticolonial struggles in Africa greatly influenced academic and popular thinking about the continent. Parsonburg, Maryland would not be one of the places touched by African anticolonial discourses, but Los Angeles, California was, particularly on the campuses of Los Angeles City College and UCLA where Everett attended.[8]

Between 1959 and 1965, Everett underwent a transformation in name, thought, and action that served as a major precursor to the creation of Kwanzaa in 1966. Everett enrolled at Los Angeles City College (LACC) in the fall semester of 1959. Everett's first semester at LACC was relatively uneventful, mainly spent attending classes and making friends. By the second semester, Everett made a name for himself on the predominantly white campus of LACC, quickly emerging as a student leader in his second year. One of Everett's first public appearances involved a speech in which he and twenty-four other students reached the semi-final round of the All-School Speaking Contest in the spring of 1960. Awaiting Everett and LACC's other potential finalists was a trip to Washington, DC. The chosen finalists were to compete against students from other colleges for the best speech on the topic "Freedom is Up to You." Everett never received a chance to give a speech in front of several members of the House of Representatives on a subject he would later have much to say about. He did not make the final round. Instead, he refocused his energies, campaigning and winning the position of vice-president of the Associated Students, LACC's student union.[9] During his tenure as vice-president, Everett tended to issues of academic freedom, human relations, and student segregation. He also helped international students adjust to life on campus. Helping international students of color adapt to the predominantly white environment of LACC paid political dividends for Everett. He asked for their support in the next election. These students, Everett remembered, became the decisive factor in his overwhelming victory in becoming the first black student body president at LACC:

> I was able to organize them in a way no one else had and that's what made my victory. People were stunned by the size of the victory. They had never seen people of color as a major active force. Whites outnumbered us then so it was something for me to organize not only Africans, who were my natural constituency, but also Third World people in general and international students in particular and even some progressive whites. . . . This was before any talk of multiculturalism.[10]

Upon winning, Everett promised to "carry out the points of the platform in which I ran," which included passing a student budget, bringing more speakers to campus, and creating programs for international students.[11] More than creating programs for international students, Everett learned about African and Third World cultures from the very students he was elected to serve.

Everett's responsibilities broadened during his time as president. He was partly responsible for bringing well-known speakers to LACC, like journalist Harry Ashmore. He traveled and regularly attended intercollegiate conferences. He became involved in student movements, such as the struggle against the use of nuclear power, helping to form a National Committee for a Sane Nuclear Policy (SANE) student chapter on LACC's campus. Everett also fought against capital punishment, held rallies in support of the Cuban Revolution, and attended fundraisers for civil rights workers in the south. Though being president of Associated Students could have easily evolved into a quiet career in student office-holding serving others, Everett used his opportunity in government to cultivate a career in student activism.[12] The first phase of Everett's reinvention from country youth to student activist was nearly complete; he would now serve himself, turning his attention to reconfiguring his personal identity from an African-American subject to an "African" who was tied to a larger black diaspora culture.

Language acquisition and studying African history and culture informed Everett's new emerging biography. African history and languages preoccupied Everett's days and nights, enlivening his activist politics and guiding his hand later on in creating Kwanzaa. During the spring semester in 1961, Everett took the first African history course offered at LACC, a class taught by Dr. Joseph E. Hearn. Some of the material covered included the history of African languages, including Swahili. An African-Asian language conference was held during the same semester by Alpha Mu Gamma, the national foreign language society. Many experts in fields of African and Asian languages from southern California colleges and universities across the country attended the LACC conference. As student body president, Everett also attended, fueling his interest further in African languages, especially Swahili. Everett placed high value in the study of African languages, and believed that African languages were an important source of pride and identity—as he witnessed from African students that attended LACC. This belief in the power of African languages and the continent's ability to offer black Americans cultural traditions was not new in the early 1960s. Paul Robeson talked powerfully about the importance of African languages in 1935, though he was in the minority at that time:

> As a first step I went to the London School of Oriental Languages and, quite haphazardly, began by studying the East Coast languages: Swahili and the Bantu group which forms a sort of Lingua Franca of the East Coast of Africa. I found in these languages a pure Negro foundation, dating from an ancient culture, but intermingled with many Arabic and Hamitic impurities. From them I passed on to the West Coast Negro languages and immediately found a kinship ... with the Negro-English dialect which I had heard spoken around me as a child. It was to me like a home-coming, and I felt that I had penetrated to the core of African culture. ... It is astonishing and, to me,

fascinating to find a flexibility and subtlety in a language like Swahili sufficient to convey the teachings of Plato, for example, and it is my ambition to
make an effort to guide the Negro race by means of its own peculiar qualities
to a higher degree of perfection along the line of their natural development.
Although it is commonplace to anthropologists, these qualities and attain-
ments of Negro languages are entirely unknown to the general public of the
Western world and, astonishingly enough, even to the Negroes themselves. It
is my first concern to dispel this regrettable and abysmal ignorance of the
value of its own heritage in the Negro race itself. . . . I am convinced that the
results will be adequate to form a concrete foundation for a movement to
inspire confidence in the Negro in the value of his own past and future.[13]

Like Robeson, Everett came to understand the importance of studying
Swahili and other African languages. He remembered checking Swahili
books out of the library and getting "headaches trying to learn it all at
once." By May of 1961, Everett's autodidacticism paid off when he was
offered a language scholarship to attend UCLA the following semester.[14]

Everett arrived on the UCLA campus that was as politicized as the one
he left behind. There were many groups and individuals stoking the flames
of racial protest that Everett would have come into contact with. The
Bruin chapters of the National Association for the Advancement of
Colored People (NAACP), Congress of Racial Equality (CORE), the
American Civil Liberties Union, the Eugene Debs Club, the Student Peace
Union, and the Young Socialist Alliance all staged rallies on campus in
support of the black freedom movement. Journalist Louis Lomax, novelist
James Baldwin, and Marxist historian Herbert Aptheker passed through
UCLA, providing students with insightful commentary on black political
struggle. Although Everett welcomed their presence on UCLA's campus,
admittedly, he was more attracted to the lectures given by the Nation of
Islam.[15] Like civil rights and leftist groups, the Nation of Islam made its
presence known at UCLA. Malcolm X, the Nation of Islam's national
spokesman, and John Shabazz, the Los Angeles captain, were invited
by student organizations in the early 1960s. Everett met Malcolm in
1962 as part of a speech the Muslim leader gave under the sponsorship
of the Bruin NAACP. The subject matter of Malcolm's lecture ranged
from the religion of Islam and African-Americans' place in it to the frustra-
tions of enforcing new civil rights laws. Malcolm also talked about police

brutality—a topic taken up in greater detail by John Shabazz four months later. Resonating with Everett the most was Malcolm's analysis of black culture. "The American Negro is a Frankenstein," Malcolm announced to six hundred UCLA students, "a monster who has been stripped of his culture and doesn't even know his own name." Malcolm's ideas about culture and self-help deeply attracted Everett to the point where he contemplated joining the Nation. But as he had with the NAACP and CORE, Everett rejected the Nation, even a personal invitation from Malcolm himself as he recalled the encounter:

> Malcolm wanted me to join the Nation. I wasn't religious. I'm concerned spiritually and in a certain way I'm concerned ethically ... but I didn't believe I should belong to an organized religion. I had just left Christianity and I wasn't interested in religion. My family is Baptist. So I had a long tradition of Baptist training and orientation. My father is a minister, and my mother is very religious. So I broke from Christianity, in terms of internal criticism and the absence of Africa in it, and the need to search for our own origin. So we talked and I raised questions about the Arab stamp on Islam as an ethnocentric project which had moral implications. So the question was always, where is Africa?[16]

After turning down Malcolm's invitation to join the Nation of Islam, Everett instead joined forces with a lesser-known organization called the Afro-American Association headed by Don Warden—one of the few black nationalist organizations in California during the early 1960s.[17]

The Afro-American Association came into existence in March of 1962 as an outgrowth of a weekly book discussion group that first met regularly in the San Francisco Bay Area, specifically on the campuses of the University of California—Berkeley and San Francisco State College. Headed by a young attorney named Don Warden, the Afro-American Association stressed the importance of cultural, social, and economic unity of the "black race." The organization also believed in building self-esteem and pride among African-Americans, using heroic examples of black people in history. Huey Newton and Bobby Seale, later of the Black Panther Party, were part of this Oakland-based group. Evidence does not indicate how Everett heard about the group. Everett, perhaps, first became familiar with the Afro-American Association when Warden visited the

UCLA campus to give a talk two weeks after Malcolm X had given his speech.[18] If Everett compared Warden's talk with Malcolm's, he would have found more similarities than differences. Only the religion of Islam distinguished the commentary of the two men. Like Malcolm, Warden criticized the inertia of civil rights laws and the overall direction of the movement. Why waste time, said Warden, trying to "integrate a few schools or elect a few representatives?" He also stressed the importance of culture, admonishing the black audience to cease using bleaching creams and the like and become proud of its African heritage. Warden identified a lack of dignity as a major reason why African-Americans failed to act in a self-determining manner. Everett must have liked Warden's message. He soon joined the organization, becoming the chairman of the Afro-American Association's Los Angeles chapter sometime in 1963. Exactly one year after Warden delivered his message of cultural revitalization, Everett appeared as Ron Karenga, a representative of the Afro-American Association on a UCLA panel entitled "Solution to the Negro Revolt."[19]

The fact that Karenga appeared on the panel in 1963 as a representative of Warden's group spoke volumes about Karenga's early black nationalist leanings and his avoidance of civil rights organizing. The 1963 movement to desegregate Birmingham, Alabama may have galvanized the rest of the Los Angeles civil rights community to engage in non-violent protest as a way of life, but not Karenga, the young nationalist. As a 1963 UCLA panel indicated, he seemed more interested in cultural self-determination. In Los Angeles, Birmingham protests prompted local affiliates of the NAACP, CORE, the Civil Liberties Union, the National Council of Negro Women, and the American Jewish Congress to "band together to give a mammoth demonstration in support of Dr. Martin Luther King, Jr." The Reverend Maurice Dawkins and attorney Thomas Neusom of the Rally for Freedom Committee argued that "we must forcefully demonstrate in a most concrete manner that citizens of Los Angeles are shocked and ashamed by the atrocities perpetrated upon women and children in Birmingham." In June of 1963, an experienced freedom rider from the South and a member of CORE showed an audience at Zion Hill Baptist Church in Los Angeles how to "double up in a ball—hands over head, legs folded under" to protect themselves from random attacks. The two men wanted to demonstrate that "violence can be met with non-violent tactics," and that physically striking back "limits one's creativity."

"The new idea," said Earl Walter of CORE, "is to resist passively and in this way create the pressure of public opinion against discrimination." When Russ Ellis of the Bruin CORE and Bob Farrell of the United Civil Rights Committee posed non-violent direct action as a solution during the UCLA panel, Karenga appeared unconvinced, even after announcing that he once participated in a non-violent demonstration in front of Woolworths. He, instead, understood the problem as an absence of self-definition. Karenga told the panel and the UCLA audience that the only way to fight oppression is for blacks to employ methods of cultural self-determination. "We must define and speak for ourselves instead of others speaking for and defining us."[20]

If 1963 represented the year Ron Everett, the "Negro" transformed into Ron Karenga, the "nationalist," then the Civil Rights Movement was clearly not the impetus. Along with the nationalist-oriented Afro-American Association, the African independence movement contributed to Karenga's evolution as an intellectual and black cultural nationalist. Since he believed power was the main ingredient in African struggles for independence, he incorporated the discourse of African independence into his own analysis, informing his knowledge about the black movement in the United States. "I said we need power," Karenga recalled, "and I'm identifying with the independence movement in Africa, that's a defining moment for me, this rise of Africa."[21] This rise of Africa proved decisive in Karenga's own autobiographical conversion in the early 1960s. It would be the leaders of African independence movements and the books they authored that both informed and shaped Karenga's thinking about identity formation and protest politics. In the case of East Africa, the lines of intellectual influence were clear. Karenga was deeply moved by Gikuyu independent schools and Kenyan nationalism. He took the description used by the Gikuyu independent school movement, "Kareng'a" ("keeper of tradition") and began using it as his last name.[22] In his influential book, *Facing Mount Kenya*, Jomo Kenyatta described how African culture and Gikuyu nationalism proved decisive in overthrowing British colonial rule in Kenya. Karenga witnessed in Kenyatta the success of an African leader as well as the power of an indigenous culture to transform an entire nation. The Gikuyu people and the Mau Mau as a form of black cultural nationalism demonstrated to Karenga that African culture could also be used as an example for black America's liberation from whites in the

United States, if only African-Americans embraced their African culture. So convinced of the power of African culture, it was after reading Kenyatta's text, *Facing Mount Kenya*, in 1963 that Ron Everett retired his family name "Everett," taking on the name Karenga. It would not be the last time Karenga was belligerently serious about his autobiography. One year later he added the title, "Maulana"—which means "master teacher" in Swahili—and placed the title in front of Ron Karenga. For the rest of the decade, he was known by the name Ron Karenga or "Maulana" Ron. Sometime in the late 1960s or early 1970s when he emerged as a national figure in the Black Power Movement, he dropped "Ron"—his given first name—and went solely by the full name Maulana Karenga (master teacher, keeper of the tradition).

Totally giving up on one's birth American name and assuming an African one was to take a page out of Malcolm X and the Nation of Islam's cultural playbook. However, assuming an African name was also to take Guinea president Sekou Toure's ideas to their most logical conclusion, particularly Toure's position of moving Guineans "towards full re-Africanization." Karenga studied the anticolonial struggle in Guinea and was intrigued with Toure's commitment and insistence on the "rehabilita-tion of African civilization and culture," through the process of "decolo-nization and de-westernization." With French operating as the dominant language in Guinea, Karenga admired Toure's position on lessening the influence of French with the hope of removing the colonial lingua franca altogether. Toure wrote: "The political Bureau has ordered the teaching of African languages in our schools, with the prospect that the future national staffs will be able, everywhere in Guinea, to speak directly to the people. . . . [but] we regret that we are not able, at present, to adopt as an official language one of the national languages of Africa." Toure's concept of re-Africanization was an attempt to ask his people in their struggle to overthrow French rule the fundamental question: "who are you?" Toure did not wait to hear his people's reply. Toure answered thunderously for them, "Soussou, Malinke, Peuth, or Toma," he said, not French. Reading Toure's book, *Toward Full Re-Africanization*, prompted Karenga to ask himself the same question: "Who am I? . . . if I am an African, why don't I know an African language?" Karenga would learn several African languages, taking full advantage of the people and institutions around him to do so.[23]

The move toward African independence on the continent was accompanied in the United States by the birth of a number of institutional sites for the study of Africa in the post-war period. In the early 1950s, Melville Herskovits founded the Center for African Studies at Northwestern University. In 1956, a varied group of scholars, writers, and activists created the American Society of African Culture. The African Studies Association was formed in 1957. And by the time Karenga reached Westwood, UCLA was one of the premier institutions of higher learning engaged in the study of Africa. As a *Daily Bruin* report noted in 1963, "for Africa is now the object of intensified study at UCLA through its African Studies Center. UCLA now offers a wider range of subjects dealing with Africa than any other university in the country." This was no empty claim by the *Daily Bruin*. African statesmen, religious leaders, peace-corps officials, and scholars of Africa passed one another on campus, in seminar rooms, and in the halls. At the center of it all stood twenty-year-old Ron Karenga who soaked up as much knowledge about Africa as he could.[24]

Karenga enrolled in classes with professors who specialized in Africa. One of his favorite professors was Councill Taylor, better known as "Count" to students and faculty. Taylor taught courses in African ethnology for eight years. Robert Singleton, who eventually became the second director of UCLA's Center of African-American Studies in 1969, remembered Karenga as a fellow undergraduate at UCLA, specifically in a class of Taylor's. "We attended a couple of classes together. This was in the sixties, '61 or '62. He [Karenga] was taking some of the teachings of Councill Taylor to the streets. Councill Taylor was an anthropologist who was introducing us to what was called Negritude: the deep thinking of black scholars in other parts of the world." Karenga also took a course in South African literature with Dr. A.C. Jordan who he says "reinforced my interest in Zulu." He continued his immersion in African subject matter, studying under the direction of Dr. Bonaface Obichere, whom he saw as the "premier African historian." He furthered his interest in African languages, attending William Welmers' course on Ibo.[25] Like Taylor, many of Karenga's professors are no longer living, but the few who remain from the period remembered him very well. Professor Sylvester Whitaker taught an upper division political science course every year called the "Politics of Africa." The course covered everything from pre-colonial African traditional systems, to the scramble for Africa, ending at the movement toward independence. Whitaker remembered Karenga as a vocal student, quick to challenge the perceived ideas about the assigned material. Though Whitaker says Karenga was unconventional and a non-conformist in the classroom, he could see Karenga was "very bright."[26]

Professor Michael Lofchie remembered Karenga taking his class on "Governments and Politics of East Africa" in 1964. As the semester progressed, the constant challenges by Karenga made it "more and more clear that our views did not coincide," says Lofchie. Lofchie also recalls an incident when Karenga came into his office to discuss Kenyan nationalism wearing a Jomo Kenyatta t-shirt. The discussion involved the dominant interpretation of Kenyatta as advanced by the Carl G. Rosberg and later John Nottingham book, *Myth of "Mau Mau": Nationalism in Kenya*. The Rosberg–Nottingham thesis argued that Kenyatta was a conservative to moderate leader forced into the role of militant nationalist by colonial rule in Kenya. Karenga flatly disagreed, reading Kenyatta's nationalism as endemic to Kenyatta's personality despite the reality of white colonial rule around him. Karenga did not buy the idea of the "myth" as a historical explanation of the movement led by Kenyatta. For Karenga, the myth dismissed Kenyatta's agency, making him an object of white scholarship instead of a subject of African history.[27]

Karenga considered the approaches by Carl Rosberg and his student Michael Lofchie as an example of the white professorate's inability to relate their subject matter to the material conditions of blacks. Recalling his experiences with white professors, he surmised that some were satisfactory but "I'd challenged them ... I don't remember that they gave me something to deal with."[28] Karenga's utilitarian approach to academics was not so much a slight against his white or black professors as it was an ongoing criticism of the entire academic enterprise. He considered political science, his own discipline, confining, and in some ways hiding behind university walls, rendering it useless. "As for political science as an academic thing," Karenga mused, "I think it's of no use. ... I remember when I was at UCLA in graduate school and we were studying international relations. ... I had hoped that this class could give me some political mottoes that I could concretely apply in my dealings with larger groups. I think we should've learned how groups can increase their power. I think that if social change is not taught in terms of how to increase power, it's meaningless."[29] Despite repeated disagreements with professors and ruminations about higher education, Karenga earned enough credits to graduate with a Bachelor's degree in political science in 1963. From the fall of 1963 to the spring of 1964, Karenga earned a Master's in African Area studies. After a year into the doctorate program with hopes of becoming an academic, the rebellion in Watts intervened. In August of 1965, Karenga terminated his studies at UCLA and refocused his energies from a life of the mind in Westwood to the organizing of black Americans in South Central Los Angeles. Holiday creation and calendar politics would play a major role in his social activism.

## THE US ORGANIZATION AND BLACK POWER IN LOS ANGELES

The ubiquity of Karenga's presence in Watts shortly after the rebellion was evident in just a few weeks that led to the formation of the US Organization. Six months prior to Watts, Karenga and others left the Afro-American Association. Warden's commitment to cultural nationalism waned. As Karenga remembered, Warden had begun participating in Republican electoral politics and increasingly saw himself as part of a larger American polity:

> We began to leave the organization by the end of 1964, and certainly by 1965 because Don had begun to talk a different kind of project. He began to speak at Republican meetings, and began to talk more about what was good for America. And so at that time, you couldn't do that, I mean you had to talk about struggle, about confrontation, about line-drawing. And so he wasn't talking this, and so most of us dropped out and began to form other organizations.[30]

On September 7, 1965, Karenga founded his own organization called US, meaning US (black people) as opposed to "them" (white people or oppressors). US began as a small cultural nationalist collective that evolved out of a study group known as the Circle of Seven. The Circle of Seven congregated at Karenga's house and at a black-owned bookstore called Aquarian during the summer of 1965. Some of the first members included Samuel Carr-Damu, Karl Key-Hekima, Hakim Jamal, Ken Seaton-Msemaji, and Karenga's first wife, Haiba Karenga. By the time Karenga and his close associates formed US three weeks after the Watts rebellion, he believed a rigidly structured and highly disciplined organization with titles, departments, holidays, and rules of conduct would be the kind of group needed to rebuild Watts—an organization akin to the vanguard African political party found in Guinea, Ghana, and Tanzania.[31]

US members, in both the leadership and the rank and file, held responsibilities in the organization and were culturally accountable to Maulana Karenga, and to one another. There was the *Maulana*—master teacher, the *Imamu*—high priest, *Mwalimu*—teacher, and the *Shahidi*—protector of the faith. US also created a youth and woman's component called the *Simba* ("Young Lions") and *Muminina*, respectively. In addition, Karenga created an internal doctrine/philosophy known as *Kawaida* ("tradition"). Holding it all together was the *Kiapo* or Oath that members embraced, accepting the responsibility of building US and remaining loyal to Maulana Ron Karenga. Finally, the *Kanuni*, the Rules, were implemented to govern personal behavior and conduct. The Kanuni forbade discussing organizational business with outsiders, engaging in gossip and forbidding profanity, smoking, drinking, and dressing "in a manner that is in conflict with the organization."[32] Rank-and-file members, or "advocates," as they were called, also changed their first or last name or both upon request from Karenga. Joining US was to fulfill Karenga's expectation of identity transformation by adopting African names. To identify with the continent of Africa meant taking on the Swahili name that most reflected your personality or past experience. For instance, on joining US, Sam Carr was known as Sam Carr-Damu (warrior), a designation given to Damu because of his military background and his service in the Vietnam War. Other members were given names similarly, reflecting a character trait Karenga identified in them: James Mtume ("messenger"); Ngoma Ali (Ngoma-drum or being musical); and Joann Kicheko ("one who brings smiles"). Naming was also part of an organizational rite of passage as witnessed in the naming or nationalization ceremony for very young children called the *Akika*. In addition to rites of passage, advocates were expected to use African cultural standards in all rituals and ceremonies, such as in weddings and funerals. The official word for wedding in Swahili is *Arusi*, and one of the first African-styled weddings occurred in 1966, performed on behalf of nine couples in the US Organization. Upon death, fallen members and their families were given *Maziko* (funeral) ceremonies. To concretize one's cultural transformation and existence in US, changing the way one physically looked meant further re-defining oneself by wearing an Afro hairstyle, and donning African clothing, like bubas and dashikis. The greatest cultural statement US members made was not so much what came out of their mouths, or what rituals they performed, but how they looked to the general public.

Inspired by the continent of Africa, US's organizational structure, the oath, rules, African attire, and name changes of members from English to Swahili were all preparatory for the coming cultural revolution. US promoted the idea of returning to what its leader and members saw as the source of cultural blackness. The continent of Africa—its philosophical and ethical systems, its myriad cultural practices, its clothing and languages—became the geographical and ideational point of departure for the new cultural nationalist wing of the American Black Power Movement led by US beginning in 1965. Africa loomed in importance and deemed the source of culture precisely because black Americans were seen by Karenga and US as an African people. "We don't borrow from Africa," Karenga stated, "we utilize that which was ours to start with." For US, white racism precluded any claim to an authentic American heritage. So, Karenga not only raised Africa as a biological point of origin, but also as a repository for a new black American culture. Thus, the US Organization's requirement of member name changes, the adoption of African-inspired weddings and funerals, and the creation of its own series of holidays all underscored Karenga's essential premise that "you must have a cultural revolution before the violent revolution. The cultural revolution gives identity, purpose, and direction."[33]

Karenga believed the organization's cultural emphasis spoke to the needs of young blacks on the streets of Watts and provided them a positive identity, a sense of purpose, and new direction. In fact, US recruited a number of "street brothers" into the organization as well as several young people from Pasadena City College in the first year. Members that hailed from the streets were part of South Los Angeles area gangs who became politicized due to the riot. In contrast, the Pasadena contingent, most notably Clyde Daniels-Halisi and James Mtume, were first-generation working- and middle-class students whose consciousness was raised as a result of a growing politically active Pasadena City College campus. The US Organization created paramilitary-style drills visible on the streets of Watts designed to teach adolescent boys in the neighborhood discipline

*Figure 1: Maulana Karenga teaching Swahili in Los Angeles, 1965.*
*Courtesy of Library of Congress, Prints & Photographs Division, Look*
*Magazine Photograph Collection, LC-L9-66-2755-W*

and how to protect their communities. Karenga could also be found in South Central neighborhoods teaching Swahili at Fremont High School's weekend adult education program and offering black history seminars at community centers.[34]

Black Power was emerging in 1966, shifting from a demonstration slogan to a protest way of life in many cities across the country. Five months before the first Kwanzaa, *Life* magazine wrote a special section on Watts in July of 1966, showcasing the new generation of Black Power leaders in Los Angeles. The cover featured young members of Karenga's US Organization—the *Simba* (young lions)—donned in organizational sweat-shirts and marching in a military-style formation. Other photographs showed black men debating in front of an anti-poverty agency, the Neighborhood Westminister Association, and full-page images of Maulana Karenga and Tommy Jacquette—the leader of an organization called SLANT (Self-Leadership for All Nationalities Today). One of the captions noted, "the power vacuum in Watts shows signs of being filled by an emerging group of leaders. . . . the nationalists have one powerful effect.

They force moderate leaders to take harder lines in dealing with whites."[35] *Newsweek* magazine also covered the new generation of black leaders, taking note of Karenga and the US Organization in a special issue on Black Power in southern California:

> Los Angeles is Karenga's city and birthplace of the movement US. It is an intense and growing movement, still small (three hundred at the hard core) but reaching out, with jammed public meetings, adult classes in Negro history and weekend drill sessions for children. Dominating it all is the evangelical presence of Karenga—his voice rhythmic, high pitched, full of frank joy of being up front, talking race pride, talking economic power, talking revolt.[36]

Karenga saw the coverage of US in the national media as a measure of both groups' growing visibility that should be recognized by local municipal authorities, commenting: "we have gained a measure of legitimacy . . . a legitimacy that says we are a force in the community, a force that must be dealt with."[37]

Introducing black Los Angeles to African culture was not an easy sell for Karenga, given his academic credentials and accomplishments at UCLA. Marnesba Tackett, a member of the Los Angeles branch of the NAACP who was older than Karenga and interacted with him periodically, criticized his approach:

> I remember saying to Ron Karenga, I said, 'Ron, you are teaching these people Swahili. But you have your Masters degree; what you need to be teaching them is hard work, study, education, so that they can enter into the mainstream. How many jobs are these young people going to get when they go downtown and say good morning in Swahili?'[38]

For Karenga, academic degrees, aspiring black youth, and rebuilding Watts were not in diametric opposition to teaching Swahili in South Central Los Angeles. Teaching Swahili and black history appeared lame in an effort to rebuild a riot-torn community; Karenga, however, worked with other groups and government officials while pursuing his cultural nationalist objectives through US. These entities included a government agency—the Los Angeles County Commission on Human Relations, two anti-poverty organizations—Westminister Neighborhood Association and the Social

Action Training Center, two community-based groups—the Sons of Watts and SLANT, and finally, two umbrella groups—the Temporary Alliance of Local Organizations (TALO) with its Community Alert Patrol, and the Black Congress. The Los Angeles County Commission on Human Relations (LACCHR) asked Karenga to work with one of its neighborhood human relations councils. Human relations workers, as they were called, were peace brokers responsible for easing racial tension deemed "a menace to peace and public welfare" on the streets of Watts and South Los Angeles. People like Karenga and other human relations workers were the heart of these councils, traversing blocks and meeting neighborhood residents to deal with their concerns. "In 1965," Karenga remembered, "I began to work with John Buggs [Director of LACCHR] . . . trying to pull people together . . . making sure that black and brown communities were in harmony, engaging in conflict resolution in the community and between communities."[39] Karenga also worked with Westminister, the Social Action Training Center, Sons of Watts, the Community Alert Patrol, and SLANT. With the help of federal anti-poverty money, Westminister hired Karenga and other young community activists to encourage neighborhood kids to attend African-American history, Swahili, math and reading classes at its headquarters at 102nd and Beach Street. Similarly, the Social Action Training Center, headed by John Davis, received a grant to teach black and Mexican youth about community organizing and conflict resolution. Karenga called the Social Action Training Center his "main base" next to US. Karenga also worked closely with social worker Billy Tidwell, who reorganized a street gang known as the "Parking Lot Boys" into the Sons of Watts. Finally, Karenga helped Tommy Jacquette, a close ally of US, found his own group, SLANT.[40] These new organizations would criss-cross between the intersections of city municipalities, social welfare agencies, and the streets of Los Angeles. Part of their brand of politics was holiday cultural nationalism.

## HOLIDAY FORMATIONS: CULTURAL AND COMMEMORATIVE NATIONALISM

Holiday formation outside of the US Organization played a significant role in Karenga's social activism. US's first public appearance was organized around the inaugural Malcolm X observance in Los Angeles. With US founded only five months from the first Malcolm observance, and a mere three months before Karenga's questioning of Christmas, Karenga and US assumed the charge of promoting Malcolm X commemorations similar to the ones promoted in New York, Boston and Washington, DC. Karenga's approach to commemorating Malcolm X would slightly differ from east coast organizations. Karenga provided a rationale for Malcolm's commemorative legacy and underscored it with a Swahili name, "Dhabihu," meaning sacrifice. Dhabihu would become the official holiday name for Malcolm X's birthday in Los Angeles. The holiday named for the Swahili word sacrifice, Dhabihu, or Malcolm X's martyrdom, immediately proved promising. At the Garden of Prayer Church on February 20, 1966, the first Dhabihu gathered two hundred black activists and a significant number of white leftists. While Malcolm X's widow Betty Shabazz was unable to attend at the last minute, most of the leading black nationalist organizations in Los Angeles came together to pay tribute to Malcolm who was assassinated one year earlier. As two candles burned at the lectern on behalf of Malcolm and slain Congolese leader Patrice Lumumba, speeches covered topics such as integration versus separation, the problem with white liberals, anticolonial struggles in Africa, and Malcolm's evolving political positions prior to his assassination. Malcolm's assassination commemoration would indeed be US's public entry into black Los Angeles politics, but the first Dhabihu also marked the beginning salvo in holiday public protest for Karenga.[41]

Karenga would play a role in popularizing another Malcolm X observance—May 19—adding a second Malcolm commemoration to black America's growing protest calendar. The first Malcolm X birthday holiday in 1967 brought out a veritable who's who in Black Power Los Angeles such as SNCC, CORE, and US. While black nationalist groups honored Malcolm X on his birthday, it was Karenga who pushed the idea of making the day a black American holiday with real commemorative import. First, Karenga attached a Swahili name to Malcolm's birthday calling it "Kuzaliwa." Second, Karenga desired more than the usual black nationalist organizations partaking in the holiday. He wanted the holiday to transcend the black protest community. Leading up to the day of May 19, Karenga and US promoted "Kuzaliwa" throughout South Los Angeles with the net effect of impacting attendance at South Central public schools. The *Los Angeles Sentinel* reported: "On Friday, a wave of absenteeism hit Los Angeles schools in a response to a call from Ron Karenga of

US to make the birthday of Malcolm X a national Negro holiday."[42] The *Sentinel* reported that one thousand five hundred Compton High School students walked out with many going to Griffith Park. Kamili Mtume, a senior at Washington High School, joined the US Organization after she both participated and encouraged fellow students at Washington High to leave school for the day. "I was active in getting and encouraging other kids not to come to school that day or walk out," Kamili remembered, "so much so that the principal . . . came to me to try to get kids to come back." Charles Johnson-Sitawisha, a Horace Mann Bond High School student and another future member of the US Organization, was questioned the next day by his teacher for being absent from school on May 19. When asked why he was not present, Johnson-Sitawisha responded to his teacher, "Because it was a holiday yesterday." Johnson-Sitawisha remembered the "whole class laughing at me," but he took Karenga's call to stay away seriously.[43]

Inaugurating holidays and expanding the black holiday tradition was no laughing matter for many African-Americans, especially Maulana Karenga. In a February 1966 interview, Karenga foretold the growing influence of Malcolm X and future black holidays and their rationale for existing: "This is going to be one of many holidays we are going to substitute for those celebrated by Euro-Americans. . . . It's a matter of intelligence and self-determination that everyone who claims to be free should determine . . . who should be the heroes and what days they should be honored."[44] Though one of the most ardent holiday boosters in Los Angeles, Karenga understood he was not acting alone in attempting to alter the American calendar-scape, reiterating to the reporter: "there will be similar observances in New York City sponsored by the *Liberator Magazine*."[45] Karenga and US maneuvered additional commemorations on the black Los Angeles calendar. Two of the most enduring observances were the commemoration of all blacks who lost their lives in the Watts rebellion on August 11, 1965. Karenga named this observance Uhuru Day, meaning "Freedom" Day. The second, an annual commemoration called the Watts Summer Festival, would last some thirty years in Los Angeles, promoted primarily by the organization SLANT.

To say that Karenga believed holidays would better black America's present is to witness Karenga operate in the moment. In 1967, however, Karenga created a Seven Year Calendar with Swahili designations in an attempt to forecast black America's future. With two years of historical retrospection behind him, Karenga labeled 1965 as the Year of New Generation (Watts Revolt): *Mwaka wa Uasi*; and 1966 as the Year of Black Power: *Mwaka wa Uwezo Mweusi*. Both the Watts rebellion in 1965 and the black community's call for "Black Power" in 1966 were watershed markers in African-American history. Uncertain about what 1967 would bring, Karenga designated it as the Year of the Young Lions, *Mwaka wa Simba Wachanga*, perhaps giving credit to the younger members in US and young people in the movement who were challenging white authority more directly than their parents' generation. On Karenga's Seven Year Calendar, 1968 marked the Year of the Black Panther, *Mwaka wa Chui Mweusi*; 1969, the Year of Reconstruction; 1970, the Year of Splitting Apart, *Mwaka wa Dabuka*; and 1971, the Year of the Guerrillas, *Mwaka wa Gaidi*. As the latter years of the 1960s, particularly 1967 and 1968, produced more black urban rebellions in Newark, Detroit, Minneapolis, and the assassinations of Martin Luther King, Jr. and Robert Kennedy, the United States appeared as if black and white America were heading for a civil war. Karenga thought it was surely inevitable, indeed predictable, that 1970 would be the year black and white America would separate along racial lines. If 1970 was the Year of Splitting Apart, then 1971 would be, as US member George Subira put it, "a big fight between US and the L.A. police and whoever . . . [whereby] some people would die and some people would go to jail."[46] US members were required to heed to the Seven Year Calendar and commemorate every aspect of the black struggle, from the US Organization's founding day on September 7, 1965 known as *Kuanzisha*, Malcolm X's assassination and birthday on February 21 and May 19, *Dhabihu* and *Kuzaliwa*, respectively, and the memory of Watts on August 11, known as *Uhuru Day*. Karenga saw such focus on calendar politics as a necessary step in systematizing and ordering black struggle chronologically and perennially. As historian Scot Brown has argued, Karenga's focus on an US internal calendar "followed the pattern of long-range social and economic central planning schemes, popularized by Third World nationalists and socialists during the late 1950s and 1960s, exemplified by Jawaharlal Nehru's five-year plans in India, Gamal Abdel Nasser's Arab socialism in Egypt, and Indonesia's use of Chinese economic planning methods."[47]

Using calendars and holidays to systematize the United States black struggle indeed paralleled cultural struggles in parts of the Third World, each giving way to a series of invented cultural traditions. The Tamil/Dravidian nationalist movement against the dominant Hindi in India during the 1960s was another telling example where Dravidian nationalists created a series of observances and insisted on Tamil becoming a recognized language alongside Hindi and English.[48] Overthrowing British colonial rule in India upset the entire social order for the better part of two decades, creating vacuums for newer invented traditions. In fact, Eric Hobsbawm and Terence Ranger have persuasively argued that newer invented traditions are likely to increase " . . . when there are sufficiently large and rapid changes" in a particular society. "It is therefore reasonable to expect," say Hobsbawm and Ranger, that "these instant formalizations of new traditions to cluster during" periods of "rapid transformation" where "social patterns for which old traditions had been designed" are weakened or destroyed. Understanding Karenga and the US Organization's preoccupation with calendar ordering and holiday invention away from American mainstream calendar observances is important. Christmas and other American holidays were far from being weak, compromised, or overturned in 1966. But at no other time, whether prior to the 1960s or during the post-Black Power period, could Christmas have been vociferously questioned. Similarly, at no other time could black calendars and holiday rituals take hold and captivate the attention of so many African-Americans. Black Power breached the hegemonic present, creating the opportunity for Kwanzaa to emerge. Hobsbawm and Ranger surmised that time matters when such invented traditions manifest: "indeed, the very appearance of movements for the defence or revival of 'traditions,' 'traditionalists,' or otherwise, indicates such a break." The Black Power Movement cleared the deck and opened the door for a series of black invented traditions, including Kwanzaa and Kwanzaa's philosophical foundation known as Kawaida.[49]

In 1965, Karenga developed a philosophy he named Kawaida (pronounced Kah-wah-ee-da), taking the Swahili word meaning "custom" or "tradition." Known as "the doctrine" to US members, Kawaida represented the foundational ideology for the US Organization. Kawaida consisted of a series of numbered philosophical or doctrine positions. All told, Kawaida contained somewhere near one hundred sixty-six points in 1965 and 1966, much of it known only to Karenga, the Mwalimu (teachers), and the Imamu (priests) in the US Organization. Some examples of

Kawaida doctrine included the Seven Criteria of Culture, the Seven Aspects of US, the Seven Basic Concepts in Brother Malcolm's Message, the Three Ends of Black Power, the Three Ends of a Culture, the Four Areas of Political Power, and the Six Character Types of White Liberals. Kawaida was Karenga's attempt to invent new knowledge and numerically order this knowledge for purposes of systematization and effective communication. For example, the Seven Criteria of Culture were defined as 1) Mythology; 2) History; 3) Social Organization; 4) Economic Organization; 5) Political Organization; 6) Creative Motif; and 7) Ethos, each bearing its own explanation. In the Kawaida framework, Mythology serves as a people's religious concept "which provide[s] an answer to the origin of things." Mythology is also the "idea of a group of people being a Chosen People, which is necessary for developing a good self-concept." History, in the Kawaida doctrine, implied a "record of events, images and issues that reinforce a good self concept." Kawaida also taught that, "only a people can write its own history." Social Organization simply meant the process of socializing through the teaching of roles within the family and group, while Political Organization referred to a "system of obtaining power by utilizing all political forces available." Economic Organization acknowledged the "ways and means of providing goods and services" in a society whether based on capitalism, communism, socialism, or African communalism. Creative Motif in Kawaida was the expression of the dominant theme or attitude in a people's art, music, and literature. And Ethos represented the dominant cultural characteristic of a group, which in the late 1960s, Karenga and US identified as "soul" for African-Americans.[50] Each of these positions contained standard answers in "outline form," where Karenga "would clarify them to his audience with witty anecdotes and insights," historian Scot Brown acknowledged.[51] A serious public reflection from Karenga, such as "we say the 'Negroes'' main problem in America is that he suffers from a lack of culture . . . [so] we must free ourselves culturally before we succeed politically," would be followed up with a witty refrain like, "All Negroes want to be capitalists—and ain't none of them got any capital."[52]

Though Kawaida points were pretty static and represented established answers, Kawaida as a whole was an "on-going synthesis" of intellectual thought. Clyde Daniels-Halisi, editor of two US Organization books, *The Quotable Karenga* (1967) and *Kitabu: Beginning Concepts in Kawaida*

(1971) wrote, "one must understand that the doctrine of Kawaida is in a continuous state of development. . . . Kawaida is not a static ideology; nor is it completely constructed. It is continuously being generated by Maulana Karenga."[53] Kawaida was never fully fleshed out because at its base, Kawaida was a cultural philosophy that integrated knowledge from Africa and black American history, knowledge from Africa's past with the lived reality of black America's present. The objective was to operationalize a new intellectual synthesis that could inform the black freedom struggle. As Karenga noted, "We base our culture on tradition and reason. We draw from the wealth of knowledge that makes up our African tradition for our foundation. Then we must use reason to organize this knowledge in terms of present needs and future reality."[54] There were pitfalls in translating knowledge and ways of being from Africa into America that Karenga and the US Organization recognized from the beginning. If African-Americans believed that African culture was indeed black America's historical tradition, then many wondered how to embrace African culture in a non-African societal context. Clyde Daniels-Halisi addressed this issue that reared itself in the late 1960s:

> We draw from [African] tradition, our cultural foundation of values and institutions. But Maulana realizes that we cannot become atavists and seek to return to a totally African past while being both in America as well as in the present. He also realizes that we cannot totally transplant African culture in an American context, therefore, we must adjust our tradition to fit and facilitate our movement herein America. Many critics of Kawaida have with empty polemics attempted to brand our organization as reactionary in the sense of wanting to return to a past state. Nothing could be further from the truth. Maulana Karenga's concept is that tradition will provide US emotional and spiritual contact with our ancestors that will allow US to establish an Afroamerican community of values in America, a community based on values different from the America society . . . [55]

Kawaida's intellectual synthesis was just as much a revolution in values as it was a cultural revolution. Kawaida was centrally about values—imported, borrowed, invented, or a combination of all three. Thus, Kawaida philosophy, as articulated by Karenga and defended by members of the US Organization, appears to embody three "overlapping" types that

Ranger and Hobsbawm have identified as being crucial to the formation of invented traditions: first, membership in a real, or in one of Benedict Anderson's "imagined" communities; second, establishing and legitimizing both institutions and relations of authority; and third, the inculcation of beliefs, values systems, and conventions of behavior. As for the first, the imagined community that Kawaida produces ranges from the micro to the macro: from the US Organization at the micro level to the macro community of Africans in the diaspora. As for the second, institutional and relations of authority exist within the US Organization—flowing from the Maulana on down; cultural nationalists in general; and the continent of Africa as the supreme authority. As for the third, the inculcation of beliefs, values systems, and conventions of behavior is probably the greatest manifestation of Kawaida's "invented-ness": a series of philosophical positions on the black struggle, a cultural critique, and a set of "black" values for "black" people in the United States.[56]

Kawaida's critique of Christianity, of which Kwanzaa is heir, bears out the black politics of inventing new traditions and reorienting values. When parts of Kawaida were created in 1965 and early 1966, the doctrine seemed like a quasi-religious attempt to challenge Christianity's authority and perhaps supersede it with its own mythology: "for the leader speaks the word (the leader being Maulana Karenga)—that word being the doctrine (the doctrine being Kawaida)—the doctrine being the basis for the structure, symbolism, and substance of the organization," wrote Clyde Daniels-Halisi, an Imamu (priest) in US. The biblical-like language in early Kawaida thought was purposeful, for Karenga directly targeted Christianity and argued that a people's conception of God should be "historical, beneficial, and like you." Karenga's notion of a historical god challenged Christianity, for it belonged to Europeans and by extension white Americans. If one pointed to the rich and vibrant history of the black Christian tradition in the United States, Kawaida's response was that religious traditions originating outside of the black experience were not valid, for gods and religious traditions "must have been historically with US," Karenga writes. Kawaida also argued that a people's religion "has to benefit US psychologically and physically." Kawaida attacked some of Christianity's basic assumptions, particularly the scriptures that directed blacks to an outer life instead of what took place on earth. "For the next life across the Jordan," Karenga wrote, "is much farther away than the growl of dogs and policemen and the pains of hunger and disease." Karenga also forced blacks to examine "Christian behavior" as manifested by white Americans. Since whites were also Christians that discriminated and victimized blacks, it followed that "the Christian is our worst enemy." "Quiet as it's kept," said Karenga, "it was a Christian who enslaved us . . . the Christian that burns us . . . the Christian that beats us down in the street . . . and it'll be the Christian that's shooting us down." "You have to face the fact," Karenga continued, "that if the Christian is doing all of this there must be something wrong with Christianity."[57] Karenga rendered a simple but harsh conclusion: "Christianity is a white religion. It has a white god and any Negro who believes in it is a sick Negro." Kawaida's last position centered on worshipping a God that looks like the people embracing it, prompting the question from Karenga, "How can you pray to a white man?" Whether the God in question was a man incarnate, such as Jesus Christ, or some other white biblical figure, it just seemed, Karenga lamented, that "everyone but the Negro has a God that looks like him." God "must be like US in form as well as in feeling. . . . The Christian god cannot do this and so therefore is invalid."[58]

Kawaida provided positions on Christianity and a number of other topics that US members believed gave them a central understanding of black oppression as well as a convenient and quick way of responding in the midst of an intellectual exchange. US members believed Kawaida to be the proper perspective in understanding the black predicament and a "comprehensive prescription for solving the problem." Kawaida points were assessments and solutions all in one, enabling the US Organization and black America "to deal with the problem [of black oppression] more effectively."[59] Kawaida provided US members with a certain confidence during debates, whether on the streets of Los Angeles, college campuses, or on local television. Karl Key-Hekima, an US advocate, remembered being asked to define various concepts and ideas in public settings. When asked specifically by a reporter about Black Power, Hekima would always give the standard Kawaida answer by saying that the Three Ends of Black Power are self-determination, self-respect, and self-defense. "We could run it off," says Hekima,

> self-determination means that we name ourselves, speak for ourselves, and
> act for ourselves; self-respect means that we respect ourselves as African

people and that we want to return to our traditional culture, to our traditional ways of doing things; self-defense means that we have the right and responsibility to defend ourselves against our oppressors and against enemies of those things we hold dear and near to us as Black People.[60]

Thus, Kawaida was, in many ways, pre-packaged black thought, a veritable intellectual lean cuisine for immediate public ingest and digest. In one of the few attempts at explaining what Kawaida actually was, Clyde Daniels-Halisi wrote, "much of Kawaida is presented as three types of this, or seven levels of that, or seven functions of the other."[61]

Though many in US were able to recite certain Kawaida points in crucial situations, few mastered the entire doctrine. Outside of Karenga, the advocates that demonstrated the best command of Kawaida were the Mwalimu, a select group of teachers in US. The Mwalimu represented one of the most important responsibilities as they were frequently charged with establishing US chapters in other cities, or at the very least, helping other black nationalist groups organize themselves. As teachers, the Mwalimu stood beside the "master teacher," the Maulana, and often appeared in public with clean-shaven heads, an US cultural trademark. In order for members to reach the level of a Mwalimu, they had to submit to a rigorous training regimen as Mwanafunzi, student-teachers. Training in the doctrine occurred within the Kawaida Committee, the section of US responsible for teaching the doctrine to its members. After training was successfully completed, the Kawaida Committee, with the approval of US's Circle of Administrators, issued diplomas and conferred Mwalimu status on student-teachers.[62]

As stated earlier, much of the original Kawaida doctrine remained internally circulated and only known by Mwalimu, Mwanafunzi, and a handful of rank-and-file US members. There were, however, various parts of the doctrine that filtered in the general public. One part of Kawaida generally known to the public was a series of terms that would soon form the basic values of Kwanzaa—the seven principles or the Swahili name subsequently given, the Nguzo Saba. When asked to define the philosophy of his organization in September of 1966, three months before the first Kwanzaa celebration, Karenga did not go into detailed aspects of Kawaida with the *Los Angeles Free Press*. He simply told the reporter "we have seven main principles."[63] These seven principles were less than a year old and became the building blocks of a new black holiday. Part of building a new holiday at year's end meant encountering the historical Christmas and the subsequent days it occupied on the calendar.

## CHRISTMAS AND THE BLACK POWER ALTERNATIVE

Black Power as a national social movement was in its early stages of articulation when the first official week of Kwanzaa commenced in December of 1966. Six months earlier, Stokely Carmichael and others attempted to define to the nation what Black Power truly meant.[64] Only weeks removed from the "Meredith March Against Fear," the media and civil rights leaders would not wait for a clear analysis and definition of Black Power from Carmichael and others.[65] These various entities seized the moment and offered versions of the term immediately at odds with its major proponents.[66] But if confusion abounded about what Black Power meant, no such national bewilderment dictated how Black Power should manifest itself during the Christmas holiday season. That is because no one anticipated Black Power's complexity and the kind of cultural work it would perform on behalf of African-Americans. Certainly, no one envisioned Black Power's challenge to the traditional year-end holiday season and few took notice of the first Kwanzaa celebration at the end of December. And why would anyone take notice of an obscure black holiday not fully fleshed out and seemingly dominated by its longstanding counterpart?

Out of all of the weeks on the American calendar, none belong to black slaves. The last week of the year "became" black America's to claim only because whites gave it. The established tradition of Christmas and the accompanying days between December 25 and January 1 certainly brought the year to a pause, allowing different regions of the country to catch their collective breath, including slaves. Though Christmas was regional in its orientation throughout the eighteenth and nineteenth centuries, individual states and the federal government eventually legalized both Christmas and New Year's Day. Prior to the Civil War, however, the African-American right to the Christmas week was not supplied by the state, but instead by white masters. On plantations and inside homes, masters temporarily "freed" slaves from their normal work routines. Slaves looked forward to both Christmas and New Year's Day, using the time to tend to matters in their own community. The number of days off varied from plantation to plantation, ranging from two to seven days. Christmas was an occasion to reconnect with loved ones on neighboring plantations and engage in festive activities. Thus, for slaves, the last week of the year was a time of leisure and the only calendrical break from the previous fifty-one weeks. The fact that Christmas week stood in stark contrast to the entire year, it was tantamount to a true holiday for slaves as explained by a first-hand observer:

> Throughout the state of South Carolina, Christmas is a holiday, together with two of the succeeding days … especially for the negroes. On these days the chains of slavery with which the blacks are loaded and in which they toil unceasingly for their masters, are loosed. A smile is seen on every countenance, and the miseries of the year seem amply recompensed by this season of hilarity and festivity. No restraint is imposed upon their inclinations, no lash calls their attention from the enjoyment of all those delights which the most unconstrained freedom profers [sic]. Children visit their parents, husbands, their wives; brothers & sisters, each other, who live at a distance. . . . [67]

Year-end folly notwithstanding, the Christmas week, particularly New Year's Day, was political as much as it was social. On December 26, 1863, the *Christian Recorder* wanted its readers to prepare for January 1, 1864—the one-year anniversary of the Emancipation Proclamation. The coming of New Year's Day in 1864 would not be an ordinary time on the calendar. Reflecting on Abraham Lincoln's war measure, the publication took the opportunity to grapple with the problem of slavery by assessing New Year's Day: "The time for the American Jubilee, the first Anniversary of Freedom's birthday in the United States, is drawing near. It is meet and proper that the recipients of the precious blessings resulting from the decree given, on the first of January, make preparations to celebrate that day in a way worthy of sons and daughters of Freedom." While leisure proved to be the sole option at the end of the year for slaves, free blacks and others politicized week fifty-two, calling into question the institution of slavery. With the black holiday tradition coalescing around January 1 celebrations, it became clear that New Year's Day provided an opportunity to opine about politics and history as much as it was a day of leisure.

Kwanzaa followed in the tradition of using the last week of the calendar year to gather socially. But Kwanzaa also used the last week to mitigate the overly leisure cast of the Christmas holiday season by making December 26 to January 1 an official black holiday in historical politics and memory with the power of perennial reinforcement. Kwanzaa's seven principles were not only designed as a set of black values for a hostile white environment, but seven days on the calendar. When Karenga placed the principles on the calendar and measured them, he was presented with two main options: one, he could begin his holiday on December 25 and end it on December 31, or he could place the first day of Kwanzaa on December 26 and have the holiday end on January 1. Karenga knew to gain a loyal black following for Kwanzaa the new holiday should not fall directly on Christmas day. No matter how oppressive Christmas appeared to black cultural nationalists, the parochial and virtually unknown Kwanzaa was no match for the well-established December 25. After all, black Americans were Christians and generational celebrants of Christmas. To place Kwanzaa on the day after would prevent it from being enveloped by Christmas, and allow Kwanzaa to operate truly as an alternative holiday. Creating a Christmas alternative was paramount, for "some of the most fundamental things that Black people lacked were holidays," Karenga argued.[68] Responding to questions about his attempt to circumvent Christmas with Kwanzaa, Karenga mused, "the white boy got enough dates for everybody."[69] By dotting the calendar-scape in and around Christmas and New Year's, Karenga, as a calendar activist and holiday-maker, "blackened" two of the most important days on the American and Gregorian calendars: the 25th and the 1st. Boxing Day, a major observance on December 26 outside of the United States, would not pose a problem for the new holiday Kwanzaa. Thus, Kwanzaa's beginning on December 26 (UMOJA) and ending on January 1 (IMANI), challenged the political, cultural, and economic might of the Christmas holiday season, and gave black America a viable alternative. Before spreading throughout black America, the idea of a Christmas alternative germinated inside the US Organization.

Three months removed from the founding of his cultural nationalist organization US in September of 1965, Christmas created a crisis for Karenga that raised the specter of fashioning an alternative holiday and diminishing Christmas' influence. US member Samuel Carr-Damu paid a visit to the home of Karenga on Christmas Day in 1965 bearing a gift in hand. The gift was a black doll, meant to bring joy and delight to Karenga's youngest daughter, Thanayi. After talking briefly with Karenga and his wife Haiba inside their Los Angeles home, Sam Damu presented Thanayi with the black doll. Karenga thanked Damu for the gift, appreciating the gesture to his daughter. But Karenga's thank you was partly compromised. Karenga's thanks to Damu was accompanied by one of the most astonishing statements to Damu—a lifelong celebrant of Christmas: "I'm sorry Damu but we don't celebrate Christmas." To say Damu was taken aback would severely understate the case. "What do we celebrate then?" Damu replied.[70] Karenga did not answer. The reason: Karenga was incapable of providing an answer to Damu on that December 25, 1965 because no answer existed. Karenga would spend the next twelve months preparing an answer for Damu and the other members of the US Organization as well as providing black America with an alternative to Christmas.

The pronoun "we" in Karenga's response to Damu, "we don't celebrate Christmas" included Karenga, his wife and daughter. The pronoun "we" also extended to his new family, members of the US Organization who positioned themselves as the foremost group that understood culture in the most political of terms. The pronoun "we" would eventually extend to all of black America where Karenga believed the key to black liberation and freedom lay in black America's ability to develop a distinct cultural way of living, celebrating, and observing far different from white America. Since Christmas dominated the calendar at year's end, engulfing black America in its crass consumerism and its images of a white Christ, Karenga believed Christmas stood in the way of black cultural advancement. Indeed, on December 25, 1965, Christmas proved to be an impediment to Karenga who was emerging not only as a social activist but as a cultural theorist with an eye for identifying what he increasingly understood as white cultural domination. Karenga's refusal to accept a doll on behalf of his daughter forced his members to question a longstanding belief with the prospect of jettisoning a family traditional celebration. Many members in the US Organization were discombobulated when they eventually received news of Christmas' demise within the organization. While many in the US Organization delighted and rejoiced in having a Black Power alternative, some members faced the prospect of either choosing or forgoing Christmas altogether. But historically, Christmas had always maintained black America's loyalty, even in the post-Kwanzaa period.

## INVENTING AND IMPORTING AFRICA: THE POLITICS OF KWANZAA'S MAKING

Invention informs the personal and transformational politics of Karenga at the level of the individual, and US, at the level of organization; quite naturally invention would inform the making of Kwanzaa. But to comprehend Kwanzaa's "making" is to understand what Kwanzaa is: *a hodgepodge of indigenous African practices placed inside a black American ritual framework.* Africa provided the inspiration and the cultural raw materials at the level of language and ritualized ceremony; black America provided seven days on the calendar. In the sense that Kwanzaa takes from Africa, it is an old-world original import. In the sense that Kwanzaa takes from nowhere in Africa, but rather is created in Los Angeles, it is imagined. The dialectic of imagined holiday and imported practices led to a cultural synthesis called Kwanzaa that was both a historic and new celebration. The right to imagine and import cultural practices lay with an understanding that black Americans were part of an African continental community and a black diaspora one. Being part and parcel of both a continental and diaspora community provided one with the right to claim, select, borrow, appropriate, use, re-configure and re-invent longstanding practices and bring them closer to the present as part of a larger synthetic enterprise. Kwanzaa's holiday DNA is continentally and diasporically shaped—permeated with a plethora of African practices, guided by cultural synthesis, and informed by syncretic dialogue with the African continent.[71] By evoking cultural syncretism in Kwanzaa's making, the quilt as a metaphor is useful, for it demonstrates the profound undertaking of layering and sewing diverse cultural practices into a novel coherent whole from a storehouse of historical information.[72] Thus, Kwanzaa is an invented tradition based on the politics of cultural syncretic practice observed in the history of the black quilt, black Protestant Christianity, and jazz in the United States; and Rastafarianism, Carnival, and Voodoo in the Caribbean.[73] Since Karenga and the US Organization believed the entire continent of Africa was the source of African-American culture, much of Kwanzaa and other attempts at "returning to the source" were African-inspired amalgamations and creative syntheses; at most, partial appropriations from specific African cultures.[74]

Out of all of the appropriations, Swahili is the most revealing in the holiday's construction. Using Swahili as a point of departure played to powerfully explosive continental and diaspora politics that united blacks across the Atlantic, as it was uniting Kenyans, Ugandans, and Tanzanians in East Africa during the 1960s. Swahili's ubiquity, at least in East Africa, attracted Karenga to the language, becoming the primary reason for black American identification: "It is an African language and it is non-tribal; we are not interested in identifying with any one tribe but with African people."[75] But choosing Swahili as a kind of official language for Kwanzaa and black cultural nationalist practices in the United States was wrought with a myriad of complexities. For one, the debate around Swahili's origins has never been settled, whether it is indigenous African, Arab, or some mixture of the two. In addition to its complicated linguistic and cultural history, Swahili represented one of thousands of languages spoken throughout the continent of Africa. Karenga felt African-Americans need not worry themselves about the dispersal of Sabaki-speaking communities or the various Swahili dialects and sub-dialects in eastern Africa. What appeared most important was the language's continental origin and its regional coverage. If Swahili could serve as a national language for some continental Africans, then Karenga and US believed Swahili could serve as an unofficial lingua franca for culturally awakening African-Americans desiring to demonstrate African roots and assume a greater African posture.[76] Karenga did not introduce Swahili to the United States; he and his organization embraced the language in the context of continental identification. Thus, Kwanzaa, whose linguistic lineage is tied to the east African language, had the potential to become one of the greatest manifestations of the "Swahilization" of black American culture.[77]

Central to Kwanzaa's invention was the manipulation of Swahili and the appropriation of celebratory elements from African harvest festivals. Language manipulation meant both adding and subtracting alphabets, altering definitions of Swahili words, and adding a lexicon of new words and phrases, such as "Kwanzaa" and the "Nguzo Saba."[78] Inspired by African harvest celebrations on the entire continent, Karenga appropriated the word "kwanza" from the Swahili phrase, *matunda ya kwanza*, with matunda meaning "fruits," and ya kwanza, meaning "first." Dropping "matunda ya," Karenga capitalized the "k" in "kwanza," then added another "a," giving the holiday its official name in the American context, "Kwanzaa."[79] Taking a word meaning "first" from the original Swahili imbued the new holiday with authenticity and cultural legitimacy. Because the name Kwanzaa was so reliably convincing and saturated with African veracity, many black Americans did not realize that the name Kwanzaa was only inspirationally African and not African in fact. Due to the growing confusion in Kwanzaa's early years, Karenga was forced to level with black America, clarifying: "Nowhere on the African continent is there a holiday named Kwanzaa."[80]

But Kwanzaa did "exist" on the African continent; it was called a thousand different names tied to the particularities of harvest celebrations in local African communities. These harvest celebrations provided Karenga with the cultural repertoire to construct and invent Kwanzaa. While reading books on the rich traditions of southern African Zulu culture, Karenga came across one particular harvest festival called Umkhosi.[81] Umkhosi was one of many first fruit ceremonies practiced in the Natal and Zululand regions of South Africa centuries before and during colonial occupation. The culmination of the harvest in Natal and Zulu regions usually occurred during the end of the year and at the beginning of the next, prompting the people in these areas to stop their daily activities and partake in the annual agricultural celebration. Umkhosi, like many first fruit ceremonies, relied on the king or chief to protect the community by sampling the crops first. Usually inoculated from a medicine prepared by the village elders, the king or chief readied himself against potentially evil forces prior to ingestion. Once evil was undetected in the harvest, the food proved ready for consumption by the rest of the village. Other features Karenga and US discovered in Umkhosi ceremonies were animal sacrifices, mock insults of the King, dance competitions among military regiments, ancestor veneration, feasting, and the in-gathering of local people. These elements in Umkhosi were both deeply cultural and spiritual. One author surmised that the name Umkhosi is a variant of the word amakhosi, a Zulu term meaning ancestral spirit.[82] The Zulu practice of ancestor worship in the form of Nkulunkulu, the Creator or first ancestor, was admired and adopted by Karenga and US in Kawaida.[83] In addition, in-gathering, feasting, drinking, and dancing were widespread practices in Zulu harvest celebrations as author T.V. Bulpin explained:

Especially at the beginning of each year these great beer-drinks were numerous. Then it was that the ceremony of the first fruits would be staged; a period of mystic ceremonial, of dancing and singing. At this time, the days of the ukuNyathela (preliminary harvest festival) and the umKhosi (royal festival) the whole nation would meet at the capital to pass greetings and, with mass hysteria, fortify the national spirit of love of their King. Then it was that the national song, the Ngomankulu, would be sung and danced in a fever of excitement. A black bull would be slaughtered . . . the King would be doctored and reinforced with sundry medicines.[84]

Karenga and US were presented with a cornucopia of cultural practices from Umkhosi. In designing the new holiday, the challenge became what to select from the many activities performed in Umkhosi harvest festivals. Certain village ceremonial activities associated with the harvest in Natal and Zululand areas were incongruent within an urban industrial context. Stripping away components of the Zulu custom unfeasible in an urban society, Karenga and US forwent Umkhosi's animal sacrifices and mock insults of the king. Nor would Karenga and US expect African-Americans to plant seeds for an agricultural harvest. However, calling out the names of ancestors, feasting, dancing, and Umkhosi's appearance at the end and beginning of the calendar year proved critical to the new holiday Kwanzaa.[85] Thus, African-Americans would celebrate Kwanzaa—a selective reproduction of Umkhosi—not Umkhosi itself or any other harvest holiday as Karenga explained, "Kwanzaa then became for US and Black people, a time and week of the gathering-in of ourselves rather than the agricultural harvests of our ancestors."[86]

Forgoing certain activities in the United States did not mean Kwanzaa lacked the performative aspects of traditional harvest celebrations. In many respects the basis of Kwanzaa's appeal lay in performance. Performativity was endemically tied to the Black Power Movement. As I argued earlier in the chapter, Black Power as a protest paradigm existed prior to the general temporal marker of 1966. What defines Black Power in the post-1966 period is ritualized performance(s). To manifest Black Power, one often had to perform it. Performing Black Power involved doing things: elaborate hand-shakes or extending the arm in the air with a clenched fist; uttering words and phrases: "brother," "sister" or "all power to the people." Similarly, performing Kwanzaa involved doing things, such as pouring libation, reciting the seven principles, or chanting "Harambee" ("let's pull together") after each daily ceremony during the Kwanzaa week. Performing Black Power ultimately meant mastering the kinesthetic and illocutionary sciences in Black Power ritual, using bodily gestures and "speech acts" to great effect.[87] The bodily gestures and verbal speech acts associated with Black Power, generally, and Kwanzaa, specifically was meant to demarcate boundaries, to identify who was inside or outside the lines of black consciousness. Black Power consciousness could not be assumed, it had to be demonstrated, which often meant acted out. Negro-to-Black conversion experiences, which were conclusive, confirmable, and irrefutable examples of the transformational process black Americans underwent to claim new subjectivity in Black Power, could only be demonstrated at the level of ritualized performance. As Catherine Bell has argued, "the power of performance lies in great part in the effect of the heightened multisensory experience it affords: one is not being told or shown something so much as one is led to experience something." Anthropologist Barbara Myerhoff concurred, "not only is seeing believing, doing is believing."[88]

If doing was believing, then the grandest event in Kwanzaa, the Karamu (feast) punctuated Black Power performance and provided Kwanzaa its greatest visual and verbal presentation. "Why is it," asked Theodore and Lin Humphrey, "that so many of our social actions . . . take place in the company of food?"[89] Kwanzaa not only answered the question by having the end of the holiday week culminate in the Karamu, the large feast on Kwanzaa's sixth day, but used the occasion to enact a collective statement of black gathering of which food played a major part. The Karamu drew its inspiration from African harvest festivals and the power to assemble large segments of the community. In Umkhosi, the context for mass gathering at year's end was the harvest. In Kwanzaa, the context for bringing people together was the feast. Food as a "catalyst for social interaction" defined black gatherings on the continent and in the diaspora. Group interaction around food has been an important component of black social activity and political activism. The consumption and preparation of food was political as much as it was social. In fact, during the late 1960s, Black Power demarcated "black" food from "white" by using one of its core concepts, "soul," redefining black food vis-à-vis white American cuisine. Some of the food prepared for the Karamu was both traditional African and black American.

Though food could typically dominate aspects of black community gatherings, the Karamu also extended beyond food politics and involved ornamental splendor and African inspired ceremony. The site of the

Karamu, home or community center, was laced in multiple black, red, and green color motifs—the black nationalist colors of Marcus Garvey and the Universal Negro Improvement Association (UNIA). The Karamu's location on December 31 was staged to make Africa real and palatable in ways that the previous five days could not. The Kwanzaa set was made visible, placed on top of a large Mkeka (mat) which took up the center of the room along with the food brought by attendees. African-based entertainment took center stage. Drummers and storytellers were employed. Members of US performed the boot dance—an appropriation of South African dancing mastered by black workers in the diamond mines.[90] Karl Key-Hekima, an US member who helped shape the early Karamu, remembered the performative aspects of those days: "We did the whole traditional thing—you brought your food, you brought your pillows and stuff to sit on the floor, you didn't eat with utensils, you used your hands. . . . We did African dances. We told African stories. . . . It was very festive."[91]

Karenga and the US Organization could not "do" or "perform" Kwanzaa without holiday symbols accompanying the ritual. In 1966, Kwanzaa began with five symbols: MKEKA (mat), KINARA (candleholder), MISHUMAA (candles), MUHINDI (ear of corn), and the ZAWADI (gifts). The MKEKA is a straw mat found in a variety of African societies. Out of the five original symbols, the MKEKA is the only one from the continent of Africa. Since it was a "traditional" item, Karenga believed it should represent the "foundation on which all else rest." As the foundation, the MKEKA was meant to spread on a low table or lay on the floor.[92] The KINARA, placed in the middle of the MKEKA, is the candleholder designed to hold the seven MISHUMAA (candles, later called MISHUMAA SABA). The seven candles correspond to the seven principles and the seven days of Kwanzaa. The KINARA contains seven holes, where three candles on both sides of one central candle are inserted. The correct way to present the KINARA and MISHUMAA is to place three red candles on the left and three green candles on the right of the center black candle, lighting one during each day of Kwanzaa in an alternate manner. The black middle candle is lit on IMANI, the last day of Kwanzaa. After a candle is lit each day, the head of the house, or an elder, explains the principle and its significance.[93]

When Karenga and US first conceived of the KINARA and the MUHINDI, they were very much consumed by African creation myths. The

KINARA was not just any candleholder, it represented the "original stalk." The original stalk or black parental origin was symbolized by the Zulu religious concept called Nkulunkulu. Nkulunkulu, in Zulu religious mythology, is referred to as the Creator or origin of man. Karenga extended the Zulu concept of Nkulunkulu to the KINARA as an "Adam-like" first born where all black people originated. Nkulunkulu was not only the original stalk in Kawaida mythology, he also gave black people the seven principles according to US Organization belief: "Nkulunkulu was the first law giver and laid down the Nguzo Saba," said Halisi. "He is considered our first ancestor who organized the first African community around the seven principles," from which the candles signify.[94] The last two original symbols are the MUHINDI and the ZAWADI. The MUHINDI (corn, originally interpreted as ear of corn by Karenga) represent the offspring of a house, or the children, who in turn become stalks or parents in the future. The MUHINDI are to sit on both sides of the KINARA, the symbol for parent. And last, Karenga and US de-emphasized the crass commercialism of Christmas and believed gift giving should be purposeful, directed mainly toward children. Gifts should be hand-made and awarded on the basis of "good acts, good thoughts, good grades . . . and how well they live up to their commitments." ZAWADI are to be distributed on IMANI, the last day of Kwanzaa.[95]

If the politics of selection contributed to the infrastructure of Kwanzaa's invention, then the politics of revision—editing, modification, elaboration, and addition—also contributed to Kwanzaa's making. When Karenga and US created Kwanzaa over the course of 1966, the holiday-set only included five symbols (Mkeka-mat, Kinara-candleholder, Mishumaa-candles, Muhindi-ear of corn, and Zawadi-gift), the seven principles (Nguzo Saba), and the feast (Karamu), all validated by the US Organization's 1960s instructional pamphlets on Kwanzaa.[96] Karenga's first published writing on the holiday in 1975 provides further confirmation on the original five symbols, the seven principles, and the Karamu as the original holiday set-up. Seemingly, there were other symbols, such as the libation cup, the color schemes of black, red, and green, and activities, like pouring libation, the Kwanzaa greeting (Habari Gani—what news?) that were part of the US panoply of cultural items and practices present during Kwanzaa's first ten years of existence. For reasons unclear, they were not included in the holiday's inventory of material items and essential activities, thus not part of the original Kwanzaa set. By the time Karenga published his second work on Kwanzaa in 1977, he added two additional symbols to the Kwanzaa set—Mazao (crops) and the Kikombe cha Umoja (unity cup). Since Kwanzaa drew its inspiration from the African harvest, the original Kwanzaa set failed to provide a representational item during the first ten years, leaving both a void and some confusion as to what the ear of corn or Muhindi symbolized. Many early celebrants mistakenly believed Muhindi (corn or maize plant) signified the harvest, but Muhindi, according to early Kwanzaa pamphlet literature, had always represented the offspring or the children in a domicile, not a harvest. Mazao, the word in Swahili meaning crops or produce, would become the symbolic representation of the harvest in the Kwanzaa setting.[97] While Karenga left the Muhindi's meaning constant, and placed Mazao alongside it, he abandoned the Kinara's original meaning completely. The Kinara is arguably the most important of Kwanzaa's holiday symbols. Its early meaning was fused with US organizational mythology and the quasi-religiosity of Kawaida. In 1966, Karenga initially made the Kinara's meaning synonymous with the South African God of creation. He rendered this obsolete nine years later: "The Kinara is a candleholder and in the traditional sense represents the original stalk or the First Born, Nkulunkulu, from which we all came. But this traditional and colorful concept runs counter to reason and we must sacrifice it for a more scientific and historical approach to our origin." Karenga felt the Kinara should not memorialize an "Adamic-like" first born, but instead African offspring (i.e. continental Africans) and those blacks who died fighting for freedom: "Thus, the Kinara must symbolize the historical . . . roots from which we rose—the African people as well as our forefathers and foremothers who struggled and died here."[98]

The seven principles of Kwanzaa (Nguzo Saba) retained all of their original meanings. However, Karenga's later interest in African ethics, particularly Egyptian ethical thought, informed his decision to elaborate on some of the principles. In 1966, Karenga and US originally identified the Nguzo Saba with the metaphysical realm and the same deity originally represented by the Kinara. "We once traced the Nguzo Saba to the First Born, Nkulunkulu," he wrote. By 1975, Karenga emphatically rejected this early premise, stating that the connection "was cultural mythology and not needed." After its metaphysical beginnings in the US Organization, the Nguzo Saba was simply understood as Kwanzaa's values, or part of the black value system. Though Karenga eliminated the "sacred and holy" from the Nguzo Saba, preferring to put "man and woman [at] the beginning of our origin," he never entirely abandoned the idea of informing the Seven Principles with sacred conceptions. Karenga removed folk metaphysical notions like Nkulunkulu from the Nguzo Saba in the late 1960s in favor of more cerebral ethical concepts in African philosophy by the 1990s. No longer would Kwanzaa be informed by African folk religion. Karenga's pursuit of a second doctorate in social ethics led him to associate elements of Kwanzaa with African moral philosophies such as MAAT of ancient Kemet (Egypt). This post-Black Power Kwanzaa was also inspired by ideas and dictums from the Cieng of the Dinka (Sudan), the Lovedu of the Transvaal (South Africa) and the Odu Ifa of Yorubaland.[99] Umoja (Unity) and Ujima (collective work and responsibility), the first and third principles of the Nguzo Saba, are illustrative of this change over time and the influence of African ethics in Kwanzaa. In 1966, Karenga defined Umoja within the context of black nationalist Los Angeles when he made the distinction between total unity, of which he offered no real explanation, and operational unity—a familiar phrase used in Los Angeles and the national Black Power Movement that meant an "alliance with all other organizations on common community problems."[100] In the next year or so Umoja was simply defined as "to strive for and maintain unity in the family, community, nation, and race," and has remained the standard definition. By the 1980s and 1990s, Karenga's foray into African moral and philosophical systems led him to see elements of African ethics in some of Kwanzaa's principles like Umoja: "Unity as principled and harmonious togetherness is a cardinal virtue of both classical and general African societies." Unity was now synonymous with harmony, a cardinal virtue of MAAT as well as its literal translation, according to Karenga. Karenga also surmised that there existed aspects of Yoruba and Lovedu ethics in Kwanzaa's third principle Ujima. Both the Yoruba and Lovedu demonstrated through prayers and other actions that personal undertakings and other forms of individuality operated contrary to the larger community. Collective work and responsibility in the Yoruba and Lovedu would preclude an individual asking "for the personal without at the same time asking for the collective." Such request in ethical systems of the Yoruba and Lovedu were "both improper and immoral."[101] Kwanzaa's seven principles, Karenga believed, were in dialogue with African ethical systems and moral philosophies, requiring slight elaboration, reflection, and revision in later years.

## The First Kwanzaa in Los Angeles

Kwanzaa's evolution and elaboration over time did not prevent the US Organization and non-US blacks from promoting the alternative to Christmas beginning in 1966. On the eve of December 24, 1966, US members received instruction from Karenga to ignore Christmas as the first official Kwanzaa holiday week approached.[102] Ignoring Christmas meant no traditional gift buying for family and children, and certainly no acknowledgment of Santa Claus, reindeer, and other "white" mythological narratives. The challenge that faced US members was twofold: to completely bypass a perennial calendrical moment so familiar in its yearly place, and then subsequently fill up the novel seven-day holiday with activities germane to the US Organization and the new political culture of Black Power. Indeed, by eschewing the dominant holiday tradition, many members suffered from what would be akin to withdrawal symptoms. But December 26 was a potent antibiotic for the cultural addiction and economic malaise Christmas imposed on all lifelong celebrants.

Kwanzaa's growth potential was evident during the holiday's first year. Cultural nationalists and non-movement blacks found themselves together during the inaugural Kwanzaa week in spaces as disparate as the Hekalu (or temple as translated from the original Swahili), and at the homes of both US members and non-members. US members left their homes on the afternoon of December 26 and headed to the Hekalu with great anticipation. As a space for official US Organization political business and as a space for leisure gatherings, the Hekalu hosted the first day of Kwanzaa. Like any other day, walking into US's headquarters was like stepping into a museum. Images of Malcolm X and other black leaders permeated the wall. African artifacts lay in every corner accompanied with colorful African and Middle-Eastern fabrics. Chairs and African stools were well positioned for purposes of display and functional use. And arriving at the Hekalu on the afternoon of the 26th were US members—the first Kwanzaa celebrants anywhere in the United States: Maulana Karenga and his wife Haiba Karenga, Oliver and Hasani Heshimu, Charles and Sufadi

Sigidi, Clyde and Asali Halisi, James and Carmelita Tayari, Sam and Regina Damu, James and Faida Mtume, Karl and Diama Hekima, Ramon and Ujima Imara, Ken and Ahera Msemaji, Buddy Rose-Aminifu and Amina Thomas, Melvin and Constance Mabadiliko, Sanamu Nyeusi and Reginald Endesha.[103]

The members roamed the Hekalu talking to one another, trading stories of how difficult it proved to convince their children about the problems with Christmas and the significance of the following day. After ruminating, they began discussing why they were there. The first day of Kwanzaa took on the form of a typical US Organization Conversation Party.[104] Conversation Parties were times set aside for intellectual exchanges on some aspect of the group's Kawaida philosophy, or dialogues on the state of black Los Angeles, black America or both. This Conversation Party on December 26, 1966 was slightly different. On the meeting agenda stood the reasons for, and significance of, the US Organization's alternative to Christmas. Karenga opened by empathizing with the members about the parental difficulties of bypassing Christmas, but he reiterated that the time had come to look ahead. Karenga explained the basics of the holiday, enumerating all of the aspects of Kwanzaa and reinforcing what the US Organization discussed in the last few months. Much of the membership had been exposed to parts of the Kawaida philosophy during the year, so the Seven Principles—a Kawaida doctrine and the holiday's principles—had an already familiar ring. What needed reinforcing were Kwanzaa's symbols, not only identifying them but understanding their larger meaning and significance in the celebration. Karenga also explained the arrangement of the symbols for maximum display effect as part of the all-important Kwanzaa set.

The Kwanzaa setting was everything in the ceremony, Karenga believed, for without the proper placement of the holiday's symbols, high standards of beauty and aesthetics could not be achieved.[105] Karenga's emphasis on the aesthetics of the Kwanzaa layout led to a contest among some US members at their respective homes. Karenga encouraged the contest as a way for members to master the art of arranging symbols for public and private display. During the next few days of the first official Kwanzaa week, members decorated a room in their homes with Sam Damu and Oliver Heshimu receiving the most praise for the settings they each produced.[106] The experimental displays in these smaller gatherings proved to be worthy educational tutorials, for on December 31, US members moved Kwanzaa out of the Hekalu and their households to promote the holiday among a larger audience.

The homes on Washington Street and Tenth Avenue near the Santa Monica Freeway stood unassumingly as they had for much of their existence. But on the evening of December 31, 1966, the house of an US supporter who had regularly attended Soul Sessions and other Conversation Parties welcomed members of the US Organization to the first Kwanzaa Karamu celebration.[107] On the sixth day of Kwanzaa, inaugural weeklong festivities culminated in one grand evening among the top leadership, rank-and-file members and their families. In addition to US members, non-organizational blacks, like the host, also attended the first Karamu. Clyde Daniels-Halisi recalled that "all of us were encouraged to bring people . . . so they would get to see the holiday and what we were doing."[108] On one level, how the US Organization conducted their New Year's Eve celebration was standard operating procedure as an early program announcement revealed: "our Karamu consists of the seven main things that feasts usually consist of: Food, Drink, Music, Dance, Conversation, Laughter, and Ceremony."[109] On another level, this seemingly festive gathering at a home on Washington and Tenth would begin a year-end tradition on the sixth day of Kwanzaa that did not merely bring in the New Year, but politicized the festive, ushering in a black politics of celebration during the dominant holiday season.

The fifty or so people who filed inside the home experienced a celebration in two parts. From approximately early evening to 12 a.m., the first half of the Kwanzaa Karamu was administered with traditional Africa in mind. Drumming served as both clarion call and unofficial greeting with rapid percussive beats filling the home. US members wore colorful African dashikis and bubas hand woven by the organization's own muminina (women). The members bowed and embraced, exchanging Swahili pleasantries to greet one another. The candles on a modified Jewish Menorah used in Hanukkah rituals were lit accompanied by the definition of Kwanzaa's seven principles.[110] Libations were poured in the name of the ancestors. US women prepared the food, and adults and children alike sat on the floor to eat with their hands. One attendee reported on the menu: "There was an emphasis on rice, chicken, vegetables, and beans . . . and many of the foods had symbolic value. . . . For example, black-eyed peas represented good luck, *jama jama* [West African-style greens] stood for prosperity. . . . Chicken was a symbol of welcome, and rice expressed wishes for an abundance of good things in life."[111]

For children, emphasis was placed on African storytelling, role-playing, and various skits on kings, queens, and other royalty: "this year we are very fortunate to have Kings and Queens from all parts of Africa visiting . . . during our Kwanzaa celebration," a Kwanzaa program for children announced. "Our first visitor is the Kikuyu King . . . with him is King of the Watusi. . . . And here we have the beautiful Thanayi, daughter of our Master Teacher, Maulana Karenga and Princess of Afroamerica."[112] Additional African royalty from southern and northern areas on the African continent were invoked in the form of role-playing performances. To conclude the youth portion of the festivities, seven children of US members were called to the front of the room to assemble with placards around their necks, representing a letter in the word Kwanzaa. All children-oriented activities took place during the African phase of the Karamu which indicated the level of importance the organization placed on establishing Africa as both a real and imaginary site for black youth. Establishing the relevance of Africa as a place to emulate cultural practices was indeed an important feature for both children and adults to learn, even if the practices were misunderstood to be universally African:

> Everything is done in the traditional manner—food is prepared in traditional African style and eaten without European utensils. We bring pillows and sit on the floor; we dance African dances, listen to African music, tell African stories, make our traditional Tambiko (libation), drink from the Kikombe (unity cup), after which we each say HARAMBEE! (Let's pull together). After the traditional African part of the Karamu, we move to a position of Afroamerican expression.[113]

If six o'clock to midnight represented an attempt to connect with a lost African past, then 12 a.m. to daybreak meant returning to the American present. Roughly twelve midnight or the late evening hours until the early morning hours encompassed the African-American portion of the celebration. The second half of the Karamu during the early morning hours of January 1, 1967 was reserved for adults as an "all-night set" and "for all those who have made adequate babysitting arrangements."[114] US members and non-members who reconvened at the house on Washington and Tenth partied and danced to the latest black music. James Brown and Curtis Mayfield, two of the earliest incarnations in Black Power Soul, blared from the stereo as Karamu attendees took to the floor. After officiating the first half of the Karamu, Karenga also let the spirit of the moment engulf him as he danced to the music. Elizabeth Campbell, a nine-year-old girl who was allowed to witness some of the adult phase of the Karamu, later recalled seeing Karenga on that night:

> During the celebration, I saw for myself what made Ron Karenga special. I must have been 9 years old, old enough to take an interest in what was going on around me. I was used to seeing Karenga lecturing from a podium, looking so stern in his black clothes and dark-rimmed glasses. But now he was on the dance floor, enjoying himself with everyone else. I was surprised to see someone so serious—a big shot down with the folks and having a good time.[115]

Young Elizabeth Campbell was the daughter of W.D. Campbell—an US sympathizer who wanted his child to experience what the Karamu had to offer culturally. A second and much older non-US member recalled attending the same inaugural Kwanzaa Karamu. Unlike young Elizabeth Campbell who took notice of the adult phase of the feast, Iya Afin was enthralled by the first half ceremonies, remembering how the event transformed her life:

> I met some people in my apartment building who invited me to a feast. The feast took place at the US organization meeting house in Los Angeles in 1967. They were celebrating a feast . . . known as Kwanzaa. The music, the food, the clothes, my people, I was entranced and captivated. For the first time in my life I felt at home in my own skin. I was listening to my people's music and dancing to my people's drums. At last I had a culture of my own. I felt a connection to my ancestors so strong that everything I had ever experienced in my whole life came back to me and I was changed forever.[116]

The kind of transformative experience undergone by Afin was exactly the effect desired by Karenga and the US Organization. Coming off the success of the first Kwanzaa, US used the early and middle months of 1967 to recruit new members by promoting the holiday. Ngoma Ali, a former Gladiator gang member prior to joining the organization, remembers Kwanzaa being used as a major strategic recruiting device, a kind of cultural initiation and enlisting into the US Organization:

> the reason I remember so much . . . is that when I got into the organization back in July, they were telling us about Kwanzaa and . . . I was ecstatic. We always celebrated Christmas . . . and it was the first time we could really celebrate our roots. . . . We were so hyped . . . we were recruiting people all the time telling them about Kwanzaa, selling them on Kwanzaa. We had never celebrated it, but we were up man.[117]

Faida Mtume, another original member of the US Organization, remembered how the first Kwanzaa was both a chance to showcase the new holiday as well as to introduce LA blacks to the organization: "that's how we drew people into the organization's membership. . . . everything we did was about recruitment . . . to get the word out."[118]

While traveling on the East Coast in 1968 preparing for the Black Political Convention in Newark and the National Conference on Black Power in Philadelphia, Karenga promoted these major Black Power gatherings along with the little-known Kwanzaa. Attempting to raise awareness about the new holiday, Karenga stressed the importance of embracing cultural alternatives in a speech at Howard University in 1968. He asked the black student body to consider exchanging longstanding family traditions based on European-derived pagan culture for something with more cultural and psychological import: "if we ask people not to celebrate Christmas then we must be prepared to give them an alternative . . . so we did some research and found a Zulu custom where people came together for about a week around the first of the new year."[119]

# CHAPTER 3

# *Kwanzaa, Cultural Nationalism, and the Promotion of a Black Power Holiday*

Getting the word out would not be solely left to the US Organization. In fact, Kwanzaa moved beyond the promotional and celebratory purview of Maulana Karenga and the US Organization as early as 1967. If Kwanzaa's 1966 birth was a result of one organization, then the early growth of the holiday from 1967 through the late 1980s was a black community effort. At the forefront of this effort were black cultural nationalists and pan-Africanists affiliated with local community-based organizations. Though the US Organization in Los Angeles breathed life into Kwanzaa, the Committee for a Unified Newark (CFUN) in New Jersey, the EAST Organization in New York, and other activist groups in Chicago, Washington, DC, Philadelphia, and New Orleans nurtured the infant holiday in urban centers. Also instrumental in establishing Kwanzaa in black neighborhoods were an assortment of groups and institutions such as black independent schools, local Kwanzaa committees, black theater companies, and the Black Student Unions (BSUs) on college campuses. In addition, black media, black churches, public schools in black neighborhoods, and local neighborhood museums played a vital role in introducing the holiday to the larger African-American community. Although Kwanzaa is presently celebrated by many African-Americans and familiar to some whites and other people of color, what follows examines Kwanzaa's local roots prior to the holiday's acceptance into the American mainstream. By centering activist men and women as well as apolitical blacks, this chapter underscores Kwanzaa's emergence as a public celebration in black neighborhoods across the United States prior to its appropriation by white corporate and mainstream public culture.[1] Kwanzaa's public presence in black neighborhoods speaks to the holiday's connection to a broad-based social movement that was national in scope but local in character.[2] To explore Kwanzaa within its black neighborhood context, however, is to acknowledge the existence of a Black Power geography.

## Toward a Black Power Geography: Cultural Nationalism and the Promotion of Kwanzaa

If Kwanzaa was to survive beyond Karenga and the US Organization, it would need safe operating spaces to grow effectively. Using Jürgen Habermas' theory of the public sphere and the Black Public Sphere Collective as points of departure, I posit the notion of a secondary and tertiary black nationalist public—spheres that existed outside the bourgeois and mainstream black public sphere of mainline denominational churches and civil rights organizations. The mainstream black public sphere was not a safe political space for Kwanzaa to evolve and mature, hence, the need arose for alternative institutional spaces to promote the holiday. The Black Public Sphere Collective succinctly outlines the boundaries of the primary black sphere:

> The black public sphere—as a critical social imaginary—does not centrally rely on the world of magazines and coffee shops, salons and highbrow tracts. It draws energy from the vernacular practices of street talk and new musics, radio shows and church voices, entrepreneurship and circulation. Its task is not the provision of security for the freedom of conversation among intellectuals, as was the case with the bourgeois public spheres of earlier centuries. Rather, it marks a wider sphere of critical practice and visionary politics, in which intellectuals can join with the energies of the street, the school, the church, and the city to constitute a challenge to the exclusionary violence of much public space in the United States.[3]

The Black Power "public" is beyond Habermas' original geographical conception, and even sits partially outside of the purview posed by the Black Public Sphere Collective. This chapter takes up the question of

Kwanzaa's promotion within the Black Power public—the secondary black public sphere of black independent schools, community-based organizations, community centers, and to some extent, the major arteries of black neighborhood. The apparatuses of Kwanzaa promotion existed within urban networks of Black Power, a political space where visionary and courageous ideas were produced and practiced, oftentimes beyond the gaze of mainstream black voices. These urban networks of Black Power consisted of a variegated set of black institutions used throughout the month of December to educate African-Americans about the new holiday. The story of the public Kwanzaa in the late 1960s, 1970s, and early 1980s is a narrative about a community of people that collectively decided to challenge the hegemony of Christmas and stake out new areas for the Black Power Movement in unique places of promotion.

The sheer number of community-based organizations and institutions annually promoting Kwanzaa underscored the holiday's ties to a larger black neighborhood public sphere—not one that resembled the Habermasian model—but a black counter-public peopled by political activists, cultural workers, ministers, educators, and ordinary blacks.[4] To understand Kwanzaa promotion in black neighborhoods, however, is to acknowledge the existence of a second-tier black counter-public—one that stood outside of both the American and occasionally, the bourgeois black public sphere. The bourgeois black public sphere consisted of the black church, civil rights organizational headquarters, black democratic clubs, black trade unions, and heavily attended black public schools, to name a few. But for African-Americans to take the freedom struggle to another critical level and sustain a holiday of their own ultimately meant capturing other avenues and geographies of publicity: not well-connected civil rights organizational branches but black nationalist meeting sites; not mainline denominational churches but nationalist houses of worship; not political clubs but community centers; not solely public schools but black independent schools; not only widely distributed black media but underground publications and off-dial radio programs; and sometimes not even physical structures themselves but the streets. This second-tier and sometimes third-tier black counter-public was not exclusively middle-class or always separate from the nationalist sphere, but represented multi-class spaces of black gathering that directed the flow of Kwanzaa traffic every year. Indeed, African-Americans were empowered by Kwanzaa and the public spaces the holiday occupied. Thus, locating a second-tier black public is not to disavow the primary one, but to recognize the overlapping of black publics, the multiplicity of black geographies, and the simultaneity of black spaces. These multi-class publics, geographies, and spaces, were the locus of black nationalist politics and Kwanzaa promotion in the late 1960s, 1970s, and the early 1980s.

The second-tier Black counter-public grew out of the multiplicity of discourses that form the larger black freedom struggle. Only one sphere, however, can represent a "dominant" or "mainstream" perspective at any given time. The silencing of voices ultimately leads to the creation of secondary and tertiary black public spheres. Historically, those additional spheres removed from the primary one have been black nationalist, black feminist, and black queer. As Michael Dawson points out, "tensions grew within the Black counterpublic as bourgeois masculinist norms were argued to be appropriate for regulating Black discourse and participation by some Black and mainly male leaders. The adoption of the norms from the dominant society shifted Black politics from the type of inclusionary participatory debate . . . to the consistent attempts . . . to limit the participation of women in Black public discourse."[5] I would like to add to Dawson's analysis the exclusion of black nationalist from mainstream black civil rights discourse and the silencing of black queer discourses from "traditional" black heteronormative discourses which led to these additional Black counter-publics. I am not arguing that Kwanzaa existed solely in a second-tier Black counter-public; Kwanzaa rather moved in and out of all black spheres throughout its history. Certainly during Kwanzaa's first two years or so, the holiday was mainly located in the third-tiered black nationalist counter-public—a kind of political off-off Broadway as it were.

Geographical divisions and spatial positionings of people, institutions, and cultural practices have always been apparent in black America in general and black neighborhoods specifically. In fact, real and metaphorical boundries like "railroad tracks," "north side"—"south side," or "the 'hood" have always provided blacks with a keen sense of their spatial position and location vis-à-vis themselves and whites. Despite our intuitive sense of the spatial, a critical geography has not been at the center of African-American history and black social movement analysis. To assess internal movement politics, power struggles, and the sheer number of voices devoted to the black freedom struggle we need to think about black America in new geographical ways. Not only is African-American history ill-served under the dominant ontological and spatial paradigm that is so familiar in African-American history: rural versus urban, but spatial homogeneity is assumed throughout black America due to the experiential reality of racism and its deleterious political, economic, social, and geographical effects. I would like to take issue with the over-determined rural versus urban dichotomy, or the lack of spatial assessments in black history in general. To get a better look at protest dynamism in black communities—communities that often performed as political ensembles but sang in different spatial harmonies—we need to peel back the geographical layers within black America at the neighborhood level to get a better look at Black protest politics.

With this being said, I would like to offer a primary reason for calling for a critical geography in Civil Rights and Black Power Movement studies. During the late 1960s and early 1970s, Kwanzaa was everywhere and nowhere. I've been perplexed by Kwanzaa's invisibility in black neighborhoods on the one hand and the holiday's ubiquity in these same urban communities. To say that Kwanzaa was both everywhere and nowhere not only suggests that "space matters" in black America, but Kwanzaa's simultaneous visibility and invisibility leads one to ponder about the geographical organization of black neighborhoods. To get at the theme and practice of promotion and to understand the development of Kwanzaa in its infancy, one has to examine how Black Power manifested spatially. Thus, to evoke a Black Power geography is to speak of a marginal space, a space defined by the simultaneous existence of more powerful black spaces in and around it. The recognition of both marginal and dominant spatial arrangements allows us to follow the contours of Kwanzaa promotion in black neighborhoods.

A beginning assessment of Black Power geography can start at the level of the built environment. In places like New York, Newark, Philadelphia, and Chicago, older tenements harkened back to an earlier industrial period where residents dwelled on top of an assortment of businesses that served them and the rest of the neighborhood. Though this still was held true by the late 1960s and early 1970s, the racial demographics in cities had shifted from white ethnic to African-American, thereby transforming the built landscape of urban neighborhoods. This newer industrial urban landscape representing African-American residents within a post-industrial setting of black businesses, churches, political clubs, fraternal organizations, and other black institutions altered the way the older urban white ethnic neighborhoods looked visually. African-Americans did not alter the built landscape by rebuilding or gentrifying the neighborhoods they increasingly moved into. As a resource-deprived community, they generally could not afford to. Old white businesses, churches, and other institutional spaces were either visually transformed or remolded to fashion a black community and institutional politic that distinguished black residents from previous whites and sometimes from other African-Americans. The visual transformative instruments used: not bulldozers or bobcats, but paint and banners that produced artistic renderings on external building walls.

Black organizations with differing protest agendas reshaped the cityscape in their own political image and interests. Though there was no discernable and identifiable Black Power architecture, physical structures were altered which manifested in a kind of Black Power landscape on some neighborhood streets. Memorials of remembrance or paintings of murdered Black Panthers like Fred Hampton and Bobby Hutton appeared in Chicago and in Oakland. Malcolm X served as a favorite image to visually represent the Black Power Movement on apartment and community center structures. COINTELPRO and the court cases against black leaders like Angela Davis furnished additional material and facilitated the further muralization of the Black Power Movement in neighborhoods. Inexpensive and direct, using buildings and wall spaces as canvasses to inscribed Black Power and cultural nationalist motifs, such as the clenched raised fist, served to politicize residents, educate young children, and remind the community of the ongoing struggle. Kwanzaa was also a frequent subject on neighborhood structures as evidenced by the building at 8th and Q streets in Northwest Washington, DC. In bright colors of red, black, and green, a black independent school displayed a large painting of the holiday's candleholder with fruit and vegetables partially encircled by the continent of Africa. Accompanying the representation of the continent were the words "Kwanzaa" and "December 26 to January 1" painted on the southeast side of the Ujamaa Shule, a black independent school operated by Baba El Senzengalkulu Zulu. In their Swahili form, the seven principles were also inscribed onto the building next to the candleholder and the continent of Africa.[6]

But black spatial politics and practices should not solely examine the built environment and physical structures. Most geographers have moved from an analysis of the built landscape, instead concentrating on how spaces are generated by interactions and interrelations of diverse people, entities, and processes, as Jonathan Murdoch suggests. The interactions in these spaces give way to novel practices and performances, and hence, new spatial identities. The rise of Kwanzaa as a new practice in black neighborhoods involved the process of spatial becoming. The task of promoting Kwanzaa was to simultaneously advance a new holiday and to elevate a new political space so that Kwanzaa and other cultural nationalist activities could grow. Thus, Kwanzaa's early promotion occurred in a marginal but very powerful alternative space, or to borrow Edward Soja's term, a "third" space that was deeply interwoven into black neighborhood and network configurations, and highly interdependent on the interactions and interrelations between diverse actors in a national black cultural nationalist network.[7]

The relational aspect of institutions and organizations is hard to appreciate without an understanding of the people and the political networks that made up this critical black geography. Black Power was a network of loose and shifting affiliations, programs, philosophies, and organizations, each with its own assessment, diagnosis, and remedy, and each vying for time and space in the black public sphere. If one could locate a vital center or an organizing principle, the idea of self-determination would represent a logical starting point. Principally, the movement writ large agreed on at least two things: African-Americans must act as the sole or primary agent in their own liberation; and that liberation is only possible with the raising of the people's consciousness. Beyond self-determination, there could be no vital center when movement endeavors could be as diverse as the elimination of white religious iconography in black churches, the creation of black independent schools, the insistence on third-party electoral politics, the forging of Third World alliances, the formation of radical black trade unions, and the creation of African-inspired holidays, all of which were conscious-raising and self-determining acts. Unlike the Civil Rights Movement that left little room for dissent from the non-violent direct action script, the Black Power Movement's strength lay in the existence of multiple centers, variegated spaces, and unregulated discourses and activities. Thus, not only were Black Power political endeavors dissimilar; so were Black Power people.

The individuals in the Black Power Movement that promoted cultural nationalism were known as cultural nationalist due to their emphasis on culture, or as pan-Africanist due to their deep affiliation and activities with people and events on the African continent. To be a black cultural nationalist generally, one of four elements, if not all four, must be present and discernable in those who identified with this part of the movement: *rebirth*, at the level of consciousness (from "Negro" to black at a minimum, and from black to "African" if possible); *renamed*, the elimination of the so-called "slave" birth name and the assumption of an African one; *reclothed*, the forgoing of Western attire for African dashikis and other continental-style clothing; and *re-educated*, the disposal of Eurocentric and other "white" knowledge and the acquisition of a new "black" intellectual reservoir. Many black cultural nationalists underwent the first and last process. What separated most cultural nationalists from other black nationalists was not only the adoption of African names, clothing, and languages, but the insistence that the cultural realm represented the primary site of resistance. Cultural nationalists believed that the repositories of culture, such as schools, churches, history books, celebrations and rituals, to name a few, should be taken out of the hands of the oppressor. For them, it was white America's hegemony over what got taught and how; how Jesus looked; what holidays were important; and who controlled the education of blacks that should be the focus of change. For cultural nationalists, it was not so much the ballot box, white financial institutions, or government entities that were most oppressive, but the areas that directly concerned the politics of representation and meaning. Black cultural nationalists wanted to change what black people thought and believed at the level of knowledge.[8]

Encountering some cultural nationalists in the 1960s and 1970s could be as pleasant (for believers) as much as it was painful (for non-believers). Cultural nationalists were knowledge-filled individuals that came to bring the light. They were well read and versed on black history, both the United States version and the emerging continental one. They never quivered from shaming blacks who knew little or nothing about black history or appeared too inundated with "white" knowledge. They prided themselves on their "Negro to Black" conversion and ridiculed others for not doing likewise. They spoke a little Swahili, some very fluently, and could also speak other African languages. Cultural nationalists also looked the part. Black men and women wore loose and colorful dashikis or bubas made up of bright yellows, reds, and purples. Women typically wore long gown-like dresses that covered the torso down to the lower legs, often accompanied with equally colorful head-wraps. Some men wore two-piece dashiki-tops and pants, but many were content to just don the dashiki or buba-top in a solid black or brown with regular Western-style slacks or jeans. Wearing African-style garb, some of which came directly from the continent, others made by black cultural nationalists in the United States, identified and marked off black Americans as Africans. Through its projection onto the naked eye, it provided an immediate symbol of identification as a non-Western and non-American subject. This politicized attire set off and demarcated cultural nationalist blacks from other African-Americans and whites. To wear African attire, to speak an African language, to learn African history, to revel in African rituals from the late 1960s through the early 1980s was to identify with African people, African politics, African beliefs, and African practices. For black Americans to do these things for any significant length of time not only meant you identified with things African, *it meant you were African*. New "Africans," that is, black Americans who identified more with an African-based nationality and less with an American one, celebrated Kwanzaa. Kwanzaa was a product of the thinking of cultural nationalists, part of an emerging intellectual and cultural reservoir from Africa, and a visible manifestation of black America's African-ness.

The missionary-like zeal of black cultural nationalists manifested in the creation of their own vehicles of promotion that carried the holiday to the masses of African-Americans. Not only did cultural nationalists use their own bodies as forms of promotion, they would create and use their own organizations and institutions; the private homes of other activists or non-activists; existing institutions like black neighborhood museums, churches, and schools; and the streets and the highways to spread Kwanzaa. Once Kwanzaa took root in black communities across the United States, black cultural nationalists and pan-Africanists would guide the holiday's promotion narrative from their organizations and institutions. Neighborhood spaces of promotion included a nexus of cultural nationalist organizations like US, the EAST, the Congress of African People (CAP), and Afram Associates; institutions like the Studio Museum in Harlem and the Anacastia Museum in Washington, DC; black national-ist houses of worship like Union Temple Baptist Church in Washington, DC; school districts like Community District 7 in the Bronx, New York; and the streets of North Philadelphia, South Chicago, South Central Los Angeles, Harlem and Brooklyn, New York where Kwanzaa parades and processions were a perennial occurrence. The neighborhood spaces and spheres of promotion would be peopled both by cultural nationalist activists and revolutionary pan-Africanists intent on furthering a cultural revolution on the one hand, and on the other, by black professionals and everyday working black people concerned about black history and the cultural well-being of the black community.

## KWANZAA ON HIGHWAY 101

Los Angeles was the birthplace of Kwanzaa. But because of Black Power's growing political and cultural capital, resonating with more African-Americans, the city could not keep the holiday to itself. Kwanzaa began traveling in many directions, first making its way onto the entrance ramp of Highway 101, heading south and north. A few members of US with family connections in San Diego brought and celebrated the first Kwanzaa there in December 1967. The first Kwanzaa in San Diego, however, was an extension of Los Angeles and bore the stamp of the US Organization.[9] More significant is Kwanzaa's move to northern California and its promo-tion by other black activists outside of the US Organization. At the center of this story is one of many Black Power gatherings that placed an unknown student organizer from the Bay Area in contact with Kwanzaa's creator.

The Western Regional Black Youth Conference in November of 1967 was part of a growing Black Power public sphere where discussions about Kwanzaa could be identified alongside more immediate concerns in the movement. The conference's institutional site, the Second Avenue Baptist Church, was transformed from a traditional place of worship to a politi-cized meeting-house drenched in Black Power conversation and accou-trements. Angela Davis, a graduate student at the University of California at Los Angeles (UCLA), attended the conference and remembered the conference's setting at the church:

> The Second Avenue Baptist Church in Watts glowed with colorful African patterns and fabrics—the women wore traditional long dresses of red, purple, orange, and yellow; the men wore bubas that rivaled in every way the fiery beauty of the women's clothes. The walls of the registration room were alive with poster art that hailed Blackness as an ancient and peerless beauty. . . . I walked around calling everyone sister and brother, smiling and elated, high on love.[10]

The major developments and news stories included an altercation leading to gunshots between Karenga's US Organization and a black Marxist group, the United Front, and a call by the Olympic Committee for Human Rights to boycott the 1968 Mexico City Olympic Games. The US Organization's confrontation with the United Front posed no serious danger to attendees or the conference itself. The call to boycott the Olympics captured the attention of the public and was front-page news.[11] Black nationalist sociology professor Harry Edwards invited sports luminaries, such as basketball's Lew Alcindor (Kareem Abdul Jabbar), and track stars Lee Evans and Tommie Smith, to serve notice to the world that African-American athletes were preparing to take a stand against black oppression. The boycott's objective said Harry Edwards was to "put the question" of white supremacy "before the United Nations" and remove it from the "sphere of civil rights . . . into the sphere of human rights."[12] Karenga spoke to conference attendees later in the day, concurring with Edwards' assessment about the need for black athletes to use the upcoming games as a forum for political redress. But unlike his Howard University speech where he talked specifically about his alternative to Christmas, Karenga said nothing to the audience about Kwanzaa, speaking instead of a "new culture, a new value system, and a new lifestyle among black people."[13]

On day two of the Western Regional Black Youth Conference, a little-known speaker named Harriet Smith from Merritt College stood at the podium to address the black student role in the Black Power Movement.[14] A native of Berkeley and student body president at Merritt College, Smith talked about organizing on campus and the need for black students, particularly at majority white campuses, to seize control of budgets and activity fees.[15] Impressed with Smith's presentation, her strategic location in the Bay Area, her mature age of thirty-nine years, and her relative obscurity within black sectarian politics, Karenga believed the key to the holiday's expansion lay in this student leader.[16] After Smith's presentation, Karenga approached her to see if she would be willing to start what he described to her as the "community Kwanzaa" in the Bay Area.[17] Smith's non-affiliation with US or other black nationalist organizations made her an ideal person to further Karenga's plans. Karenga's ambition was driven by his desire both to see Kwanzaa grow and to inject his personal brand of Black Power in areas that the Black Panthers geographically and ideologically controlled. Remembering the interest of so many non-US members at the first Kwanzaa in Los Angeles, Karenga desired to spread Kwanzaa to the wider black public: "we will eventually be national in scope . . . but first we want to influence things right here . . . in California."[18] The US Organization's altercation with the communist United Front over ideology and movement direction reminded Karenga of the urgency to spread his beliefs of black cultural nationalism. Thus, the "community" Kwanzaa articulated by Karenga to Smith simply meant Kwanzaa celebrations practiced by African-Americans outside of the sphere of the US Organization.

The brief meeting about Kwanzaa and its potential efficacy in the Bay Area ended with Karenga giving Smith yards of material to make African-style clothing, a new name, and instructions on how to perform a Kwanzaa ceremony. After attending the first two days of the Western Regional Black Youth Conference in standard American attire, Smith took the ninety yards of gabardine and newspaper pattern provided by an US member and made bubas the night prior to the last day of the conference. "I made two uniforms. . . . I made one for Leon Williams and one for the host, who was my cousin. . . . This is November 1967 when we attended that conference."[19] Noticing certain leadership qualities in Smith through her presentation, Karenga also referred to her as "Sister Makinya"—defined by him as a black woman with strength and dignity. "He just blurted it out," Smith remembered, "yeah . . . call that sister, Sister Makinya, she's Sister Makinya."[20] Smith's three-day politicization in Black Power ideology and practice ended when she and the Merritt College contingent returned to northern California. The spatial politics of Black Power, however, forced Smith to discard the African attire before reaching the Oakland-Berkeley area because of the potential danger the clothing posed in areas controlled by the Black Panthers. If the dashikis and bubas did not make it to the Bay Area, then Kwanzaa certainly did, traveling north with Smith on Highway

101 as part of a stack of conference papers and flyers collected over the last three days.

One month after meeting Karenga, Sister Makinya decided to attempt a private Kwanzaa celebration among family and friends on December 26, 1967. Sister Makinya never intended to seriously examine the Kwanzaa instructions given to her by Karenga until cajoled to do so by Fred T. Smith, another student leader who accompanied her to Los Angeles. The first Kwanzaa in the Bay Area was held at her Berkeley home and like the first Kwanzaa in Los Angeles a year earlier, proved very experimental. The mimeographed outline lacked instructions on where to place the holiday's material items. Makinya improvised, arranging the symbols and pre-prepared foods on a table according to her own personal taste. Activities integral to Kwanzaa celebrations, such as pouring libation and the passing of the Unity Cup, were absent from this inaugural festivity, according to Sister Makinya. Thus, with only the rudimentary instructions and materials of a new holiday celebration before them, Sister Makinya and company "giggled through the first Kwanzaa."[21]

After Kwanzaa's private debut in Berkeley, it did not take long for the holiday to spread throughout the area. From 1968 to 1971, Sister Makinya became the contact person for Kwanzaa celebrations on both sides of the Bay from 1968 to 1971. She created the Kwanzaa Organizers in 1968—a Bay Area consulting organization that trained interested blacks how to perform Kwanzaa celebrations in Berkeley, Oakland, and San Francisco. After providing interested parties with information, Sister Makinya encouraged them to form their own organizations and hold annual Kwanzaa celebrations in their respective homes and neighborhoods. In Oakland, Fred T. Smith organized a Kwanzaa celebration in 1968. Thomatra Scott, trained by Sister Makinya and later a close associate of the US Organization, began conducting Kwanzaa celebrations in 1969 under the auspices of his group Young Adults of San Francisco. Other Makinya trainees included Akilimali in 1969, Debbie O'Neal in 1970, and John Hill and the Berkeley Youth Alternative from the Bethlehem Community Church in 1970.[22]

The Bethlehem Community Church in Oakland found itself as one of the early sponsors of Kwanzaa due to the younger church members' politicization in Black Power. In 1970, the Berkeley Youth Alternative invited Sister Makinya to the black Lutheran church to perform a

Kwanzaa ceremony for the young members in the congregation. After performing a short Kwanzaa program in December of 1970, the young members convinced the church hierarchy to maintain a relationship with Makinya, who had become more conversant with Kwanzaa and the Black Power Movement since 1967. The ongoing relationship between Makinya and the church led to a six-week summer project in July and August of 1971. The summer project involved traveling to northern states and educating African-Americans about the movement. Sister Makinya, John Hill, a church member and driver, and the Berkeley Youth Alternative put together a Kwanzaa pamphlet and gathered other material to distribute to African-Americans in Portland and Seattle. As part of their summer effort to promote black nationalist endeavors, Makinya and the Berkeley Youth Alternative packed up a station wagon and headed north on Highway 101. "We left here and went up through Oregon . . . to Seattle, and the brother that lived in Seattle came here first to leave with us," Sister Makinya remembered.[23] Most visits were coordinated with an institution prior to arrival, such as a community center in Portland, or a black bookstore in Seattle where African-Americans in these cities were in leadership positions of local organizations, and others, just curious about the movement and its particulars. Makinya remembered promoting Black Power in the main, which sometimes included Kwanzaa and at other times did not: "We weren't trying to sell the idea of [Kwanzaa]," said Sister Makinya, "these were people eager to know anything about the movement. Not that they wanted to know something about Kwanzaa, they may have never known about it. But they wanted nationalist education. . . . and to know more about Africa, that was the main thing, getting back to our roots. . . . that's . . . what we were doing."[24]

What seems clear is that this particular trip and the promotion of Kwanzaa inside Bethlehem did not give black church officials any causes for alarm. In fact, Kwanzaa was not an important year-end activity of Minister Kirstwood and church officials at Bethlehem. The Black Power Movement had only impacted the Berkeley Youth Alternative. The church supported the projects of the Berkeley Youth Alternative by providing funds, vehicles, church equipment, and the use of the building. As Sister Makinya recalled: "they just did things for us . . . like providing the car. . . . they provided the facilities for us to do what we wanted to do. And in order to make this trip worthwhile, they felt we should have something to hand out to people; to leave with people when we left."[25] Providing full support in resources and preparation did not mean the church endorsed Kwanzaa or Black Power. They did not. Much of what the Berkeley Youth Alternative requested—from the services of Sister Makinya to a station wagon—never completely consumed the minds of Bethlehem church officials. As Itibari Zulu, a member of the Berkeley Youth Alternative, remembered, "they didn't take it serious. . . . and they said 'oh this is something nice, let's see what they are going to do.'"[26] What Kwanzaa and Bethlehem Community Church demonstrates is the way in which the holiday existed in a second-ary black public sphere—not up on the pulpit or in the pews but rather down in the basement, perhaps off in another part of the church, or even outside of the church under feeble and unsubstantial church sponsorship.

Kwanzaa soon blossomed, becoming the featured annual event in other Bay Area organizations like Pan-African Peoples Organization (PAPO), the Street Academy (a group of black postal employees), the Nairobi Kwanzaa Committee, the Bay Area Kwanzaa Committee, the Pan-Afrikan Secretariat, the Kwanzaa Celebrants, and the Wo'se Community Church in Oakland. An early PAPO invitation attempted to set the tone for 1972 Bay Area Kwanzaa celebrations and future gatherings: "The Pan-African People's Organization proudly extends a warm welcome to all its beautiful Black brothers and sisters at Kwanza and throughout the years to come."[27]

As the Bay Area Kwanzaa representative with the longest history asso-ciated with the holiday, Sister Makinya's facilitation of public Kwanzaa celebrations in the 1970s and 1980s awarded her the unofficial title the "mother of Kwanzaa." The "mother of Kwanzaa" was able to bring various groups together during the perennial holiday week. When celebrations were small and manageable, each Kwanzaa organization would pick a day during the seven-day holiday and stage a celebration in a Bay Area city. One group would hold the first day of Kwanzaa in Berkeley, another group in Oakland on the second day of Kwanzaa, a third group on the third day in East Palo Alto, the fourth night in San Francisco, and so forth. By the mid- to late 1970s, Kwanzaa celebrations grew so large, sometimes upward of a few hundred persons at a single location, organizers agreed to have Kwanzaa festivities in multiple locations on the same night. Sister Makinya and other organizers turned down many groups that wanted to participate in coordinated Kwanzaa efforts. In a just a few short years,

Kwanzaa's popularity exploded with more groups interested in Kwanzaa than the seven calendar days could accommodate. Despite Kwanzaa's growth, eventually moving beyond the oversight of Sister Makinya, she was still remembered as the woman who brought the holiday to northern California: "Makinya Sibeko Kouate devised the first Kwanzaa for the Oakland-Berkeley area which was held on December 26, 1967."[28]

Throughout the 1970s and 1980s, Sister Makinya continued to promote Kwanzaa while working as an educator in the Berkeley Unified School District after graduating with a BA from California State University—Hayward in 1972. Downstate in southern California, Kwanzaa continued despite Karenga's incarceration in 1971.[29] The early growth of Kwanzaa in the Bay Area, however, was something of an anomaly. First, it began under the direction of a non-US member. Second, Sister Makinya, though politically conscious, was not a Kawaida cultural nationalist—a member or sympathizer of the US Organization. And lastly, she was an older woman in a public arena dominated by younger black men. Kwanzaa provided Sister Makinya, as a black woman in the movement, with a tremendous amount of agency, particularly in terms of organizing and educating the black public about Black Power. Most, if not all, high-profile spokespersons that promoted Kwanzaa in the late 1960s and early 1970s were men. Though she promoted Kwanzaa with zest and zeal, achieving notoriety in the Bay Area Black Power community, Sister Makinya in many ways remained an outsider to Black Power generally and the history of Kwanzaa. Due to historical erasure, Makinya has been marginalized in the memory of Kwanzaa's early development. The organizations and spokespersons remembered as having sustained Kwanzaa in its early years were Kawaida cultural nationalist, groups affiliated with the US Organization in major cities across the United States.[30]

## BARAKA, THE CONGRESS OF AFRICAN PEOPLE, AND KWANZAA

Amiri Baraka lived and breathed the philosophy of Kawaida. In 1968, he reoriented his political and cultural ideals around Kawaida, becoming one of the strongest supporters of Maulana Karenga. As COINTELPRO exacerbated the internecine tensions inside the Black Panther Party, Baraka ascended the Black Power mount, becoming the most vocal and visible black nationalist in the country. Baraka's two-step leap into Kawaida cultural nationalism involved renouncing the Bohemianism of the Greenwich Village beat scene he was so much a part of prior to 1965. After leaving the Beats, he embraced the new Black Power sentiment, emerging as a foundational figure in the Black Arts Movement in Harlem and Newark. Two years into the development of the Black Arts Movement, he accepted the tenets of Kawaida. Between 1965 and 1968, Baraka transformed himself from LeRoi Jones—the beat poet, to Ameer—the Black Arts theorist and Sunni Muslim, to Amiri—the Kawaida cultural nationalist. He would evolve once more in 1974 by exchanging Kawaida cultural nationalism for Marxist–Leninism–Maoism. From 1968 to 1974, Baraka not only raised the significance of Kawaida and Kwanzaa, but became the premier spokesperson for the cultural nationalist wing of the Black Power Movement during Karenga's incarceration.

Like Karenga, Baraka's brand of revolution was culturally driven and a major preoccupation in his politics, informed primarily by the Black Arts Movement. The Black Arts Movement emerged as an intellectual space for the production of radicalized black art and knowledge. The knowledge produced by the Black Arts Movement was "*more* than the process of making art, of telling stories, of writing poems, or performing plays," said Larry Neal, one of the movement's primary theorists. The Black Arts Movement was "concerned about the cultural and spiritual liberation of black people." When black artists talked about the cultural, spiritual, and mental liberation of black people, they meant the "destruction of white ways of looking at the world." Destroying the white world took black artists like Baraka and Neal on searches for "new systems of moral and philosophical thought." In this sense, the Black Arts Movement was partly akin to Mao's Cultural Revolution, which entailed the internal purging of liberal bourgeois elements in China. Baraka and Neal severely criticized black artists operating outside of the confines of the Black Arts Movement with an attempt to destroy "Negro literature and civil rights literature. . . . masturbating before white audiences." Thus, the Black Arts Movement was part of a broader cultural revolution that sought to make a "greater leap forward" into a spiritual aesthetic based on black values for the "psychic survival of black people."[31]

In its early incarnation, Baraka's idea of cultural revolution privileged an aesthetic based on black music, drama, and poetry, not an Africa filled with rituals. Baraka's first act of cultural revolution was the opening of the

Black Arts Repertory Theater/School (BARTS) in Harlem. BARTS culti-
vated new poets from the community like Sonia Sanchez and featured
older writers from Cooper Square in New York, such as Ishmael Reed.
Baraka subsequently became involved in HARYOU, a summer arts and
culture antipoverty program at the famed Hotel Theresa on 125th Street.
He brought in a number of artists from the jazz world to participate in a
HARYOU street festival: Pharoah Sanders, Archie Schepp, Sun Ra, John
Coltrane, and Cecil Taylor. In 1966, he published a collection of essays
entitled *Home* that not only signified his immersion into a newly acquired
black aesthetic, but a return to his familial roots in Newark, New Jersey.[32]
Other personal highlights included a visiting professorship in the
country's first Black Studies department at San Francisco State College in
1967. But despite his successes, Baraka felt politically discombobulated
after meeting Karenga, first in Newark in the summer of 1967, and shortly
again in San Francisco, and in Los Angeles when Baraka attended the
Western Regional Black Youth Conference. Though Baraka was the more
accomplished cultural worker, he believed Karenga possessed a tremendous amount of political aptitude and self-assurance. To Baraka, Karenga
embodied the political discipline needed to advance the black freedom
struggle forward. According to Baraka, his lacking in this area sent him on
a self-reflective journey:

> Because I was so self-critical, especially from a black nationalist perspective,
> the fact of the US Organization—i.e., that it was an organization and not just
> a bunch of undisciplined people taking up time mostly arguing with each
> other about what to do, or what method to use—that I was drawn to US and
> Karenga. He was quick-witted, sharp-tongued, with a kind of amusing irony
> in his putdowns of white people, America, black people, or whatever, that I
> admired. Plus, there was no doubt, when you were around Karenga, as to who
> was the leader, even if you weren't in his organization. . . . Also, [because]
> Karenga's whole premise was of cultural revolution, I was pulled closer. Being
> a cultural worker, an artist, the emphasis on culture played to my own
> biases.[33]

After meeting Karenga in 1967 and embracing Kawaida in early 1968,
Baraka assumed the role as the most ardent promoter of US Organization
doctrine, making Kawaida the guiding philosophy in his organizations. In

effect, Baraka became the first east coast spokesperson for Kawaida and Kwanzaa.[34]

Baraka epitomized the dialect that existed within the cultural nationalist wing of the Black Power Movement: Black Arts versus Kawaida, the former reveling in an aesthetically centered and black improvisational United States, the latter inspired by the African continent. Though the two were in no ways mutually exclusive, it is difficult at times to discern what strand of cultural thought proved more influential to the other. Though James Edward Smethurst, the foremost authority on the Black Arts Movement, locates the thrust of Black Arts history in the Old Left avant-garde, which occurred much earlier than Baraka's BARTS and Karenga's Kawaida philosophy, Smethurst still concluded that "... Baraka, Sonia Sanchez, Larry Neal, and others would draw on conceptions of history influenced by Maulana Karenga's version of cultural nationalism while at the same time employing their long-standing model of a continuum of African American culture, including popular culture, that was at odds with Karenga's vision of a pre-historic neo-African counterculture."[35] Smethurst further surmised that Karenga and the seven principles "provided the most sophisticated (and most usable) ideological scaffolding for the early visions of a mythic history advanced by Baraka, Neal, (Askia) Toure, and others ..."[36] If there were major contradictions between Black Arts and Kawaida philosophy, Baraka refused to play them up for the sake of unity in the cultural nationalist movement. Baraka's critique of Kawaida as "reactionary" and "static" would come several years later.[37] Regardless of what side had the greater impact on the other, this convergence proved critical to Kwanzaa's success and the holiday's promotion in institutions that doubled as cultural and political organizations like Baraka's Committee For a Unified Newark (CFUN) and the Congress of African People (CAP).

Karenga's influence on Baraka immediately manifested in Baraka's organizations, activities, and his cultural outlook. Baraka's CFUN mirrored Karenga's US Organization in internal discipline, departments, titles, and highly regimented activities for members. CFUN members were required to respect the different levels of membership: *Maulana*—master teacher, *Shahidi*—protector of the faith, *Imamu*—spiritual leader, *Saidi*—elders, *Muminina*—women. Members were expected to understand *Swahili*, abide by the organization's *Kanuni*, rules, and partake in traditional African ceremonies, such as an *Arusi*, wedding. Then, there were the holidays that CFUN recognized and promoted: *Kuanzisha*—the founding of the US Organization, *Uhuru Day*—the Watts rebellion, *Kuzaliwa*—Malcolm X's birthday, *Dhabihu*—Malcolm X's assassination, and Kwanzaa, which was celebrated at Baraka's Black Arts institution, Spirit House in Newark, for the first time in December 1968. From 1968 Baraka nationally promoted Kwanzaa's seven principles (Nguzo Saba) as a black value system for all of black America to embrace. Believing that "the minds of the people are the most important factor of any movement," Baraka advanced the idea that the seven principles were a manifestation of the "black mind expanding, trying to take control of its own space."[38] For Baraka, capturing mental space by freeing the mind was just as critical as acquiring physical space for movement activity. Baraka argued a value system not of one's own forces a people to "do exactly the same things as the oppressor-people."[39] Arguing that a "nation is only as good as the values it *actually* practices," Baraka issued a clarion call in 1969 about the growth of Kwanzaa's seven principles:

> The Nguzo Saba is the first, the basic, primary teaching. The rest of the doctrine, covering the completeness of modern experience is a Black ideology in toto, is a path itself to Blackness and Nationhood. The doctrine now is in the head and hands mostly of organization people ... and student leaders around the country. But soon it will be ... available to most of us. It is the central ingredient of the new Nationalist organization. It will transform Black people and by doing this, transform yes, America. You better get ready for it.[40]

Getting ready for Kwanzaa meant giving Kwanzaa national exposure in a major conference. Conference organizing on the local and national level became a Baraka staple. Realizing that Black Power activists lacked a national structure to continue the work of the three previous Black Power conferences, Baraka gathered a significant group of local, national, and international black political activists in 1970, one year after announcing the coming of Kwanzaa. The conference in Atlanta, Georgia known interchangeably as both the Atlanta and African Congress, featured Civil Rights Movement veterans like Ralph Abernathy, Whitney Young, and Jesse Jackson; religious figures such as Louis Farrakhan; newly elected black mayors such as Richard Hatcher of Gary, Indiana and Kenneth Gibson of Newark, New Jersey; and many leaders from African anticolonial struggles. More important than who attended, the Atlanta Congress held workshops on key areas of concern in the Black Power Movement. The Political Liberation workshop highlighted pan-Africanism as a possibility for an independent black nation. The workshop also called for releasing African prisoners of war. The Education workshop established definitions for education and assessed the viability of Black Studies programs, BSUs, black teachers and administrators, black colleges, and independent black schools. Other workshops featured sessions on black theater and poetry, black technology, religion, community organization, law and justice, history, and communications. The Creativity workshop included papers on black theater and poetry. The 1970 African Congress also held a workshop on Social Organization, which included a seminar on Kwanzaa.[41]

The Kwanzaa seminar began with a short synopsis of the holiday. The presentation emphasized Kwanzaa's fundamental connection to celebrations of the harvest. Kasisi Washao, the seminar's instructor and CFUN member, explained to the class that during the harvest season, "our people in Africa came together to give thanks. Songs were sung, dances danced, food was eaten, and drinks were drunk, in a word, life was lived in sheer enjoyment." Washao also described in detail the symbols of Kwanzaa: the straw mat (*mkeka*), the candleholder (*kinara*), the ear of corn (*muhindi*), and the gifts (*zawadi*). After a detailed explanation of the symbols, the instructor explained how the symbols were to be arranged: "after the mkeka has been spread out, place the kinara in the center. Then place the muhindi around or on the sides of it. Place the zawadi on the mkeka in any arrangement that is artistic. Finally, the mishumaa (candles) should be placed at the far right of everything so that they might be available for daily lighting." Washao ended the seminar by describing the evening prior to the last day of Kwanzaa, the Karamu. Washao cautioned that the Karamu should be held "at the largest house" among the celebration's participants because it is "traditionally an all night set" mainly for adults, consisting of "food, drink, music, dance, conversation, laughter, and ceremony." Before concluding, Washao told seminar attendees that Kwanzaa is CFUN's "holiday [based] upon tradition and reason. ... To us it is a sign of self-determination and self-respect. ... Surely by things like this, we provide ... something of value."[42] Thus, in just a few short years, Kwanzaa had graduated from organizational ritual in a small number of community-based groups to an important plenary session at a major Black Power gathering, touching hundreds of people at one time.

The major offspring of the Atlanta meeting was not Kwanzaa, however, but the Congress of African People (CAP). CAP institutionalized Kwanzaa in the United States. Over a hundred groups from more than twenty-five cities attended the 1970 Atlanta meeting, most leaving as local CAP affiliates. A CAP report explained the importance of local organizations: "the base of the CAP operation has been the Local Organizations. Leadership, kazi (work), and policy have emerged from local activities. These bodies based in African communities around the western hemisphere will be carrying out the daily work of CAP. To local folk, these groups represent the CAP message."[43] Part of the CAP message for local affiliates was to return home and promote Kwanzaa in black neighborhoods. CAP locals that returned with a mandate to spread Kwanzaa were Haki Madhubuti and the Institute for Positive Education (Chicago); Jitu Weusi and the EAST Organization (New York); Kalamu ya Salaam and Ahidiana (New Orleans); Reginald Mtumishi and Maisha Ongoza of the Urban Survival Training Institute (Philadelphia); Thomatra Scott and the Young Adults of San Francisco (San Francisco); Ron Daniels of Freedom, Inc. (Youngstown, Ohio); and Vernon Sukumu of the NIA Organization (San Diego), to name a few. Recalling the importance of his organization's role in spreading the new Black Power holiday, Baraka declared, "if it were not for CFUN and the later Congress of African People ... the seven principles and the holiday Kwanzaa would never have been as widely known as they are."[44]

But Baraka would only be around shortly to take note of the holiday's flowering he helped promote. On October 7, 1974, Baraka officially made his "public notice to the world of our socialism." Baraka renounced Karenga's doctrine of Kawaida and all of its accompanied rituals, including Kwanzaa, driving a wedge in the movement. Despite Baraka's public departure from Kawaida cultural nationalism, Kwanzaa continued to flourish. The holiday was already entrenched in the Black Power community, remaining behind in local cultural nationalist groups that refused to follow Baraka into Marxist–Leninism.[45]

## KWANZAA AND HOLIDAY NATIONALISM IN BLACK NEIGHBORHOODS

The organizations that refused to disavow cultural nationalism and continued to celebrate Kwanzaa were the EAST Organization in New York, the Institute for Positive Education in Chicago, the Urban Survival Training Institute in Philadelphia, to name a few.[46] Some organizations existed solely to promote Kwanzaa. Most groups, however, tied Kwanzaa to the larger process of controlling the institutional life of black neighborhoods. The men and women in community-based nationalist and non-nationalist organizations believed in creating their own schools, community centers, and publishing houses, reflecting their own Black Power politics. For them, Kwanzaa was just one in a series of activities that validated their struggle for institutional independence and cultural autonomy. Promoting Kwanzaa was an extension of building an independent school, a community center, or participating in Third World political struggles.[47]

Downtown Brooklyn bustled with commercial, government, and leisure activity on a typical day in the 1970s. The urban landscape was made up of majestic court buildings and high rise office towers that housed various private sector industries like commercial banks. Residential brownstones where wealthy white Brooklynites resided stood only a few blocks away. Less than a half of a mile at the very edge of downtown Brooklyn was home to African-Americans who lived in the neighborhoods of Fort Greene and Bedford-Stuyvesant, two black neighborhoods in the shadows of downtown. On one of those streets, just a stone's throw away from downtown Brooklyn, was where Kwanzaa dwelled every year under the guardianship of the cultural nationalist group called the EAST Organization. Certainly, one could walk down neighboring streets and not know anything about Kwanzaa, Black Power, or the EAST. But if one spent any time on Claver Place, near the main downtown artery of Fulton Street, one could encounter cultural nationalism and the organizational source of Black Power change as one publication noted: "On 10 Claver Place, a narrow side street in the Bedford-Stuyvesant section of Brooklyn, an old, renovated three story building stands almost unseen in the belly of the ghetto. However, inside its doors burns the fiery embers of 400 years of strife, now kindled by the winds of a new hope—the EAST, a model toward the foundation of a black nation."[48]

In Brooklyn, New York, home to one of the largest black populations in the United States, the EAST Organization labored every year to get the word out about Kwanzaa. "If you know something about Kwanza already, spread the word," wrote Basir Mchawi of the EAST, "our greatest communications vehicle is our mouths." For the EAST, no single place proved more appropriate than another for the introduction of Kwanzaa. Members believed Kwanzaa could be held just about anywhere: "Support and initiate Kwanza programs in your community, at day care centers, schools, community centers, your home, etc." All African-Americans should "try to make Kwanza a household word."[49]

Promoting Kwanzaa in black urban neighborhoods oftentimes meant confronting the popularity of Christmas within the black community. EAST publications during the month of December were filled with articles about blacks and Christmas, often chastising African-Americans for rampant holiday season consumption: "Now you fool where do you think you're going? Just come back here . . . sit down and let us put some sense in your head. . . . There are over $400 worth of outstanding bills which you still have from last year, including Christmas."[50] The EAST felt that Christmas shopping for blacks was akin to slavery, extolling African-Americans to "break the chains." "Once again, its time for us to PLAY THE FOOL. . . . MAS-X SEASON is here, better known as XMAS. The time for us to sigh, buy, cry, grin, and PURCHASE, purchase, PURCHASE! All for the hippie-dippey Christ and his OLD new year. TAKE THE CHAINS OFF YOUR BRAIN BLACK PEOPLE!!!"[51] The EAST annually called for a boycott from Christmas shopping and asked African-Americans to consider the cultural alternative to the main holiday tradition, admonishing: "As the holiday season approaches us again, when our monies are most likely at an all time low, we Afrikans had better seriously consider the alternative to the Christmas rip off—Kwanza." Understanding the generational politics in black families where most members were wedded to the traditional Christmas season, the EAST cautioned black parents, "if you can't handle Kwanza, give it to your children. The young folks will love you for it and respect you more than Santa." The EAST summed up their feelings about Christmas and the new Kwanzaa holiday: "Kill Santa Claus, relive Kwanza, bring forth the cultural revolution."[52]

Public announcements every December notwithstanding, Kwanzaa promotion in black neighborhoods manifested in large public events such

as Kwanzaa parades, pre-Kwanzaa workshops, concerts, and large community feasts. In 1974, the EAST moved their normal Kwanzaa activities from
their headquarters on 10 Claver Place to accommodate a larger crowd.
After the children's Kwanzaa festival on December 20, and the follow-up
family Kwanzaa activities from December 26 through to December 29, the
EAST reported that on December 31, "over 1,000 Brothers and Sisters . . .
participated in . . . activities held at the Sumner Avenue Armory." By
moving to a larger site, the EAST was able to commission nationally
known artists, dramatists, and musicians such as poet Sonia Sanchez,
musician Lonnie Liston Smith, and actors from the National Black
Theater to help promote Kwanzaa at its 1974 celebration. The EAST
reminded those unable to attend: "If you missed Kwanza '74, we'll be back
when Kwanza lands again. Be sure you catch it this year. Kwanza '75 will
be a sure nuff smoka."[53]

While the EAST made Kwanzaa an annual ceremonial event in
Brooklyn, different institutions promoted Kwanzaa in different parts of
New York City. One of the earliest groups to sponsor public Kwanzaa cele-
brations was a social service agency called the Harlem Commonwealth

*Figure 2: Children's Kwanzaa celebration in school. Courtesy of Library of
Congress, Prints & Photographs Division, Look Magazine Photograph
Collection, LC-L9-695396-II*

Council located on 125th Street. The Harlem Commonwealth Council typically held annual Kwanzaa festivities at the Studio Museum in Harlem and at area public schools. In December of 1971, the Harlem Council assembled fifty elementary students at the Studio Museum from Public School 68 to teach them about the new holiday. To enliven and embolden the message of roots, identity, and African cultural connection, as well as to reduce the generational gap between the messenger and the students, the Council commissioned a sixteen-year-old ordained minister and director of the National Youth Movement named Al Sharpton to educate the students about Kwanzaa. The young, "heavy set" Sharpton, as the *New York Times* described him, wore an African dashiki and opened his talk by explaining to the students, "today you're going to learn something about Kwanza." In the trademark raspy voice he would become known for as an adult, Sharpton went on to explain in the simplest of terms the holiday's connections with the African past, telling the students, ranging from seven to nine years old, that Kwanzaa is "a spiritual ceremony" and that "harvesting . . . is traditional in Africa." After Sharpton provided a lesson on Kwanzaa's material symbols and the correct way to enunciate the holiday's Swahili terminology, the students were provided gifts, and seven of them were chosen to light the seven candles on the kinara. The following year in 1972, the Council gathered three hundred more students at the Studio Museum to hear another lecture on Kwanzaa.[54]

While independent organizational efforts were common among groups like the EAST, coalition-led Kwanzaas were a major feature of year-end holiday ceremonies in some cities. In 1971, the Confederation of Pan-African Organizations formed to stage citywide Kwanzaa galas in Chicago. Haki Madhubuti and a few others had been performing Kwanzaa ceremonies in their organizations since the late 1960s, but the Confederation recruited a broad cross-section of Chicago black nationalists to further popularize the holiday: Madhubuti and the Institute of Positive Education; Hannibal Afrik and the Shule Ya Watoto; Musa Kenyatta and the Republic of New Africa; Ife Jogunosimi and Mansong Kulubally of the Black Body; the United Africans for One Motherland International (UFOMI); the Chicago chapter of the Provisional Government; and Conrad Worrill—educator, columnist, and later the Chicago chair of the National Black United Front.[55]

One of the most significant developments to come out of the Chicago Confederation was the Karamu Ya Imani—a community feast meaning the feast of faith. Proposed by Hannibal Afrik as a community-wide promotional and educational campaign, the first Karamu Ya Imani was held at the Ridgeland Club on January 1, 1973. Typically, children performed in the early afternoon. During the evening, the ritual phase for adults was held. Evening activities included pouring libations to the ancestors, lighting candles, and making commitments for the New Year. As customary, food was prepared by volunteers, delivered, and placed in the center of the room for consumption. The 200-person gathering included much of the Chicago nationalist community but also a steady stream of apolitical blacks from Chicago's south and west side. Black cultural nationalists also represented visually, appearing in colorful African clothing whereas others wore jeans, slacks, suits, and dresses. Remarks about the importance of embracing "African" culture were made by Hannibal Afrik and Haki Madhubuti, both of whom reiterated how important it was to instill a new set of values in African-Americans, particularly black children. All speakers agreed to the importance of the Karamu Ya Imani and announced that the Confederation would institutionalize Kwanzaa in the windy city by holding annual Feasts of Faith.[56]

In the years following 1971, an increasing number of participants forced the Confederation of Pan-African Organizations to move the Karamu Ya Imani to different locations in Chicago: the Viking Temple, the Young Men's Christian Association, the South Shore Cultural Center, the DuSable Museum, and the Packing House on 49th and Wabash. The growth of the Feast meant that more blacks in Chicago had come to embrace Kwanzaa, which also produced setbacks occasionally. By late 1978, the Confederation found it increasingly hard to finance the Karamu Ya Imani, resulting in the dissolution of the Confederation of Pan-African Organizations as the major promotional head of Kwanzaa. Two years without unified Kwanzaa ceremonies led to the creation of a second umbrella group. In 1980, a few of the original organizations in the Confederation along with a number of newer groups reorganized as the African Community of Chicago and continued the tradition of the Karamu Ya Imani in the new decade.[57]

In Washington, DC, the same spirit of cooperation existed among Kwanzaa organizations united to promote the new Black Power holiday. Again, the black cultural nationalist community took the lead in the city's Kwanzaa publicity campaign. The district's first Kwanzaa celebration was

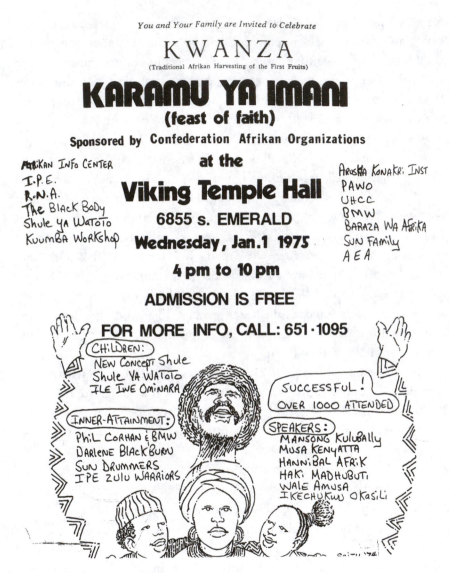

Figure 3: Karamu Ya Imani held in Chicago—one of the largest public Kwanzaa celebration during the 1970s. Courtesy of Mansong Kulubally

held at the home of local activist Sister Woody (Nia Kuumba) in December 1970. Wider public festivities soon spread to the black independent school, the Ujamaa Shule, under the direction of Baba El Senzengalkulu Zulu, and to nationalist houses of worship like the Temple of the Black Messiah and Union Temple Baptist Church pastored by the Reverend

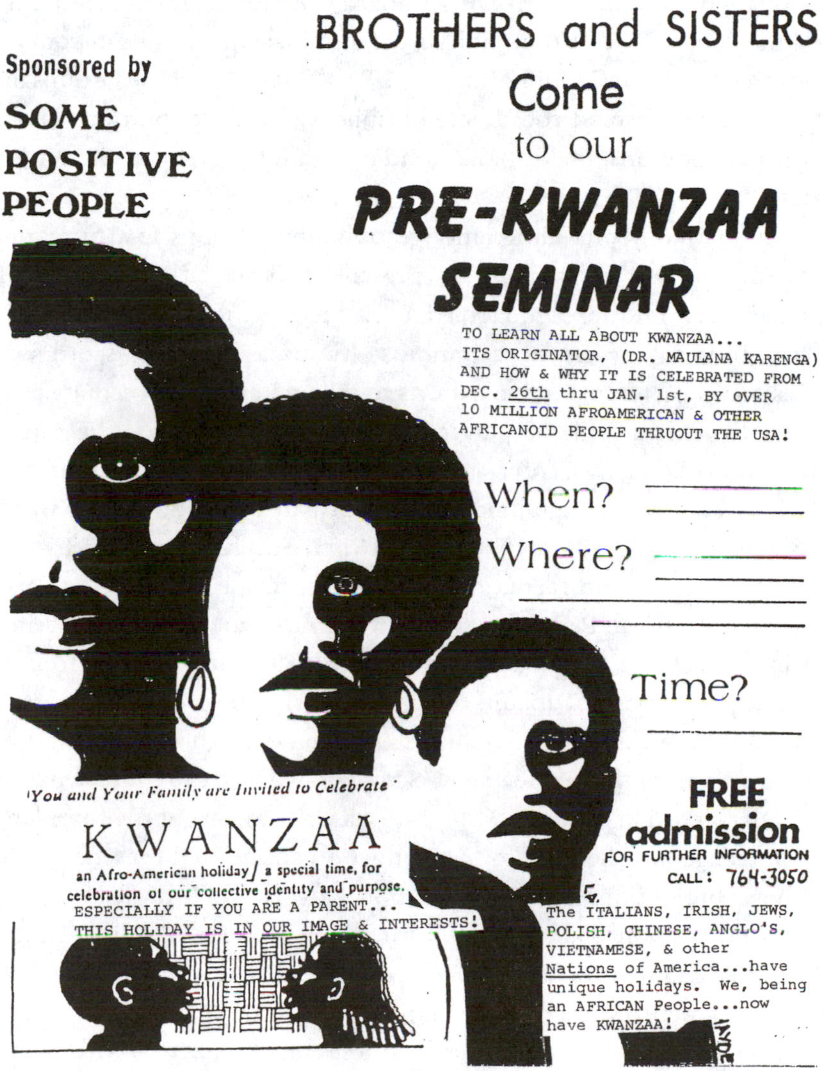

*Figure 4: Some Positive Party Organization promoting pre-Kwanzaa Workshop in 1980 in Jacksonville, Florida. Courtesy of Mansong Kulubally*

Willie Wilson. Unlike church officials at Bethlehem Community in Oakland, religious leaders in the Temple of the Black Messiah at Union Temple in Washington, DC embraced Kwanzaa in an attempt to bridge the spiritual with the cultural. The Museum of African Art under the educational direction of Amina Dickerson, the Reverend Ishakamusa

Barashango, Ayo Handy, the DC Kwanzaa Committee, the Watoto Shule, and the United Black Community were also instrumental in introducing Kwanzaa to the DC public in the 1970s. Many of these groups and institutions sponsored coordinated public Kwanzaa celebrations at their respective locations, making the holiday an annual event in the nation's capital.[58]

The harmony prevailing among community groups in Chicago and Washington, DC was not always present in other cities. Occasionally, Kwanzaa organizations squabbled over the staging and promotion of events. In vying for the most grandiose Kwanzaa festivity, discord sometimes prevailed, forcing organizations to call on Karenga to mediate differences. In Philadelphia, separate organizations, such as the African Community Learning Center, the Marcus Garvey Shule, the Temple of the Black Messiah, and the Ujima Unit participated in individual Kwanzaa activities during the late 1970s. The Urban Survival Training Institute (USTI)—Kawaida cultural nationalists and the former local affiliate of the Congress of African People—was one of the first groups to hold Kwanzaa celebrations in Philadelphia dating back to 1969.[59] The principal founders of USTI were Yokoba Tubiani—a kasisi (priest) of US's Kawaida doctrine, Reginald Mtumishi, Maisha Sullivan-Ongoza and her husband Kauli Ongoza. Some of the members in USTI migrated into the Ujima Unit after USTI disbanded in the mid-1970s. Maisha Ongoza, one of the founders of USTI, recognized the need for a stronger organizational presence behind Kwanzaa promotions in the city. In 1980, Ongoza and Mtumishi created a new organization called the Kwanzaa Cooperative. The Kwanzaa Cooperative sought the status as the city's official authority on the holiday with the power to gather various Philadelphia groups to institute annual citywide Kwanzaas. Feeling somewhat hesitant, Ongoza and Mtumishi of the Cooperative sought advice from Maulana Karenga. Karenga encouraged them to build a united-front organization that could bring the Philadelphia Kwanzaa community together. After consulting with Karenga, founding members issued this statement to the black public:

> Recently, at the urging of Dr. Maulana Karenga, creator of the Afro-American holiday known as Kwanzaa, a local Kwanzaa Co-Operative was formed. The purpose of the Kwanzaa Co-Operative is to coordinate citywide Kwanzaa activities, and to serve as the local authority on the celebration of Kwanzaa so

as to preserve and perpetuate the original spirit, purpose, and value of Kwanzaa. The Kwanzaa Co-Operative welcomes all organizations and individuals who would like to be a part of this historical project.[60]

A group called the Afro-Cultural Preservation Council liked the idea of a Philadelphia confederation and initially participated in organized Kwanzaa festivities with the Kwanzaa Cooperative. In December 1983, the Afro-Cultural Preservation Council wanted to add something new to the holiday season: Philadelphia's first Kwanzaa parade. The parade route would begin in front of the Afro-American Historical and Cultural Museum at Seventh and Arch Streets and end on 18th and Diamond at the Church of the Advocate. The parade would feature dancers, drummers, and performers from the NuTec Uptown Theater group. The feature of the parade would be actors in each section representing one of the seven principles of Kwanzaa.[61]

After the Afro-Cultural Preservation Council announced the proposed parade, the plan became embroiled in controversy with some members in the Kwanzaa Cooperative vehemently objecting to the idea. A meeting was called consisting of the city's Kwanzaa organizations. All groups under the umbrella of the Kwanzaa Cooperative, minus the Preservation Council, including Marcus Garvey Shule, Harambee, the Pan-African Studies Community Education Program (PASCEP), and the Ile Ife voted not to have the parade. The organizations objecting argued that a parade would operate contrary to the spirit of Kwanzaa, which should never manifest into a mockery display of black life on the streets. Kwanzaa, they believed, should represent a time of individual recommitment and community self-reflection, not street theater. Members in the Kwanzaa Cooperative also argued that Philadelphia was just too cold in the month of December to conduct a parade.[62] Publicly, the Afro-Cultural Preservation Council capitulated to the objection. It was soon determined that the Preservation Council was clandestinely proceeding with parade plans despite widespread objection and opposition. When evidence of the Council's plan surfaced, it set off a barrage of criticism between Ongoza of the Kwanzaa Cooperative and the Council. Informing Skobi Jambo of the Preservation Council about her knowledge of his organization's plan, Ongoza wrote:

I unfortunately have been informed by a co-board member of the Marcus Garvey Shule of your involvement with the Kwanzaa parade. My brother from

Marcus Garvey said he saw you on Monday October 22, and that you actively tried to recruit the Shule's support and participation in the parade. You encouraged him to attend the next planning meeting, and you also criticized the members of the Kwanzaa Co-Operative. We in the Kwanzaa Co-Operative, the Marcus Garvey Shule and others attended the meeting of the Afro-Cultural Preservation Committee in good faith and cooperative unity. All who attended ... voted against the parade. We believed at the time that the vote would be honored. To our dismay it wasn't.[63]

The belief that the vote was dishonored proved to be true. The Afro-Cultural Preservation Council had written Karenga one month prior, informing him of its plan to stage a Kwanzaa parade and some of the problems the organization had encountered:

Dear Dr. Karenga, for many years ... some of us have felt a desire to see and participate in an annual Kwanzaa parade and gala festival ... here in Philadelphia. This idea is not new and various organizations have tried to organize this celebration at various times ... with various human conflicts always blocking the success of it actually happening. We know that this is an ambitious undertaking ... of course, there are always those in our community who ... would try to discourage ... it [from] actually happening.[64]

Part of what infuriated Ongoza was not the behind the scenes consultation with Karenga, but the covert tactics employed by the Afro-Cultural Preservation Council. The Council sought to pressure Ongoza to go through with the parade by clandestinely communicating with her supervisors at Temple University, Ongoza's employer:

Having private meetings with whom your group considers my superiors at Temple University to try and get them to stop my lack of support and organizing against the parade. My position on the parade is open, my membership in the Kwanzaa Cooperative is long-standing and on the record. Temple does not control any part of my commitment to Kwanzaa, and no one at Temple can change my value system, which is the Nguzo Saba. My history with Kwanzaa will hold up to anyone in Philadelphia.[65]

For Ongoza and the Kwanzaa Cooperative, the worse part of the Council's parade was white financial support. The first annual Kwanzaa parade in Philadelphia represented an early attempt by corporate America to appropriate the holiday:

> One of the worst offenses of your committee is the seeking of "white money" from Bell Telephone to fund our sacred Afrikan Holy Day. This has sickened everyone who has heard about this. This is against the basic tenets of Kwanzaa, the Nguzo Saba. The Kwanzaa Cooperative is made up of some of the founding members of Kwanzaa in the tri-state area, people who have, through hard work and dedication, helped to make Kwanzaa the recognized holiday that it is. The Kawaida advocates, as you put it, are very protective of not only Kwanzaa, which is based on the doctrine, but all cultural, political, and social events that affect Afrikan people.[66]

Despite vociferous objection from the Kwanzaa Cooperative the parade went forward. The Afro-Cultural Preservation Council conducted Kwanzaa parades in Philadelphia for the next several years without the support of Ongoza and the Kwanzaa Cooperative.

While there is no evidence that Karenga ever attempted to settle this particular dispute in Philadelphia, he was familiar with Kwanzaa parades. He had dealt with a similar proposal by members of his own organization in 1968. Parades, like large community feasts and other public displays of the holiday, had been present from the very beginning. One of the earliest was the Bay Area Kwanzaa Parade held in East Palo Alto in the early 1970s consisting of black cowboys, clowns, dancers, drummers, and marchers from a multitude of African-American cultural groups.[67] But Los Angeles started its own Kwanzaa parade tradition. Samuel Carr-Damu—a high-ranking official in the US Organization, along with members Yuseff Majahliwa and Karl Key-Hekima originally proposed a plan for a Kwanzaa parade. After Karenga rejected the idea, Damu, Majahliwa, and Hekima—all three who had left the organization by 1970—joined forces with Akile Washington-Kosi and Sheila Ward (two individuals closely associated with the US Organization but never formal members) to make the parade a reality. Though the parade idea in Los Angeles was hatched in 1968, it would take ten years for the parade to come to fruition. Damu and Hekima stepped aside, which allowed Majahliwa to proceed with

Washington-Kosi and Ward in creating an independent Kwanzaa parade organization called the Kwanzaa People of Color. The Kwanzaa People of Color and its annual parade in South Central Los Angeles would represent a major vehicle for Kwanzaa promotion in Los Angeles and one of a few public expressions of Kwanzaa outside of the US Organization in southern California during the 1970s.[68]

Local Kwanzaa community organizing, such as parades, served as sustained educational campaigns toward African-Americans. One of the most common forms of protracted promotional strategies were pre-Kwanzaa celebrations. These celebrations consisted of workshops, forums, and mini-celebrations that started at the beginning of December and lasted up to the first day of Kwanzaa. Pre-Kwanzaa ceremonies in the first three weeks of December were designed to spread the word about Kwanzaa events taking place prior to the official holiday week in addition to publicizing activities during the last week of the year. Not only did these events allow blacks to purchase hard-to-find Kwanzaa materials, or provide instructions on how to stage a Kwanzaa ceremony, pre-Kwanzaa gatherings helped demystify the holiday in a variety of ways. Some African-Americans in Chicago who never heard of Kwanzaa and did not interact with the city's black nationalist community harbored thoughts about an anti-Christian holiday ritual in their midst. Hannibal Afrik, founder of the black independent school, Shule Ya Watoto, and co-founder of the African Community of Chicago, remembered encountering these obstacles in the 1970s and early 1980s:

> In those early years there was some hostility and resentment about Kwanzaa because it was felt by some that it was in opposition to Christmas and therefore was pagan . . . and church people should not get involved with it. Because it was African, most people didn't know that much about African culture and so there was some resentment to the terminology, the method of practicing Kwanzaa . . . so it was important that we take our message to the community to help inform them and to solicit their support.[69]

Afrik and other promoters made and distributed Kwanzaa materials, published calendars in black newspapers, and read Kwanzaa events aloud on black radio programs like the Lu Palmer Show on WVON—all to publicize events taking place in the city and help clear up any misrepresentations about the Black Power holiday.[70]

Although Kwanzaa entered the 1980s with institutional vigor via official Kwanzaa week celebrations and December-long pre-Kwanzaa events that gathered more adherents each year, the Black Power Movement stumbled out of the 1970s as a result of government repression, the exile of leaders, internal struggles, deaths, and an overall loss of focus by national organizations. But to invoke the death of the Black Power Movement in a linear manner is to understand Black Power only in its national dimension. Kwanzaa and local promotional efforts remained examples of Black Power's continued resilience and relevance in black neighborhoods during the decline of the national movement. It can be argued that the Black Power Movement survived because its cultural offspring, Kwanzaa, evolved and matured, becoming an independent entity whose charge was to educate a community about the African roots of black American culture. The enormity of the publicity campaign in black urban neighborhoods across the United States was nothing short of extraordinary in the late 1960s, 1970s, and early 1980s. Many persons, organizations, and institutions respectively partook in this Black Power endeavor: Ahidiana in New Orleans, SHAPE Community Center in Houston, Some Positive People in Jacksonville, Florida, the Boston Kwanzaa Committee, and the Metro Atlanta Kwanzaa Association (formerly the Atlanta Kwanzaa Committee). Additional Kwanzaa promoters included black independent schools—the Shule Ya Watoto in Chicago, the Uhuru Sasa in New York, the Aisha Shule in Detroit, the Kazi Shule in Houston, and the Council of Independent Black Institutions (CIBI), which served as an umbrella organization for all black independent schools. Others that publicized Kwanzaa early on were politically conscious black teachers in public schools like Betty Anne Jackson in Community School District Twelve in the Bronx, New York and the Department of Elementary and Secondary Education in the Milwaukee Public Schools. Some houses of worship with black nationalist ministers made Kwanzaa part of their institutional politics: Reverend Albert Cleage's Shrine of the Black Madonna in Detroit, Augustus Stallings' Imani Temple, and Jeremiah A. Wright, Jr.'s Trinity United Church of Christ in Chicago. BSUs fighting for Black Studies programs and departments made Kwanzaa a staple activity on campuses like University of Wisconsin—Madison and the University of Pennsylvania. And finally, black theater groups did much to raise public awareness about Kwanzaa: Baraka's Spirit House Movers in Newark, the

Theater of Afro-Arts in Miami, the Sudan Arts/Southwest of Houston, the Kuumba Workshop in Chicago, the Free Southern Theater of New Orleans, the Mafundi Institute in Los Angeles, and Concept East of Detroit.[71]

The conglomeration of groups and organizations were all instrumental in helping Kwanzaa take root in black neighborhoods. But the history of publicity is multi-layered with Kawaida cultural nationalists most often leading the way in promoting Kwanzaa alongside cultural nationalists with no affiliation with Karenga or Baraka, existing simultaneously with a third cohort—African-Americans that knew nothing or very little about the Black Power Movement. This is not to suggest that only Kawaida cultural nationalists played a major role in publicizing Kwanzaa. Quite the contrary, from the holiday's inception, a dialectic between Kawaida cultural nationalists and non-Kawaida personalities existed in the promotional effort. The activities of Sister Makinya (a non-Kawaidaist) and Amiri Baraka (a former Kawaidaist) bear this out.

The most visible area of promotional convergence is seen in black media where movement and non-movement sympathizers promoted Kwanzaa annually. The introduction of Kwanzaa to television, radio, magazine, and newspaper audiences proved critical to the spread of Kwanzaa in cities across the United States. During the late 1960s and early 1970s, some black media engaged in activist programming—broadcasting a broad range of subjects and events directly related to the black community, including Kwanzaa. Key radio personalities promoting Kwanzaa during the 1970s and 1980s were Frankie Crocker on WLBS in New York; Gary Byrd of WLIB-New York, who began his morning weekday show, the Global Black Experience (GBE), with a recitation of the seven principles; Bob Law's *Night Talk* WWRL-New York; and Lu Palmer of WVON-Chicago. Amiri Baraka and CAP hosted a weekly radio program called *Black Newark* on WNJR that not only talked about Kwanzaa, but also provided an annual critique of Christmas. Television reporter Gil Noble hosted a Sunday morning public affairs program called *Like It Is* on WABC-New York that began showcasing Kwanzaa as early as 1968. And John H. Johnson's *Ebony* magazine and *Ebony, Jr.* as well as *Essence* magazine began featuring stories perennially in the 1970s.

By the mid-1980s and early 1990s, Kwanzaa was entrenched throughout black America. As a result, a second generation of Kwanzaa celebrants emerged in the post-Black Power period, some of whom were unfamiliar with the progenitors that brought Kwanzaa to their respective cities. Ahidiana, a cultural nationalist group, introduced Kwanzaa to the black New Orleans community in 1971. By the time Ahidiana disbanded in the mid-1980s, the West Bank Kwanzaa Coalition assumed the position as the city's leading promoter. Like Ahidiana before it, the West Bank Kwanzaa Coalition acquainted new people to the holiday, some of whom may not have been aware of Kwanzaa's existence in the Crescent City as one resident's words underscored: "Here in New Orleans, [Kwanzaa] is one of the last places for it to be celebrated. I have family in Detroit, Houston, and Dallas, and everybody is celebrating Kwanzaa."[72] Contrary to the statement, New Orleans was one of the first cities to embrace Kwanzaa, proving that the holiday's expansion, indeed, caught many off-guard.

As Kwanzaa began turning over to new organizations, both newer and older celebrants would have to confront the holiday's commercialization. Coming to terms with the complexity of commercial activity would prove complicated due to the number of people involved and the positions they took on the issue. Some black nationalists and former Kawaida cultural nationalists saw the economic realm as a way to further promote Kwanzaa to the public. Other blacks invited major white corporations to take part in annual commercial/promotional campaigns. Many in the community vehemently disagreed with the varying mercantile enterprises, underscoring Kwanzaa's sanctity and reverence as an anti-commercial holiday, and seeing the commodification of Kwanzaa as a major threat to the celebration. A divergent set of views and activities existed around the issues of promotion and profit, exploitation and appropriation, and markets and multiculturalism. What's for sure is that the issues of commercialization and merchandising were more than a simple story of black versus white as the next chapter will show.

# CHAPTER 4

# *Holiday Marketing, Multiculturalism, and the Mainstreaming of Kwanzaa*

After locating one of the leading 1970s Kwanzaa promoters and Black Power stalwarts in his office on a cold December Chicago afternoon in 2000, he immediately knew who I was, why I suddenly appeared, and what kind of information I was looking for. "You're the brother who emailed about coming to Chicago to talk to me about Kwanzaa." "Yes, I am," I replied with great anticipation that Conrad Worrill wanted to talk about one of his most cherished activities. Instead of allowing a few minutes to go by for a formal introduction and interview set-up, Worrill shouted out: "Kwanzaa is dead . . . we've lost it." Worrill's words on the surface appeared tongue in cheek, somewhat facetious to his visitor, but I quickly realized there was a level of earnestness in Worrill's humor. Worrill's referencing of Kwanzaa's "death" and the black community's loss spoke not so much to a physical loss, but rather what he saw as perhaps more detrimental: Kwanzaa's commodification and appropriation outside of the sphere of black America.[1]

## POST-MORTEM BLACK POWER

During the 1970s and early 1980s, Kwanzaa was everywhere and then nowhere; everywhere in places that many black people frequented—community centers, public and independent schools, etc.—and nowhere white people typically ventured—neighborhood cultural nationalist gatherings etc. But if locating Kwanzaa during the Black Power Movement proved difficult for some blacks and many whites, then note Kwanzaa's ubiquity during the 1990s: "Unity, Purpose, Creativity, Faith, Heineken Beer is proud to celebrate Kwanzaa and everything it stands for," read one advertisement in 1998.[2] Consider some others: "When preparing for Kwanzaa, Be Prepared for the Clean-up, No Other Dishwashing Liquid Removes Greasy, Stuck on Food Easier!" Palmolive announced in 1998.[3] The *Advertising Supplement*, a publication of MPI Distribution based in Sacramento, California, called for "Kwanzaa Super Savings!" on Oatmeal Crisp, Honey Nut Cheerios, and Trix cereals.[4] Have you ever been sent a Kwanzaa greeting card? Chances are it's from the Hallmark Corporation, the number one maker of Kwanzaa greeting cards.[5] Many of Kwanzaa's hand-crafted wood candleholders look like they're made in Africa (and many of them are), but some of the candleholders are from India commissioned by the white-owned Los Angeles-based company, Designs for Better Giving.[6] And then, there are the Kwanzaa stamps produced by the United States Postal Service—a government entity yes, but a for-profit corporation whose competition is FedEx and the United Parcel Service (UPS).[7] For a brief period, the Chase Banking Corporation issued Kwanzaa checks and debit cards prior to an avalanche of criticism arriving. And then there is General Motors, Avon, AT&T, Circuit City, and the McDonald's Corporation—all have sponsored large Kwanzaa commercial expositions, serving as major underwriters and boosters.[8]

Still not convinced that Kwanzaa is everywhere and has hit the mainstream running, then take note of where Kwanzaa is being talked up and promoted and where the holiday now appears. Two decades ago Kwanzaa was the stuff of home-made pamphlets and Black Power periodicals like the *Black Scholar* and *Black News*, but now Kwanzaa can be found in *Time, Newsweek,* the *Economist,* and *American Demographics*. When only the *New York Amsterdam News,* the *Chicago Defender,* and the *Los Angeles Sentinel* ran stories on Kwanzaa in the 1970s, black newspaper publications had to share Kwanzaa in the 1990s with the *New York Times*, the *Wall Street Journal*, and the *Washington Post*. Likewise with *Ebony* and *Essence*. Representing the first two magazines to ever feature stories on Kwanzaa in the 1970s, Kwanzaa later occupied the pages of *Glamour* and *Ladies' Home Journal* in the 1990s. There was a time when Kwanzaa children's literature used to be made of stencil and mimeographed paper by black teachers and community-based organizations in the 1970s. Some twenty odd years later, Kwanzaa children's books flooded the market in the 1990s due to the commercial efforts of white publishers.[9] It is no longer necessary to go into the heart of an urban black neighborhood to attend a Kwanzaa celebration; you can take a trip to the Smithsonian. Feel like attending a year-end holiday cornucopia where Kwanzaa is featured alongside Christmas and Hanukkah? A visit to the First Unitarian Universalist Church in Detroit will do the trick. Albuquerque, New Mexico played host to the "Festival of Friends" holiday gala in 1999 where a white a cappella group sang a twelve-part Kwanzaa song at the Emmanuel Presbyterian Church. Perhaps, if we were lost at the northernmost fringes of the state of Wisconsin in late December near the Canadian border in a town called Minocqua, we would stumble on an all-white elementary school. In and of itself, nothing about an all-white school in northern Wisconsin is unusual. Maybe a classroom full of white students, right arm extended in the air and a clenched fist chanting Kwanzaa's ending slogan 'Harambee' would be somewhat of an oddity. Or maybe not. This was Kwanzaa's reality in the 1990s and at the turn of the century, a far cry from that first Kwanzaa celebration in 1966 by the US Organization.

As Kwanzaa moved further into the 1990s, turned over to new organizations, acquired new adherents, and settled into new institutional spaces, the holiday's commercial potential and overall appropriation loomed as a threat for some first-generation Kwanzaa celebrants. But the commercialization and the "selling" of Kwanzaa proved complicated given the various entities involved. Black nationalists saw the economic realm as a way to promote Kwanzaa to the black public as well as to create a sustainable black entrepreneurialism. Some of these activists who had been part of the Black Power Movement invited major corporations to take part in annual commercial/promotional campaigns, merging black entrepreneurship with white commercialism. Others disagreed partnering with white business interests, underscoring Kwanzaa's sanctity and reverence as an anti-commercial holiday and seeing the "commodification" of Kwanzaa for profit as a major threat to black cultural integrity. What is fascinating about the appropriation of Kwanzaa is that the story appears more complex than blacks and whites on the opposite sides of the commercial divide.

The attempt to keep Kwanzaa "pure" and protected from commercial activity has been a futile exercise from the beginning of Kwanzaa's existence. Certainly by the late 1980s and early 1990s, the black holiday that came one day after Christmas proved too irresistible for corporations, such as Hallmark, Inc. and General Motors. After two decades of attempting to control the Kwanzaa market exclusively, black businesses and entrepreneurs began to lose their grip in the very small market niche the holiday afforded them. In the 1990s, white-owned companies and retail stores suddenly recognized the holiday's commercial potential. As *Ebony* magazine noted, "Kwanzaa, the 34-year old holiday focusing on African American families, communities, and culture has proved to be far more than a fad. Its popularity has expanded enough to attract attention from the nation's biggest retailers. In short, the selling of Kwanzaa is becoming big business."[10] This newfound recognition by big business not only signaled an awakening of Kwanzaa's commercial potential, but pointed to a new direction in late twentieth-century capitalism: the marketing and merchandising of race, multiculturalism and diversity via racial and ethnic holidays.[11]

The presence of white-owned corporations in racial markets like Kwanzaa underscored the confluence of multiculturalism and commodification in the last two decades of the twentieth century. As America buried the political vocabulary of the 1960s and 1970s—freedom, rights, power, revolution—multiculturalism of the 1980s and 1990s rested on the notions of inclusion, diversity, and recognition. The rise of multiculturalism in the 1980s opened up spaces to people of color in the American public sphere, making African-Americans, Latinos, Asian-Americans politically, culturally, and economically visible and viable.[12] Multiculturalism's emphasis on the importance of race and ethnicity turned votes into a political commodity for politicians running for office. Likewise, multiculturalism made race and ethnicity an economic commodity for merchants, retailers, and corporations. It was not surprising that ethnic and racial customs, particularly annual calendar events, had become major occasions for buying and selling in the last two decades of the twentieth century. Even more than the standard American holidays like Christmas and Thanksgiving, racial and ethnic festivities enabled corporations to penetrate specialized markets. Racial holiday markets like Kwanzaa provided companies a chance not only to increase profits, but to engage in the politics of public relations by peddling the ideas of diversity, inclusion, and recognition to the communities they serve in the marketplace.[13]

But the marketplace was not only the purview of economic actors. Institutions, such as churches, museums, and schools also partook in ethnic and racial consumption by making Kwanzaa a standard year-end activity. In the name of diversity and goodwill, major white institutions discovered many potentially important features in Kwanzaa: the holiday's ability to diversify annual programming that caters to an overwhelmingly white audience; its potential to augment the museum- and church-attending public; and its ability to recast the museum, the church, and the school as racially and ethnically inclusive institutions. All of these desires are self-serving marketplace values without the overt profit-making motive. However, the fact that the end game is not profit for museums, churches and schools does not hide the absence of marketplace and consumption behavioral intent. On the contrary, cultural institutions often have a bigger stake in promoting identity-based marketing and consumption designed to remake internal institutional politics in the realm of public relations while promoting the broader goal of diversity and inclusion of racial and ethnic minorities in society.[14] So Kwanzaa, with seemingly no monetary exchange value in these contexts, equally became a fetishized and reified commodity similar to durable goods. What this ultimately meant was that Kwanzaa as commodity seemed understood by all involved: black nationalists, small black entrepreneur, black advertising copywriter, black greeting card maker, the Afrocentric boutique, white corporation, white bank, white museum, white church, Jewish synagogue, suburban white school, white media, the United States Postal Service, etc. What this also meant was that Kwanzaa's growing visibility in late twentieth-century American public culture appeared endemically tied to the marketplace decision-making and appropriation of corporate, cultural, and media institutions.

## PROMOTION, PROFIT, AND PUBLIC RELATIONS: THE STRUGGLE OVER A NEW HOLIDAY MARKET

In no way am I suggesting that all forms of Kwanzaa appropriation are synonymous with one another; that the suburban white school's celebration of Kwanzaa is somehow akin to an African-American family partaking of Kwanzaa at home. Or that Kwanzaa debit cards from Chase Manhattan Bank is similar to a black woodcraftsman making vinara and selling them at a local black bookstore. But to place in the same context the corporation, the bank, the museum, the house of worship, the school, the media, the black nationalist organization, and the black entrepreneur is to identify a political economy of culture and to provide what Bill Ryan has called "an institutional analysis of the culture industry."[15] In other words, we have to understand how market forces driven by institutional politics have brought Kwanzaa into the mainstream in both its commoditized and non-commoditized forms. As Ryan has pointed out, "it seems fundamental to recognize the distinctiveness of the culture industry. . . . not simply capitalist production . . . [but] cultural production organized along capitalist lines."[16] Ryan shifts our attention away from the entity of the company and allows us to focus on the "corporate form of capitalist cultural commodity production" that can take place in a variety of institutional settings. I want to suggest that capitalist cultural commodity production does manifest in corporate and non-corporate spheres, at least in regards to Kwanzaa. Recognizing the ubiquity of capitalist commodity production in variegated institutional spaces, Ryan identifies them as "corporations of culture."

Ryan's concept, "corporations of culture" is very useful here, for it is not restricted to the corporation in the limited organizational sense, but goes beyond the private sector to get at the very nature of capitalist logic that is inherent in most, if not all, institutions in the United States. Getting at the heart of Kwanzaa appropriative politics means institutionally "elucidating the distinctive characteristics of a particular form of organization, its constituent objects, and their logics, their rules of combination."[17] Ryan goes on to describe how these institutions operate:

> Some are given by the general conditions of profitability which impact upon companies, cultural and otherwise; others operate through trading or ownership linkages to major corporations in other spheres of industry; other links reach out into the periphery of the culture industry, in direct and short-term sub-contracting relations with independents and individuals in creative projects, and indirectly through licensing and distribution agreements, and into the amateur sphere which provides an ongoing pool of talent. 'Corporations,' therefore, is used in this analysis as an institutional term which has empirical referents only as the complex of corporate offices, subsidiaries and divisions articulated through various transactions, sub-contracts and engagements to other sectors of the economy. Furthermore, the 'corporate' form of cultural practice instituted 'inside' the corporations of culture, in some cases, flows

over into non-corporate spheres, variously and in different ways and with different effects.[18]

Ryan's analysis on the political economy of the culture industry forces us to grapple with the question: is Kwanzaa appropriative politics a story about blatant exploitation by the "corporations of culture," that is, white America writ large? If so, how are we to understand the racial dynamics of corporate and institutional exploitation and appropriation? Are all forms of appropriation exploitative? The entry of white corporations and cultural institutions into the Kwanzaa market blurred the lines between white and black. Thus, I argue the marketing of Kwanzaa by entities outside of the black community cannot simply be seen as an example of white appropriation and exploitation. The problem with this view is that too many actors were involved on both sides of the racial appropriation equation. Black graphic artists and advertising copywriters worked for major white companies that merchandised and commoditized Kwanzaa. To create and subsequently promote their Kwanzaa products, Fortune 500 and smaller companies retained the services and expertise of black marketing and advertising firms. Black visual artists worked with in-house corporate production teams and as consultants. Small black entrepreneurs—many sole or two-person proprietorships—staged large annual commercial expositions with open solicitations to white-owned corporations and financial institutions for sponsorship support. What seemed at first glance an example of cooptation by major white companies could be interpreted as nothing more than a synergistic arrangement between economic actors in a free-market economy, albeit unequally. Acknowledging the power differential that exists between black and white economic subjects, and that the corporate form of cultural practice flows over into white institutions in the non-corporate spheres provides us with a broad understanding of cultural and institutional appropriation, not just a simple explanation of white taking from black. It also provides a lens to see, if not a bare-knuckle struggle over the Kwanzaa market, perhaps, the holiday's utility in different settings and the "positionings" of various actors involved in marketing Kwanzaa for different purposes.

One hundred years ago, a diverse array of voices spoke on the subject of black economic nationalism. The first spokesperson said that "the mass of Negroes must learn to patronize business enterprises conducted by their own race, even at some disadvantage. ... The large industry, the department store and the trust are making it daily more difficult for the small capitalist with slender resources."[19] The second echoed the first saying "if we wish to bring the race to a point where it should be, where it will be strong, and grow and prosper, we have got to, in every way possible, encourage it. We can do this in no better way than by cultivating that amount of faith in the race which will make us patronize its own enterprises."[20] The third rhetorically asked a question, "How can we otherwise succeed? Some would say that this was drawing the color line. Jews support Jews, Germans support Germans, Italians support Italians. Negroes should now begin to support Negroes. Don't delay this, but begin today."[21] The last voice summed up the sentiments of the first three by declaring "a race that is solely dependent upon another for its economic existence sooner or later dies. ... The thing for the Negro to do therefore, is to adjust his own economic present, in readiness for the future."[22] These respective clarion calls from W.E.B. Du Bois, Booker T. Washington, Fred Moore, and Marcus Garvey expressed displeasure over the place of African-Americans in the economy and conveyed a closing-ranks philosophy of black economic self-help. As the twentieth century moved forward, other black economic nationalists, such as Elijah Muhammad and Malcolm X adopted their ideas about commercial self-sufficiency as the key to black advancement. Further diagnosis on black economic stagnation came from Maulana Karenga via Kwanzaa's fourth principle, *ujamaa*:

> Ujamaa (cooperative economics) specifically requires control, not only of the economics of Kwanzaa, but also the very economy of the Black community in a mutually-beneficial process of shared work and shared wealth. No serious celebrant of Kwanzaa can support a corporate control of the economy of the Black community or the economics of Kwanzaa. Nor can they in good conscience drive small-scale community artists, producers, and vendors out of business by buying corporate products and aiding their penetration and domination of the Kwanzaa market.[23]

Currents of black economic thought swirled around every period of the twentieth-century Black Freedom Movement, with each casting liberatory projections and offering to take African-Americans to commercial places they had never been. Kwanzaa added to the debate by introducing the socialist and African communitarian concept called *ujamaa*. Kwanzaa's conception of *ujamaa* was infused with a heavy dose of American black nationalist thought that resembled the economic ideas of Du Bois, Washington, and Garvey more than Tanzanian president Julius Nyerere who popularized it.[24] Thus, the creation of Kwanzaa in 1966 had two immediate effects: it revisited a century-old discussion on black economic nationalism, and secondly, Kwanzaa ushered in a brand new holiday market.

But a strange occurrence happened to black America on its path to freedom that sixties spoken-word artist Gil Scott-Heron intuitively understood. The death of Jim Crow and political liberation opened up American society. Freedom, however, was a two-way street. If African-Americans gained access without, that meant the dominant society also obtained liberty to move in. Under Jim Crow, the color-line was fixed, final, and for all intents and purposes, permanent, although whites could, and did cross it, when it proved commercially and politically beneficial. The Civil Rights Movement and Black Power Movement broke the color-line, allowing unfettered access to both dominant and subaltern communities in their respective spheres. Thus, to talk of a fortressed Kwanzaa market was to hearken back to an era where black entrepreneurs had no other choice but to maximize their commercial efforts within the community. The Civil Rights Act of 1964 and the Voting Rights Act of 1965 were the more familiar outcomes of the movement and pointed blacks toward a more inclusive society; but likewise did Community Development Corporations, Black Capitalism, and black Chambers of Commerce rapidly move African-Americans closer to the economic mainstream. For sure, many blacks wanted to be as far away from white society as possible even after the passage of the Civil Rights Act and Voting Rights Act of 1964 and 1965, respectively. There were an equal number of African-Americans, however, who welcomed a chance to enter the open society. As for white capital, it was always looking for new markets. Hence, the Scott-Heronian irony of the "revolution not being televised" may have temporarily provided black America some internal humor, but as in the words of historian Robert Weems, the revolution, indeed, was on the road to being marketed.[25]

The development of an economic market for Kwanzaa proceeded at a snail's pace during the first fifteen years of the holiday's existence. In fact, in the late 1960s and 1970s, a market for Kwanzaa barely existed at all. What did exist was a series of attempts to both promote and profit from the holiday by marketing home-made Kwanzaa greeting cards, how-to-Kwanzaa pamphlets, posters, pins, buttons, home-produced children's literature, bumper stickers, and other ephemeral material. Additionally, Kwanzaa ceremonial symbols, particularly the kinara (candleholder), were a part of a budding Kwanzaa market but produced by small-scale black woodcraftsmen and commissioned by black nationalist and community-based organizations. What immediately stood out about the merchandising of Kwanzaa in the late 1960s and the 1970s was the holiday's promising but very limited commercial potential. Thus, black economic activity around Kwanzaa in the early part of the holiday's history can be generally summed in the following phrase: Kwanzaa in a pushcart.[26]

The pushcart Kwanzaas were organizational and home-spun mail-order efforts to both market and promote the holiday from the position of black economic nationalism. Kwanzaa Arts, a small business that began in Los Angeles, typified early Kwanzaa entrepreneurial efforts. Kwanzaa Arts began when three original celebrants from the late 1960s and early 1970s came together to promote Kwanzaa by marketing a free Kwanzaa catalog containing various items. The catalog items included an "I Love Kwanzaa" bumper sticker, a Kwanzaa pin to wear on clothing, and magazine articles about the holiday. To publicize the holiday, Kwanzaa Arts advertised their catalog in major black newspapers. Couching their catalog as part of a free promotional campaign, Kwanzaa Arts wanted to profit from the holiday by attempting to solicit interest in their seven greeting cards priced at $4.95 a set: "At last you can celebrate this unique Afro-American Holiday by sending creatively designed Kwanzaa cards to family and friends . . . Just $4.95 for 7 beautiful Kwanzaa cards and matching envelopes. Satisfaction guaranteed . . . Mail your order now to Kwanzaa Arts."[27] Other commercial/promotional mail-order business appeared in Baltimore, marketing comparable items: "Kwanzaa Unlimited is proudly offering 3 authentic Kwanzaa celebration pins to be worn or given as gifts during the holiday season for just $9.99."[28]

Similar commercial practices occurred in New York City. In Harlem, community-based organization Afram Associates sold everything from Kwanzaa how-to pamphlets ranging from $1.00 to $2.00, a 17 x 24 Kwanzaa Calendar for $1.50, a Kwanzaa record at $6.98, holiday settings and material objects (candleholder, mat, and candles) between $25 and $40, and greeting cards for $0.40 each or 30 for $5.00.[29] Afram Associates went a step further by selling a Kwanzaa Directory. Pricing their Directory at $1.00, Afram revealed the contents of the inventory on its first page and the Directory's target audience: "The Kwanzaa Directory published December 26, 1973 ... is a collection of all known available kwanza resources—books, films, kwanza kards, kwanza setting." The Directory is a "useful document for schools, churches, community groups, and editors."[30] One black independent school affiliated with the cultural nationalist EAST Organization, the Uhuru Sasa Shule, marketed its own Kwanzaa items, using the theme of black overconsumption during Christmas as an advertising technique to push their own products:

> Brothers and sisters as you may already know, deadly "X-Mas" season is approaching. This is a time of the year above all others when the economic exploitation and cultural devastation of American society plunder and ravish our black communities. Enclosed we have sent you a complimentary sample of a button available for Kwanza as well as a brochure explaining the meaning and content of Kwanza. As long as supplies last, we can make available buttons at $.50 each ($.40 for amounts from 10–50 and $.30 for 50 and above). Brochures are available at a token cost of $.5 each. We also have Kwanza Kards and Kwanza Kits if you are so inclined. Please let me hear from you on this urgent matter ... for children and community. The struggle continues.[31]

Black Power organizations like the EAST felt equally responsible for the black community's commercial well-being, or perhaps, their own. Amiri Baraka's Congress of African People (CAP) engaged in commercial uplift by supplying the market with Kwanzaa ceremonial items from the point of production, distribution, and final sale. For CAP, to serve as Kwanzaa's major booster in the realm of cultural politics also meant controlling Kwanzaa's material property in the realm of marketplace politics. A 1973 CAP report explained how the Black Power organization produced Kwanzaa ceremonial items and who would make the final determination on how the symbols should look. "Man is casting kinara with seven principles on it," an internal report noted, and "will send to Imamu Baraka before going into production. . . . Imamu Baraka needs to see models of everything and prices." The man in the memorandum is never identified by name or occupation, but it can be safely assumed that the individual, probably a skilled woodcraftsman, was commissioned by CAP and entrusted to create a design acceptable to Baraka and the organization. The same report determined where and how Kwanzaa Kits would be delivered to individuals and merchants in the African-American community: "Camden will be the distribution center." Local CAP-affiliated organizations will have vinara and kits available for the African-American community, but "orders will be filled in Camden" for wholesalers and at "retail to people with no local CAP office." To eliminate confusion and difficulty in obtaining Kwanzaa ceremonial items, and to ensure proper distribution and pricing, it was important for the national distribution center in Camden, New Jersey to be in sync with local merchants, organizations, and people as the same memo noted: "must get whole financial setup between local and national . . . can be done as soon as [we] have whole cost on items."[32] Indeed, CAP went a step further by setting prices for individual items and full ceremonial kits. As part of the Kwanzaa Kit, individual vinara (candleholders) were priced at $5.50 a piece, the vikombe (unity cups) at $1.88, the mikeka (mats) at $1.40, and the mishumaa (candles) at $.70. CAP also offered Kwanzaa cards at $1.05 a piece and a Kwanzaa kitabu (a how-to-perform pamphlet) at $.15. The total price for the Kwanzaa Kit totaled $10.68, but CAP set the retail price at $17.50, making a gross profit of $6.82 per Kit. CAP also turned a profit on individual vinara, pricing them separately from the Kit at $11.00 a piece and knowing that as the single most important ceremonial item and the costliest to manufacture, many celebrants would only seek to buy Kwanzaa's candleholder and make do without other key symbols.[33] CAP kept a close watch on vinara and other products by having each local CAP-affiliated organization send back an accounting of that year's Kwanzaa inventory. The group Nyumba Ya Ujamaa reported that between December 22 and December 31, 1972 it sold fifty-three Kwanzaa Kits at $17.50 a piece for a total of $927.50. The EAST Organization reported back to CAP headquarters that it sold ninety-seven vinara, sixty mikeka, seven hundred mishumaa, and forty cover boxes for a total profit of $701.50. The organization Asili Kawaida reportedly sold seven hundred and fifty-six Kwanzaa cards at $.15 totaling $113.40. Nyumba Ya Ujamaa sold two hundred Kwanzaa cards.[34]

With CAP and its local affiliates controlling every Kwanzaa-related item from idea/concept to production/manufacturing and from distribution to sale, Kwanzaa as new market and new holiday appeared firmly in the hands of African-Americans. But since the Kwanzaa market yielded very little financial return, the intent of CAP, Afram Associates, and Kwanzaa Arts centered on Kwanzaa promotion while simultaneously remaining hopeful that money could be made from the holiday in a sustained fashion. In most small business enterprises involving Kwanzaa in the 1970s and 1980s, promotion and profit often overlapped. As Bernard Hoyes, the graphic artist for Kwanzaa Arts explained, "what I was trying to do was to market the whole idea of Kwanzaa from a utilitarian point of view. Kwanzaa wasn't going to be mass distributed unless you put it in a form to be mass distributed." Hoyes made promotion synonymous with profit, recognizing that Kwanzaa could also gain a following through economic enterprise and "not just in diatribes of political thought."[35] Thus, profit and promotion emerged early in Kwanzaa's history with an aim at keeping Kwanzaa circumscribed within the commercial boundaries of the black community and protecting the holiday from mainstream market forces. No doubt, this nascent marketing of Kwanzaa was indeed about profiting, but it was conducted in the spirit of promoting the holiday via bootstrap black entrepreneurialism—self-help, self-sufficiency, and economic uplift—thoroughly eschewing any and all white capital.[36] Ultimately, 1970s black entrepreneurs publicized Kwanzaa and used the holiday as a way to enter the marketplace and the world of business traditionally inhospitable to them as producers.

The pushcart as a metaphor and signifier for black homespun commercial efforts was reality for most black business ventures in the Kwanzaa market. To understand this legacy is to comprehend the sociology of entrepreneurship, ethnic and racial enterprises, middle-men minorities, undercapitalization, and the duel economy.[37] Black businesses and sole proprietors operating in a peripheral economy usually means manufacturing, distributing, and selling goods within a restricted market based on race. Black businesses in restricted racial markets often use outdated techniques of production, are encumbered by having only a few channels of distribution for their products, and remain powerless to reduce or eliminate the forces of competition. In every period of Kwanzaa's history, black commercial activity related to the holiday remained part of the peripheral economy while larger white-owned companies marketing Kwanzaa received their lifeblood from the mainstream economy. With the creation of a new holiday market, Kwanzaa indeed opened up a commercial space for aspiring black entrepreneurs; the problem, however, was that much of the space had long been occupied by large white companies. The greeting card industry is illustrative of this point.

The words "holiday market" immediately open a discussion about the greeting card industry. The industry is dominated by a small conglomerate of greeting card companies like Hallmark, American Greetings, and Gibson, and policed by the trade group, the Greeting Card Association. To add the modifier "new" to holiday market meant that the consortium of Hallmark, American Greetings, Inc. and Gibson were well positioned to penetrate and augment a novel niche market to increase profit margins. Their positioning and entry into the black card market proved well timed as social conditions dictated new commercial opportunities. The mainstream greeting card industry's penetration into black America is owed to the success of the Civil Rights and Black Power Movements. Black Power's political and cultural revolution created a commercial revolution by opening up a new market—the "soul" market—a name given at the time by the culture industry. Various American corporations hovered over this new racial market, strategically positioning themselves to offer many goods and services. White greeting card companies assessed the market's potential and began issuing greeting cards to the liberated black public in 1968 as *Newsweek* reported:

> For blacks, greetings cards have always been white. To celebrate a birthday, to mark an anniversary or simply to say "Happy Valentine," the Negro was forced to settle for cards created by and for white America. In a $800 million-a-year industry . . . not one greeting card pictured a black face. Now . . . the major card companies have introduced a black line. Essentially, it is a white line in blackface. American Greetings, Inc., offers Negro family scenes like skating on a frosty pond. Gibson sells such birthday greetings as a bright-eyed black moppet standing in a field of daisies with her beribboned kitchen. Hallmark's saccharine poetry remains intact although the white faces have acquired a sepia tone. Typical is one teen-age girl on the cover of a birthday greeting, who could pass for Doris Day in burnt cork.[38]

With their unlimited resources, white greeting card companies attempted to capitalize on the new "soul" market. Though Hallmark, Gibson, and American presently make cards exclusively for African-Americans, they were "outperformed" in the 1960s and 1970s by new black greeting card makers like Goodie Products in Philadelphia and Stanita in New York whose cards reflected the new Black Power aesthetic—Afros, dashikis, clenched raised fists, and the slogan "black is beautiful."[39]

Not to be perturbed by an initial lack of understanding of 1960s and 1970s Black Power politics—with its various signifiers, slogans, and insular ways of doing—white greeting card makers capitalized on another commercial avenue created by the culture industry: the "multicultural market." The multicultural market was a 1980s and 1990s phenomenon characterized not by oppositional politics, but a new brand of pluralism based on diverse histories, respect, and recognition. Multicultural pluralism prided itself on the inclusion of people of color: their bodies, their markets, their votes, their histories, and certainly, their money. Often, this translated into greater representation of African-Americans and other people of color in corporate and mainstream institutional structures who now had some input on how best to market to communities of color. When the 1960s and 1970s garnered only one or two token jobs for blacks or a single black voice, the 1980s and 1990s witnessed a steady stream of employed persons of color as professional salaried staff and/or consultants helping corporations market to racial and ethnic consumers. Thus, racial and ethnic holidays became big business for corporations in this new multicultural commercial setting—a setting characterized by heavy involvement and much greater representation of blacks and other people of color inside the culture industry.

As profits leveled off in the mainstream card market, white greeting card makers competed directly with the handful of national black card companies that emerged in the 1970s and 1980s: Broom Designs, Carole Joy Creations, Blacksmiths Cards, Love, Auntie Cheryl Greetings, L'Image Graphics, Kofi Tyus, and Kuumba Collectibles. Not only did white-owned greeting card companies directly compete by merchandising racial celebrations in the name of multiculturalism, they also eliminated or severely reduced competition from some of these black greeting card firms. Before Hallmark released its signature Mahogany product line of black greeting cards in 1991—produced by a black and white staff—the company test-marketed Kwanzaa cards in 1987 by allowing a few black producers to sell their cards in Hallmark stores and in chain supermarkets contracted to sell the Hallmark brand exclusively. Initially, Hallmark reported it was not interested in producing Kwanzaa cards, only making them available to their African-American customers. Kwanzaa cards did well in Hallmark's stores, prompting the company to change its policy the following year. Black visual artist Synthia St. James was contracted by Hallmark after Jewish-owned EthnoGraphics used her designs for its Kwanzaa cards. Hallmark also tested cards by inspirational author Iyanla Vanzant before contracting them permanently under its Mahogany line. Love, Auntie Cheryl Greetings, Inc., a small black card company, obtained a licensing agreement from American Greetings only to be dropped a few years later after American began its own line of black cards. Aspiring to become the "black Hallmark," Love, Auntie Cheryl Greetings, produced only for American, which caused the small company to fold after American terminated their relationship. In the mid-1990s, Recycled Papers, the fourth largest greeting card company in the United States, acquired L'Image Graphics, one of the most successful black greeting card companies since 1983. In a five point six billion dollar greeting-card industry, profits for black card makers in the multicultural market should have risen to new heights by 1995 according to Vivian Broom, owner of Broom Designs: "White companies have become interested in targeting the African American market. Because they have their foot already in the door, they're getting the big bucks and we're not." But Jose Martinez, product manager of ethnic cards at American Greetings, argued that it is impossible to keep mainstream greeting card companies from niche markets like Kwanzaa: "Where there is growth is where everyone wants to be." Paul Quick, general manager of Hallmark's Ethnic Business Center, took it a step further, arguing that with over seven hundred artists, designers, writers, and photographers on its staff, and the hiring of black artists and writers as consultants who make Kwanzaa and other cards, "I see the Mahogany line as helping to create some exposure for African American artists and getting their work out there. We're not working against them—we're supporting them."[40]

Placing unlimited resources in the area of multicultural card production has been a formula used by Hallmark, Gibson, and American to reduce competition and put small black greeting card manufacturers out of business. Kwanzaa represented only one in a series of racial and ethnic holidays merchandised by these large corporations. The area of multicultural card production included extensive research on communities of color, uncovering population statistics and disposable income. Ethnic business centers were established to aid ongoing research. In-house production or product teams made up of black artists, designers, and writers tracked the latest trends in all areas of the media as Hallmark's Melissa Bolden explained:

> I keep up with the latest publications, television programs, and retail catalogs targeted to our customer and I love to immerse myself in cities where the African American population is high. It helps me get outside of my own "black" experience because as with all cultures, there is a wide range of styles, forms of language, and attitudes that mainstream America sometimes overlook.[41]

This kind of effort has allowed Hallmark to produce eight hundred cards related to the African-American experience, ranging from holidays, historical personalities, everyday occasions, and birthdays. Beginning with one Kwanzaa card in 1992, Hallmark annually produced ten different cards for Kwanzaa by the end of the decade. Already controlling nearly eighty percent of the general greeting card market along with American and Gibson, Hallmark's entry and steady progress in racial card production made the existence of black greeting card companies exceedingly tenuous.[42] *Black Enterprise* magazine wrote about the difficulties black card makers faced in the 1990s:

> Remember "Cousin Mattie's Daddy's Sister's People," the line of black greeting cards with life-size soft sculpture dolls depicting scenes from everyday African American family life? Their creator, Cheryl D. Munson, was pictured with some of the characters she created in the December 1989 issue of *Black Enterprise*. Ever wonder why you can't find the cards in your local store anymore? In 1991, six years after Munson's cards went on the market, Love Auntie Cheryl Greetings, Inc. went bankrupt. Munson's story is not unusual. Of the 17 black-owned greeting card companies listed in that story, about one-third can't be traced today. And many of those that are still around are fighting to stay in business. In fact, the challenge may be greater today than it was six years ago.[43]

*Figure 5: Kinara made by Ngoma Ali of Los Angeles; Ali is one of a handful of black kinara manufacturers in the United States. Courtesy of Keith Mayes*

Skilled wood artisans and black kinara manufacturers faced a similar dilemma. Ngoma Ali, a former member of the US Organization, and one of the founders of Kwanzaa Arts, had apprenticed under Buddy Rose-Aminifu—the first kinara maker in the United States. Ali perfected his skill at woodcarving at Sarritos Junior College in Los Angeles, becoming one of a handful of national black kinara makers in the country. By the late 1980s and early 1990s, Ali witnessed an increase in kinara importers and wholesalers, some of whom were white. Designs for Better Giving, a white-owned company, outpaced all small-scale black producers to become one of the largest distributors of vinara in the country, importing their candleholders from India. Black kinara manufacturers either produced candleholders in the United States, Africa, the Caribbean, or Suriname, South America. With the emergence of Designs, not only were kinara wholesalers white, but the very hands that constructed the most sacrosanct item in the Kwanzaa setting were non-black. What really allowed Designs to thrive in this market were greater financial capital, its ability to mass-produce vinara, and its wider distribution channels. Additionally, like white greeting card manufacturers, Designs used the ideal of multiculturalism as a major selling point, merging diversity and consumption together. Disguising their racial identity via advertisements, Designs offered an assortment of black-related items, including greeting cards and vinara, created specifically by in-house African-American artists under the marketing label, "multicultural cards and gifts." Commissioning design templates from African-American artist Carlotta Swain-Ward, Designs for Better Giving employed wood artisans from India to hand-carve Swain-Ward's Kwanzaa candleholders. In a promotional campaign, Designs proudly advertised its black conceived vinara and the artist that produced them: "Our original hand-carved wood vinara with its accompanying hand-carved cup were inspired by the kinara design in Carlotta Swain-Ward's 'First Kwanzaa.' Made out of solid mango wood, these vinara will be cherished by your family for generations." Designs for Better Giving offered at least seven types of vinara made by Swain-Ward and other black artists. Designs' inventory also included Japanese prints, Latin and Haitian art as well as cards and gifts for every conceivable event communities of color partake in.[44]

Competition from private mail carriers forced the United States Postal Service (USPS) to conceive of ways to merchandise Kwanzaa, ethnic holidays, and historical personalities. The move to commoditize cultural events, perennial occurrences, and historical persons coincided with the Postal Reorganization Act of 1970 which transformed the agency from a subsidized tax-supported federal entity into a business financially supported through correspondence, business advertising, and stamp sales. With annual operating revenue at $63 billion and a workforce close to eight hundred thousand employees, the USPS would qualify as one of the largest Fortune 500 companies. While the size of the USPS reached unprecedented proportions in the 1990s, it has long been eclipsed by the private mailing industry with combined annual revenue reaching $155 billion and employing over six million people. The USPS's continued loss of revenue and the inability to sustain itself through tax-supported dollars made the agency cognizant of competitors and other ways to expand. One road to new growth came from augmenting its stamp selection process, using subjects and events with high rates of marketability.[45] Thus, in 1996, the USPS created a holiday stamp series beginning with Hanukkah. One year later, under the direction of its Stamp Advisory Committee, the USPS issued a Kwanzaa stamp with the help of the holiday's creator, Maulana

Karenga and black artist Synthia St. James who designed the stamp.[46] On October 22, 1997, the stamp was unveiled in several US cities, with the major kickoff occurring in Los Angeles.[47] The Natural History Museum of Los Angeles County gathered two thousand people for a stamp dedication ceremony, including Karenga, LeGree Daniels of the USPS Board of Governors, James L. Powell, Executive Director of the museum, and artist Synthia St. James. During Karenga's keynote speech, traces of Black Power rhetoric familiar to Kwanzaa's origin and early years were barely heard. Instead, Karenga used the moment to recast Kwanzaa as a multicultural ceremony:

> [Kwanzaa] is a reaffirmation of the country's need to respect, celebrate, and build on the rich resource of its diversity of peoples and cultures; to see itself as an ongoing multicultural project to create a truly just and good society; and to embrace an ethics of sharing—shared space, shared wealth; shared power, and shared responsibility of all peoples—African, Native American, Latino, Asian, and European—to conceive and build the world they want to live in.[48]

Other ceremonies were held throughout the month of November in places like Sacramento, Chicago, and Washington, DC with the stamp's image unveiled on lapel pins, greeting cards, and pre-paid phone cards.[49]

Engaging in niche racial markets have not only made the corporations of culture successful marketers but appear as though they are supporters and promoters of marketplace inclusivity. Being "inclusive" economic actors in racial commercialism provides the corporations of culture with the cover of being responsible capitalists, thereby lessening the sting of indictments around white exploitation. Increasing in-house staff, diversifying product teams, contracting well-known artistic personalities, and creating racially thematic product lines has allowed the culture industry to gain and maintain an edge in cultural commodity production by making blacks and other people of color the public face of their appropriation. Bill Ryan has rightly observed that the "project team form of labour organization . . . is the corporate form's single most important characteristic." The project team has indeed given African-Americans a place at the table, particularly when it comes to the production and circulation of black cultural representations. Though African-Americans may appear as key decision-makers, and in many cases they are, what is most valued about this class of black professionals is not necessarily their ideas and labor, but the legitimacy they are able to provide in creating and circulating black culture. Hence, retaining black artists and black professionals is "no longer carried out for purely artistic purposes but [is] overlaid by the logic of capital."[50]

The logic of capital that Ryan underscores has been the culture industry's ability to elevate the black artist, the black marketer, the black craftsmen, the black in-house staff, and other "performers" to the "position of directed executant" in the Kwanzaa market. Thus, within a multicultural atmosphere white commercial appropriation of Kwanzaa required black faces and voices. Nowhere is this more evident than in the corporate underwriting of Kwanzaa commercial expositions.

## Black Ujamaa and Corporate Underwriting

The struggle of black entrepreneurs to maintain their stake in the Kwanzaa market and the holiday's financial and symbolic appeal to corporations ultimately meant the pairing of black entrepreneurs and large white corporations. The combination of black entrepreneurship and corporate interest in Kwanzaa reached its most significant stage with annual commercial expositions, later called Kwanzaa fests. Commercial expositions placed black entrepreneurs and consumers in direct contact with one another for the sole purpose of buying and selling. The fests also afforded corporate structures a degree of public visibility to black consumers in a show of community support and potential profit. The presence of huge corporate logos in close proximity of black entrepreneurs selling Afrocentric clothing represented a major turning point for both late twentieth-century capitalism and black nationalist economic enterprise.[51]

Kwanzaa expos or fests date from the early 1980s, but their history is directly tied to black self-help economics of the early and mid-twentieth century. Kwanzaa introduced a new catch phrase in the history of black commercial self-help called "cooperative economics," a philosophy that would seem familiar to Booker T. Washington, W.E.B. Du Bois, Marcus Garvey, Carlos Cooks, Elijah Muhammad, Malcolm X, Louis Farrakhan, and Roy Innis. Though not self-proclaimed nationalists, Booker T. Washington and W.E.B. Du Bois advocated a separatist economics.

*Figure 6: Billboard in Minneapolis, Minnesota promoting the largest Twin Cities annual Kwanzaa celebration at Pantages Theater. Courtesy of Mikiesha Terrell*

Washington founded the National Negro Business League in 1900. In the early 1930s, Du Bois advocated for a black cooperative enterprise, which resulted in his termination from the National Association for the Advancement of Colored People (NAACP). Marcus Garvey and his disciple Carlos Cooks preached and practiced economic self-sufficiency by creating businesses to uplift black America. Despite Washington's death, Du Bois' dismissal, and Garvey's deportation, black economic self-help continued. Tired of being underemployed in areas they lived, urban black consumers in New York City and Detroit organized "Buy Black" campaigns against white-owned retail stores in the 1930s and 1940s. Through Elijah Muhammad's Nation of Islam, the idea of commercial self-help flourished in the modern era as Malcolm X further popularized the notion of a separate economic sphere for African-Americans. By 1966 when Karenga formulated Ujamaa—a strict and exclusive economic cooperation between black buyer and seller through the fourth principle of Kwanzaa—he drew on a well-spring of knowledge on nationalist economics and black entrepreneurship in the marketplace.[52]

Operating squarely within the tradition of nationalist economics, Karenga believed Kwanzaa should establish sound commercial practices in black America, specifically between black entrepreneur and black consumer. Indeed, part of Kwanzaa's commercial history is the practice of Ujamaa. In the post-Black Power era, however, black economic enterprise around Kwanzaa resembled less the exclusive "Buy Black" campaigns of the 1930s and 1940s and more a partnership between black entrepreneurs and corporate America. Black visionaries looking to promote Kwanzaa through commercial expos successfully facilitated the union between corporate America and black entrepreneurs in the last decade of the twentieth century.

Since 1981, Kwanzaa expositions occurred annually in Oakland, Chicago, and St. Louis, but New York City had always staged the largest one called the Kwanzaa Fest with the most black entrepreneurs, consumers, and corporate sponsors.[53] In 1981, Jose Ferrer and Malik Ahmed, two long-time community activists who worked for a social service agency, the New York Urban Coalition, persuaded the organization to use Kwanzaa as a vehicle for community uplift.[54] Similar to Kwanzaa Arts, Ferrer and Ahmed created an idea where Kwanzaa and its principles were promoted via commercial interaction rather than through politic pronouncements. Ferrer and Ahmed shied away from proselytizing the holiday's principles to African-Americans and instead pitched the idea of Kwanzaa through economic enterprise. Ferrer and Ahmed's desire to promote the holiday commercially initially had to do with the difficulty blacks faced in finding Kwanzaa ceremonial items. But trying to stage a commercial venture during the week of Kwanzaa proved difficult for Ferrer and Ahmed. By the start of Kwanzaa on December 26, most black consumers had already spent their holiday money. Black consumers interested in purchasing goods from black vendors told Ferrer and Ahmed that the expositions occurred too late in the holiday season. After failing to compete commercially with Christmas in 1981 by reaching a significant number of black consumers, Ferrer and Ahmed decided to move the Kwanzaa expo from the last week of the year to early December, where it had remained a fixture for twenty years.[55]

The Kwanzaa exposition quickly exceeded Ferrer and Ahmed's expectations. After the inaugural fest at Harlem's John B. Russwurm Elementary School in 1981, the two men moved the gathering to the City College of New York's (CCNY) gymnasium the following year. Twenty black vendors were present at Russwurm in 1981 and about fifty at City College in 1982. With more black vendors and entrepreneurs demanding space at the following year's Kwanzaa fest, Ferrer and Ahmed moved the expo to the 369th Armory located on 142nd Street and the Harlem River Drive. The 369th Armory was not big enough to keep the expo in Harlem. It was moved to the Borough of Manhattan Community College (BMCC) by mid-decade, remaining there for a few years. The fest continued to grow in the number of vendors, entrepreneurs, and overall visibility. The Museum of Natural History asked Ferrer to bring the expo there in 1990. After a successful expo, the directors of the museum were dismayed that black vendors competed directly with its gift shop and other museum merchants. The Museum of Natural History asked Ferrer to significantly scale back the number of entrepreneurs for Kwanzaa expo 1991. Refusing, Ferrer secured the Jacob Javits Center on 34th Street and 12th Avenue as a final home for the fest in 1991.[56]

From 1991 to 2000, the expo changed dramatically. First, Ferrer and Ahmed's resignation from the New York Urban Coalition in 1990 took the annual commercial exposition from the social service organization. Second, Ahmed, Ferrer's partner in the 1980s, moved to St. Louis and started another Kwanzaa exposition in that city.[57] Third, with Ferrer left as the sole organizer, the Kwanzaa expo in New York incorporated as a family-owned business under the name Kwanzaa Fest Unlimited, Inc. Last and most important, Ferrer, as owner and president of Kwanzaa Fest Unlimited, Inc., secured about ten major corporate sponsors and several media boosters.[58]

Between 1981 and 1991, the Kwanzaa expo remained true to the spirit of Kwanzaa's fourth principle—commercial exchange between black buyer and seller free of white economic intermediaries. But keeping black entrepreneurs and consumers together in the spirit of Ujamaa as the expo grew exponentially eventually meant securing outside support. With black businesses and corporations lacking sufficient resources to serve as commercial sponsors, white-owned interest seized on the opportunity to partner with Ferrer and the Fest.[59]

The *New York Daily News* became Ferrer's media partner, promoting the expo on its pages and creating an annual supplement in one of its December Sunday editions. Perhaps seeking to rehabilitate its image in the black community or to increase its black readership, the *Daily News* embraced the Fest to a far greater degree than black media outlets, such as Inner City Broadcasting and the *Amsterdam News*.[60] Inner City Broadcasting, owners of WBLS and WLIB, served as a minor media partner before and after the *Daily News'* arrival in 1991. Wilbert Tatum's *Amsterdam News* covered the Kwanzaa expo in its pages. But in contrast to Inner City and the *Amsterdam News*, the *Daily News* went a step further by not only partnering with the Fest, but also giving Ferrer the titles of publisher and editor of its supplement. Ferrer had control over all content and the solicitation of advertising, making the supplement the official publication of the Fest. In addition to print and radio coverage, Ferrer also convinced ABC's Good Morning America and FOX's Good Day New York to broadcast their weather forecast live on the opening day of the Fest. The initial publicity given to the Fest by the *Daily News* allowed Ferrer to procure other corporate sponsors.[61]

The Fest's major sponsors included some of the biggest corporations and retail stores in the United States. Ferrer's most constant sponsors included General Motors, Kraft Foods, Fleet Bank, Chase Manhattan Bank, Philip Morris, AT&T, Anheuser-Busch, and electronic giant Circuit City. Corporate sponsors underwrote the Fest throughout the 1990s, paying overhead costs that could not be met solely through admission fees. This corporate revenue stream put the Fest on a permanent footing, freeing Ferrer from the need to put up his own money, as he says, with "no guarantee that it's going to come back."[62] Paying the bills, indeed, gave corporate America an entry to the market of black consumers via Kwanzaa.

While sponsor logos graced all areas of the Jacob Javits Convention Center, the small black entrepreneur stood at the center of attention. Streams of people, mainly African-American consumers, strolled six aisles of carnival and consumption, passing by African art, jewelry, cosmetics, books, and an occasional dance performance. Two to three hundred black businesses had a chance to pitch their products to the thirty thousand people that passed through the aisles of the convention during the annual four-day event.[63] Music blasted from the resident radio station WBLS-FM; children's plays were performed; and Nguzo Saba award tributes were given to influential people in the community. Ferrer saw the Fest as a mixture of festivity and black economic self-sufficiency, a confluence, as he called it, of education, culture, and commerce:

> There is a direct correlation between education, culture, and commerce. These relationships have allowed other groups to succeed despite obstacles, in an often hostile environment. Many groups have used their culture as a means for economic growth and as a way to establish vibrant, comparatively self-sufficient communities. There's no logical reason why we shouldn't be the beneficiaries of our own economic might. The concept of black economic self-sufficiency is not new. Great leaders like Marcus Garvey and the Honorable Elijah Muhammad advocated it generations ago. The beauty of Kwanzaa . . . is that it addresses all of the components necessary to empower a people—economics, culture, and spirituality. Kwanzaa Fest is our small way of helping to bring about that reality.[64]

Viewing the Fest as a form of black economic self-sufficiency, as Ferrer did, only captures part of the story. The Fest was also a prime example of business colonization. American companies were not only sellers of goods and services at the Fest; they were sponsors of festival, providers of culture, and facilitators of community relations. Corporate partnership of the Fest legitimized Kwanzaa and its racial politics. At the same time, the racial politics of corporate-sponsored Kwanzaa destroyed the holiday's identity as cultural resistance. Corporate sponsorship made Black Power and Kwanzaa's fourth principle distant memories. The problem with Kwanzaa in this setting was not that it had been co-opted, absorbed, or ripped-off. There were signs that all three occurred. Kwanzaa was beginning to resemble the official culture it was created to subvert. Though the Kwanzaa Fest represented the largest example of black Ujamaa, it also had become the biggest corporate takeover of black cultural expression. As Leslie Savan pointed out in another context, it is a pity "how easily any idea, deed, or image can become part of the sponsored world."[65]

## The Marketing and Merchandising of Holiday Multiculturalism

Kwanzaa is one of many cultural entities up for grabs in the new multicultural marketplace. The appropriation and marketing of black hair care products, rap music, ethnic Barbie dolls, and clothing style all punctuate the salience of race as an important part of contemporary capitalism in the last twenty-five years. Rap music and hip-hop culture's transformation, from an indigenous expressive form in black neighborhoods of the Northeast, to a commercialized product of corporate America paralleled Kwanzaa's own commodification. From the mid-1970s up until the mid-1980s, rap music was almost entirely controlled by African-Americans and Latinos who bartered cassettes of live park performances with one another. Blacks and Latinos owned independent record labels that showcased neighborhood hip-hop acts. As rap music became more popular, not only did live performances in inner city parks give way to major concert venues, white-owned record labels purchased most of the black independent record companies and signed black and Latino rap artists directly.[66]

The story was the same for toys, where the confluence of race and commerce made Mattel the number one provider of ethnic dolls. Mattel's history in black doll manufacturing began in the 1960s, ironically, after the Watts rebellion. Seeking to help rebuild Los Angeles, Mattel donated $150,000 to a black self-help organization known as Operation Bootstrap. Part of Operation Bootstrap's mission was to counter the negative images of young black children by offering them alternative dolls through their Shindana Toys division. After Mattel provided seed money, it watched the market in black dolls grow. In 1967, Mattel put out its own product called Colored Francie, and another doll named Christie in 1968. Though the Civil Rights and Black Power Movements had an effect on the creation of Colored Francie and Christie, the racial politics of doll making at Mattel had its limits. Barbie, the all-American white doll, was Mattel's preeminent product. Colored Francie and Christie became Barbie's friends; no black Barbies appeared in the 1960s.[67]

If the Civil Rights and Black Power Movements signaled a minor shift in the racial politics of doll making, then the early 1980s emphasis on multiculturalism and a diverse America pointed to another shift with commercial implications. Witnessing Shindana's sales climb into the millions by the mid-1970s, Mattel, like Hallmark in the greeting card market, decided to become the leader in ethnic doll production. Mattel ceased production of black Barbie companions, like Colored Francie and Christie, and allowed Barbie to appeal to young girls of all races and ethnicities. After 1980, Barbie would never be exclusively white again, as the doll historian Cynthia Roberts explained:

> At this point in America's social development, it's no longer necessary or desirable for an icon like Barbie to be identified exclusively as a Caucasian. So this year [1980], rather than expanding the ethnic base of Barbie's line by creating new "friends," Mattel simply comes out with black and Hispanic Barbies. It's an important moment in the doll's history. Now little girls of varied backgrounds can relate directly to Barbie.[68]

Mattel's mission in providing young girls with a new sense of ethnic identity held serious repercussions for black doll makers—many who existed in the peripheral economy. With all of their resources and channels of distribution, Mattel's entry into the ethnic doll market signaled the demise of black doll manufacturers, including Shindana, which folded in 1983.[69]

No longer sanctified possessions of specific communities of color due to their profitability, ethnic cultural products and practices in the late twentieth century became sites of contestation in the legal arena. In 1993, Shark Products, a white-owned hair care company in New York City, sued black B&J Sales Company of Fayetteville, Georgia for using the word "African" on its hair care products. The Shark lawsuit joined suits already settled, pending, or planned against other black hair care companies like Walbert Laboratories in California, and the Bonner Brothers of Atlanta. Shark Products argued that B&J's use of the term "African Natural" was too close to its own "African Pride." Shark also claimed that Walbert Laboratories' "Mother Africa" line copied its "trade dress," which not only included the word "African" but the same red, black, and green color sequence. While Shark settled out of court against Walbert, it withdrew its suit against B&J after black hair care manufacturers across the country united against Shark. "How the heck can he [president Brian Marks of Shark], a white man try to patent the word 'African'? What's next? We'll have to ask his permission to call ourselves African-Americans?" an angry black hair care manager wondered. This display of indignation was not simply directed at Brian Marks. The underlying problem was competition from an array of white-owned hair care companies that had entered the black hair care market since the early 1980s: All Ways, TCB, Dark & Lovely, Right-On Curl, Let's Jam, and Kenya Products.[70]

White-owned hair care companies, Mattel, Hallmark, and other American firms in markets of color were part of the growing trend in multicultural marketing, a phenomenon unheard of thirty years prior. Ethnic marketing agencies like Multicultural Marketing Resources, Inc., the Chisholm-Mingo Group, Cultural Access, Graham Gregory Bozell, and Mosaica facilitated corporate access to race-specific celebrations and products. These groups exist in order to put corporations like AT&T, Hallmark, and General Motors in touch with ethnic consumers. A company profile of the Chisholm-Mingo Group, one of the oldest black marketing and advertising firms, explains that its aim is to help corporate entities "leverage their ethnic roots and expertise by creating a pre-emptive emotional bond between the consumer and the client's products and services."[71] So-called emotional bonding with a particular product is supposed to establish the company brand as a top purchase choice for the targeted community.

Cementing a bond between consumers of color and white-owned corporations can be a tricky proposition, especially if the relationship historically involved aggressive marketing techniques and charges of exploitation.[72] Many multicultural marketing firms have concluded that the way to build healthy relationships with ethnic communities is by engaging in public relations rather than marketing. Public relations, or what is sometimes referred to as corporate image advertising, proved important during and immediately after the tumultuous Black Power period. According to a *Black Enterprise* magazine study, "some of the earliest campaigns commissioned were intended to strengthen the image of corporate clients in the black community."[73] Lisa Skriloff, president of Multicultural Marketing Resources, Inc., surmised that the "essence of good marketing . . . is tying into something that is important to the consumer."[74] By promoting ethnic festivities and engaging in community affairs programs, corporations seek to establish a presence in communities of color that pays bigger dividends in the long run.[75] The *New York Times* noted McDonald's use of this technique in relation to Kwanzaa: "the McDonald's Corporation is running Kwanzaa ads created by Caroline Jones Inc . . . that does not show a single Big Mac. The message is not so much about French fries and burgers as it is to show the company as understanding and respecting African-Americans' sense of family and community. One commercial . . . shows families in festive settings, including a choir performing to a jubilant congregation."[76]

Multicultural Marketing Inc., the Chisholm-Mingo Group, and others have peddled the idea of difference to big business, making them see the advantages of marketing celebrations originating from communities of color: "Certainly there are opportunities where marketers reach out to the general market, whether its President's Day sales or a seasonal holiday shopping opportunity," says Skriloff. "It is the smart marketers who are looking for opportunities that are not overexploited and where they can cut through the clutter."[77] Some marketers of color see their role as educating uninformed corporate clients about untapped racial and ethnic markets. Caroline Jones, a former partner in the Chisholm Group before branching out on her own, remembered: "most clients are not organized to look at the black consumer market in any long-term way, so we have to do it for them. And we want to do it. If we don't do it . . . we won't have a client."[78]

Commercial institutions were not the only ones who felt this way. Cultural institutions, like museums and churches, also practiced a client-based philosophy and used Kwanzaa to get more African-Americans in the doors. Kwanzaa found a place in African-American museums as early as the 1970s, but by the 1990s, year-end attendance increased at places like the Charles H. Wright Museum of African-American History in Detroit, the African-American Historical and Cultural Museum of the San Joaquin Valley in California, the DuSable Museum in Chicago, and the African-American Museum in Philadelphia. No less significant was the Smithsonian Institution in Washington, DC, the American Museum of Natural History in New York, the Kansas City Museum, the Philadelphia Museum of Art, and the Children's Museums of Indianapolis and Tampa. Even more than museums, Kwanzaa seemed ever-present in a variety of Protestant denominations including the Faith United Methodist Church in Los Angeles, the Kwanzaa Presbyterian Church in Minneapolis, the Nineteenth Street Baptist Church in Washington, DC, the First Unitarian Universalist Church in New Orleans, the St. Matthew's Episcopal Church in Delray Beach, Florida, and the African-centered Wo'se Community Church in Sacramento.

No longer sites limited to high culture, museums in the 1990s had become places featuring ever-broadening forms of popular culture, notably cultures of performance. As art critic John Zeaman observed, "there has been a shift in recent years away from exhibits of a purely historical nature to those focusing on the creative arts."[79] The existence of creative arts and other real-time performances occurred all year round in museums but particularly during holidays. "If you walk into the African-American Museum in Hempstead on December 31," wrote an observer, "you'll be greeted by the chanting of singers and the rhythm of drummers. Seven large candles will flicker in a narrow wooden kinara (candleholder), and brightly dressed dancers will demonstrate traditional dances of Nigeria. Welcome to the museum's annual observance of Kwanzaa."[80] In the last two decades of the twentieth century, museums used holiday occasions to display the culture of "real people," or as one author put it, to showcase "contemporary culture ... within living memory."[81] Thus, Kwanzaa represented one of many attempts at the "museumification" of American holidays through performance.[82]

Long before the museum appropriation of Kwanzaa, there already existed a connection between the holiday and performance. Kwanzaa had always entailed ritualized activities, such as pouring libation, reciting the seven principles, unity chants, etc. Whenever these core rituals were conducted inside museums, they now shared equal time with other performances and entertainment productions tangential to the core of the Kwanzaa celebration. These public Kwanzaa performances in museums comprised storytelling, African-style dancing, and choir singing, just to name a few. For example, the Charles H. Wright Museum in Detroit featured an assorted Kwanzaa production in 1998 where the Millvall Youth Choir sang gospel songs on Umoja, the first day of Kwanzaa. The museum also conducted doll- and quilt-making workshops on Kujichagulia and Ujamaa, the second and fourth days of Kwanzaa, respectively. In addition, the Charles Wright Museum included a presentation by Phylis Anderson of the Detroit Association of Black Storytellers.[83]

Every year since Kwanzaa of 1992, the Philadelphia Museum of Art showcased the Keepers of Culture, a local black storytelling organization. The Philadelphia Museum of Art annually commissioned the Keepers of Culture to hold a number of workshops on the black storytelling tradition that culminated with a grand performance inside the Van Pelt Auditorium. The workshops explored the history of African griots, techniques in movement and body language, the story as an instrument of education, and the preservation of family history. Another workshop focused on arts, crafts, and Kwanzaa gift making. Finally, the Van Pelt

Auditorium played host to a performance by nationally known black storytellers, Charlotte Blake Alston and Kala Jojo. Local storytelling artists included Saundra Gilliard Davis, Angela Willie, Brother Robb "As-Salaam" Carter, Wanda Gigetts, and Tahira.[84]

The American Museum of Natural History in New York City staged Kwanzaa celebrations since the mid-1980s, devoting the entire Hall of Ocean Life to performance and entertainment every last Saturday of the year. Rudimentary in its beginnings by only offering one or two acts, the museum's 1990s Kwanzaa celebration included Vozolo, an African dance and drumming troupe and the renowned Forces of Nature Dance Theatre Company. Kwanzaa at the American Museum of Natural History also featured Yvette Glover and Friends—a tap dancing group, Makanda Ken McIntyre—a jazz trio, and Voices of Inspirational Praise—a contemporary gospel ensemble from Emmanuel Baptist Church. The museum also held a family visual arts workshop where children learned about the seven principles of Kwanzaa via watercolor paintings. In addition, the museum employed the services of Harlem Textile Works, offering children a chance to create their own Kwanzaa hand-made gifts with silk.[85]

For the American Museum of Natural History, Kwanzaa and other living traditions were part of the institution's educational and multicultural programming. Educational programming created a sense of public understanding about New York City's diverse ethnic communities. As facilitators of public culture, museums like American felt obligated to teach and inform audiences about a variety of communities through performance. A recent American Museum of Natural History announcement explained:

> Through presentations on the living cultural traditions, contemporary life, and cross-cultural exchanges, voices from many cultures can be experienced through performances, artist demonstrations, films, lectures and panels. Special events and programs of temporary exhibitions offer the opportunity to learn through unique and multiple experiences, the music, dance, rituals, songs, folklore, and artistry of a particular culture, some of which are seldom seen or heard in the United States.[86]

This statement by the American Museum of Natural History crystallizes the fine line between education and entertainment, a synergy understood by black nationalist celebrants of Kwanzaa who have long called the connection between the two, "edu-tainment."[87]

But staging performances around Kwanzaa meant more than exhibiting living cultural traditions and educating an uninformed public. Museums used Kwanzaa to enter into the business of ethnic representation and engage in the politics of inclusion, making their appropriation of Kwanzaa partly self-serving. "We want to represent, as much as we can, the entire community with the holidays that are celebrated," said Andrea Ellis, a representative for the Kansas City Museum. Kwanzaa "is a culture we wanted to be sure we didn't miss out on," she continued.[88] The Chicago Children's Museum shared Ellis' concern about the representation of Kwanzaa. The museum included the holiday within its tree-trimming production in 1997, an event attended by the Governor of Illinois' wife. As part of its Tree of Lights ceremony that year, a Children's Museum official said Kwanzaa was a "wonderful representation of the important role our cultural heritages play in the celebration of this festive season."[89]

As a legitimate part of the festive celebration season in museum corridors, Kwanzaa had indeed arrived in the name of diversity and goodwill. The 1990s was the decade Kwanzaa rose to the level of other traditional celebrations in visibility, if not in stature. As *The Age* reported in 1994, "Thanksgiving is a distant memory, the Hanukah menorahs have been put away, and the Christmas trees are destined to become recycled mulch. On America's crowded festive calendar that means one more thing: time to deck the halls for Kwanzaa."[90] Kwanzaa was part of a growing movement toward holiday multiculturalism in the 1990s, oftentimes appearing alongside more traditional celebrations as well as less familiar ones. In 1989, the Chicago Public Library Cultural Center conducted four holiday ceremonies in the month of December that included Kwanzaa, Hanukkah, Christmas, and the Feast of Babaluaiye.[91] In 1993, the Children's Museum in Tampa, Florida offered its own holiday cornucopia by staging Kwanzaa, Hanukkah, the Mexican celebration of Las Posadas, and the Swedish celebration of St. Lucia.[92] In 1995, the Oakland Museum of California presented its annual "Winterfest: A Celebration of Family Tradition," which included Kwanzaa, Hanukkah, Italian American Christmas, Japanese American New Year, and Las Posadas.[93] Though the presentation of Kwanzaa and other celebrations was done in the name of diversity and cultural recognition, museums sometimes camouflaged their holiday celebrations in the language of heritage and history: "Though different, all of the holidays mean more than just swapping gifts. They put people back in touch with their family heritage, teaching them about their forefathers. The Smithsonian knows this, that's why it's kicking off a six-day 'Holiday Celebration' to show how Christmas, Hanukkah, Kwanzaa, and the New Year are celebrated in America."[94] Kwanzaa's elevation in status not only suggested the holiday had arrived, but that museums had also changed too by "opening themselves up to use by diverse communities," and showcasing cultures "which would previously not have been thought 'museum-worthy.'"[95]

If Kwanzaa became a museum-worthy attraction, then the holiday appealed to churches and other religious-based institutions on similar grounds. Like museums in the 1970s, only a few churches featured Kwanzaa, specifically those churches sympathetic to the cause of Black Power. The Reverend Al Sampson of Fernwood United Methodist Church in Chicago was one of the first ministers to embrace Kwanzaa in the 1970s. Twenty years later, Reverend Sampson still featured yearly Kwanzaa ceremonies at Fernwood. He encouraged other African-American Christians to demand their churches do likewise: "challenge the church to weave these principles inside the pastor's message on the one side, inside the Sunday school on the other ... and set aside a block of time inside the worship service for Kwanzaa. Have several Sundays where you practice the entire ritual of Kwanzaa," the Reverend Sampson reiterated.[96] Minister Imhotep Akebulaun of the four-year-old African-centered Wo'se Community Church in Sacramento admonished his parishioners along similar lines but went one step further, stating: "Kwanzaa is not all about partying, its about using the seven principles of Kwanzaa everyday ... we can't afford to simply go to celebrations, we must do something afterwards."[97]

While some black churches with activist clergy thought more along the lines of empowerment, white houses of worship saw Kwanzaa as a vehicle to bring people together. For white religious institutions Kwanzaa could be everyone's holiday. This form of holiday multiculturalism bore itself out in a variety of white denominations. In 1998, the First Unitarian Universalist Church in Detroit staged a single worship service that included most of the year-end holidays. "We recognize the Solstice, Hanukkah, Christmas, and Kwanzaa," interning pastor Jean Darling stated. "We feel that we have to do this ... it's best to be inclusive of everyone's customs and beliefs rather than choosing to celebrate one tradition over the others," she continued.[98] The themes of holiday diversity and inclusion also manifested in Sacramento's Church of Scientology during the 1999 holiday season. Kwanzaa was one of several holidays featured in an event entitled "The Festival of Friends." The festival was designed to "create increased understanding and affinity between the people who make up the richly diverse Sacramento community."[99] The Church of Scientology used different ethnic foods, stories, and art as a part of its "Festival of Friends." In a similar presentation, the Emmanuel Presbyterian Church in Albuquerque, New Mexico determined that music would better suffice in creating a greater understanding between the races. From 1999 to 2001, Emmanuel Presbyterian commissioned De Profundis, a white a cappella men's choir to sing the Music of Advent, Christmas, Hanukkah, and Kwanzaa, "in genres ranging from the Gregorian Chant to a 12-part 'Harambee' (Kwanzaa)."[100]

Some churches elected not to hold joint holiday celebrations. Many white churches conducted single Kwanzaa services with the hope of showing how the holiday transcended race. In 1998, a reporter noted in amazement the number of different ethnic groups attending a Kwanzaa ceremony in the predominantly white St. Lawrence O'Toole—a Catholic Church located in the Chicago suburb of Matteson: "look out over the crowd and see how many non-African-American faces there are . . . children of different colors were running around the parish hall at St. Lawrence O'Toole on Sunday while their parents took time to socialize after the ceremony. Half of the hundred or so in attendance were non-African-American." Andrew Lyke, one of the festivity's organizers recognized the importance of Kwanzaa to the few black members of the church, but noted unabashedly, "when we decided to do this, we didn't do it for the African-Americans in our parish. It's a way of sharing our culture," he said.[101] Walter Johnston, organizer of the fourth annual Kwanzaa celebration at the Unitarian Universalist Church in St. Petersburg, Florida, concurred, saying Kwanzaa's principles appeal to all ethnic groups. When there is common ground, said Johnston, "people of different cultures ought to celebrate one another's cultural events."[102] A similar thought was echoed by a member at Louisville, Kentucky's First Unitarian Church, which celebrated their tenth straight Kwanzaa in 1998: "I think so many people believe Kwanzaa and things like that are just set aside for black people . . .

it's for all people, and it's defeating the purpose of Kwanzaa if you segregate it."[103]

Church denominations included Kwanzaa within their year-end holiday festivities with a desire to make meaningful connections between Christianity and Kwanzaa. The Reverend Thelma C. Mitchell of Wilkinsburg Baptist Church outside of Pittsburgh posited the idea that God can speak to people in a multiplicity of ways, including through Kwanzaa. "I really see us moving to appreciate all the ways in which God speaks in and through his people. Perhaps Kwanzaa can reflect a little corner of what the kingdom of God will look like." For Mitchell, God possessed the ability to reach beyond the world of the sacred and metaphysically impact everyday life. She believed that manifestations of God occurred throughout the larger society. "Oftentimes you cannot separate religion from culture in society," she noted. "The secular and the sacred coexist."[104] Reverend Derrick Harkins of the Nineteenth Street Baptist Church in Northwest Washington, DC echoed Mitchell's assessment about the relationship between religion and culture, arguing, "culture and religion can augment one another; for us to talk about Afrocentricity makes sense because of the Christian context of the black church. Kwanzaa is one expression of that sojourn."[105]

This general notion of the secular and the sacred, or specifically, Kwanzaa's principles and Christian religious doctrine coexisting became more pronounced in the last decade of the twentieth century. The appeal of Kwanzaa had not only to do with its growing status as a holiday, but also with the universal applicability of its principles. Kwanzaa and its seven principles found a common narrative of melioration among religious denominations and social service organizations. The ubiquity of declension narratives in regards to the breakdown of families, and a lack of values and morals afforded Kwanzaa some legitimacy in late twentieth-century cultural and religious politics. Kwanzaa's value-based system of principles cohered well with biblical liturgy and scripture as Zaudie Abiade, a Christian observer, underscored: "Though the festivity of Kwanzaa was founded by Dr. Maulana Karenga during the late 1960s, its origin is rooted in biblical principles."[106]

Some Christians went further, often discerning a Christian foundation in most, if not all, of Kwanzaa's seven principles. Abiade, the same Christian individual that claimed Kwanzaa's origin was rooted in the bible, believed the antecedents of Ujamaa, Kwanzaa's fourth principle meaning cooperative economics, were contained in Acts 4:32–37. These verses in Acts recount the story of Joseph or Barnabas selling his field and giving the money to those less fortunate after the apostles' testimony encouraged the community to do so. The overall spirit of giving worldly possessions to the community during the early Church period resonated with Abiade who argued, "Kwanzaa challenges us to be giving to others in the community. That is what pure cooperative economics can produce." Immaculate Heart, a catholic home school in Pennsylvania, also found Kwanzaa's fourth principle to be very useful but mainly to other fellow Christians, cautioning, "buy from Christians, support Christian businesses, buy from a secular source only if a Christian source is not available. If it is only available from a blatantly anti-Christian source, make your own or do without."[107]

Abiade believed that Kwanzaa's fifth principle Nia (purpose) could be found in Romans 8:28 and Kuumba (creativity), the sixth principle, in the first several chapters of Genesis. But out of all the principles, Imani (faith) was "the most significant aspect of Kwanzaa," for Abiade and other Christians: "This is the night we most discuss our relationship with Jesus Christ and salvation," she said. Though secular adherents of Kwanzaa end the holiday (January 1) with a day of assessment and a feast the night before, Christians "end Kwanzaa with the scripture that is the basis of our faith," from Hebrews 11:1–3, "by faith we understand that the world was created by the word of God, so that what is seen was made out of things which do not appear," and especially from Romans 10:9, "If you confess with your lips that Jesus is Lord and believe in your heart that God raised Him from the dead, you will be saved." Karenga's definition of imani in Kwanzaa meant faith and belief in black people, parents, teachers, leaders, and the righteousness of black struggle. Catholics at the Immaculate home school, however, wanted to take the definition a step further by slightly altering Kwanzaa's last principle, announcing, "this statement should be rewritten as 'to believe with all our hearts in our God'. We as Christians have to believe that [things] will get better, maybe not until we are reunited with Jesus . . . we must keep the faith."[108]

Chike Akua, a member and part-time pastor of Victory Baptist Church in Stone Mountain, Georgia, also attempted to "facilitate an understanding of Kwanzaa's principles using the Scriptures." Like Abiade and the Catholics at Immaculate home school, Akua provided examples in the bible where God and Jesus actualized the seven principles. Umoja was understood not as unity among black people but rather "interdenominational unity" contained in I Corinthians 1:10: "Now I beseech you, brethren, by the name of our Lord Jesus Christ, that ye all speak the same thing, and that there be no divisions among you; but that ye be perfectly joined together in the same mind and in the same judgement." Akua believed Kwanzaa's second principle, Kujichagulia (self-determination) was most manifested in the story of Moses in the book of Exodus, Ujima (collective work and responsibility) in Nehemiah 4:6, Ujamaa (cooperative economics) in Acts 4:34–35, Nia (purpose) in Jeremiah 1:4–5, Kuumba (creativity) in Psalms 150:3–6, and Imani (faith) in Hebrews 11:1.[109]

Kwanzaa and its principles also found their way into Christian sermons, workshops, national religious conferences, and Sunday school services. The National Black Catholic Congress used its annual conference in 1993 to explore Kwanzaa's principles in conjunction with Jesus' Sermon on the Mount (Matthew 5:3–11).[110] The Reverend Dr. Lynn Collins of the Episcopal Church Center in New York City preached a yearly sermon since the mid-1990s that equated Kwanzaa with Christian spirituality, stating, "Kwanzaa is a spiritual experience. . . . we must experience Christ at all levels of life . . . Kwanzaa offers another level of spiritual expression."[111] A Unitarian Sunday school at the North Parish Church in North Andover, Massachusetts, convinced its congregants that Kwanzaa's principles had something to offer the predominantly white membership, but recognized the limitations the holiday placed on white people who desired to officiate a Kwanzaa ceremony: "Even if we are not African-American, there is a lot that the candles of Kwanzaa have to teach us. . . . As a white person, I can't be a part of the remembering . . . I will not light the candles, for they are not mine to light. I will, however, honor the struggle for justice by speaking a history, the story of a people which is not often enough told in our society."[112]

Some clergymen hesitated before associating Kwanzaa with Christianity. Some thought the mere fact that much evidence could be marshaled to discern biblical antecedents in Kwanzaa's seven principles was enough reason to reject Kwanzaa or at least be cautious of it. The Reverend William L. Banks, the *Philadelphia Tribune*'s religious columnist, disagreed with Karenga's claim that Kwanzaa was a non-religious holiday. He believed Kwanzaa was a weak attempt to revise many of the moral tenets of Christianity under the guise of a cultural celebration. "The claim that Kwanzaa is a non-religious holiday is false . . . it is religious through and through." Adding insult to injury, Banks also believed Kwanzaa's separatist origins worked against African-Americans' ongoing attempt to enter mainstream American society, calling Kwanzaa a "hinderance," at efforts toward inclusion.[113] Other ministers displayed a similar degree of trepidation. Reverend Thomas Shepard of Delray Beach's St. Matthew's Church explained his initial feeling about Kwanzaa: "my primary concern was that the seven principles of Kwanzaa would conflict with and contradict the twelve days of Christmas as we observe them in the Episcopal Church." After giving the principles a thorough reviewing, Rev. Shepard's initial concern was finally assuaged: "but I discovered that the principles of Kwanzaa actually support Christian ideas and values."[114]

If Kwanzaa were a poor substitute for Christian ideals, then at least Kwanzaa's presence in churches and museums introduced some people to a holiday for the first time. Lateefah Doxey attended her first Kwanzaa production in 1994 at the Kidspace Museum in Pasadena, California. The pervasiveness of Christmas in her upbringing precluded an initial acceptance of Kwanzaa: "since I already celebrated Christmas, I wasn't ready to receive it into my mind."[115] For others like seventy-nine-year-old Charlie Mae Ranson and eighty-year-old Louise Caver, the holiday was still a mystery despite its growing stature in American public culture. They both attended their first Kwanzaa celebration in 1998 at the St. Paul Methodist Church in Dallas. After attending her first ceremony, Caver said, "I had heard of it, but never really knew what it was about . . . it was very enlightening." Ranson also confessed that she had not "celebrated it before," but even at the age of seventy-nine, "may start now."[116] Darlene Sanders, an African-American woman who attended the 1998 St. Lawrence O'Toole Kwanzaa in Matteson, Illinois, also admitted that she and her family had "never been to a Kwanzaa celebration before. . . . This is the first time we've been part of this. . . . But it was something. Next year, we'll probably do something at home too."[117]

For many newer adherents, doing something at home often meant celebrating both Kwanzaa and Christmas. Melva Parhams, a resident of South Central Los Angeles, makes sure she gives herself enough time to prepare for the family's Christmas and Kwanzaa celebrations, respectively. Parhams' home is usually decorated with a Christmas tree, red stockings, a fruit basket that signifies the African harvest, and a very large kinara—Kwanzaa's candleholder. Since incorporating both holidays in her family tradition since the early 1990s, Parhams has never felt conflicted about recognizing the two most important occasions for African-Americans. "Some people don't like to mix the two holidays," said Parhams, "but we celebrate both … Kwanzaa gives African-Americans something of their own to celebrate, but it doesn't stop Christmas. You can incorporate both holidays, back to back." Celebrating both, however, can lead to some confusion. Parhams has to continually remind her children what gifts are for Christmas and what gifts have been designated for Kwanzaa. "On Christmas, I have to tell the kids, 'no, no, you can't open those presents over there yet, those are for Kwanzaa.'"[118] Other potential confusions arise when one of the days of Kwanzaa falls on the Sabbath for practicing black Christians. As a Seventh-day Adventist and a Kwanzaa celebrant for fifteen years, Johari Rashad avoids Kwanzaa celebrations from sundown on Friday to sunset Saturday, reserving this period for the tenets of her religion.[119]

While confusion arose from linking Kwanzaa and Christmas, Kwanzaa and Hanukkah went together more smoothly. Joint Kwanzaa and Hanukkah celebrations bridged the divide between African-Americans and Jews, allowing both groups to share in the memory of suffering. Cultural institutions like Bowers Museum in Santa Ana, California noted the connections and seized on the opportunity to bring the two groups together. In 1993, Bowers along with the Orange County Cultural Exchange sponsored a joint Kwanzaa and Hanukkah celebration, gathering two hundred people inside the museum. The two-hour ceremony featured several speakers explaining the history of both Kwanzaa and Hanukkah. Performances included Jewish folk songs, African-American spirituals, and an appearance by the Israeli Dance Troupe. The most poignant part of the ceremony was a joint lighting of the kinara and menorah accompanied by commentary on what united blacks and Jews instead of various differences and miscommunications between them. "This is the first time that we've done something like this," explained Randi Rubenstein of the Orange County Cultural Exchange. "You have the lighting of the candles with both Hanukkah and Kwanzaa." Similarly in the 1990s, joint Kwanzaa and Hanukkah gatherings were held in other parts of the state and at a Hebrew Congregational Day School in Baltimore.[120]

Kwanzaa's appearance with Hanukkah and Christmas provoked objections to Kwanzaa's elevation alongside traditional religious celebrations. Jim Dodd, a resident of southern California, wrote the *Union-Tribune* to express his displeasure with Kwanzaa's growing ubiquity:

> I am disturbed that you would run an article in your paper that puts the recently invented secular socialist "cultural holiday" Kwanzaa on the same level as Christian Christmas, Jewish Hanukkah, and Islam's Ramadan. This is an insult to those Peoples of the Book and to their faiths. People who worship political correctness may think Kwanzaa rises to the level of comparability to the world's great religions, but it is a clumping together of borrowed things forced together that actually obscure the principles of those same religions.[121]

Newspapers were often the targets of Kwanzaa's growing popularity while museums and churches usually escaped criticism. But most readers' letters seemed mild compared with the virulent comments made by Robert Ulrich, a white Texaco executive, whose thoughts about Kwanzaa were caught on tape in 1996: "I'm still having trouble with Hanukkah, now we have Kwanzaa . . . fucking niggers, they have shitted all over us with this."[122]

Though museums and churches were free to set their own agenda, public schools did not possess the same flexibility and also proved a convenient target for Kwanzaa's critics. "One of my alert readers called me the other day to inform me that the public schools in New Jersey aren't allowed to celebrate Christmas but are celebrating Kwanzaa," wrote Paul Mulshine in an op-ed piece in the *Newark Star-Ledger*. If the state disavowed religious ceremonies in public schools, then "public schools should not be pushing certain cultural practices," he continued. For Mulshine, the problem with Kwanzaa was not its quasi-religiosity, but its overt multicultural politics: "the idea of Kwanzaa fits firmly within multiculturalism . . . and however you feel about multiculturalism, you must admit that it is a political movement and . . . should not be supported with tax dollars." The fight to keep Kwanzaa out of schools was part of a major culture war to curtail multiculturalism. As in the case of school curriculums and literary canons in the early 1990s, the drive for a multicultural America also established Kwanzaa as a permanent fixture in American public culture, legitimizing the holiday in public schools. Although multiculturalism raised the stakes for Kwanzaa, there was one fundamental difference between Kwanzaa and its holiday companions: "Kwanzaa isn't a religious holiday," explained Ed Martone of the America Civil Liberties Union. "It doesn't have the same restrictions as Chanukah or Christmas."[123]

Beside museums, churches, and schools, various organizations and individuals did their part to elevate Kwanzaa's stature in the last decade of the twentieth century. Not only were people calling for a national Kwanzaa celebration, the holiday was declared a smoke-free occasion on the calendar and recognized in similar health-conscious respects. Kwanzaa was also used in various rites of passage programs and other areas of black community uplift. Kwanzaa received various proclamations from local city governments and was recognized annually by President Bill Clinton. Though Kwanzaa had always cut across class lines, the black middle class increasingly embraced Kwanzaa more in the 1990s. Hence, Kwanzaa not only became multicultural, the holiday proved more utilitarian, used by different persons and groups for varied purposes.

One of the many ironies about Kwanzaa in the 1990s was its use against the effects of cultural isolation experienced by some blacks living in predominantly white suburbs. For many black middle-class suburbanites, Kwanzaa was one of the few occasions that helped mitigate against a perceived diminishing "blackness." Henry Louis Gates, Jr. of Harvard University's Afro-American Studies department, termed these feelings in many middle-class blacks a "resulting cultural alienation" and a bad case of "the guilt of the survivor." Gates said of his generation of upwardly mobile African-Americans, "we were the first large-scale number of black people to come to historically white institutions" and live in white suburbs. Gates believes the inability of the black suburban middle class to frequently connect with other blacks and black culture placed a greater burden on them to prove their sense of racial self-worth. Thus, the black suburban desire to embrace "Kwanzaa and kente cloth are part of proving you're not running away from being black, which is what you're likely to be accused of by other blacks," noted Gates' colleague, Professor K. Anthony Appiah of Princeton University.[124]

With an increasing number of black middle-income earners in the United States since 1970, Kwanzaa witnessed a steady growth of newer celebrants from higher-income levels. Some of these middle-class blacks lived in suburbs where the black population remained small, isolated, and scattered. Seeking ways to connect their children to other younger blacks, many parents founded Kwanzaa clubs, Jack and Jill clubs, and other race-conscious black middle-class organizations. One example was the Kwanzaa Club created in the mid-1980s in Allison Park, Pennsylvania, a suburb in northern Pittsburgh. Connected to the Young Women's Christian Association Center for Race Relations and the North Hills NAACP, the Kwanzaa Club was a way to help black teenage students "find their niche in white communities in the North Hills" section of Pennsylvania. Matt Griffin, a junior at North Allegheny High School, remembered the impact the Kwanzaa Club had on him when his family moved to McCandless, a neighboring Pittsburgh suburb: "I knew no one. Then my mom learned about the Kwanzaa Club and I started coming. At first it was a social thing. Then as I got older, I began to learn about our culture and hanging out with other kids like us who go to all-white schools." Fifteen-year-old William McCoy, who also attended North Allegheny High, said the Kwanzaa Club was more than a place "to meet new people," but a site "to get with other black kids." Ted Roberts, executive board member of the North Hills NAACP, even encouraged his sixteen-year-old son to take advantage of the Club, saying, "Kwanzaa gave my son a chance to meet with kids of similar backgrounds and similar cultural needs."[125]

## RESISTING WHITE APPROPRIATION, RESTORING KWANZAA'S PRINCIPLES

The kind of holiday consumption practiced by middle-class blacks was generally given a pass by black critics of Kwanzaa's appropriation. But there emerged a growing resistance to Kwanzaa's commercial exploitation by holiday purists directed at both African-Americans and whites. If Skriloff's Multicultural Marketing, the Chisholm-Mingo Group, and Caroline Jones attempted to cash in on the popularity of race and ethnicity, feeding people of color and their cultural expressions to big business, then the International Black Buyers and Manufacturers Expo and Conference (IBBMEC) and MATAH, two black-owned marketing and trade firms, represent the opposite end of the spectrum.[126] IBBMEC and MATAH belong to a body of African-Americans in the 1990s intent on preventing the exploitation of Kwanzaa. Born out of the temporary dissolution of the African-American Greeting Card Collective and the permanent folding of their magazine, *Ba Papyrus*, IBBMEC was co-founded in 1995 by Tonyia

Rawls, president of a Washington, DC-based marketing and advertising consulting firm, along with Sala Damali and Alexander Medley, Jr., co-owners of Kuumba Kollectibles, an African-centered greeting card company. In 1995, the three co-founders of IBBMEC discovered a need to bring together black manufacturers and retailers on an annual basis. Requiring that all black commercial interests at its yearly trade show be at least fifty-one percent black owned, IBBMEC sat squarely in the tradition of separatist economics. One of its primary aims in 1995 was the protection of the Afrocentric market. IBBMEC took a hard-line stance against white-owned businesses appropriating Kwanzaa. Calling on black businesses, buyers, and trade associations to "Buy Black," IBBMEC drew a line in the retail sand and claimed Kwanzaa for African-American merchants and consumers: "Kwanzaa by its very nature demands that we shop Black! Buying Kwanzaa cards, kinaras, mats, etc. made by white companies flies in the face of the entire concept of KWANZAA. SHOP BLACK and support self-determination."[127] In 1997, three African-American men formed a marketing and trade networking group known as the MATAH. Al Wellington and Ken Bridges,[128] graduates of the Wharton School, and attorney Greg Montgomery used marketing research surveys conducted at the Million Man and Woman marches to revitalize the idea of black cooperative economics. With an unapologetic race-first philosophy, the MATAH decided to combine Kwanzaa's principles with the estimated annual $500 billion in black economic spending power to restore the "Buy Black" ideal. As a MATAH profile explained:

> We did see from the research done at the Million Man March and the Million Woman March that if we developed a business format that could motivate us to practice the principals of Kwanzaa 365 days of the year, we would have our True Freedom in relatively short order. It became clear that we would have to practice the second principle of Kwanzaa, Self-Determination, to create a new business format to satisfy our unique needs and circumstances. We call this business format True Cooperative Economics or Kwanzaa in Action.[129]

Echoing these sentiments were a number of community activists, merchants, Black Power nostalgists, and even the creator of Kwanzaa, Maulana Karenga.

Corporate America's interest in Kwanzaa forced Karenga to address the question of commercialization directly. He warned African-Americans of white-owned interests selling Kwanzaa-related items, but cautioned blacks to be more aware of "standard enticements," and "ethnic imagery" in corporate advertisements. He believed the corporate manipulation of holiday "language and symbols" was an attempt to "redefine the meaning and focus of Kwanzaa." Karenga feared Kwanzaa would follow the path of all holidays, which was complete commercialization. This conscious manipulation of Kwanzaa's principles and symbols in magazines, on billboards, and through television would move the holiday from the control of "small-scale African-American producers and vendors," and make the occasion "another holiday of maximum and compelling shopping." By adhering to the philosophy and principles of Kwanzaa, Karenga believed, "black people can and do pose a strong will against the waves of commercialization which affect all holidays in this market culture which is essentially a culture of sales and consumption." Karenga concluded that a distinction must be made between "normal Ujamaa," as practiced by black entrepreneurs and consumers, and the "white corporate world's" attempt to dominate the Kwanzaa market. "The first is appropriate," says Karenga, "the latter is exploitive and should be resisted."[130]

One of the most vocal groups against any commercial tampering with the holiday has been the National Coalition to Preserve the Sanctity and Integrity of Kwanzaa. Conrad Worrill and Hannibal Afrik, the two men responsible for popularizing Kwanzaa in Chicago in the early 1970s, led the National Coalition. Advocates of Black Power, Worrill and Afrik have remained committed to cultural nationalism and pan-Africanism. For them, Kwanzaa represents one of the purist forms of black cultural nationalist expression. They believe Kwanzaa to be one of the last sacrosanct creations of the Black Power period. Their long-standing role in the racial politics of Black Power and citywide Kwanzaa celebrations provides them the authority to oppose all forms of commercial appropriation.

The National Coalition to Preserve the Sanctity and Integrity of Kwanzaa warned black Chicagoans in 1994 of a consortium of white-owned companies marketing an "authentic African Kwanzaa punch" recipe. The recipe was not only advertised on radio, but sold at five OMNI Super Stores in the Chicago area. Domino Sugar, Canfield's Soda, Dole Pineapple, Tropicana and Minute Maid Orange Juice sponsored the recipe. After the initial advertisements ran on WVAZ-V103 FM in December of 1994, the National Coalition encouraged listeners of black radio stations to call up WVAZ and express their dismay. Hundreds of calls to the radio station forced a meeting between Worrill's National Coalition and V103's general manager Barry Mayo. After the meeting, Mayo cancelled the advertisement.[131]

Worrill and the National Coalition did not limit their attacks to white radio stations. They went after black advertising agencies, many of which were responsible for such ads. Burrell Advertising and Proctor and Gardner, two of the biggest black advertising and marketing firms, felt the wrath of Worrill and the National Coalition for creating Kwanzaa ads for white-owned companies. Burrell produced a Kwanzaa clothing advertisement for K-Mart. Proctor and Gardner helped long-time client Jewel Food Stores reorient Kwanzaa's principles to create the idea of family festivity during the holiday season. Worrill saw both advertisements as blatant attempts to debase Kwanzaa. He expressed his displeasure to a Burrell project coordinator and to Barbara Gardner Proctor, president of Proctor and Gardner. Representatives from both Burrell and Proctor expressed sympathy with the National Coalition's concern and even pledged to work with Worrill's organization. Though the National Coalition gained sympathetic partners in their fight to protect Kwanzaa, the Coalition's actions did not result in a cancellation of either account.[132]

After losing the battle with black advertising companies, the National Coalition approached Hallmark, Safeway Grocery Stores, and Jose Ferrer, chairman of Kwanzaa Fest Unlimited. Recognizing the practice of black ujamaa at Ferrer's expo, Worrill deplored the presence of corporate sponsors. The National Coalition asked Jose Ferrer to reconsider the use of corporate sponsors at the expo. Worrill said: "We spoke to Jose Ferrer . . . who admitted he had been working to make Kwanzaa acceptable to major white corporations." "It was clear from our conversation that he intends to continue this kind of exploitation of Kwanzaa." After receiving information about Ferrer's plans to expand the Kwanzaa expo to other US cities, the National Coalition mounted an additional challenge against Ferrer's corporate sponsors: "We are preparing to challenge any white corporations that do business with Mr. Ferrer and his National Kwanzaa Holiday Expo project." Given the commercial potential of Kwanzaa to corporate America, Worrill was not surprised by the lack of support. "So far," Worrill wrote, "only Time/Life and AT&T have sent letters of apology."[133]

Like Ferrer and black ad agencies, Karenga also raised the ire of the National Coalition by participating in the United States Postal Service's Kwanzaa commemoration stamp. Karenga said that he was not involved in the initial idea of a postal stamp but lent his knowledge to the effort to bring a sense of historical and cultural integrity to the endeavor. During the unveiling of the stamp in 1997, Karenga said the stamp would give African-Americans greater recognition in the public sphere. Worrill disagreed, pointing to Kwanzaa's origins in the Black Power Movement as a major reason why Karenga should not join in any exercise that commercialized the holiday. Worrill saw recognition, respect, and integration into American society as the thrust of the Civil Rights Movement, not the Black Power Movement. "We have always seen Kwanzaa as a different kind of project that has become sacred to the Black Nationalist Movement," he said. "Kwanzaa is not the kind of African-American celebration that should be sold to corporate America or one that needs endorsement of public government agencies like the U.S. Postal Service."[134] Part of Worrill's criticism of the stamp revolved around the symbols of African-American nationalist history, notably the inversion of the colors on the black nationalist flag. In 1920, Marcus Garvey used the colors red, black, and green as a symbol of the ongoing black freedom struggle. In the 1960s, Karenga and the US Organization reoriented the colors to black, red, and green. Karenga not only changed the color pattern, he slightly altered the color's definitions. As an US organizational symbol, Karenga's black, red, and green flag remained virtually unknown until the flag became part of the Kwanzaa pantheon of symbols in the late 1980s and 1990s. Artist Synthia St. James used Karenga's rendition of the nationalist flag in the design of the stamp, causing black activists to cry foul. Unaware of Karenga's flag prior to the stamp's appearance, Worrill and other critics assumed that the USPS had reoriented the colors of the flag on its own.[135] The reconfiguration and merchandising of Garvey's flag on the Kwanzaa postal stamp made Worrill and other critics realize Kwanzaa had reached the commercial point of no return. The holiday had spurred the creation of Kwanzaa Claus figurines, Kwanzaa teddy bears, and puzzles.[136] The ubiquity of Kwanzaa commerce was so evident in the 1990s that Dawad Philip, senior editor at the *Daily Challenge*, wondered, "when they're going to announce a big Kwanzaa clearance sale." Some critics denounced the retailing of Kwanzaa as the very "commercialization of our soul."[137]

One of the grandest attempts at mitigating the commercialization of Kwanzaa was to nationalize the holiday and hold annual spiritual retreats. Four professional black men, some of whom were former Black Power adherents, founded a group called the National Black Wholistic Society (NBWS) in 1981 and started the first national Kwanzaa celebration ten years later. The Society included David Hall, a professor of law (former Dean of the Law School at Northeastern and current Provost), Haki Madhubuti, a Kwanzaa celebrant since 1969, professor of English at Chicago State University and owner of Third World Press, John Howell, an engineer from Philadelphia, and Walter Drummond, also an engineer. Five other men later joined them: Jack Thomas, an urban planner, Chester Grundy from the University of Kentucky's Office of Minority Student Affairs, Jesse Carter, a laborer, Kamau Jawara, a former New York City transit worker and presently a professor in New York, and Morris Jeff, president of the National Black Social Workers Association.[138]

The goal of the National Black Wholistic Society was to regenerate the ideals of the Black Power Movement as well as find solutions to mounting black problems during the first Reagan administration. The four original founders had always talked about the role black men should play in rebuilding the community. Instead of using some of the traditional solutions from the Civil Rights and Black Power eras, they decided to hold summer retreats for spiritual self-empowerment. The goal was to bring black people together from all walks of life and allow them to interact with one another on the basis of the concepts of holism and self-regeneration. Many of the founders of the organization, or the "Brothers," as they became affectionately known, were not simply successful middle-class professionals, but health-conscious vegetarians that believed the struggle around personal well-being was the next level of black empowerment.[139]

To enact their plan, the National Black Wholistic Society held annual summer retreats beginning in 1984. During the first four years, the organization rented space at a Pennsylvania ski resort, bringing scores of African-Americans from different parts of the country. As the annual July retreats grew larger in people and revenue, the NBWS moved from Pennsylvania to Kings Lodge, a black-owned resort in Otisville, New York. By moving the annual summer retreats to Kings Lodge in 1988, the Society was able to convince more black people who not only believed in spiritual regeneration but black economic empowerment to join in their cause.

Regular attendees now numbered in the hundreds, which convinced the leadership to create two more retreats during the calendar year. One of the newest retreats was a call for a national Kwanzaa celebration in the month of December. Though eager to promote Kwanzaa nationally, the leadership of the NBWS realized that the Catskills proved inhospitable for a large gathering during the winter. In 1991, they decided to forgo Kings Lodge, the resort that had become the group's home, and hold the very first national Kwanzaa ceremony on Jekyll Island, Georgia.[140]

In 1991, five hundred people gathered on an island off the coast of Georgia for the first of three national Kwanzaa celebrations. Kwanzaa festivities took place over the three-day period, including all of the holiday's core ritual activities, such as lighting the candles on the kinara, reciting the seven principles, pouring libation to the ancestors, and the Karamu Ya Imani (a special feast made famous by the Kwanzaa community in Chicago). In addition to these core Kwanzaa rituals, summer retreat activities were merged with the first national Kwanzaa. Participants had their choice of Egyptian yoga classes, nutrition workshops, hair-sculpting seminars, brotherhood and sisterhood sessions, storytelling shows for children, and sporting events. Maulana Karenga, the creator of Kwanzaa, officiated the first national Kwanzaa ceremony with help from keynote speakers, Dr. Na'im Akbar, a clinical psychologist and professor at Florida State University, and Dr. Francis Cress Welsing, a specialist in general and child psychiatry. Other guest speakers at the Kwanzaa retreats included Dr. Betty Shabazz, the widow of Malcolm X, Susan Taylor, former editor-in-chief of *Essence* magazine, and Iyanla Vanzant, inspirational speaker, author, and television talk show host.[141]

The most interesting phase of the three national Kwanzaas on Jekyll Island were the yearly rituals held by the ocean. One of them was a ritual of remembrance for the last slaves ever brought to the United States. In 1858, *The Wanderer*, a slave ship carrying over four hundred African men and women, landed at Jekyll Island. The NBWS immediately sought to connect this 1858 Jekyll Island experience with the present. Appropriating the legacy of the Goree Island slave fort in Senegal, specifically the "Door of No Return," where thousands of Senegalese Africans passed through on their way to the New World, the NBWS created a ritual during the first national Kwanzaa called "Closing the Door," a memorial to those last victims of the Atlantic slave trade. The participants at the first national

Kwanzaa dressed in all white as they marched down to the ocean singing a variety of freedom songs. They also secured a huge flowerpot from the Jekyll Island museum that was originally on board *The Wanderer*. Bringing the pot to the ocean, participants performed libations, planted seeds, and engaged in other symbolic acts that allowed them to viscerally connect to the ship's occupants. Out of this experience, the NBWS created an ancestral book of life where all of the national Kwanzaa participants wrote the name of a significant person who had passed on. Betty Shabazz was given the honor of writing Malcolm X's name as the very first entry.[142] In 1993, the NBWS held its final Kwanzaa retreat. The NBWS leadership was unable to sustain the level of participation that had been steadily growing since the summer retreats of the mid-1980s. Mounting expenses coupled with fatigue caused the permanent dissolution of the national Kwanzaa celebrations. These problems also led to a four-year organizational hiatus. In 1997, the NBWS resurrected itself along with one of its summer retreats. Though optimistic about future retreats, the organization's national Kwanzaa celebrations have yet to resume as of the present day.

Kwanzaa continued twisting and turning its way through the last years of the twentieth century and into the twenty-first as evidenced by the attempt to nationalize the holiday and to return it to some original state. But Kwanzaa's evolution begs the question of how does the holiday measure in comparison to other black observances. Kwanzaa has raised the black holiday bar to the degree to which there is a growing tendency to ask the question: "how popular is Kwanzaa among blacks?" Answering this all important question is something we should attempt to do.[143] However, I have found it fascinating that we do not ask the same question of other black holidays. When have you heard, "how many African-Americans observe Martin Luther King, Jr. Day or Juneteenth or Black History Month?" Asking that question of Kwanzaa and not asking the question of other black observances says something about the work Kwanzaa has performed and its impact on the calendar—both the American and the black protest calendars. Kwanzaa's mainstream appearance and success, indeed, made us obsessive about the number of celebrants; Kwanzaa's greatest impact, however, has been the generation of holiday copycats like alternative black Thanksgivings—Umoja Karamu and Gye Nyame (last Friday in November); an alternative black Easter—A Day of Praise (March 26); an alternative black Valentine's—Black Love Day (February 13); an alternative black Columbus Day—African Holocaust Day (October 12); and Black Solidarity Day—an alternative Election Day observance. Indeed, these black holidays represent Kwanzaa's competitors in American public culture, with the men and women who created them, desiring a similar growth and recognition. But in the last twenty years Kwanzaa's greatest holiday competitors have not been necessarily those above, but rather Martin Luther King, Jr. Day, Black History Month, and to a lesser extent, Juneteenth. To ask questions about the popularity of some black holidays is to ascertain holiday winners and losers and what black holidays have real calendar legitimacy in black America and in American culture, the subjects of the final chapter.

# CHAPTER 5

# *Black Holidays and American Calendar Legitimacy*

Imitation is the highest form of flattery. Never has this been truer than within the black holiday tradition. Kwanzaa accomplished several things for African-Americans and for the black holiday tradition. Certainly, it gave blacks a holiday of their own; it allowed many blacks to re-examine their African roots; it provided African-Americans a year-end holiday alternative to Christmas; and lastly, Kwanzaa served as a bridge to other black holidays that came before and after. The fact that Kwanzaa was a bold experiment in holiday alternativity and calendar placement made other black holiday-makers believe they could accomplish similarly. As we saw in Chapter 1, Kwanzaa sits at the middle of the tradition, bridging other black holidays that came before and inspiring others that have come since. The last three chapters detailed Kwanzaa's early beginnings, its internal promotion, and its external appropriation. This chapter will discuss newer holidays Kwanzaa helped inspire, mainly the alternative Valentine's called Black Love Day (February 13), the alternative Easter named A Day of Praise (March 26), and the alternative Memorial Day named Ancestor Honor Day (May 25). As a nod to Kwanzaa's success and impact, these holidays have augmented the black holiday tradition and continued Kwanzaa's political and cultural work of de-emphasizing mainstream calendar observances by sitting alongside Valentine's Day, Easter, and Memorial Day, respectively.

But in many ways these new holiday incarnations have yet to perform the work of Kwanzaa. Some have only begun to catch on, while others are under-promoted and remain within the cities in which they originated.

Though many black alternative holidays failed to move beyond their local neighborhood origins, the newer holidays have nonetheless provided African-Americans a yearly opportunity to discuss and debate historical and current social issues. Indeed, novel black observances in the post-Black Power period were important for what they intended to accomplish, but Kwanzaa's holiday "competitors," however, have not been Black Love Day, A Day of Praise, or African Holocaust Day (alternative Columbus Day), but rather those with greater calendar legitimacy, such as Martin Luther King, Jr. Day, Black History Month, Malcolm X Day, and Juneteenth. Chapter 5's main objective is to juxtapose various black observances within the tradition and offer some insight about the political and educational potential of black holidays. If black holidays are to do their greatest and most effective work—bring people together; remember the past; critique the present; and point a people to a brighter future—they must attain what I call calendar legitimacy. Not all black holidays have achieved this. Many of the holidays' creators and communities care not to.

Mainstream calendar legitimacy is not why black holiday-makers make holidays. Black holiday-making speaks to a process that requires temporal reflection and usually calls for action to ameliorate some aspect of the black condition. Black observances come to fruition when social problems and historical injustices have metastasized, yet have not been fully adjudicated or remedied. Like the nineteenth and early twentieth centuries, getting black social issues on some calendar—whether it's the provincial black protest calendar or the American calendar—allows the issues an annual airing in public with the potential for resolution. Kwanzaa addressed black geographical rootlessness and re-imagined Africa as home; emancipation celebrations like Juneteenth spoke to the need to remember the horrors of slavery and the benefits of black freedom; Negro History Week addressed the absence of African-American history in schools and in American public culture; and Black Solidarity Day reminded African-Americans of their political power in voting and economic power in boycotting. More than mainstream or "white" holidays, black observances narrate all aspects of the black freedom struggle. Black holiday-makers understood very early that the calendar could be used to perennialize black political, social, cultural, and economic issues indefinitely, even if it meant their observances would remain a feature of the black protest calendar. But holidays need nurturing, often requiring some legitimizing agent to keep them growing. Thus, at the end of the day, standing calendar placement with growing calendar legitimacy (either official or unofficial) for black holidays means greater awareness, larger audiences, more adherents, and perhaps most significantly, survival.

## HOLIDAY "CIVIL RIGHTS" IN THE POST-BLACK POWER ERA

The decade of the 1980s was a political windfall for those who identified the 1960s and 1970s as fiscally wasteful; a time of bloated governments—both national and state; a period of unabashed liberal policies; and a moment of unchecked progressive leftist protest. The Republican revolution, rewriting the policies of the 1960s and 1970s, made conservative politics of smaller government and supply-side economics the dominant party position in the 1980s. Conservatives called for a break on so-called liberal spending at the very least, and a roll-back of Democratic and progressive public policies at most. The net effect of their policies was that central cities suffered from a retraction of social services, leaving a void in black neighborhoods across the country. The safety-net policies of the 1960s and 1970s had come to an end. Part of the result was an unceasing number of black-on-black crimes and a drug epidemic wreaked by crack cocaine that destroyed many individuals and families. In this post-Black Power context of the 1980s and 1990s, black activists and community organizers used perenniality and calendar politics as an organizing tool to address social ills inflicting black communities. When masses of black people could be mobilized at a moment's notice during the 1960s and 1970s, assembling people for a call to action would prove more difficult in the post-Black Power period. For black community organizers, one of the most effective ways of rallying people and addressing present-day concerns in the Reagan–Bush–Clinton eras was black holidays.[1]

In the period between 1976 and 1983, black holidays sat at the forefront of the Black Freedom Movement and stood as hotly contested issues in the larger black and American public. Two events demonstrate the political importance of holiday recognition and holiday denial: first, America's Bicentennial—which fostered a Black History Month movement, and second, the grassroots insurgency to make Martin Luther King, Jr.'s birthday into a federally recognized holiday. In 1975 as the United States readied itself for local and national Bicentennial festivities, *Ebony* magazine posed several questions about African-Americans and the observance. To the question, "should they participate in the Bicentennial?" the answer was mixed but the responses that dissented received the greatest attention. Historian and *Ebony* magazine editor Lerone Bennett was one of the dissenting voices: "Let there be no mistake about it, I speak here as an American, and it is precisely as an American that I say Americans have nothing to celebrate." On the heels of the three-decade-old Civil Rights and Black Power Movements, Bennett and others saw the Bicentennial as an example of a cultural revolution incomplete: as a denial of new knowledge about blacks that the movement ushered in; and as another year to prohibit blacks from the American historical narrative. Black Bicentennial critics argued that 1976 would perpetuate long-standing historical myths that the movement fought so hard to eliminate. "As Black Americans," said Bennett, "we dare not participate in the nostalgic, hypocritical ... old myths of American history. ... For us to do so would be blasphemy and sacrilege."[2] If nothing else the Bicentennial proved the ultimate transformation of the American story would take much longer to achieve than other forms of civil rights. Carter G. Woodson's Association for the Study of Negro Life and History agreed with Bennett's assertions. As the most influential promoter of black history in the country, the organization used black Bicentennial invisibility and led the fight to extend Negro History Week to a full month.[3] Thus, the few voices of dissent and rejection against the American Bicentennial snowballed into a national cry leading to both a critique of black historical invisibility and a recalibration of the one-week "set-aside" observance in the beginning of February into a full-fledge month of black observances.[4] This three-week addendum to the calendar proved watershed, and could have only come through a critique of the American Bicentennial's lock-out of black America's contributions to United States history.[5]

The same sentiment that attempted to circumscribe Negro History Week/Black History Month emerged in the 1970s and early 1980s to prevent the passage of congressional holiday legislation for Martin Luther King, Jr. Day. Holidays are bottom-up movements, first achieving recognition at local levels. It was at the local level beginning a few days after King's assassination that the King Holiday Movement began. In 1971, Ralph Abernathy and the Southern Christian Leadership Conference delivered three million petition signatures to Washington, DC; Congress, however, remained unimpressed. Representative John Conyers of Michigan presented King holiday bills every year in the House to no avail. Most Republicans and a few conservative Democrats rejected any holiday legislation designed to honor the memory of the civil rights leader. By the late 1970s and early 1980s, however, the King Holiday was recognized by many school districts, municipalities, and a few states. In 1975, the New Jersey State Employees Association and the New Jersey Civil Service Association filed suit against the state, charging that New Jersey's failure to declare January 15 a holiday violated their employee contracts.[6] In many states, King holiday advocates typically won concessions in unions, school districts, and counties only to be rebuffed by the state:

> The Fairfax County school board voted last night to make the January 15 birthday of the Rev. Dr. Martin Luther King, Jr. a county school holiday starting next year. The state does not add an additional school holiday but shifts to Jan. 15 the existing Jan. 18 state holiday observance of the birthdays of Stonewall Jackson and Robert E. Lee. The vote makes the 15th the observance for all three men, at least for county schools. Virginia Gov. John N. Dalton recently vetoed a bill that would have made the civil rights leader's birthday a state holiday.[7]

The governor's veto in Virginia was part of a larger white counter-movement to prevent a King observance at state and federal (congressional) levels. Opponents, such as Senator Jesse Helms, provided several reasons, from "too costly" to King's supposed ties to communism.[8] Despite opposition, a grassroots holiday insurgency increased with each passing year, ballooning to a national movement by the early 1980s.

The first National Martin Luther King, Jr. Birthday March took place in Washington, DC one week before President Reagan's inauguration in January 1981. Organizers and promoters of the King federal holiday felt a new sentiment against Civil Rights Movement initiatives with the ascendancy of the conservative Republican Ronald Reagan to the presidency. Reagan's victory caused the King Holiday Movement to widen their efforts, creating a grassroots coalition consisting of blacks, whites, labor unions, teachers, public officials, activists, and a host of other people that cut across race, class, and gender. Despite the King Holiday Movement kicking in high gear when Reagan took office, most people felt that King

## Come To Atlanta For This Historic Occasion!
# KING WEEK '82

### THE FIFTY-THIRD BIRTHDAY OF MARTIN LUTHER KING, JR.
### FOURTEENTH ANNUAL BIRTHDAY OBSERVANCE
### THE DEDICATION OF THE FREEDOM HALL COMPLEX

The Freedom Hall Complex

*The Martin Luther King, Jr. Center for Nonviolent Social Change, Inc.*
*449 Auburn Ave., N.E. / Atlanta, Georgia 30312 / (404) 524-1956*
*Coretta Scott King, President*

*Figure 7: King Week '82 flyer in Atlanta, Georgia. Courtesy of*
*Ayo Handy-Kendi*

forces were "holiday-dreaming" with a conservative Congress coupled with a conservative executive. Only a few people, including Congressman John Conyers, remained optimistic that the holiday would become a reality under Reagan's leadership: "People think that we're now in a conservative year and that the King holiday bill doesn't have a chance but I don't think that's necessarily the case."[9] Alfred King, nephew of the civil rights leader, reiterated Conyers' point, saying, "Let's not judge Reagan before he even begins. We'll have to wait and see what he does."[10] The black community did not have to wait. On the campaign trail in Philadelphia, Mississippi, Reagan reiterated his unwavering commitment to cutting government programs for the poor and returning the country back into the direction of states' rights.[11] During the same presidential election year in 1980, singer Stevie Wonder recorded and released the song "Happy Birthday," which quickly emerged as *the* King Holiday anthem. With its upbeat tempo, the song grabbed the attention of the listener and forced him or her to think about King's legacy in the very first verse: "You know it doesn't make much sense; there ought to be a law against; anyone who takes offense; at a day in your celebration."[12] As the song played on black and white radio in late 1980 and early 1981, generating popular support for the holiday in the United States and abroad, Stevie Wonder followed up the song by leading National King Day rallies every January in Washington, DC. The first National King Day rally coincided with President Reagan's inauguration. Five days after the marchers left the nation's capital, Reagan's inaugural gathering could still hear the reverberating echoes of millions of people shouting, "We Want a Holiday! We Want a Holiday!" as he was sworn in.

The National King Day rallies in 1981, 1982, and 1983 drew an average of twenty-five thousand people to the public square between the Lincoln and Washington monuments. The rallies' parallel aims were memorializing King and keeping the civil rights struggle alive by addressing social issues in the black community. Beside the panoply of speeches and admonitions about Reagan's policies, the racially mixed crowd heard speeches on the importance of the Civil Rights Movement in United States history. When it was to the speaker's advantage in other public contexts to minimize King and maximize the efforts of other leaders, many commentators at these rallies did the opposite, taking their opportunity to lionize and reify Martin Luther King, making the Civil Rights Movement more King-centric than ordinarily. There was a perfect explanation for lifting King above the movement. Grassroots organizations, activists, labor and public officials had the difficulty of persuading Reagan and congressional lawmakers that King and his legacy approached the stature of former presidents.[13] In fact for that very reason, President Reagan was hesitant about a King holiday. He told the media he thought such gestures were designated for presidents who passed away long ago. Save for Columbus (who was neither an "American," nor a former president), the only other American figures bestowed a day on the calendar were presidents George Washington and Abraham Lincoln. As one member in the crowd at the 1981 national rally said of the American holiday calendar, "if it's good enough for George, it's good enough for Martin."[14] The comparison of Presidents' Day and a potential King Day mirrored some arguments made by advocates of black history about black children identifying with black leaders. "It is King . . . with whom black children too young to remember the time are learning to identify," said a Baltimore man who attended a King rally in 1978. "If we're going to remember people's birthdays, I can't think of anyone whose birthday I'd rather remember than King's," he continued.[15] Mayor Marion Barry put it more poignantly: "King was to the black revolution what George Washington was to the birth of the nation."[16] Comedian Dick Gregory felt that there were too many white holidays, honoring King would "be doing the calendar a favor."[17] A King Day was not only a time on the calendar to memorialize the Baptist preacher, but to address the most central issues of the day. The 1981 national rally pressured Congress into extending the Voting Rights Act with certain provisions expecting to expire the following year.[18] Rally participants also protested in front of the South African Embassy in Washington, DC, criticizing South Africa's Apartheid regime. Operation PUSH's Jesse Jackson, the National Association for the Advancement of Colored People's Benjamin Hooks, the Reverend Ben Chavis (who had been released from prison a year earlier when a federal appeals court overturned the verdict in the Wilmington Ten case), and a host of other black leaders used King's occasion to take President Reagan to task for his administration's budget cuts. As the *Washington Post* reported, much of the oratory was about present conditions and what the thousands that gathered each January 15 should do about them: "The old warriors present at yesterday's march were eager to seize the moment and move the big crowd on the west steps of the Capitol beyond talk of a national holiday toward something more sharply focused [on] direct action."[19]

The grassroots holiday movement paid off. In 1983, both houses passed their respective King holiday bills. The law passed with bi-partisan support with thirty-seven Senate Republicans voting for the measure, including Senators Howard Baker (Tennessee), Al D'Amato (New York),

John Danforth (Missouri), Bob Dole (Kansas), Dick Lugar (Indiana), Ted Stevens (Alaska), and the repentant Strom Thurmond (South Carolina). Dissenting and voting against the King measure were democratic Senator John Stennis (Mississippi) and Senate Republicans Barry Goldwater (Arizona), John McCain (Arizona), Jesse Helms (North Carolina), and Orin Hatch (Utah).[20] Republican Senators Bob Dole and Jack Kemp provided two of the most powerful reasons why the country should honor Dr. Martin Luther King, Jr. with a federally recognized holiday. Both men evoked history, Dole by referencing slavery and Jim Crow: "To those who would worry about the cost, I would suggest they hurry back to their pocket calculators and estimate the cost of 300 years of slavery, followed by a century or more of economic, political and social exclusion and discrimination," and Kemp, linking the founding of the United States with the tumultuous decades of the 1950s, 1960s, and 1970s: " . . . the American Revolution will not be complete until we complete the civil rights revolution."[21] The legislation established the third Monday in January as the official federal holiday. The King Holiday was signed into law by President Reagan on November 3 in a Rose Garden ceremony with Coretta Scott King and congressional lawmakers looking over his shoulder. Jesse Jackson, who announced earlier in the day that he would enter the 1984 presidential campaign, said that Reagan "institutionalized" the Civil Rights Movement with the signing of the bill, and that "this is one of his [the President's] high moments."[22] In 1984, Congress passed an additional law establishing the Martin Luther King Federal Holiday Commission to coordinate and oversee the holiday's first observance in 1986, and subsequent commemorations in the 1980s and 1990s.

By 1991 only Arizona and New Hampshire refused to recognize the King Holiday. While the state of New Hampshire attempted to work out a compromise, proposing a holiday called Civil Rights Day instead, Arizona remained recalcitrant. Part of the opposition in Arizona involved playing various groups against one another. In 1989 Governor Rose Mofford was pressured into signing legislation eliminating a Columbus Day paid holiday for a King paid holiday. Opponents of a King Holiday were not generally Italian groups, but Italian-Americans found themselves caught in the middle—on the one hand distancing themselves from King holiday antagonism but seeking ways to restore Columbus Day to the state holiday fold. Organizations such as the Sons of Italy and the Arizona Columbus

Day Committee started a petition drive and forced the issue on the ballot in 1990. Proposition 301 (paid King Day; unpaid Columbus Day) and Proposition 302 (paid King Day and paid Columbus Day) were put to the voters. Arizonians rejected Proposition 301, thereby nullifying the previous year's King Holiday legislation signed by the Governor, and also rejected 302, leaving the state with neither observance. In 1992, proponents of a King holiday were able to place Proposition 300 to the voters, which finally passed. In 1993, Arizona joined the other forty-nine states in honoring King with a holiday.[23]

While the King Holiday Movement thrived in the 1980s, Malcolm X commemorations floundered, not growing much beyond their original capacity since the late 1960s and 1970s. In Omaha, Nebraska, Malcolm X's birthplace, the city did designate as a local landmark the home where Malcolm was born on 3448 Pinkney Street, one week prior to President Reagan signing the King bill into law.[24] With much of black America swept up in the euphoria of a King federal holiday, there were some groups in the country who urged others, particularly King holiday supporters, not to forget about the legacy of Malcolm X. February 21, 1985 marked the twentieth anniversary of Malcolm's assassination and it was time, argued a Chicago-based group calling itself the Cooperative Research Network in Black Studies, that African-Americans took a closer look at the Muslim leader's life's work.

> In recent history most people in the USA have recognized the contribution of Martin Luther King or soon will because the day of his birth becomes a legal public holiday in 1986. It is our responsibility to turn our focus to the life of Malcolm X. Malcolm X was just as important as Martin Luther King, and must never be forgotten. *Can we afford to let the next generation of Black people forget Brother Malcolm X?* NO! Again, now is the time to turn our focus to the life of Malcolm X. In 1985 we celebrate the 60th anniversary of his *birth*—May 19, 1925 and rededicate ourselves to struggle on the 20th anniversary of his *assassination*—February 21, 1965.[25]

The Remember Malcolm Campaign sponsored by the Network in Black Studies used Malcolm's speeches and books in study groups and panel discussions to demonstrate his individual transformation and evolution from Malcolm Little to Detroit Red to Malcolm X to El Hajj Malik El Shabazz, and to answer the question, "Why Remember Malcolm in the

*Figure 8: Malcolm X Day flyer in New York City, 1979.*
*Courtesy of Ayo Handy-Kendi*

1980s?" Groups like the Network in Black Studies were indeed important; but without the cross-sectional support of whites from all walks of life that the King Holiday Movement enjoyed, the drive for a Malcolm X Day needed greater support from the world of black entertainment and black popular culture.

With King Day as the new black holiday standard bearer and with Kwanzaa's increasing emergence in the public sphere, Malcolm X Day observances received their own boost from rap music's turn to black nationalist and Black Power themes in the late 1980s. If Stevie Wonder is the critical link to the King Holiday Movement, then arguably rap group Public Enemy galvanized the national Malcolm X Day holiday protest. From 1987 to 1992, Public Enemy reveled in Black Power thought, inspiring a younger generation to become students of the black nationalist 1960s. With hit songs, such as "Prophets of Rage," and "Rebel Without a Pause," Public Enemy's lyrics were played in every corner of black America, providing history lessons such as:

Power, equality and we're out to get it . . . This party started right in '66 with a pro-Black radical mix; Then at the hour of twelve some force cut the power and emerged from hell; It was your so-called government that made this occur, like the grafted devils they were; J. Edgar Hoover and he coulda [*sic*] proved to you; He had King and X set up also the party with Newton, Cleaver, and Seale, he ended, so get up; Time to get them back, get them back on track, word from the honorable Elijah Muhammad, know who you are to be black.[26]

Rap music produced groups that front-loaded their songs with political messages prior to Public Enemy, KRS-One, Rakim, or De La Soul. What appeared different in the late 1980s and early 1990s was the turn toward black history, particularly recent Black Power history. In the song "Fight the Power" on Spike Lee's movie soundtrack, *Do the Right Thing* (1989), Chuck D of Public Enemy not only blasphemed John Wayne and Elvis Presley, arguing that "most of my heroes don't appear on no stamps," he urged black listeners to "get down to business" regarding knowing who their leaders were in history.[27]

Public Enemy's music dovetailed with ongoing activities associated with Malcolm X Day. "Today, his name, face and words are alive on T-shirts and rap records," the *Washington Post* reported. "Academicians are leading a new movement to declare Malcolm X's birthday, May 19 a de facto African-American holiday. The long planned Hollywood movie based on 'The Autobiography of Malcolm X' seems ready to happen. A battle is brewing in New York City over the future of the boarded-up Audubon Ballroom.[28] Meanwhile, a 79-year woman, Rowena Moore, is responsible for buying up 10 acres of land around Malcolm X's birthplace."[29] Between 1990 and 1992, a host of commentators and writers marveled privately and publicly about the nation's growing obsession with Malcolm X. Many wondered, what is fueling this growing devotion or why the sudden change of heart when "just a few short years ago, Malcolm X was said to be promoting separation, hate and violence among other things."[30] The answer certainly lay in large Malcolm X Day commemorations in cities like Washington, DC, as well as current black music and film, particularly the excitement around Spike Lee's movie *Malcolm X* (1992) that began production in 1990. In addition, the emergence of national organizing bodies promoting the idea of a national Malcolm X Day capitalized on the nation's re-discovery of Malcolm X.[31]

The last decade of the twentieth century witnessed increased efforts by grassroots organizations to promote Malcolm X Day. In 1990, the National Malcolm X Commemoration Commission (MXCC) was founded by the African American Progressive Action Network, an organization established by activist Ron Daniels. Created on February 21, 1990, another holiday organization called the Malcolm X Holiday Commission (MXHC) came into existence. These two groups were joined by a third in 1992, the Malcolm X Commemoration Committee, started by some of the original members in both of Malcolm's organizations, the Muslim Mosque, Inc. and the Organization of Afro-American Unity. Many Malcolm X holiday promoters were long-time activists in the black freedom struggle. Ron Daniels, co-chair of the MXCC, has been one of the leading advocates of black alternative holidays, bringing a wealth of organizing and promotional experience from the National Black Convention in Gary, Indiana, the National Black Independent Political Party, and the National Rainbow Coalition. Not only do some of the conveners of national Malcolm X Day groups have activist histories, they are cross-celebrants and promoters of black holidays such as Kwanzaa, African Liberation Day, and even King Day. In fact, the MXHC advanced the position of creating a more ritualized celebration for Malcolm X observances similar to Kwanzaa: "On Malcolm X Day there is the displaying of the black, red, and green flag and the lighting of the black candle. The Africa Cup and the Diaspora Cup are used in the Malcolm X Unity Ritual."[32] Much of the organization's promotional and memorializing efforts involved annual petition drives and Malcolm X conferences. As with other holidays, promoters also took the opportunity to protest present injustices; in the case of MXHC it was the brutal beating of Rodney King in Los Angeles, and with the Malcolm X Commemoration Committee it was the release of political prisoners. Though these groups engaged in gargantuan efforts in keeping the idea of a Malcolm X Day alive, and in many ways expanded the earlier grassroots holiday efforts that began in the late 1960s, by the turn of the twenty-first century, the holiday drive for Malcolm had not moved beyond the early 1990s. Not only had Malcolm X Day observations leveled off, no overwhelming evidence existed suggesting any real push for a federally recognized holiday from boosters.[33]

As one of the oldest black observances, Juneteenth waxed and waned its way through the twentieth century, getting a boost from both the Civil

Rights and Black Power Movements and from the general inclination to make black alternative holidays a national practice in the United States. The overwhelming groundswell generated by the King Holiday Movement coupled with the efforts of black state legislator Al Edwards hastened the creation of the first official state Juneteenth holiday on January 1, 1980 in Texas. It was befitting that Texas would become the first state to recognize the holiday given General Granger's Order Number 3 that told the last remaining slaves on June 19, 1865 they were free from bondage. Similar to Malcolm X Day groups, national Juneteenth holiday organizations emerged in the 1990s, most notably the National Association of Juneteenth Lineage under the leadership of Lula Briggs Galloway, a long-time celebrant of Juneteenth and other freedom holidays. National Juneteenth groups worked closely with local organizations that sponsored Juneteenth observances in major cities like Minneapolis and Milwaukee. One of the aims of Juneteenth promoters was to lobby public officials to make the holiday a national observance. Republican Representative J.C. Watts of Oklahoma carried the fight for a national Juneteenth holiday in Congress. As a state with one of the longest histories of Juneteenth celebrations, Watts not only partook in these holiday observances growing up, he understood what the holiday meant for Oklahomans and for the nation. Watts reiterated to his congressional colleagues that "history is to be regarded as a means for understanding the past and solving the future." Watts also argued that slavery's history did not solely belong to blacks: "the celebration of the end of slavery is an important and enriching part of the history and heritage of the United States." Recognizing the role of grassroots organizations in promoting larger Juneteenth efforts, Watts concluded, "a copy of this joint resolution should be transmitted to the National Association of Juneteenth Lineage as an expression of appreciation for its role in promoting the observance of the end of slavery."[34] Though Juneteenth gained momentum in the 1990s, proving important to many state legislatures and a few members in Congress, Kwanzaa's influence could not be measured similarly. No state has yet to recognize Kwanzaa as state holiday. Kwanzaa's influence is measurable by its impact on other holidays.

The Kwanzaa holiday script proved inspirational as new black holiday formations followed Kwanzaa's lead in de-emphasizing mainstream American observances. If Valentine's Day represented a day for cupid's arrows, red hearts, and an individualized understanding of romantic love, then African-Americans would reassess how much import Valentine's Day had for a suffering community. Since "love" lies in contradistinction to "suffering," it was inevitable that African-Americans would begin recasting Valentine's Day to speak to the needs of African-Americans. One *Chicago Defender* editorial argued that black-on-black love covered many areas of care and affection and went on to identify areas of improvement inside and outside of the home, such as eliminating gang-related violence and domestic abuse. Much of the violence that manifested in black communities across the United States was tied to the post-industrial malaise that transformed the urban political economy and permanently tossed black males out of the labor market, the retrenchment of civil services from shrinking Reagan federal government that provided less money to states, and a crack-cocaine epidemic that haunted black neighborhood streets. Black men and women stood up and addressed the issue directly, creating Stop-The-Violence and Black-on-Black Love campaigns in cities with high murder rates among young black males.[35] Within the context of Reagan–Bush–Clinton domestic priorities and an unabated black-on-black violence, a new alternative holiday emerged on February 13 called Black Love Day.

Ayo Handy, a native of Washington, DC, created Black Love Day and held the first observance of it on February 13, 1993. Handy did not create Black Love Day without any prior involvement with black holidays and grassroots activities. Her interests since the early 1970s involved employment in social service institutions, engaging in community organizing, and working in areas such as mental health, all of which laid the foundation for her brand of holiday-making. Born in 1951 in the nation's capital, Handy graduated from Anacostia Senior High School in 1969 and moved to Okinawa a year later to join her boyfriend turned husband, Damini Handy, who was in the US military stationed at the Naha Air Force Base in Japan. Okinawa not only provided them with a glimpse of US racism, which they both experienced while living among fellow Americans in Japan, but the experience made them more racially conscious and militant. Okinawa was also where Handy and her husband were introduced to drugs, particularly heroin and cocaine. Returning to the United States in one year after her husband received a general discharge for "non-adaptability," the couple soon had two children. Drugs eventually destroyed the couple's marriage, which sent Ayo on a search to find herself and reconnect with her family. While seeking aid from chemical dependency by engaging in holistic healing, meditation, fasting, and prayer, Ayo immersed herself in a number of social justice causes in the Washington, DC area and started the *Positive Energy Newsletter* in 1980 to promote black empowerment through personal healing. Black personal empowerment at the level of meditation and diet cohered with the larger Black Power politics occurring in Washington, DC.[36] Ayo embraced the local Black Power community, becoming involved in district-wide Kwanzaa celebrations throughout the 1970s and 1980s. As one of Washington, DC's major Kwanzaa promoters, she created the African-American Holiday Expo in 1982—an annual economic self-help gathering that brought black producers and consumers together, similar to the expositions in other cities. The success of the Holiday Expo led Ayo to start the non-profit African American Holiday Association in 1989 as "value-centered alternatives to traditional overly commercialized holidays." Ayo not only created the African American Holiday Association to promote Kwanzaa and other black holidays; she would use the Association to conceive and establish new holiday alternatives.[37]

Spike Lee's movie, *Malcolm X* (1992), especially the assassination at the end, and the incessant violence in Washington, DC black neighborhoods provided the impetus for Black Love Day. Handy desired for blacks to "make an effort to do more than sit back and say, 'we are just falling apart as a race of people.'" As she rode the bus home from the movie, Ayo thought: "what, if, for 24 hours, the shooting ceased, the cussing and fussing stopped, the man on the stoop got up and swept the street, a mother hugged her child a little longer and the neighborhoods crews made peace? What would the day be like? What would Washington be like?"[38] Ayo had no way of knowing if black Washington, DC and black America would embrace the observance and its tenets. But the success of Kwanzaa confirmed that African-Americans would support a grassroots holiday. It seems the situation in "chocolate cities" grew acute with each passing year, with the murder epidemic even touching Handy herself when she lost her seventeen-year-old son Rashid to violence on a northwest DC street two years after the first Black Love Day. "I'm real mad," says Handy "that people are taking the deaths of so many of our young people as business as usual."[39] Tired of waiting for public officials, Ayo took matters in her own hands and created Black Love Day. Handy asked blacks to "perform five acts of love during the 24 hours" of every February 13, which would form the basis of annual Black Love Day observances. "Romantic Love is not enough for Valentine's Day," said Handy. "We need more. . . . We need a holistic approach to all of our loving relationships."[40]

The first Black Love Day was held at McKinley Tech High School on 2nd and T Streets NE and featured a number of seminars including "Dealing with Abusive Relationships," "Blended Families—Yours, Mine, Ours," "Letting Go—Releasing Relationship Pain," "Teenage Love and Sexuality," "Boys and Men Without a Male Parent," and "The Challenge of an Interracial Relationship." The first Black Love Day, like subsequent celebrations, commissioned well-known speakers and area experts in the black community. Ayo Handy used the seminar sessions to deal with the complexities of love, moving beyond the provincialism of Valentine's Day that focused only on individuals. The reason Valentine's Day was called into question was mainly fourfold. First, Valentine's Day "does little to speak to the specific needs of the black community." Second, Valentine's Day "encourages unhealthy attitudes of depression if you are not in a positive relationship . . . " Three, the history of Valentine's Day is tied to a European pagan ritual and "many undocumented legends as to the true identity of the Saint and how his name became associated with the celebration on February 14th." And finally, Valentine's Day discourages the development of black purchasing power while encouraging African-Americans "to act merely as consumers buying the customary items for such observances . . . "[41] Not only did Black Love Day offer constructive criticism of Valentine's Day, the observance pushed blacks to demonstrate "five acts of service toward the Creator, toward oneself, within the family, in the community, and for the race." Handy envisioned a holiday observance steeped in celebration and drowning in reconciliation, atonement, and healing, not romantic love.

Similar to Kwanzaa, Black Love Day is ceremonial, ritualistic, and participatory. In public Black Love Day ceremonies, participants greet one another with *Nya Akoma* (pronounced Knee-ah Ah-coma) from the language of the Akan people in Ghana with the phrase defined as "be patient, get a heart and return to love, consistency and faithfulness." Next, participants are asked to pray and meditate during a deep breathing phase that entails listening to the heart and mind, envisioning pain, and communing with the Creator. Third, individuals are to write their need for

*Figure 9: Ayo Handy, Black Love Day founder, pouring libation during the ceremony. Courtesy of Ayo Handy-Kendi*

reconciliation on paper and place it inside a charcoal burning urn. According to Handy, this allows participants to "release pain, helps us reconcile, atone, forgive or seek forgiveness." Next, the congregation stands in a circle. Participants are "anointed with a mix of sandalwood, frankincense, bitter herbs and honey," stepping forward and offering public apology and testimony in front of community members. Public as well as private ceremonies also require the demonstration of five acts of love contained in the nine-part Black Love Day pledge: 1) to show love for the Creator; 2) to love myself first and to erase all traces of self-hatred; 3) to develop moral principles to stand on; 4) to forgive myself for past acts of unloving behavior; 5) to show love for my family; 6) to show love for my community; 7) to show love for my race; 8) to show love for myself, the community, and race; and 9) to commit to the "Nguzo Saba" and to practice these principles on a daily and year-long basis and not just during Kwanzaa. In another nod to Kwanzaa, Black Love Day has its ceremonial colors: instead of black, red and green like Kwanzaa, Black Love Day's colors are purple and black—"purple representing spirituality and black signifying the blend of all colors."[42]

*Figure 10: Kwanzaa kinara and Akoma ritual symbols in the Black Love Day ceremony. Courtesy of Ayo Handy-Kendi*

After the first holiday celebration in 1993 Black Love Day gained new adherents annually. Black Love Day caught on with a sizable segment of the black Washington, DC population and also among black college students at Howard University, Morgan State University, and at Florida Agricultural and Mechanical University (Florida A&M). Though evidence suggests that Black Love Day has expanded beyond Washington, DC, no firm numbers exist on how many people celebrate Black Love Day nationally. Despite the holiday's recognition from local government officials, such as Wilma R. Harvey, Ward 1 Representative in the District of Columbia, and Harry L. Thomas, Councilmember from Ward 5, the holiday exists mainly at the grassroots level and still remains a product of the black protest calendar. Black Love Day's "success" in some quarters in the black community prompted Ayo Handy to create other black alternative holidays to challenge mainstream observances and help blacks reorient the way they think about annual celebrations. In 1998, A Day of Praise and Ancestor Honor Day were designed to redefine and expand the original conception of both Easter and Memorial Day, respectively. Like its Easter counterpart, A Day of Praise evoked spirituality. Instead of privileging solely Christian conceptions of resurrection and re-birth, A Day of Praise recognized, observed, and memorialized other under-appreciated deities celebrated in United States communities of color. Similarly, since Memorial Day narrowly commemorated the past efforts of those who sacrificed their lives on foreign and domestic battlefields, Ayo Handy attempted to augment the boundaries by acknowledging the physical sacrifice of "non-military" persons who "worked and died for freedom, justice, and equality" writ large. Using Black Love Day as a point of departure in opening up other alternative commemorative possibilities, Ayo Handy took similar action against Easter and Memorial Day: A Day of Praise would not be solely reserved for Jesus Christ just like Ancestor Honor Day would not solely recognize fallen soldiers.[43] To promote old and novel black holidays, Ayo Handy-Kendi used the first national holiday organization to advance black alternative observances.

The African American Holiday Association (AAHA) was incorporated in 1989 as a 501 (c) (3) whose mission was to "perpetuate and preserve culture through traditional and non-traditional holidays, celebrations and rituals." As a long-time community activist, Handy-Kendi coalesced all of her past and present activities under the AAHA, using it as her primary vehicle of holiday promotion. As a black holiday-maker, not only did the AAHA provide Handy a larger platform; the organization solicited the involvement of local and national citizens to take part in a broader holiday movement. The AAHA is a member organization of community groups, individuals, and institutions in Washington, DC and across the United States that believe in the future growth and development of black holiday alternatives. Offering a number of services to the public, including holiday lectures, Kwanzaa Griot (storytelling), racial reconciliation healing, and officiating African weddings, the AAHA stands as an example of organizational diversity in the ongoing Black Freedom Movement. Some of the organization's past efforts include the coordination of the African American Holiday Expo in Washington, DC, waging holiday public relations campaigns locally and nationally, organizing for the Martin L. King, Jr. holiday bill, participating in the Free D.C. Movement, galvanizing the Jericho '98 initiative (freedom of political prisoners), and serving as local sponsors of the Million Man and Woman marches.[44]

The AAHA owes its existence to a number of holiday developments but mainly three are very significant: the growing popularity of Kwanzaa in the 1970s and 1980s, the evolution of Negro History Week to Black History Month in 1976, and the passage of congressional legislation making Martin Luther King, Jr. Day a federal holiday in 1983. This black holiday drive in the late twentieth century is telling about the state of the Black Freedom Movement. The growth of black holidays suggests both a nadir in civil rights and black power politics and a shift in movement concerns. On the one hand, the drive to make Negro History Week into Black History Month, King into a federal holiday, and even Juneteenth and Malcolm X into national observances, was part of the movement's unapologetic emphasis on cultural and historical recognition. It also can be argued that holidays are not the meat and potatoes of political movements. The fact that holiday-making assumed a greater role in black movement politics suggests a diminution of sorts, a sense that the thrust of the 1960s and 1970s had crashed and burned at worst, or at best, shifted priorities. I take issue with the former and argue the latter. As we have seen with Kwanzaa and earlier black observances in the nineteenth century, holidays have and remain political products, brought into existence not under subterfuge but as overt statements about a people's place in society. Holidays are communiqués or bulletins about a people's sacred past and what work ought to be done about a community's present condition and its future. Thus, black holiday-making and promotion was part of a broader civil rights struggle in the late twentieth century.

## CALENDAR LEGITIMACY: TOWARD A THEORY OF BLACK HOLIDAYS

Calendar legitimacy is rooted in the cross-over desires of black holiday-makers and boosters. Black holidays are similar to popular/top forty and rhythm and blues songs. Analogous to the pop and R&B music charts, many black artists and musicians either deliberately attempt to gain wider appeal among whites, or some serendipitous god allows a song to appeal to a more mainstream audience without artist intent. The black protest calendar is akin to the R&B charts, with its organic music pouring out of the efforts of artists longing to have their music heard and appreciated by their own people. Likewise the black protest calendar is filled with organic holidays that are neighborhood and community based, hold a limited audience, and like many R&B songs, are only known by a small faithful few. Most black holidays and observances start as endemic features of the black protest calendar—Kwanzaa, Malcolm X Day, Juneteenth, Black Love Day, Black Solidarity Day, Umoja Karamu, Martin Luther King, Jr. Day, and Negro History Week—just as most soul music evolves and is tested on the R&B charts before going pop. Many black holidays, however, do not remain standards of the black protest calendar. Some black holidays, like Kwanzaa, find that mainstream audiences have identified something appealing in them and have thought proper to embrace and promote them for a myriad number of legitimate and self-serving reasons. Other black holidays have made it their raison d'être to achieve national, federal, and mainstream recognition. The King Holiday was a grassroots observance beginning in 1968, but after the congressional stamp by Congress in 1983, King Day quickly crossed over onto the American calendar. Some observances, such as Black History Month, have crossed over at a much later historical period from their dates of origin. Juneteenth is an example of a black holiday existing on the black protest calendar for much of its 140-year history but has sought American calendar legitimacy in the last twenty years from major boosters.

Similar to the Black Power period with the creation of Umoja Karamu (alternative Thanksgiving created in 1970) and Black Solidarity Day (the alternative Election Day created in 1969), Kwanzaa's mainstream appearance and success has generated black holiday copycats in the post-Black Power era: an alternative Valentine's—Black Love Day (February 13); an alternative Memorial Day—Ancestor Honor Day (third Monday in May); an alternative Easter—A Day of Praise (Easter Saturday); and an alternative Columbus Day—African Holocaust Day (Sunday before Columbus Day). Indeed, these black holidays represent Kwanzaa's competitors in American public culture, with their creators hoping for a similar growth pattern within black communities as well as recognition beyond the boundaries of black America. But in the last twenty years Kwanzaa's greatest holiday competitors have not been those above but more Martin Luther King, Jr. Day, Black History Month, and to a lesser extent, Juneteenth and Malcolm X Day. Black holidays, new and old, proved effective in providing a narrative of counter-memory that spoke to black community concerns, particularly when they sat alongside well-established white American observances. Well-established black observances like Negro History Week used the moment of America's Bicentennial in 1976 to remind the country that African-Americans were excluded from the main narrative of United States history despite the attention the Civil Rights and the Black Power Movements place on black history. The Association for the Study of Negro Life and History and other boosters of Negro History Week not only demanded more calendar space, but sought calendar legitimacy by having President Jimmy Carter declare the entire month of February as Black History Month and provide it with annual policy recognition. These moves toward black holiday officialdom were actively pursued by other promoters of black holidays, such as the backers of Juneteenth, Martin Luther King, Jr. Day, and Malcolm X Day, all seeking and achieving greater national recognition but at vastly different levels.

What is clear about the Black Holiday Movement is that some form of legitimacy appears to be the overarching goal, legitimacy either by the "people," by the "state," by "institutions" (public or private) or by all three. Legitimacy in the holiday context means holiday audience—who are the celebrants of a particular observance and how large is the circle of those that embrace any one holiday. In order for holidays to have the greatest impact, they must touch as many people as possible; hence, in many ways, the greater a holiday's audience, the greater its legitimacy. Throughout the history of black holidays, however, there are some people who have invested in the racial politics of black holiday validation. For some, race matters in matters of black holiday creation, expansion, recognition, and approval. For others, only one process of holiday legitimation matters: mainstream acceptance and American calendar recognition. These two polar extremes dominate the history of black holiday thinking, particularly the former.

Consider journalist Claude Lewis' assessment of black holiday-making in the 1980s. Lewis' analysis of black holiday creation in general and Martin Luther King, Jr. Day specifically is interesting in two respects. One is the particular time period in the history of King Day he focused: 1983—the year Congress passed the King Holiday bill and President Reagan signed it into law. And two, the words he chose to use in describing where and how the black community erred in the King Holiday Movement. Two weeks after the last of the three national King Day rallies in 1983, Claude issued this reading of the movement:

> For several years, Stevie Wonder the musical genius has been leading the
> effort to establish a national holiday in the name of Dr. Martin Luther King,
> Jr. It occurs to me that Stevie and all of those who believe Dr. King's birthday
> ought to be memorialized each year, are going about it the wrong way. The
> way to establish a national holiday is simply to *take* it.[45]

Lewis' conception of "take" is akin to a capture, an acquisition, a seizure
of sorts. Taking or seizing in Lewis' conception is a hostile act, an act of
legitimation that cannot come through the opposite process of "*asking*"
for a holiday. "The way to create a holiday is to *seize* the [calendar]
day," said Lewis. "It seems to me that asking *permission* to establish a day
in Dr. King's memory is a sign of weakness and insecurity. By *taking*
the holiday, you create it officially." Holiday seizure for Lewis meant
blacks "should simply stay at home on January 15, or least stay away
from the workplace." If African-Americans took a day on the calendar
by "staying" home, said Lewis, black holidays "will automatically be
established."[46]

Lewis is only partially correct in his analysis of the black holiday tradition. The black holiday tradition has always been about taking days—
establishing and maintaining times on the calendar related to important
historical events as well as appropriating calendar space before or after
dominant American holidays to create new black observances. The duel
existence of the black protest calendar and the American calendar over
hundreds of years bears this out. The black protest calendar is invisible to
many, provincial to most, and even radical to a few. The black protest
calendar with its limitations does not mean it is unable to perform the
work that it needs. It has always allowed African-Americans to "take" and
"seize" days, in essence, to have holidays of their own. History has demonstrated that American calendar acceptance at the very beginning of a black
holiday's existence is not possible. The black protest calendar as the first
representative of the black holiday tradition has never allowed African-
Americans to come "hat-in-hand" as Lewis maintains: "the call to celebrate
January 15 should begin with the Black community and spread outward.
It makes little sense to go hat-in-hand to the very individuals and institutions who openly thwart our efforts . . . " What Lewis failed to assess was
the black holiday tradition in its entirety or even examine the King Holiday
Movement closely. Almost every black holiday in the tradition, including

Martin Luther King, Jr. Day, has been established by grassroots organizations and activists as part of an endogamous beginning before moving beyond community boundaries. Some have come into the larger American public sphere by external appropriation and validation at the behest of blacks, whites, and others. The appearance of black holidays in American public culture, however, does not make them less black or weak. Neither does external validation of black observances force blacks to relinquish ownership. What Lewis and others have confused is official government recognition with holiday sell out, a presidential proclamation with holiday watering down, a commercialization or a wider societal appropriation with holiday loss or a death. Assessing black holidays at the point of state or institutional intervention and action decouples official holiday recognition—that is, school district, city council, municipality, county, state, executive proclamations, and congressional holiday laws—from their more important grassroots histories. Very few holidays, black or white, have procured state or mainstream public culture approval without a grassroots holiday struggle waged first. In most cases, the grassroots involvement never ceases even after official holiday policies and procedures are put into effect by corporate and cultural institutions, municipalities, states, or the federal government. When Karenga postulated a similar argument to Claude Lewis' by saying, "Unlike Martin Luther King Day, the established order has nothing to do with this holiday [Kwanzaa]," he too perpetuated a myth about King Day and belied how black holidays evolve and grow in popularity, including his own Kwanzaa.[47]

Arguably, both grassroots and official involvement in black holiday creation and promotion has augmented the function of black holidays. For all groups, especially marginalized communities, annual holidays operate as perennial histories. Given that black history has not become a policy reality in most public school districts, despite being taught by many well-meaning teachers, black holidays loom in importance for reasons of curriculum impact. Since no official uniform educational policy exists on the mandatory teaching of black history in public schools, black holidays have served as proxies for the teaching of black history in many districts. This fact was not lost on the *Washington Star* when it reported that without a King Day, "one thousand years from now, even 100 years from now, the tumultuous civil rights movement of the 1960s may rate only part of a chapter in history books. The name of Dr. Martin Luther King, Jr. may appear only in a paragraph."[48] Unfortunately, for many schools in the United States this has become a reality. Since the 1960s and certainly the 1920s, the United States has not advanced much beyond what I call black "holiday-history"—allowing only what can be considered a modicum recognition of the black experience during the "long" Black History Month: from Kwanzaa (December 26) to February 28. In 1926, Negro History Week was initiated; and from the 1960s to the present, African-Americans gained Martin Luther King, Jr. Day in January and three more weeks in February. For many years, these calendar occasions were the only moments when the black experience manifested inside classrooms. Even outside the classroom, black history is synonymous with black holidays. In 1997, Congressman Ron Dellums informed his fellow House representatives about the growing black calendar, placing Malcolm X's birthday within the long Black History Month and asking lawmakers to understand the holidays' pedagogical import:

> Mr. Speaker, I rise today in commemoration of Black History Month. The observation of Black History Month dates back to 1926 when African-American historian and scholar Carter G. Woodson introduced "Negro History Week," traditionally observed during the second week of February to coincide with the birthdays of Abraham Lincoln and Frederick Douglass, a personal hero. In 1976, this was expanded to include the entire month of February. In many communities, this has also been expanded with celebrations beginning with Kwanzaa in late December, continuing in January with the birthday celebration of Dr. Martin Luther King, Jr. through February, culminating in May with the birthday of Malcolm X. Of course, it goes without saying that black history is relevant everyday especially in the United States since it is inextricably linked to the history and development of this nation.[49]

Black holidays proved to be important calendrical gains as outlined by Congressman Dellums to be sure; but on the flip side, black holiday pedagogy is a sad commentary on the state of black history in the United States at the turn of the twenty-first century.[50] At the very least, however, black holiday perenniality allows debates to surface yearly on the state of black historical, social, and political subjectivity. But black holidays are no substitute for transformative black history.

The fact of the matter is that the larger the audience for black holidays the greater impact they can have to memorialize the past, to assess the present, and to stake out a brighter future. Holiday growth and survival is important to the expansion of the black holiday tradition. Holiday growth is also necessary to individual observances transcending beyond and moving off the black protest calendar, or like black crossover music, perhaps simultaneously occupying two chart/calendar spaces at once. Consider the three most popular observances in the tradition that have done just that: Kwanzaa, Martin Luther King, Jr. Day, and Black History Month. What is appealing about these observances and has fostered their endurance is their import beyond the original holiday audience, their capacity to speak to multiple audiences, their connection with broad-based social movements, and their association with American progress. The social movements of the 1960s and 1970s are instrumental in all three. Kwanzaa was created in the context of the Black Power Movement, a time when much of black America re-evaluated their history and identity. Martin Luther King, Jr. was and still is a signifier for the civil rights revolution, cut down way before the revolution fulfilled its objectives. And though Negro History Week was a product of the Harlem Renaissance 1920s, Black History Month benefitted from and came to fruition via Black Power's critique of the American Bicentennial. Similarities can also be discerned from the holidays' original audience and their broader appeal. When Karenga and the US Organization created Kwanzaa and the holiday's seven principles, they were known as the seven principles of blackness. On closer examination there is nothing black about the Nguzo Saba. Whites and other people of color can exercise unity and faith; be creative, self-determining, and purposeful; and work together collectively. Likewise, Martin Luther King's legacy does not belong to blacks solely, but rather to the ideal of American and human progress. And Black History Month not only serves the purpose of educating African-Americans about their own history; Black History Month laid the foundation for American calendrical diversity as witnessed by the months designated for women and ethnic minorities on the American calendar. But how did Kwanzaa and the Black Power Movement "make" the black holiday tradition? Surely it can be argued that Martin Luther King, Jr. Day or Black History Month equally compelled the African-American holiday tradition to further development. Kwanzaa did not create the tradition. However, unlike the other black holidays, Kwanzaa and the Black Power Movement turned much of the tradition toward holiday alternativity, inspiring other black holidays to challenge dominant calendar positions and put more days on the black protest calendar, and subsequently, the American holiday calendar.

# Notes

## 1 THE BLACK PROTEST CALENDAR AND THE AFRICAN-AMERICAN HOLIDAY TRADITION

1 Frederick Douglass, "The Meaning of July Fourth for the American Negro," in Philip S. Foner, ed. *The Life and Writings of Frederick Douglass*, vol. 2 (New York: International Publishers, 1950), 188–89.

2 Basir Mchawi, "Kwanzaa, By Any Means Necessary," *Black News*, December 1974, reprinted in *Black News*, December 1976, 6–8.

3 Matthew Dennis, *Red, White, and Blue Letter Days: An American Calendar* (Ithaca: Cornell UP, 2002), 15.

4 Ellen M. Litwicki, *America's Public Holidays, 1865–1920* (Washington, DC: Smithsonian, 2000), 3.

5 J. Walker McSpadden, *The Book of Holidays* (New York: Thomas Crowell, 1958), 4–5.

6 Dennis, *Red, White, and Blue Letter Days*, 144.

7 Ibid., 230–36, 240–50; Litwicki, *America's Public Holidays*, chaps. 1, 3.

8 Dennis, *Red, White, and Blue Letter Days*, 150.

9 "Monday Holidays," *Congressional Record*, House of Representatives, 90th Congress, 2nd Session, May 8, 1968–May 15, 1968, vol. 114, part 10.

10 Jacques Derrida, *Writing and Difference* (Chicago: University of Chicago Press, translated by Alan Bass, 1978).

11 "Monday Holidays," *Congressional Record*, May 8, 1968–May 15, 1968.

12 Molefi Kete Asante, ". . . And Then There Was Columbus," *Essence*, October 1991, 144.

13 Ibid.

14 J. Zamgba Browne, "Reject Columbus Day? The People Speak," *New York Amsterdam News*, October 9, 1993, 34; Marta Vega, ". . . And Then Columbus," *New*

*York Amsterdam News*, April 20, 1991, 13; for a Native American reading of the Columbus Quincentenary, see Michael J. Major, "Dancing to a Different Drummer: How Native Americans View the Columbus Quincentenary," *Public Relations Journal*, November 1992.

15 "Holidays the Afrikan Way," *Kuumba Report*, November–December 2003, 1.

16 Ayo Handy, "What Does St. Patrick's Day Have to Do with Black Folks?" (March 1990?), personal papers of Ayo Handy-Kendi; Ron Daniels, "Celebrating Holidays: An Afro-Centric Perspective," *Vantage Point: Articles and Essays by Ron Daniels*, December 26, 1988; Jill Nelson, "Armageddon is Now: Some Sobering Reflections on What the Fourth of July and the War of Independence Really Mean to Us," *Essence*, July 1986, 81.

17 Susan G. Davis, *Parades and Power: Street Theatre in Nineteenth Century Philadelphia*. Philadelphia: Temple University Press, 1986, 16–17.

18 J. Walker McSpadden, *The Book of Holidays*. New York: Thomas Y. Crowell, 1958, v; Jane M. Hatch, *The American Book of Days*. 3rd edn. New York: H.W. Wilson, 1978, v.

19 Len Travers, ed. *Encyclopedia of American Holidays and National Days*, vols. 1 & 2 (Westport: Greenwood Press, 2006), vol. 1, x.

20 William H. Wiggins, Jr. *O Freedom!: Afro-American Emancipation Celebrations*. Knoxville: University of Tennessee Press, 1987, xix.

21 Shane White, "'It Was a Proud Day': African Americans, Festivals, and Parades in the North, 1741–1834," *Journal of American History* 81 (June 1994).

22 Quote taken from Philip S. Foner, "Black Participation in the Centennial of 1876," in *Freedom's Odyssey: African American History Essays from Phylon*, eds. Alexa Benson Henderson and Janice Sumler-Edmond (Atlanta: Clark Atlanta UP, 1999).

23 Leonard Sweet, "The Fourth of July and Black Americans in the Nineteenth Century: Northern Leadership Opinion Within the Context of the Black Experience," *Journal of Negro History* 61 (July 1976); Len Travers, *Celebrating the Fourth: Independence Day and the Rites of Nationalism in the Early Republic* (Amherst: University of Massachusetts Press, 1997).

24 William B. Gravely, "The Dialectic of Double-Consciousness in Black American Freedom Celebrations,1808–63," *Journal of Negro History* 67 (Winter 1982).

25 Mitchell Kachun, *Festivals of Freedom: Memory and Meaning in African American Emancipation Celebrations, 1808–1915* (Amherst: University of Massachusetts Press, 2003).

26 W.E.B. Du Bois, "The Jubilee of Emancipation," *The Crisis*, May 1915, 31–32.

27 Geneviève Fabre, "African-American Commemorative Celebrations in the Nineteenth Century," in *History & Memory in African-American Culture*, eds. Geneviève Fabre and Robert O'Meally (New York: Oxford University Press, 1994), 86.

28 "Requesting the President to Proclaim February 1 as National Freedom Day," 80th Congress, Senate, 1st Session, July 25, 1947; "Requesting the President to Proclaim February 1 as National Freedom Day," 80th Congress, House of Representatives, 2nd Session, June 17, 1948.

29 "Negro History Week to Begin Tomorrow," *Washington Post*, February 7, 1926; "Negro History Week Praised as Beneficial," *Washington Post*, February 10, 1926.

30 Carter G. Woodson, "Negro History Week: A National Celebration," *Journal of Negro History* 12 (1928), 2.

31 Ibid., 1.

32 Ibid., 1.

33 Ibid., 4.

34 Ibid., 5–6.

35 "Negro History Hailed: Week of Feb. 12–18 Proclaimed by Dewey in Honor of Race," *New York Times*, February 11, 1945, 34; "Black History Month," *Washington Post*, February 19, 1977, A-12.

36 John Hope Franklin, et al., "Black History Month: Serious Truth Telling or a Triumph in Tokenism?" *The Journal of Blacks in Higher Education* (Winter 1997–98), 87–92; "Afrikan History Month '81, Calendar of Events," Center for Black Studies, Wayne State University; "Why African Heritage Month?" African Heritage Committee of the Woodson-Banneker-Jackson Bey Division 330 of the UNIA-ACL.

37 "The Beatification of Malcolm X," *Time*, March 1, 1968, 16.

38 "Whose Version of History?" *Christian Science Monitor*, February 16, 1968, 18.

39 "Thousands Attend Rites for Malcolm X," *The Sunday Star*, February 28, 1965, B-4.

40 Ibid.

41 "Where Was Mrs. X?" *Pittsburgh Courier*, May 22, 1965, 1.

42 "Negro Pupils Extend Tribute to Malcolm X," *The Evening Star*, February 22, 1969.

43 "Memory of Malcolm X Honored at AU," *Washington Post*, February 22, 1968.

44 "College Students Remember Malcolm X," *New York Amsterdam News*, February 20, 1971, 1, 33; "Negro Pupils Extend Tribute to Malcolm X," *The Evening Star*, February 22, 1969; "Few Stores in D.C. Honor Malcolm X," *Washington Post*, May 21, 1968.

45 "School Holiday Urged on Birthday of Malcolm X," *Congressional Record*, House of Representatives, 90th Congress, 2nd Session, May 16, 1968–May 24, 1968, vol. 114, part 11. Early Malcolm X commemorations were a by-product of the Black Power Movement's ability to capture schools and other educational institutions. Black commemorative observances held sway over many schools. As local institutions, public schools served a narrow constituency of students and parents. Schools in cities with large black populations were beholden to their populations in ways other public and private institutions were not.

46 HR 16510, "A Bill to Designate the Birthday of MLK as a Legal Public Holiday," 90th Congress, 2nd Session, April 8, 1968.

47 Senate Joint Resolution 159, "Introduction of Joint Resolution Designating January 15 of Each Year as Martin Luther King Day," *Congressional Record*—Senate, April 8, 1968.

48 Ibid.

49 "Store Closings Asked As Malcolm X Tribute," *Washington Post*, May 17, 1968; "Few Stores in D.C. Honor Malcolm X," *Washington Post*, May 21, 1968.

50 "A Memorial to Brother Malcolm X," flyer from Malcolm X Memorial Committee.

51 "King Memorial Service at Coliseum," *Los Angeles Sentinel*, April 11, 1968, 8A.

52 "Honoring King and Malcolm X," *Washington Post*, February 2, 1974.

53 Daphne Sheppard, "Black Solidarity Day," *New York Amsterdam News*, October 11, 1969, 1, 4; "Solidarity Day and How it Was," *New York Amsterdam News*, November 8, 1969, 1, 14; Daphne Sheppard, "Solidarity Day Observance Causes Job Loss By One," *New York Amsterdam News*, November 8, 1969, 25; Douglas Turner Ward, *Happy Ending and Day of Absence: Two Plays by Douglas Turner Ward* (New York: The Third Press, 1966).

54 Daphne Sheppard, "Solidarity Observance Causes Job Loss By One," *New York Amsterdam News*, November 8, 1969, 25.

55 "Black Solidarity Day Activities Planned," *Bay State Banner*, May 14, 1970, 7.

56 Rev. Ishakamusa Barashango, *Afrikan People and European Holidays: A Mental Genocide, Book I* (Silver Spring, MD: Fourth Dynasty Publishing Company, 1980), 1.

57 Ibid., 52.

58 "Committee Prepares African Liberation Day," *Muhammad Speaks*, May 9, 1972; "African Liberation Day: Washington May 27," *Muhammad Speaks*, June 2, 1972; "African Liberation Day!: Over 25,000 U.S. Blacks Demonstrate Support of Motherland Liberation Struggles," *The Black Panther*, June 3, 1972.

59 Litwicki, *America's Public Holidays*, 3.

60 David Cressy, *Bonfires and Bells: National Memory and the Protestant Calendar in Elizabethan and Stuart England* (London: Weidenfeld and Nicolson, 1989), xii.

61 Black Love Day is covered in detail in Chapter 5.

## 2 MAULANA KARENGA, THE US ORGANIZATION, AND THE MAKING OF KWANZAA

1 Clifford Geertz, *The Interpretation of Cultures* (New York: Basic Books, 1973).

2 Peniel Joseph, *Waiting 'Til the Midnight Hour: A Narrative History of Black Power in America* (New York: Henry Holt, 2006).

3 William E. Cross, Jr., "The Negro-to-Black Conversion Experience: Toward a Psychology of Black Liberation," *Black World*, July 1971.

4 V.Y. Mudimbe, *The Invention of Africa: Gnosis, Philosophy, and the Order of Knowledge* (Bloomington: Indiana UP, 1988), 22–23; V.Y. Mudimbe, *The Idea of Africa* (Bloomington: Indiana UP, 1994).

5 Quote taken from Adelaide Cromwell Hill and Martin Kilson, eds. *Apropos of Africa: Sentiments of Negro American Leaders on Africa from the 1800s to the 1950s* (London: Frank Cass, 1969), 14–15.

6 Michel Foucault, *Power/Knowledge: Selected Interviews and Other Writings, 1972–1977*, ed. Colin Gordon (New York: Pantheon Books, 1980), 98–99.

7 Orlando Patterson, *Slavery and Social Death* (Cambridge, MA: Harvard UP, 1982).

8 "Interview with Maulana Karenga," February 9, 1999; Scot Brown, *Fighting for US: Maulana Karenga, the US Organization, and Black Cultural Nationalism* (New York: NYU Press, 2003).

9 "25 Orators Reach Speech Semi-finals," *Los Angeles Collegian*, May 13, 1960, 1; "AS Elections Begin Tues: Top 4 Positions Uncontested, None Vie for AWS, ICC Heads," *Los Angeles Collegian*, May 20, 1960, 1; "Issues Top Ballet, Offices Unopposed, Steve Bein, Everett Present Qualifications for Top Posts," *Los Angeles Collegian*, May 24, 1960, 3.

10 "Interview with Maulana Karenga," May 12, 2000, 3.

11 Ron Everett, "Student Body Veep Explains School Role," *Los Angeles Collegian*, December 6, 1960, 2; Mike Keller, "Everett Wins: VP Defeats AS Treasurer, Record Crowd Turns Out to Support New AS Prexy," *Los Angeles Collegian*, January 13, 1961, 1.

12 "AS Prexy Attends Intercollege Confab," *Los Angeles Collegian*, March 14, 1961, 1; "AS President Breaks Tie, Names Perlin as Delegate," *Los Angeles Collegian*, March 24, 1961, 1; "Five Delegates Attend Student State Confab," *Los Angeles Collegian*, April 14, 1961, 1; Richard Tripp, "Editor Hits Educational Standards," *Los Angeles Collegian*, April 21, 1961, 1; "Interview with Maulana Karenga," May 12, 2000, 9.

13 Paul Robeson, "African Culture," in Cromwell Hill and Kilson, eds. *Apropos of Africa*, 134–35.

14 "African History Course Offered Next Semester," *Los Angeles Collegian*, December 16, 1960, 1; "Society to Focus Attention on Afro-Asian Languages," *Los Angeles Collegian*, March 17, 1961, 1; "Africa, Asia, Accented By Conference," *Los Angeles Collegian*, March 21, 1961, 1; "Interview with Maulana Karenga," September 15, 1999, 12.

15 "Forty UCLA Students Join Sit-In," *UCLA Daily Bruin*, November 11, 1963, 1; "CORE Picket Lines Draw 25 from UCLA," *UCLA Daily Bruin*, June 14, 1963, 9; Elinor Sigler, "Journalist Raps Negro Leaders," *UCLA Daily Bruin*, March 27, 1963, 1; Nancy Copeland, "Novelist Baldwin Talks About Racial Problem," *UCLA Daily Bruin*, May 13, 1963, 1; "Blame Capitalism for Prejudice," *UCLA Daily Bruin*, October 24, 1963, 1.

16 "Interview with Maulana Karenga," September 15, 1999, 8–9.

17 David Shaw, "'Negro a Monster Stripped of His Culture'—Malcolm X," *UCLA Daily Bruin*, November 29, 1962, 1; "Black Muslim Indicts Whites for Prejudice," *UCLA Daily Bruin*, March 25, 1963, 1; Scot Brown, "The US Organization: African-American Cultural Nationalism in the Era of Black Power, 1965 to the 1970s" (PhD dissertation, Cornell University, 1999), 51.

18 Vic Pollard, "Clean Ghetto is Issue for Negro, Warden Asserts," *UCLA Daily Bruin*, December 10, 1962, 1; Thomas Addo Quaynor, *A Documented History of Black Consciousness* (New York: Vantage Press, 1986), 133–41.

19 Pollard, "Clean Ghetto is Issue for Negro, Warden Asserts," *UCLA Daily Bruin*, December 10, 1962, 1; Don Harrison, "Panelists Ponder Integration," *UCLA Daily Bruin*, December 13, 1963, 1.

20 Harrison, "Panelists Ponder Integration," *UCLA Daily Bruin*, December 13, 1963, 1.

21 "Interview with Maulana Karenga," September 15, 1999, 11.

22 Jomo Kenyatta, *Facing Mount Kenya: The Tribal Life of the Gikuyu* (New York: Vintage Books, 1962).

23 Sekou Toure, *Toward Full Re-Africanization* (Paris: Presence Africaine, 1959), 58–61; "Interview with Maulana Karenga," September 15, 1999, 6–7.

24 "UCLA Tops Africa Study," *UCLA Daily Bruin*, July 30, 1963, 1; Diane Smith, "Must Separate Races in South Africa—Zulu: Clergyman Speaks to UCLA Students

on African Racial Problem," *UCLA Daily Bruin*, March 21, 1963; "65 Commence Peace
Corps' African Course," *UCLA Daily Bruin*, October 1, 1962, 1; "Africans Curious
About U.S. Politics," *UCLA Daily Bruin*, February 19, 1963, 1.

25 Dave Lawton, "Another Professor Fired: Bosses Silent on Ouster of Local
NAACP Sponsor," *UCLA Daily Bruin*, February 13, 1963, 1; "Interview with Maulana
Karenga," September 15, 1999, 11–12; "Black Leadership in Los Angeles: Robert
Singleton," *UCLA Center for African-American Studies*, Oral History Program, 1999, 165.

26 "Interview with Professor Sylvester Whitaker," audio recording, November 6,
2000.

27 "Memories," Michael Lofchie to Keith Mayes, email, October 12, 2000.

28 "Interview with Maulana Karenga," February 9, 1999, 2.

29 Quote taken from Armstead L. Robinson, Craig C. Foster, and Donald H.
Ogilvie, eds. *Black Studies in the University: A Symposium* (New Haven: Yale University
Press, 1969), 46.

30 "Interview with Maulana Karenga," September 15, 1999, 6–7.

31 Brown, "The US Organization," 78–95.

32 Quoted from US Cultural Organization Kanuni (Rules), reprinted in Brown,
"The US Organization," 96.

33 Clyde Halisi and James Mtume, eds. *The Quotable Karenga* (Los Angeles: US
Organization, 1967), 7, 11; Brown, "The US Organization," 126–27.

34 Brown, "The US Organization," 81–82, 86–87.

35 "Watts Today," *Life*, July 15, 1966.

36 "We Have Only One Power—To Disrupt Things," *Newsweek*, July 22, 1966; Jack
Sherpard, "In Burned-Out Watts: It's Now Baby," *Look Magazine*, June 28, 1966,
94–100.

37 *Los Angeles Free Press*, September 2, 1966.

38 "Black Leadership in Los Angeles: Marnesba Tackett," *UCLA Center for African-
American Studies*, Oral History Program, 1988, 142.

39 "Interview with Maulana Karenga," February 9, 1999, 7; "Interview with
Maulana Karenga," September 15, 1999, 2; John A. Buggs, "On Human Relations,"
*Los Angeles Sentinel*, July 25, 1965.

40 "Westminster Neighborhood Agency, We Believe in Power," *The Movement*
(January 1966), in *The Movement, 1964–1970*, ed. Clayborne Carson (Westport:
Greenwood Press, 1993), 98; Sherpard, "In Burned-Out Watts: It's Now Baby," *Look
Magazine* 30 (June 28, 1966), 94–96, 99–100; Terence Canon, "A Night With the Watts
Community Alert Patrol," and "A Meeting With Brother Lennie, There is a Necessity
For Brothers Being in the Streets Looking Out For Their Brothers," *The Movement*
(August/September 1966), in Carson, ed. *The Movement, 1964–1970*, 140, 151;
"Interview with Maulana Karenga," February 9, 1999, 7.

Though a cultural nationalist, Karenga and US worked in coalition with
traditional civil rights groups and other black nationalist organizations like the new
Oakland-based Black Panther Party that opened a chapter in Los Angeles in 1967.
The younger groups along with the more vetted NAACP, CORE, and black church
leaders all united under two umbrella organizations—the Temporary Alliance of Local

Organizations (TALO) and the Black Congress—for the sake of organizational unity and improving conditions for blacks in Los Angeles. As one account reported, "when TALO was formed it was the only organization in the history of Los Angeles that succeeded in getting the bourgeois Negro, CORE, SNCC [Student Nonviolent Coordinating Committee], US, SLANT . . . the Slausons and the Businessman to sit down and try to do something positive for this community in the way of keeping the violence down." ("Westminister Neighborhood Agency, We Believe in Power," in Carson, ed. *The Movement: 1964–1970*, 98).

United under phrases popularized by Karenga, such as "operational unity," and "unity without uniformity," the coalition met frequently to strategize about a number of solutions for the rebuilding of local black neighborhoods (A.S. Young, "Ron Karenga Speaks Up on 'Unity Without Uniformity,'" *Los Angeles Sentinel*, April 11, 1968, B5).

Two proposals in particular show the extent to which the influence of the younger leadership had grown in Los Angeles. TALO created a Community Alert Patrol to monitor police practices in Watts and surrounding black neighborhoods. Operating as an independent civilian force, volunteers, who were mainly young blacks, traveled in cars equipped with two-way radios, recording the actions of the police and reporting back to responsible social agencies. The Community Alert Patrol would serve as a basis for other city civilian patrols as well as for the future police monitoring strategies of the Black Panther Party. TALO also proposed to secede Watts from Los Angeles to ensure that black Angelenos received fair municipal representation and services. As an idea hatched by SNCC inside of TALO, "Freedom City" was a proposal that would allow Watts to exist as a separate city with powers of incorporation. The idea attracted a high degree of support from civil rights leaders and public officials. Norman Houston of the NAACP believed that Freedom City would help foster black political power. Black City Councilman Billy G. Mills called Freedom City "exciting." So committed to the police patrols and the idea of Freedom City, traditional civil rights groups refused to allow police chief Parker and Mayor Yorty to prohibit TALO's younger organizations from a planned meeting to discuss the matters as the *Los Angeles Times* reported: "local heads of the NAACP, CORE, and other groups refused to enter the commission room in protest against what they called an ignoring of the Temporary Alliance of Local Organizations" by City Hall (Jack Jones, "Police Hearing Boycotted by Rights Groups," *Los Angeles Times*, June 11, 1966). If city officials attempted to ignore the presence and ideas of the younger cohort in TALO, then the national press certainly took notice of their emergence.

Though TALO represented a force to be reckoned with, internal strife caused the dissolution of the coalition by the end of 1966, giving rise to another united-front umbrella organization a year later, called the Black Congress. The Black Congress would contain the major civil rights organizations, community-based groups, and nationalist organizations, including the Los Angeles NAACP, SNCC, CORE, SLANT, United Parents Council, Operation Bootstrap, Black Students Alliance, Black Anti-Draft, US, and the Black Panthers. The Congress also united and held the support of Hispanic community activists, most notably, Cesar Chavez and Reies Tijerina, creating a black and brown alliance as well. Walt Bremond, a former employee in the Office of Economic Opportunity under President Kennedy, was elected as chairman because of his non-affiliation with any of the member organizations. Bremond could be found at the Black Congress headquarters on 73rd and Broadway in South Central, making sure an office bustling with organizational activity ran smoothly. As an observer reported, "The Simbas of US are practicing Swahili chants in the back room. The Black Panthers are meeting across the hall. Members of Black Perspectives . . . are banging out press releases on clacking typewriters. People are wandering in and out. Wives, in search of husbands last seen huddling with the ever-meeting executive councils are pressed into answering telephones and cutting stencils." ("Black Congress Ask Medi-Care Funds Be Cut," *Herald-Dispatch*, September 27, 1967, 1.)

Besides day-to-day activities, the Black Congress often took to the streets, organizing one rally in support of Huey Newton, indicted in late 1967 for the killing of Oakland police officer John Frey. The "Free Huey" conference took place at the Los Angeles Sports Arena on February 17, 1968, attracting five thousand blacks, whites, and Latinos. Presiding over the rally was James Forman of SNCC. The Reverend Thomas Kilgore, Bobby Seale, Karenga, and Reies Tijerina—the Mexican-American protest leader, attended the rally and provided commentary. Discussions ranged widely from retaliatory confrontations with the police, the "misguided war" in Vietnam, operational unity, and the defense of Huey P. Newton. Some speeches focused so much on confronting the police, Karenga tried to keep the focus on Newton's plight, telling the interracial crowd, "that's what we are here today for—to discuss . . . the defense of Huey Newton." (Doc Stanley, "Black Power, Every Negro is a Potential Blackman," *Herald-Dispatch*, February 22, 1968, 3.)

The US and Black Panther partnership under the auspices of the Black Congress turned sour as a result of the growing influence of both organizations in the coalition and in the southern California region. Specifically, Karenga, according to Congress member Ayuko Babu, was known to criticize the Panther's revolutionary rhetoric during Black Congress meetings, announcing once "I don't understand bloods. You all talk revolution all day long. If you really want to fight the white man, wait until the sun goes down, we'll be ready, US is always ready." (Babu quoted in Brown, "The US Organization," 164, 268.) Karenga's statement implied that the Panthers were more talk than action, filling Congress meetings and sponsored events in Los Angeles with revolutionary verbosity. Likewise, the Panthers never appreciated the cultural approach taken by Karenga and the US Organization, stating "those who believe in the 'I'm Black and Proud' theory—believe that there is dignity inherent in wearing naturals; that a buba makes a slave a man; and that a common language, Swahili, makes all of us brothers." (Linda Harrison, "On Cultural Nationalism," in Philip Foner, ed. *The Black Panthers Speak* (New York: Da Capo Press, 1995 [1970]), 151.) Though both groups raised the banner of Black Power in Los Angeles and nationally, the Panthers' approach to solving the problems in African-American communities differed from solutions proposed by Karenga's US Organization, giving way to what historian Scot Brown called "competing vanguard conceptions and strategies" that ended in deadly consequences (Brown, "The US Organization," 164, 268).

The Los Angeles press discerned the developing confrontation between the Panthers and US when one newspaper reported in August of 1968 that "the Black Panther organization, based in Oakland [is] . . . trying to muscle in on the Los Angeles scene." ("Strange Man is Savior," *Los Angeles Sentenel*, August 22, 1968, A1.) The Panthers' presence in Los Angeles, however, was not solely organizational. Like some US members, Panthers attended southern California colleges, most notably UCLA. Black Panthers Alprentice "Bunchy" Carter, John Huggins, and Elaine Brown were UCLA students, with Huggins acting as campus organizer and one of the founders of the Black Student Union at the university. The Black Student Union became the center of a dispute involving the creation of a Black Studies program in 1968 and 1969. The Panthers and US disagreed over who would direct the newly founded Center of Afro-American Studies at UCLA. Each group supported a different candidate for Executive Director. On January 17, 1969, a Black Student Union meeting at Campbell Hall erupted into a spontaneous gun battle between US and Panthers, leading to the deaths of Huggins and Carter. Three members of Karenga's US Organization, George Stiner-Ali, Larry Stiner-Watani, and Donald Hawkins-Stodi, were tried and convicted for murder. In New York City at the time of the incident, Karenga was not legally implicated, but the Panthers and the media vilified him in the court of public opinion. The incident sparked a wave of retaliatory shooting incidents by Panther members and led to the resignation of Walt Bremond from the Black Congress on January 30, 1969. The coalition in the Black Congress had unofficially come apart.

The incident at UCLA proved to be a prelude to more trouble for Karenga and the US Organization. A year later, Karenga was charged with assaulting two women in his organization. According to the trial testimony of Karenga's estranged first wife, he believed the women had attempted to poison him with crystals. One of the victims testified that Karenga and a few members of his organization retaliated by placing the women's toes in vise grips and torturing them with a water hose and soldering iron. Karenga and supporters contended that the charges were fabricated as part of the larger campaign of state repression of black nationalist groups as carried out by J. Edgar Hoover's COINTELPRO. Evidence does suggest that Karenga and his organization were a priority of the FBI, successfully fomenting bad relations between the Panthers and US. Karenga was convicted of assault, and beginning in 1971, he spent four years at the Men's Colony in San Luis Obispo, California. (Ron Einstoss, "Black Militant Chief Karenga Arrested on Torture Charges," *Los Angeles Times*, October 7, 1970, pt. 1, p. 3; "Karenga's Wife Tells All at Trial," *Los Angeles Sentinel*, May 20, 1971, A1, A4; David Lamb, "Karenga, Two Others Found Guilty of Torturing Woman," *Los Angeles Times*, May 30, 1971, section B, p. 3; Kenneth O'Reilly, *Racial Matters: The FBI's Secret File on Black America, 1960–1972* (New York: The Free Press, 1989), 305–9; Imamu Clyde Halisi, "Maulana Ron Karenga: Black Leader in Captivity," *Black Scholar* 3 (May 1972), 27–31; "The State: Parole Application," *Los Angeles Times*, May 3, 1973, 2; Celeste Durant, "The Watts Rebuilding Dream is a Dream Deferred, A Quest for Change Goes On," *Los Angeles Times*, March 23, 1975; Brown, "The US Organization," 312–14. For a complete history of the US versus Panther conflict see Brown, *Fighting for US*.

41 "Observance Set for Malcolm X," *Los Angeles Sentinel*, February 3, 1966, A1, A4; "First Annual Memorial Staged for Malcolm X," *Los Angeles Sentinel*, March 3, 1966, A11; former US member and a relative of Malcolm X, Hakim Jamal staged Malcolm X commemorations on the black Muslim leader's birthday on May 19 called Kuzaliwa, with his former colleagues in US, but particularly after Jamal's departure from the organization in 1967. Hakim Jamal, "Celebration Planned for Malcolm X," *Los Angeles Sentinel*, May 16, 1968, B9. For US's first public appearance, see Clay Carson, "A Talk with Ron Karenga, Watts Black Nationalist," *Los Angeles Free Press*, September 2, 1966, 12.

42 "Riot Disrupts Malcolm X Meeting . . . ," *Los Angeles Sentinel*, May 25, 1967, A3.

43 Quoted in Brown, *Fighting for US*, 76–77.

44 "Observance Set for Malcolm X," *Los Angeles Sentinel*, February 3, 1966, 4.

45 Ibid.

46 Quoted in Brown, *Fighting for US*, 68.

47 Brown, *Fighting for US*, 68.

48 Marguerite Ross Barnett, *The Politics of Cultural Nationalism in South India* (Princeton: Princeton UP, 1976).

49 Eric Hobsbawm and Terence Ranger, eds. *The Invention of Tradition* (Cambridge: Cambridge UP, 1983), 4–5, 8.

50 Clyde Halisi, ed. *Kitabu: Beginning Concepts in Kawaida* (Los Angeles: Temple of Kawaida, 1971), 6.

51 Brown, *Fighting for US*, 51.

52 Halisi and Mtume, eds. *The Quotable Karenga*, 2.

53 Halisi, ed. *Kitabu*, 1, 5fn, 7.

54 Ibid., 7.

55 Ibid., 7, 12fn.

56 Hobsbawm and Ranger, eds. *The Invention of Tradition*, 9.

57 Halisi and Mtume, eds. *The Quotable Karenga*, 26–27.

58 Halisi, ed. *Kitabu*, 7; Halisi and Mtume, eds. *The Quotable Karenga*, 25.

59 Halisi, ed. *Kitabu*, 1.

60 Quote taken from Brown, *Fighting for US*, 9–10.

61 Halisi, ed. *Kitabu*, 2fn; Brown, "The US Organization," 97–99. Brown writes that in Kawaida, even the numbers themselves had meanings. The number 7 was considered the black man's number, or the numbers 7, 5, and 3 were pro-black while the number 6 was designated for and about whites.

62 Brown, "The US Organization," 101–2.

63 Carson, "A Talk With Ron Karenga, Watts Black Nationalist," *Los Angeles Free Press*, September 2, 1966, 12.

64 Massachusetts Review (Sept. 1966) contained in *Stokely Speaks: Black Power Back to Pan-Africanism* (New York: Random House, 1971), 31–43; for Carmichael's longer and more thoughtful reflection on Black Power, see Stokely Carmichael and Charles Hamilton, *Black Power* (New York: Vintage, 1967).

65 James Meredith, one of the first African-Americans to bring national attention to the issue of desegregation in higher education, integrated the University of Mississippi in 1962 by becoming the first black to attend. As a result of his protest at

"Ole Miss" and his ongoing participation in southern civil rights protests, he decided to conduct a "March Against Fear" in June of 1966. On his 200-mile journey from Memphis, Tennessee to Jackson, Mississippi he was shot and wounded. Major civil rights leaders, such as Martin Luther King and Stokely Carmichael, decided to continue the march for Meredith. In Greenwood, Mississippi, the SNCC field secretary Willie Ricks and Stokely Carmichael engaged in a call-and-response routine with marchers that involved discontinuing the famous civil rights slogan, "Freedom Now" for the new "Black Power" chant. During a rally in Greenwood Carmichael announced: "The only way we gonna stop them white men from whuppin' us is to take over. We been saying freedom for six years and we ain't got nothin'. What do you want?" The marchers yelled, "Black Power! Black Power! Black Power!" The new Black Power chant would suddenly move from slogan to a sophisticated analytical assessment about the direction the Black Freedom Movement should assume.

66 "Negro Cry: 'Black Power!'—What Does it Mean?" *U.S. News & World Report*, July 11, 1966; "A Negro Congressman Talks About 'Black Power': Interview with Representative Adam Clayton Powell," *U.S. News & World Report*, August 15, 1966.

67 Eugene Genovese, *Roll Jordan Roll: The World the Slaves Made* (New York: Pantheon, 1972), 578.

68 Darius Anthony, "Kwanzaa: A Holiday Tribute to Africa," *Soul*, December 25, 1978.

69 Halisi and Mtume, eds. *The Quotable Karenga*, 1.

70 "Interview with Clyde Daniels-Halisi," April 30, 2001; "Interview with Karl Key-Hekima," April 24, 2001.

71 Charles Stewart and Rosalind Shaw, eds. *Sycretism/Anti-Syncretism: The Politics of Religious Synthesis* (New York: Routledge, 1994).

72 Gladys Marie Fry, *Stitched from the Soul: Slave Quilts from the Antebellum South* (New York: Dutton Studio Books, 1990); Maude Southwell Wahlman, *Signs and Symbols: African Images in American Quilts* (New York: Studio Books, 1993); Barbara Brackman, *Facts and Fabrications: Unraveling the History of Quilts and Slavery* (Concord, CA: C&T Publishing, 2006).

73 Timothy E. Fulop and Albert Rabateau, eds. *African-American Religion: Interpretive Essays in History and Culture* (New York: Routledge, 1997).

74 Toure, *Toward Full Re-Africanization*, 7–8.

75 Halisi, ed. *Kitabu*, 14

76 Derek Nurse and Thomas Spear, *The Swahili: Reconstructing the History and Language of an African Society, 800–1500* (Philadelphia: University of Pennsylvania Press, 1985); Adhama Kijembe, "Swahili and Black Americans," *Negro Digest* 18 (July 1969), 4–8; also see Swahili lessons given in several issues of the *Black Collegian* in the early 1970s. "Swahili Lesson," *Black Collegian*, May/June 1973, 50–51.

77 Alamin Mazrui, *Swahili Beyond the Boundaries: Literature, Language, and Identity* (Athens: Ohio University Press, 2007), 1–14. James de Vere Allen, *Swahili Origins* (Athens: Ohio University Press, 1993); Wilfred Whiteley, *Swahili: The Rise of a National Language* (London: Methuen & Co., 1974 [1969]), 101; see a very cogent essay on gender and the appropriation of African traditions, E. Francis White, "Africa on My

Mind: Gender, Counter Discourse and African-American Nationalism," *Journal of Women's History* 2 (Spring 1990), 73–97.

78 During the first half of 1966, Karenga identified seven principles he believed could potentially make life better for African-Americans. These principles were not new, but part and parcel of Kawaida thought. Like other doctrinal points or positions, he applied Swahili names to them, giving the seven principles definitions as was customary in Kawaida. Before the seven principles assumed the authority of values in a new holiday, they were commonly held as the seven principles of blackness. Though part of the original Kawaida framework, the definitions of the seven principles remained static, retaining much of their meaning with only slight modifications when they were transferred over to the Kwanzaa holiday.

The first, and probably the most important principle of Kwanzaa was **UMOJA** derived from the word MOJA, which means "one." From MOJA, or one, Karenga defined it as **UNITY**. In 1966, Karenga explained, "we are interested in two types of unity; total unity, which is an idea for the future, and operational unity, that is alliance with all other organizations on common community problems in order to solve them." Operational unity was the catch phrase Karenga used on the streets of Los Angeles in the mid-1960s to form working coalitions with other civil rights and black nationalist groups. Several years later, he de-contextualized the concept and gave it a more general definition for Kwanzaa: *to strive for and maintain unity in the family, community, nation, and race* (Carson, "A Talk with Ron Karenga, Watts Black Nationalist," *Los Angeles Free Press*, September 2, 1966, 12; Imamu Clyde Halisi, ed. *Kwanzaa: The First Fruits* (Los Angeles: US Organization, unpublished pamphlet, 1968?), 9; Maulana Ron Karenga, *Kwanzaa: May Your Holiday Be with Much Happiness* (San Diego: Kawaida Publications, 1975), 4.)

The second principle is **KUJICHAGULIA**, from the word CHAGUA, meaning choose. CHAGUA could also mean elect or select. When the word KUJICHAGULIA is directly translated, it means self-choice. Karenga applied the word to the African-American experience in the 1960s, defining it as **SELF-DETERMINATION**. "We believe," Karenga insisted, "that it is ultimately important that *we define and speak for ourselves instead of always being defined and spoken for by others*." Karenga's KUJICHAGULIA was partly motivated by the call of Black Power and the movement's emphasis on closing ranks and internally determining its own direction (Carson, "A Talk with Ron Karenga, Watts Black Nationalist," *Los Angeles Free Press*, September 2, 1966, 12; Halisi, ed. *Kwanzaa*, 9).

The third principle is **UJIMA**. UZIMA is the closest word in Swahili, meaning life, but this Swahili term is far from Karenga's UJIMA, which he defined as **COLLECTIVE WORK AND RESPONSIBILITY**. By collective work and responsibility, Karenga envisioned the black community building and maintaining itself from within or as he said, "*to make our brother's problems ours and solve them together*." In 1966, Karenga cast UJIMA as a critique against American individualism, announcing, "we believe that individualism is non-functional. It is a cancer in the black man's community. It has taught him to say 'I can make it,' and forget the others. Individualism is a non-African value, a Western value that we cannot afford to assimilate." (Carson, "A Talk with Ron Karenga, Watts Black Nationalist," 12; Halisi, ed. *Kwanzaa*, 9.)

The fourth principle of Kwanzaa is **UJAMAA**, derived from the root JAMAA, meaning one's family. The history of the word UJAMAA developed in the East African country of Tanzania where President Julius Nyerere popularized the term during his struggle to overthrow British rule. Appropriating the word that meant family or familyhood, Nyerere redefined UJAMAA as Tanzanian socialism. Nyerere rightly admitted that UJAMMA was not a direct translation for socialism, explaining "nor did this word result solely from the desire to find a Swahili equivalent for the word socialism." But Nyerere believed socialism was built on a form of African communalism, an indigenous economic system of shared wealth. "By use of the word ujamaa," Nyerere said, "we state that for us socialism involves building on the foundation of our past, and building also to our own design." Karenga took Nyerere's approach of building on the foundation of the past, and also adopted the word UJAMAA as the fourth of Kwanzaa's seven principles to mean **COOPERATIVE ECONOMICS**. Initially, the basis of Karenga's cooperative economics was to form cooperatives so "we can have meaningful competition with the outsiders who control the economy of our community." He subsequently de-emphasized cooperatives and instead labeled his brand of UJAMAA as a commitment *to build and maintain black businesses*, spend money with one another, and "*to profit together from them*." (Carson, "A Talk with Ron Karenga, Watts Black Nationalist," *Los Angeles Free Press*, September 2, 1966, 12; Halisi, ed. *Kwanzaa*, 9; Julius K. Nyerere, *Freedom and Socialism / Uhuru Na Ujamma: A Selection from Writings and Speeches 1965–1967* (London: Oxford University Press, 1968), 2.)

**NIA** represents the fifth principle Karenga used in Kwanzaa. NIA has multiple meanings and uses in Swahili: objective, motive, intention, and the word Karenga decided to use as its definition: **PURPOSE**. Karenga defined purpose as collective vocational community building, or nation building—a task he thought should be for all African-Americans. NIA resembles UJIMA in the sense that it advocates communal responsibility, that of obligating social purpose. Moved by Frantz Fanon's assessment that "each generation must . . . discover its mission, fulfill it or betray it," Karenga believed the common purpose of blacks was to "participate in creating a context of maximum freedom and development" for other African-Americans, ultimately restoring them to what he understood as their traditional greatness before European or American interruption (Carson, "A Talk with Ron Karenga, Watts Black Nationalist," *Los Angeles Free Press*, September 2, 1966, 12; Halisi, ed. *Kwanzaa*, 9; Frantz Fanon, *The Wretched of the Earth* (New York: Grove Press, 1968), 167; Maulana Karenga, *Kwanzaa: A Celebration of Family, Community, and Culture* (Los Angeles: University of Sankore Press, 1998), 60.)

The sixth principle is **KUUMBA** from the root UMBA, which means create, build, make, or shape. As black culture manifested itself in various forms during the mid-1960s, the idea of creativity permeated the cultural politics of the period, forcing Karenga to define his concept in a familiar 1960s tone: "the next thing we are interested in is Kuumba, which is **CREATIVITY**. We believe in Soul, which is an emotional quality that is the source of our creativity." For many artists, "soul" proved explicitly important in black creativity. Karenga, however, subsequently left KUUMBA an open-ended concept, expressing it in the following way: *"to do as much as we can, in the way we can, to leave our community more beautiful and beneficial than we inherited it."* The final principle, **IMANI**, also included multiple meanings in Swahili, such as compassion, confidence, and belief. It also means **FAITH**, which Karenga applied to Imani to mean *faith in parents, teachers, and leaders, as well as the "righteousness" of the black freedom struggle*. With each individual principle defined, Karenga subsequently translated the concept, *"Seven Principles"* in the original English into the Swahili, *Nguzo Saba* (Carson, "A Talk with Ron Karenga, Watts Black Nationalist," *Los Angeles Free Press*, September 2, 1966, 12; Halisi, ed., *Kwanzaa*, 9). For early definitions of the Seven Principles see Carson, "A Talk With Ron Karenga, Watts Black Nationalist," 12; Halisi, ed. *Kwanzaa*, 9.

For later uses of the Nguzo Saba in African-American communities as a form of black psychotherapy and cultural uplift, see Frederick B. Phillips, "NTU Psychotherapy: An Afrocentric Approach," *Journal of Black Psychology* 17, no. 1 (Fall 1990): 55–74; and Pamela M. Foster, Frederick Phillips, Faye Z. Belgrave, Suzanne M. Randolph, and Noel Braithwaite, "An Afrocentric Model for Aids Education, Prevention, and Psychological Services within the African American Community," *Journal of Black Psychology* 19, no. 2 (May 1993): 123–41.

79 Karenga and the US Organization's creation of new Swahili words in the United States by altering existing Swahili words and phrases from the East African context caused some confusion with the black Americans in regards to the holiday's spelling. The US Organization used two a's from the holiday's inception. The two a's as opposed to the original one 'a' was a way for Karenga and US to brand their new holiday as slightly different from the word's African roots. Moreover, two a's cohered with Karenga's preoccupation with things adding up to seven. There were seven days, corresponding to seven principles, that better corresponded with seven letters (Kwanzaa) and not six (kwanza). Karenga also added to the 'two a' theory by positing the desire on the part of one child in 1966 during the very first Kwanzaa celebration who felt left out of an activity where six kids were chosen to represent the letters of the holiday by holding placards of each letter. According to Karenga, his desire to include the child in the ceremony precipitated the adding of another 'a' to the word. This perhaps may be apocrypha and US Organization lore but the fact is that Kwanzaa had always been spelled with two a's by Karenga and his organization. Most Black Power groups followed US's lead and spelled Kwanzaa with two a's. In the late 1960s and early 1970s other Black Power organizations, such as the Committee for a Unified Newark (CFUN) and the Congress of African People (CAP) spelled Kwanzaa with one 'a' (Kwanza). During the first decade of the holiday's existence, the spelling of Kwanzaa appeared to remain an organizational choice. By the 1980s and 1990s, almost all persons and organizations used the original US Organization version. For Karenga's 'two a' theory see Karenga, *Kwanzaa* (1998), 17.

80 M. Ron Karenga, *Kwanzaa: Origins, Concepts, Practices* (Inglewood, CA: Kawaida Publications, 1977). Toure, *Toward Full Re-Africanization*.

81 It is important to note that Karenga's initial understanding of African cultural practices came via books, not from first-hand observations. He would visit Africa for

the first time during the Second World Black and African Festival of Arts (FESTAC) in Lagos, Nigeria in 1977. See Brown, *Fighting for US*, 159.

82 Eileen Jensen Krige, *The Social System of the Zulus* (Pietermaritzburg: Shuter & Shooter, 1965 [1936]), 249.

83 Ibid., 280–82.

84 T.V. Bulpin, *Natal and the Zulu Country* (Cape Town: Books of Africa, 1966), 200.

85 Krige, *The Social System of the Zulus*, 249–60; Henri A. Junod, *The Life of a South African Tribe*, vol. 2 (2 vols. New Hyde Park, NY: University Books, 1966), 28; W.C. Willoughby, *The Soul of the Bantu* (London: Student Christian Movement, 1928), 225–50. Although Karenga drew heavily from Zulu and other South African first fruit ceremonies, other harvest festivals in different regions in Africa also inspired him. See D.G. Coursey, "The New Yam Festival Among the Ewe," *Ghana Notes and Queries* (December 1968), 18–23.

86 Karenga, *Kwanzaa* (1977), 25.

87 John Searle, *Speech Acts* (Cambridge: Cambridge University Press, 1969); Richard Bauman, "Verbal Art as Performance," *American Anthropologist* 77, no. 1 (1975), 290–311; William L. Van Deburg, *New Day in Babylon: The Black Power Movement and American Culture, 1965–1975* (Chicago: University of Chicago Press, 1992), 216–24.

88 Catherine Bell, *Ritual: Perspectives and Dimensions* (New York: Oxford University Press, 1997), 160. Barbara Myerhoff quote taken from Bell, 160.

Much of where Kwanzaa derives its power is at the level of signs, not symbols. Kwanzaa's holiday symbols—the mat, the candleholder, the candles, the corn, the cup, the crop, the principles—are ordinarily simple, and if made to function independently, appear arbitrary and uncommunicative. But as cultural linguists have taught, it is at the level of signs that rituals are provided with their communicative thrust and authority. Catherine Bell neatly summarizes the difference between symbols and signs:

> A symbol evokes a metaphorical, paradigmatic, or synchronic relationship between itself and what it refers to. A sign, on the other hand, involves a metonymical, syntagmatic, or diachronic relationship between itself and its referent. Signs, as opposed to symbols, do not occur in isolation; they are always contiguous with other signs that together form part of a set; it is only as part of a set that a sign can communicate information. For example, a green light means "go" only as part of the set of juxtaposed colored lights, red, yellow, and green (65).

Kwanzaa's candleholder is illustrative here as a "sign," for the Kinara not only represents the origin of where African people came from, but the Kinara's seven holes, representing that the seven days of Kwanzaa cannot function without its seven red, black, and green candles. The red candles inside of the left three holes represent the blood of blacks spilled on slave ships, southern plantations, and in Jim Crow trees. The green candles inside of the right three holes represent the continental birthplace of Africa. The middle black candle represents the struggle of African-Americans waged against white supremacy in the United States. Pull the candles out of the Kinara and place them idly on the table, the entire sign ceases to function. The candles as well as the Kinara are reduced to the level of symbol. Thus, syntagmatic associations, like the Kinara, the straw mat it sits on, the candles, and the ear of corn, "are chainlike relationships among elements in a type of series, such as the relationship among letters that make up a word, the musical notes that make up a melody, or the words that make up a poem." Bell, *Ritual*, 64–5.

89 Theodore C. Humphrey and Lin T. Humphrey, eds. *We Gather Together: Food and Festival in American Life* (Ann Arbor: UMI Research Press, 1988).

90 A staple activity of the US Organization's Taifa Dance Troupe was the performance of the boot dance—a traditional dance created by black diamond mine workers in South Africa who trekked in and out of the mines making music and dance with their rubber boots. South African songstress Letta Mbulu and her musician–composer husband Caiphus Semanya helped the US Organization learn a number of songs and Zulu dances in the late 1960s. For the relationship between South African artists and the US Organization as well as the importance of black musical culture see Brown, *Fighting for US*, 132–44.

91 Quote taken from Brown, *Fighting for US*, 71; Karenga, *Kwanzaa* (1998), 103–5.

92 Halisi, ed. *Kwanzaa*, 5.

93 Ibid., 7, 9.

94 Halisi, ed. *Kitabu*, 7, 13fn; Krige, *The Social System of the Zulus*, 280–81.

95 Halisi, ed. *Kwanzaa*, 11, 13.

96 Ibid.

97 Halisi, ed. *Kwanzaa*; Karenga, *Kwanzaa* (1975); Karenga, *Kwanzaa* (1977). The Kikombe, the Swahili word for cup, was not technically a new symbol as cups had been used for pouring libations in the name of the ancestors since the very first Kwanzaa. What made the Kikombe new by 1977 was its inclusion in the pantheon of major Kwanzaa symbols. Similarly, Marcus Garvey's revised black nationalist color scheme of black, red, and green had always played an important role in Kwanzaa decorative arrangements. In his second Kwanzaa publication dated 1977 as in earlier Kwanzaa pamphlets, Karenga advised all celebrants to "keep in mind that décor must be in an African motif and that Black, Red, and Green should be prominent colors in it." He repeated the same instruction in the 1988 publication. However, it was not until 1998, his latest work on Kwanzaa, that a Bendera (flag) bearing those colors appeared, becoming an official symbol in Kwanzaa settings. Karenga, *Kwanzaa* (1977), 51; Maulana Karenga, *The African American Holiday of Kwanzaa: A Celebration of Family, Community & Culture* (Los Angeles: University of Sankore Press, 1988), 103; Karenga, *Kwanzaa* (1998), 88–89, 107.

The activities of Kwanzaa also followed a changing course. In the 1960s and early 1970s, the Karamu was the only activity referenced in Kwanzaa instructional literature. However, evidence suggests that during the early Karamus in the US Organization, other ceremonial exercises took place, such as libations (Tambiko), ancestor naming, candle lighting, the official greeting of Habari Gani (what news? and its accompanied response, Njema), as well as the Harambee—an East African call-to-unity chant defined by Karenga, meaning "let's pull together." Though present during Kwanzaa's first ten years, these occurrences were not recognized as major activities until 1977. Between 1977 and 1988, two other activities were added: the Day of Meditation (Siku ya Taamuli) on January 1 for purposes of self-reflection, and Umoja Night—a candle-lighting ceremony by community leaders. "1969 Kwanzaa Program," US Organization, School of Afroamerican Culture, Education Committee, n.d.; Karenga, *Kwanzaa* (1977), 24–25; Karenga, *The African American Holiday of Kwanzaa*, 99–100.

98 Karenga, *Kwanzaa* (1975), unpaginated.

99 Karenga, *Kwanzaa* (1975), unpaginated; Karenga, *The African American Holiday of Kwanzaa*, 36–38; Karenga, *Kwanzaa* (1998), 37–41; Maulana Karenga, "MAAT – The Moral Ideal in Ancient Egypt: A Study in Classical African Ethics" (PhD dissertation, University of Southern California, 1994); Maulana Karenga, *Selections from the Husia: Sacred Wisdom of Ancient Egypt* (Los Angeles: University of Sankore Press, 1984); Maulana Karenga, *Odu Ifa: The Ethical Teachings* (Los Angeles: University of Sankore Press, 1999).

100 Carson, "A Talk With Ron Karenga, Watts Black Nationalist," *Los Angeles Free Press*, September 2, 1966, 12.

101 Karenga, *Kwanzaa* (1998), 45, 54.

102 "Interview with Karl Key-Hekima," April 24, 2001, 4–5.

103 "Interview with Faida Mtume," audio recording, side A, February 3, 2004.

104 "Interview with Oliver Heshimu," audio recording, side A, February 16, 2004.

105 Karenga, *Kwanzaa* (1998), 106.

106 "Interview with Clyde Daniels-Halisi," April 30, 2001, 14; "Interview with Oliver Heshimu," audio recording, side A, February 16, 2004.

107 The memory of some original US members is fuzzy as to the name of the gentleman who opened his home to the first Karamu. Scot Brown's book on the US Organization mentions a man named Noble Hanif, but no clear consensus on the name of the man was reached by original members of US when interviewed. The consensus is that it was an US supporter, someone who attended Sunday afternoon Soul Sessions, but not an official member of the organization.

108 "Interview with Clyde Daniels-Halisi," April 30, 2001, 4.

109 The US Organization, School of Afroamerican Culture, Education Committee, "1969 Kwanzaa Program," n.d., 5.

110 Two original US members recall Karenga searching for a candleholder with seven holes. Unable to find one in Los Angeles in 1966, Karenga and the US Organization used a Jewish Menorah and plugged up two holes for the first Kwanzaa. The very first Kwanzaa candleholder, the Kinara, was made for the following year's Kwanzaa in 1967 by US member Buddy Rose-Aminifu. Early photographs confirm the rudimentary nature of the first Kinara—a wooden log with holes drilled into it. "Interview with Buddy Rose-Aminifu," May 23, 2001; "Interview with Clyde Halisi," April 30, 2001.

111 Elizabeth Softky, "A Kwanzaa Memory: Growing Up with Dr. Karenga," *Washington Post*, December 20, 1995, E4.

112 "1969 Kwanzaa Program," 7.

113 Ibid., 6.

114 Ibid., 5.

115 Softky, "A Kwanzaa Memory," *Washington Post*, December 20, 1995, E4.

116 Iya Afin and Ayobunmi Sangode, *Rites of Passage: Psychology of Female Power* (Brooklyn, NY: Athelia Henrietta Press, 1999), 9–10.

117 "Interview with Ngoma Ali," May 15, 2001, 5.

118 "Interview with Faida Mtume," audio recording, side A, February 3, 2004.

119 "In Perspective: Karenga's Mission is for Posterity," *The Hilltop*, January 5, 1968, 3.

## 3 KWANZAA, CULTURAL NATIONALISM, AND THE PROMOTION OF A BLACK POWER HOLIDAY

1 To privilege the "public" Kwanzaa is not to deny the existence of "private" Kwanzaa ceremonies. But during the late 1960s and 1970s at the height of the Black Power Movement, it was difficult to separate the two given the politically charged atmosphere of black nationalism. In many cases, the private was often public due to the affiliations and ideological leanings of those who would stage such celebrations both in their homes and in public. This is not to suggest that every private Kwanzaa staged during the Black Power period had movement implications. But I posit that the private Kwanzaa realm, void of any deep movement undertones, was generally a product of a later post-black nationalist moment.

2 For an example of the interplay between national and local manifestations of Black Power, see Komozi Woodard, *A Nation Within a Nation: Amiri Baraka (LeRoi Jones) & Black Power Politics* (Chapel Hill: University of North Carolina Press, 1999) and James Edward Smethurst, *The Black Arts Movement: Literary Nationalism in the 1960s and 1970s* (Chapel Hill: University of North Carolina Press, 2005).

3 "Preface" in *The Black Public Sphere: A Public Culture Book*, ed. Black Public Sphere Collective (Chicago: University of Chicago Press, 1995), 2–3.

4 My use of the black public sphere has been greatly shaped by the essays contained in the Black Public Sphere Collective, eds. *The Black Public Sphere*, particularly Houston A. Baker, Jr., "Critical Memory and the Black Public Sphere," Michael Dawson, "A Black Counterpublic?: Economic Earthquakes, Racial Agenda(s), and Black Politics," Regina Austin, "'A Nation of Thieves': Consumption, Commerce, and the Black Public Sphere," Rosemary J. Coombe and Paul Stoller, "X Marks the Spot: The Ambiguities of African Trading in the Commerce of the Black Public Sphere," and Thomas Holt, "Afterword: Mapping the Black Public Sphere."

5 Michael Dawson, "A Black Counterpublic?: Economic Earthquakes, Racial Agenda(s), and Black Politics," in the Black Public Sphere Collective, eds. *The Black Public Sphere*, 204.

6 Joann Stevens, "A Lifestyle Called Kwanzaa, Black Maryland Families Celebrate a Week of Ceremonies That Reflect Age-Old African Traditions," *Washington Post*,

December 27, 1979, Md3; Edward D. Sargent, "Alternative Festival, 'Kwanzaa' Celebrates Spirit of Community and Heritage," *Washington Post*, December 25, 1980, DC4; Eugene L. Meyer, "Kwanzaa Reaffirms Roots, Holiday Lets Americans Honor African Heritage," *Washington Post*, December 26, 1986, C1; Pam Carroll, "Celebrating an African Companion to Christmas," *Washington Post*, December 24, 1987, DC1.

7 Edward Soja, *Thirdspace: Journeys to Los Angeles and Other Real-and-Imagined Places* (Cambridge, MA: Blackwell, 1996); Edward Soja, *Postmodern Geographies: The Reassertion of Space in Critical Social Theory* (London: Verso, 1989); Jonathan Murdoch, *Post-Structuralist Geography: A Guide to Relational Space* (Thousand Oaks, CA: Sage, 2006); Doreen Massey, *Space, Place, and Gender* (Minneapolis: University of Minnesota Press, 1994).

8 William E. Cross, Jr., "The Negro-to-Black Conversion Experience: Toward a Psychology of Black Liberation," *Black World*, July 1971.

9 Vernon Sukumu, future chair of the US chapter in San Diego, remembered the first Kwanzaa in 1967: "We had it in [Joe] Chochezi's house; some brothers from Los Angeles came down and officiated the ceremony." Vernon Sukumu, interview by author, Carson, CA, May 12, 2001, 3. For an assessment of San Diego's US chapter see Scot Brown, *Fighting for US: Maulana Karenga, the US Organization, and Black Cultural Nationalism* (New York: NYU Press, 2003), 44.

10 Angela Davis, *Angela Davis: An Autobiography* (New York: International Publishers, 1988 [1974]), 158.

11 Douglas Hartmann, *Race, Culture, and the Revolt of the Black Athlete: The 1968 Olympic Protests and Their Aftermath* (Chicago: University of Chicago Press, 2003), 56–59; Amy Bass, *Not the Struggle But the Triumph: The 1968 Olympics and the Making of the Black Athlete* (Minneapolis: University of Minnesota Press, 2002), 90–92, 203.

12 Quote taken from Hartmann, *Race, Culture, and the Revolt of the Black Athlete*, 57.

13 Davis, *Angela Davis: An Autobiography*, 159.

14 Smith enrolled at Oakland's Merritt College in 1965. Her entry into Merritt College coincided with the growing sentiment toward Black Power in the Bay area and around the country. Smith came to Merritt at the same time as Black Panther Party members Huey Newton and Bobby Seale. Though Smith never became a Black Panther, she gravitated toward the black student organization at Merritt called the Soul Students' Advisory Council (SSAC) of which Newton and Seale were members. "I became a member there in February of 1966," Smith recalled, "and was introduced to the new way of thinking about [being] black on a predominantly white campus." Smith remembers the meeting in the SSAC when Newton and Seale announced their intention to leave the SSAC to form a new organization called the Black Panther Party for Self Defense. "Interview with Makinya Sibeko-Kouate," June 26, 2000, 2.

15 Smith served as a student council representative in the fall of 1966 and was elected the first black president of the student body in May 1967. One of her aims was to take control of student budgets controlled by white campus organizations. "Smith Elected President, Five CSR Candidates Win," *Merritt College Reporter*, June 1, 1967.

16 Smith was born in 1925 and graduated from Berkeley High School in 1943. After working as a grocery checker in the 1950s and with the Berkeley Housing

Authority in the 1960s, Smith decided to obtain a college education at the age of forty. At age forty-one at the time of her meeting with Karenga, she was sixteen years his senior and someone he believed mature enough to promote Kwanzaa seriously.

17 "Interview with Makinya Sibeko-Kouate," June 26, 2000, 2.

18 Dan Wakefield, "Supernation at Peace and War," *Atlantic Monthly*, March 1968, 70–72.

19 "Interview with Makinya Sibeko-Kouate," December 29, 2000, 20.

20 "Interview with Makinya Sibeko-Kouate," April 2, 2001, 13–14.

21 "Interview with Makinya Sibeko-Kouate," June 26, 2000, 3.

22 Sister Makinya [Harriet Smith—Slave Name], "Asante Sana for the Organizing of the Kwanza Ceremonies in the San Francisco Bay Area," (1972?), personal papers of Makinya Sibeko-Kouate.

23 "Interview with Makinya Sibeko-Kouate," April 2, 2001, 10.

24 Ibid., 11.

25 Ibid., 10.

26 "Interview with Itibari Zulu," February 10, 1999, 3. Itibari Zulu and his brother Hurumu Zulu were members of the Berkeley Youth Alternative and accompanied Sister Makinya on the trip.

27 "An Invitation from the Pan-African People's Organization" (1972?), personal papers of Sister Makinya.

28 Delvin Walker, "Kwanzaa, An Original Afro-American Holiday Just For You," *Pamoja*, December, 1980, 23; "Bay Area Communities Celebrate Kwanzaa," *California Voice*, December 19, 1986, 1–2; Marilyn Bailey, "Kwanzaa, An Afro-American Holiday Evolves," *Oakland Tribune*, December 26, 1992, E1, E5; "Interview with Hurumu Zulu," April 12, 2000, 2.

29 For the details of Karenga's incarceration see Brown, *Fighting for US*, 121–29.

30 When asked by the author about the role Sister Makinya played in popularizing Kwanzaa in the Bay Area, Karenga said he did not remember her. He recalled being more familiar with the work of Thomatra Scott (known as Scotty) of the Young Adults of San Francisco in relation to the spread of Kwanzaa in the Bay Area. "Interview with Maulana Karenga," February 9, 1999, 8; "Interview with Makinya Sibeko-Kouate," June 26, 2000, 10.

31 Larry Neal, "Any Day Now: Black Art and Black Liberation," in *Black Poets and Prophets*, eds. Woodie King and Earl Anthony (New York: New American Library, 1972), 148–65. For a larger study of the Black Arts Movement, particularly its regional development, see Smethurst, *The Black Arts Movement*.

32 Amiri Baraka, *The Autobiography of LeRoi Jones* (Chicago: Lawrence Hill Books, 1997 [1984]), 306–7; LeRoi Jones, *Home: Social Essays* (New York: William Morrow & Co., 1966).

33 Baraka, *The Autobiography of LeRoi Jones*, 358–59.

34 For a detailed assessment of Kawaida see Chapter 2. For a thorough treatment of black cultural nationalism and Karenga's impact see Algernon Austin, *Achieving Blackness: Race, Black Nationalism and Afrocentrism in the Twentieth Century* (New York: NYU Press, 2006), 74–109.

35 Smethurst, *The Black Arts Movement*, 58.

36 Ibid., 79.

37 Amiri Baraka, *Daggers and Javelins: Essays, 1974–1979* (New York: Quill, 1984), 97, 106–7.

38 Imamu Amiri Baraka (LeRoi Jones), "A Black Value System," in King and Anthony, eds. *Black Poets and Prophets*, 143.

39 Ibid., 142.

40 Amiri Baraka, *Kawaida Studies: The New Nationalism* (Chicago: Third World Press, 1972); Baraka, *The Autobiography of LeRoi Jones*, 383, 385; "Interview with Imamu Amiri Baraka," *Black Collegian*, March/April 1973, 31; Woodard, *A Nation Within a Nation*, 109; Scot Brown, "The US Organization: African-American Cultural Nationalism in the Era of Black Power, 1965 to the 1970s" (PhD dissertation, Cornell University, 1999), 89–91, 126–27.

41 Imamu Amiri Baraka, ed. *African Congress: A Documentary of the First Modern Pan-African Congress* (New York: William Morrow & Co., 1972); Congress of African People, "Structure Report, 1972," Amiri Baraka Papers; Alex Poinsett, "It's Nation Time!: Congress of African People Proposes Models for Worldwide Black Institutions," *Ebony*, December 1970; for a complete assessment of the Atlanta Congress and Baraka's political endeavors, see Woodard, *A Nation Within a Nation*, 160–69.

42 Baraka, ed. *African Congress*, 183–86. In the late 1960s and early 1970s, CFUN and later the Congress of African People (CAP) spelled Kwanzaa with one "a" as did other groups. Evidence suggests that Karenga and the US Organization had always spelled Kwanzaa with two a's. Karenga maintained the reason he spelled Kwanzaa with two a's was to accommodate a child wanting to take part in the celebration. Whether that is true or not, both the photograph of the Kwanzaa children's play in 1966 and US Organization literature from 1966 to 1969 validates the US Organization's use of two a's. There were other organizations that spelled Kwanzaa with two a's, and like CFUN and the later CAP, with one "a" during this early period, perhaps desiring to keep to the original spelling. The spelling of Kwanzaa remained an organizational choice in the 1970s. Most individuals and groups used two a's by the 1980s and 1990s. See photo of first Kwanzaa in Maulana Karenga, *Kwanzaa: A Celebration of Family, Community, and Culture* (Los Angeles: University of Sankore Press, 1998).

43 Congress of African People, "Structure Report, 1972"; for a list of cities and organizational attendees see Baraka, ed. *African Congress*, 469–75.

44 Baraka, *The Autobiography of LeRoi Jones*, 387.

45 Ibid., 433–36, 445; Amiri Baraka, "Why I Changed My Ideology: Black Nationalism and the Social Revolution," *Black World*, July 1975, 30–42; Haki Madhubuti, "Enemy: From the White Left, White Right, and In-Between," *Black World*, October 1974, 36–47; Kalamu ya Salaam, "Tell No Lies, Claim No Easy Victories," *Black World*, October 1974, 18–34.

46 Jitu Weusi wrote, "In 1970, The EAST had a brief alliance with Amiri Baraka's Committee for a Unified Newark (CFUN), a group based in Newark, New Jersey. We adopted Kwanzaa from that relationship and thus became the first institution east of

the Hudson River to practice and observe Kwanzaa." Jitu Weusi, "The EAST Legacy," *International African Arts Festival—25th Anniversary*, Brooklyn, NY 1996 (brochure), personal papers of Segun Shabaka.

47 Kwasi Konadu, *Truth Crushed to the Earth Will Rise Again: The EAST Organization and the Principles and Practice of Black Nationalist Development* (Trenton: Africa World Press, 2005).

48 Weusi, "The EAST Legacy," *International African Arts Festival—25th Anniversary*, Brooklyn, NY 1996 (brochure), personal papers of Segun Shabaka.

49 Basir Mchawi, "Which Way Kwanza," *Black News*, December 1975, 8.

50 "Christmas Nigger," *Black News*, November 15, 1969, 1.

51 "Black People and the X-MAS Ripoff," *Black News*, December 1973, reprinted in *Black News*, December 1976, 4–5.

52 Segun Shabaka, "Kwanza," *Black News*, December 1975, 16.

53 "Kwanza in Brooklyn," *Black News*, January 31, 1974, 2; Segun Shabaka, "Symbols of Kwanza," *Black News*, December 1975, 16.

54 Charlayne Hunter, "Spirit of Kwanza—Time of Giving: Harlem Pupils Told of Ritual Celebrating Harvest," *New York Times*, December 24, 1971, 28; Barbara Campbell, "Harlem Pupils Get Early Start on Kwanza," *New York Times*, December 20, 1972, 47; Judith Cummings, "City Blacks Begin Fete of Kwanzaa," *New York Times*, December 27, 1973, 41; Carrie Mason-Draffen, "In Kwanzaa, Two Festive Traditions," *New York Times*, December 24, 1986; Cedric McClester, "Editor's Comments," and "Kwanzaa: A Cultural Reaffirmation," *Kwanzaa Magazine* (1984–85 edition), 6, 13. By the time the Harlem Commonwealth Council and the EAST Organization began to lose institutional muscle in the late 1970s and early 1980s, Jose Ferrer, Malik Ahmed, and the New York Urban Coalition emerged as one of New York City's major organizers of public Kwanzaa celebrations, particularly Ferrer with his annual Kwanzaa Fest—a perennial economic bazaar and exposition.

55 Baba Hannibal Afrik and Conrad Worrill, "The History, Origin, and Development of Kwanzaa in the City of Chicago," November 26, 1999 (unpublished manuscript), 1–2, personal papers of Conrad Worrill; "Interview with Mansong Kulubally," October 10, 2000, 2–3; "Interview with Conrad Worrill," December 13, 2000; Haki Madhubuti published one of the earliest Kwanzaa how-to-books, *Kwanzaa*: A Progressive and Uplifting African American Holiday (Chicago: Third World Press, 1972).

56 Afrik and Worrill, "The History, Origin, and Development of Kwanzaa in the City of Chicago," 3–5.

57 Ibid.

58 Stevens, "A Lifestyle Called Kwanzaa, Black Maryland Families Celebrate a Week of Ceremonies That Reflect Age-Old African Traditions," *Washington Post*, December 27, 1979, Md3; Sargent, "Alternative Festival, 'Kwanzaa' Celebrates Spirit of Community and Heritage," *Washington Post*, December 25, 1980, DC4; Meyer, "Kwanzaa Reaffirms Roots, Holiday Lets Americans Honor African Heritage," *Washington Post*, December 26, 1986, C1; Carroll, "Celebrating an African Companion to Christmas," *Washington Post*, December 24, 1987, DC1; Rev. Ishakamusa

Barashango, *Afrikan People and European Holidays: A Mental Genocide, Book I* (Silver Spring, MD: Fourth Dynasty Publishing Company, 1980), 81.

59 In December 1969, the USTI held one of the first Kwanzaa celebrations in Philadelphia at its original location on North Broad Street. *Kwanzaa* (unpublished pamplet, 1970), personal papers of Maisha Ongoza.

60 "Kwanzaa Co-Operative," Public Service Announcement, December 1, 1983, personal papers of Maisha Ongoza.

61 Afro-Cultural Preservation Council, "Let's Pull Together: First Annual Kwanzaa Parade and Karamu Festival," (1984?), personal papers of Maisha Ongoza. At the beginning of the parade, the first principle of Kwanzaa (umoja or unity) would have participants dressed up with chains attached to them signifying black unity under brutal historical conditions. Kwanzaa's second principle (kujichagulia or self-determination) would witness women carrying children on their backs in traditional African style with black doctors, ministers, and other black professionals walking behind them. The third section of the parade corresponding to the third principle (ujima or collective work and responsibility) would display fictitious alcoholics and drug addicts with various social service organizations trailing, indicating their availability. In the fourth section of the parade (ujamaa or cooperative economics), the Preservation Council proposed to have people carry signs, balloons, and buttons that read, "Buy Black, Support Black, Create More Black Businesses." The fifth section of the parade (for kuumba or creativity) would have people dressed up with trash over their bodies and walking around with tobacco or marijuana cigarettes in their mouths with others behind them carrying signs that read "cancer, don't smoke." The sixth section (nia or purpose) would feature cardboard paintings of Egyptian symbols with the name of black American slaves who contributed to black progress. The last section of the parade (imani or faith) would have people of different class backgrounds being led by those in the community with leadership qualities: elders, teachers, and ministers all wearing some form of red, black, and green and carrying floats of black martyrs.

62 "Interview with Maisha and Kauli Ongoza," October 15, 2000, 16.

63 Letter from Maisha Ongoza to Skobi Jambo, October 24, 1984, personal papers of Maisha Ongoza.

64 Letter from the Afro-Cultural Preservation Council to Dr. Maulana Karenga, September 1, 1984, personal papers of Maisha Ongoza.

65 Letter from Maisha Ongoza to Skobi Jambo, October 24, 1984.

66 Ibid.

67 Walker, "Kwanzaa: An Original Afro-American Holiday Just For You," *Pamoja*, December 1980, 20–24.

68 Melva Joyce Parhams, "Kwanzaa and Its People," *LA Community Coupon Clipper*, December 1989; "Life Story of One Who Has Departed—In Love and Memory of Ngao Damu," *Obituary*, January 27, 1995, personal papers of Ngoma Ali. The first Kwanzaa Gwaride Parade was held in December of 1978, beginning on Adams Street and Chrenshaw Blvd, terminating at Leimert Park with an all-day festival. The Kwanzaa Gwaride Parade became so popular in Los Angeles, Mayor Tom Bradley issued a proclamation in 1989 that read: "Whereas, the Kwanzaa Parade was initiated in 1978 by

priest Yuseff Majahliwa along with numerous Kwanzaa committees and community forums . . . I, Tom Bradley, Mayor of the City of Los Angeles . . . do hereby proclaim December 31, 1989 as 'Kwanzaa Parade Festival Day' in Los Angeles." Parhams, "Kwanzaa and Its People," *LA Community Coupon Clipper* (December 1989). Another example of Kwanzaa's growing appeal beyond US in Los Angeles was the birth of a charity organization called the Kwanzaa Foundation in 1973 started by actresses Marla Gibbs and Esther Rolle. Kwanzaa Foundation activities received coverage in major media publications, "Merry Kwanza," *Newsweek* (December 19, 1977), p. 103. *Newsweek* reported "In Los Angeles, comedian Red Foxx and jazz artist Gil Scott-Heron will participate in a $50-a-plate Kwanza disco dinner show to raise money for poor families."

69 Afrik and Worrill, "The History, Origin, and Development of Kwanzaa in the City of Chicago," 4.

70 Afrik and Worrill, "The History, Origin, and Development of Kwanzaa in the City of Chicago," 8, 12; "Kwanzaa Happenings in the City," *Chicago Defender*, December 27, 1997, 15.

71 Mtumishi St. Julien and Kalamu ya Salaam, "Ahidiana Operating Principles" (1973) contained in Mtumishi St. Julien, *Upon the Shoulders of Elephants We Reach the Sky* (New Orleans: Runagate Press, 1995); "The Occasion of the 30th Anniversary of the S.H.A.P.E. Community Center," House of Representatives, 106th Congress, 2nd Session, *Congressional Record Extensions*, May 11, 2000; Mansong Kulubally, ed. *We Must Come Together*, vol. 4 ( Jacksonville, FL: Some Positive People, 1992); Some Positive People, "Kwanzaa Flyer," December 1982, personal papers of Mansong Kulubally; "Seventh Kwanzaa Celebration to be Held at Edward Waters College Dec. 26," *Jacksonville Free Press* (December 23, 1998), 1; "A Kwanzaa Vision for Atlanta," Resource Guide & Souvenir Book, 1993, Metro-Atlanta Kwanzaa Association, Kwanzaa Collection, Library of Congress; Ronald Roach, "Area Blacks Celebrating Kwanzaa Days," *Atlanta Journal-Constitution*, December 31, 1988, C03; David G. Yosifon, "Kwanzaa Taking Root in Boston Community," *Bay State Banner*, December 24, 1998, 1; the Black Student Union (BSU) at the University of Wisconsin—Madison used Kwanzaa's seven principles as a rallying cry for organizing black student strikers, *Black Journal Strike Bulletin*, February 1969.

72 Richard Sine, "Kwanzaa Grows on West Bank," and "Traditions of Kwanzaa," *New Orleans Times-Picayune*, December 31, 1998, 1F, B1.

## 4 Holiday Marketing, Multiculturalism, and the Mainstreaming of Kwanzaa

1 "Interview with Conrad Worrill," December 13, 2000.

2 *Kwanzaa Fest '98 (New York Daily News)*, December 1998, 2.

3 Ibid.

4 "Kwanzaa Super Savings," MPI Coupon Inserts, *Advertising Supplement*, December 1993.

5 "Fast Facts about Mahogany Cards," Hallmark Press Room, www.pressroom.hallmark.com (accessed 2009).

6 "Kwanzaa Ceremonial Items and Gifts," www.designsforbettergiving.com (accessed 2009).

7 www.usps.com (accessed 2009).

8 *Kwanzaa* Fest '98 *(New York Daily News)*, December 1995; "Christmas & Kwanzaa," *Avon Boutique*, 1996.

9 *The Rugrats' First Kwanzaa*, adapted by Stephanie Green (New York: Simon Spotlight/Nickelodeon, 2001); Lola M. Schaefer, *Kwanzaa* (Mankato, MN: Pebble Books, 2001); Nancy Williams, *A Kwanzaa Celebration Pop-Up Book* (New York: Little Simon, 1995); Juwanda G. Ford and Ken Wilson-Max, *K is for Kwanzaa: A Kwanzaa Alphabet Book* (New York: Scholastic, Inc., 1997); Andrea Davis Pickney, *Seven Candles for Kwanzaa* (New York: Dial Books for Young Readers, 1993); Garen Eileen Thomas, *Santa's Kwanzaa* (New York: Hyperion Books for Children, 2004).

10 "Kwanzaa Becomes $700 Million Business," *Ebony*, December 2000, 42.

11 Marilyn Halter, *Shopping for Identity: The Marketing of Ethnicity* (New York: Schocken Books, 2000); also see Ann DuCille, *Skin Trade* (Cambridge: Harvard University Press, 1996); Viviana A. Zelizer, "Multiple Markets: Multiple Cultures," in *Diversity and Its Discontents: Cultural Conflict and Common Ground in Contemporary American Society*, eds. Neil J. Smelser and Jeffrey C. Alexander (Princeton: Princeton University Press, 1999); Susan Willis, "I Want the Black One: Being Different—Is There a Place for Afro-American Culture in Commodity Culture?" in *Cultural Remix: Theories of Politics and the Popular*, eds. Erica Carter, James Donald, and Judith Squires (London: Lawrence & Wishart, 1995). Two of the earliest books marketed to the adult market were Eric V. Copage, *Kwanzaa: An African-American Celebration of Culture and Cooking* (New York: Quill/William Morrow, 1991) and Dorothy Winbush Riley, *The Complete Kwanzaa: Celebrating Our Cultural Harvest* (New York: HarperCollins, 1995).

12 Arlene Dávila, *Latinos, Inc.: The Marketing and Making of a People* (Berkeley: University of California Press, 2001).

13 For a more historical treatment of the commercial appropriation of American holidays see Leigh Eric Schmidt, *Consumer Rites: The Buying and Selling of American Holidays* (Princeton: Princeton University Press, 1995).

14 Sharon MacDonald and Gordon Fyfe, eds. *Theorizing Museums: Representing Identity and Diversity in a Changing World* (Oxford: Blackwell Publishers, 1996).

15 Bill Ryan, *Making Capital from Culture: The Corporate Form of Capitalist Cultural Production* (Berlin: Walter de Gruyter, 1992), 7–8.

16 Ibid., 13.

17 Ibid., 8.

18 Ibid., 10–11.

19 W.E.B. Du Bois, *The Negro in Business* (New York: Arno Press, 1968 [1899]).

20 Booker T. Washington, *The Negro in Business* (New York: AMS Press, 1971 [1907]), 359–60.

21 Fred T. Moore's speech at 1904 Business League Convention. See August Meier, *Negro Thought in America: Racial Ideologies in the Age of Booker T. Washington, 1880–1915* (Ann Arbor: University of Michigan Press, 1988 [1963]).

22 Marcus Garvey, "The Negro as an Industrial Makeshift," in *The Philosophy & Opinions of Marcus Garvey*, compiled by Amy Jacques Garvey (Dover: The Majority Press, 1986), 48.

23 Maulana Karenga, *Kwanzaa: A Celebration of Family, Community, and Culture* (Los Angeles: University of Sankore Press, 1998), 120.

24 Julius K. Nyerere, *Ujamaa: Essays on Socialism* (New York: Oxford University Press, 1968).

25 Gil Scott-Heron, "The Revolution Will Not Be Televised," *Small Talk at 125th Street and Lenox* (1970); also on Scott-Heron's album *Pieces of a Man* (1971); Robert Weems, "The Revolution Will Be Marketed: American Corporations and Black Consumers During the 1960s," *Radical History Review* 59 (Spring 1994): 94–107; see also, Robert Weems, *Desegregating the Dollar: African American Consumerism in the Twentieth Century* (New York: NYU Press, 1998).

26 I am indebted to John Sibley Butler for the pushcart metaphor. John Sibley Butler, *Entrepreneurship and Self-Help Among Black Americans: A Reconsideration of Race and Economics* (Albany: State University of New York Press, 1991).

27 *Los Angeles Sentinel*, December 11, 1981. The main purpose of the free catalog was to tap into the untested market of Kwanzaa greeting cards. Every item in the catalog, including the bumper stickers and pins, was free, except the Kwanzaa greeting cards. Kwanzaa Arts would use the greeting cards to economically capitalize on the holiday's relative obscurity by couching the catalog in the language of holiday promotion. Created by a young graphic artist and painter named Bernard Hoyes, Kwanzaa Arts issued a test card in 1975, showing the profile of a black woman with an Afro hairstyle, inset with a smaller black man's face staring straight ahead. Next to the man's face and behind the woman's image is a kinara, an ear of corn, and a talisimu—an US Organization symbol. Encasing the entire image on the front of the card is the phrase "Happy Kwanzaa," with the Nguzo Saba and a brief description of Kwanzaa inside. Following the test card in 1975, Hoyes and Kwanzaa Arts released seven different greeting cards in 1977 corresponding to the seven principles. The seven cards amounted to a full package offered by Kwanzaa Arts. Sold mainly in 5" x 9" and 6" x 9", each card included the seven principles inside with an image on the front corresponding to one principle. These full-color cards were sold as a set, encased in black heavy paper with gold foil on the cover of the containing package. As one of the first Kwanzaa greeting cards made, Kwanzaa Arts attempted to make their cards available to a wider audience, but most major white distributors refused to market the card, citing the "esoteric" nature of the cards' images. Instead, Kwanzaa Arts sold their greeting cards directly to black bookstores in Los Angeles, Atlanta, and Brooklyn, New York, which readily promoted them to annual celebrants and newcomers to the holiday. According to Kwanzaa Arts founder Ngoma Ali, black school teachers purchased and used them as teaching tools in the classroom. Despite some interest, Kwanzaa Arts never sold the greeting card package beyond its first printing. In fact, it took six years to sell the initial production of 1,200, underscoring the difficulties of black distribution channels and how small the Kwanzaa market was in the mid- and late 1970s. "Interview with Bernard Hoyes," July 29, 2001. "Interviews

with Ngoma Ali," May 9 and May 15, 2001. Kwanzaa Arts greeting cards in the personal papers of Ngoma Ali.

28 *Baltimore Afro-American*, December 5, 1984.

29 Afram Associates, Inc., "Kwanzaa Materials" (1973), Kwanzaa Micro Fiche 002, 697, 1925–74, Schomburg Center Clipping File, Schomburg Library.

30 Afram Associates, Inc., "Kwanzaa Directory" (1973), Kwanzaa Micro Fiche 002, 697, 1925–74, Schomburg Center Clipping File, Schomburg Library.

31 Jitu Weusi, "Kwanza," November 25, 1974. Kwanzaa Micro Fiche 002, 697, 1925–74, Schomburg Center Clipping File, Schomburg Library.

32 "CAP Conference Call," October 2, 1972, Amiri Baraka Papers, Moorland-Spingarn Research Center, Howard University.

33 K. Mtetezi to Amiri Baraka, "Kwanza Kit Costs," memorandum, January 2, 1973, Amiri Baraka Papers, Moorland-Spingarn Research Center, Howard University.

34 K. Mtetezi to Imamu Amiri Baraka, "Report on Sale of Kwanza Kits," January 8, 1973, Amiri Baraka Papers, Moorland-Spingarn Research Center, Howard University; from Nyumba Ya Ujamaa to Kaimu Mtetezi, "Financial Report for Kwanza Kits Sold in Nyumba from 12/22/72 to 12/31/72," January 3, 1973, Amiri Baraka Papers, Moorland-Spingarn Research Center, Howard University.

35 "Interview with Bernard Hoyes," July 29, 2001.

36 Lisa J. Servon, *Bootstrap Capital: Microenterprises and the American Poor* (Washington, DC: Brookings Institution Press, 1999); Jawanza Kunjufu, *Black Economics: Solutions for Economic and Community Empowerment* (Chicago: African American Images, 1991).

37 Bulter, *Enterpreneurship and Self-Help Among Black Americans*; Robert T. Averitt, *The Duel Economy: The Dynamics of American Industry Structure* (New York: W.W. Norton, 1968); Kilolo Kijakazi, *African-American Economic Development and Small Business Ownership* (New York: Garland Publishing, 1997).

38 "Soul Cards," *Newsweek*, May 5, 1969, 101.

39 Ibid.

40 Yanick Rice Lamb, "Sentimental Returns: Black Owned Greeting Card Companies Meet Special Challenges to Get Their Share of the Holiday's Profits," *Black Enterprise*, December 1989, 79–80, 82; Marjorie Whigham-Desir, "Boom in Black Greeting Cards," *Black Enterprise*, December 1995, 104; Sala Damali, telephone interview with author, July 18, 2001.

41 "Meet Designer Melissa Bolden," www.hallmark.com (accessed 2009).

42 "Fast Facts about Mahogany Cards," and "Kwanzaa 2000 Facts," www.pressroom.hallmark.com (accessed 2009); Whigham-Desir, "Boom in Black Greeting Cards," *Black Enterprise*, December 1995, 104.

43 Whigham-Desir, "Boom in Black Greeting Cards," *Black Enterprise*, December 1995, 104.

44 "Interview with Ngoma Ali," May 9, 2001; "Kwanzaa Items: Carved Kinaras," "Multicultural Cards and Gifts," www.designsforbettergiving.com (accessed 2009).

45 "USPS Five Year Strategic Plan," and "Postal Facts," www.usps.com (accessed 2009).

46 "Postal Service Observes 'First Fruits' With Kwanzaa Stamp," September 18, 1997, www.usps.com (accessed 2009).

47 Cythnia L. Webb, "Kwanzaa Holiday Honored," *Los Angeles Sentinel*, November 5, 1997, A1.

48 Dr. Maulana Karenga, "Why a Stamp for Kwanzaa is a Good Thing," *Chicago Defender*, November 3, 1997.

49 "Kwanzaa Stamp to be Introduced Locally: Post Office Honors African-American Celebration with Gala Ceremony," *Sacramento Observer*, October 29, 1997, G1; "New Kwanzaa Stamp Unveiled Here," *Chicago Weekend*, October 30, 1997, 1; "Kwanzaa Stamp Unveiled at Union Temple," *Washington Informer*, November 19, 1997, 22.

50 Bill Ryan, *Making Capital from Culture: The Corporate Form of Capitalist Cultural Production* (Berlin: Walter de Gruyter, 1992), 126.

51 The corporate appropriation of oppositional culture in the last two decades of the twentieth century is covered in Thomas Frank and Matt Weiland, eds. *Commodify Your Dissent: Salvos from The Baffler* (New York: W.W. Norton, 1997); on corporate America's latest attempt to foster business relations with black companies, see Roger O. Crockett, "Reaching Out to Growing Markets," *Group Notes*, November/December 1998, 5.

52 Louis Harlan, "Booker T. Washington and the National Negro Business League," in *Booker T. Washington in Perspective: Essays of Louis Harlan*, ed. Raymond W. Smock (Jackson: University of Mississippi Press, 1988); Fred Moore, an editor for the *New York Age* and the *Colored American Magazine*, announced at the 1904 National Negro Business League convention that black businesses and consumers should support one another: "How can we otherwise succeed? Some would say that this was drawing the color line. Jews support Jews, Germans support Germans, Italians support Italians. Negroes should now begin to support Negroes. Don't delay this, but begin today." Quote taken from Meier, *Negro Thought in America, 1880–1915,* 125–26. For a history of the "Buy Black" campaigns during the 1930s and 1940s, see Cheryl Greenberg, *Or Does It Explode?: Black Harlem in the Great Depression* (New York: Oxford University Press, 1991); for Carlos Cooks and the Nation of Islam, see a 1955 speech by Carlos Cooks, "Speech on the 'Buy Black' Campaign: Hair Conking, Buy Black," and a 1965 speech by Elijah Muhammad, "From a Program for Self-Development," both in William Van Deburg, ed. *Modern Black Nationalism: From Marcus Garvey to Louis Farrakhan* (New York: New York University Press, 1997); in his brief time as a nationalist, CORE national director Roy Innis posited similar ideas. See Roy Innis, "Separate Economics: A New Social Contract," in *Black Economic Development*, ed. American Assembly (Englewood Cliffs: Prentice Hall, 1969); see also Butler, *Entrepreneurship and Self-Help Among Black Americans*.

53 Daryl Bell, "Kwanzaa Expo '94," *Philadelphia Tribune*, November 8, 1994, 1B; "11th Annual African-American Holiday Expo and Kwanzaa," *Oakland Post*, November 26, 1995, 4; "African-American Business Exchange Presents Holiday Expo and Kwanzaa Celebration," *Sun Reporter*, November 23, 1995, S2. Since the beginning of the 1990s, Ferrer has sporadically staged a Kwanzaa expo in the City of Philadelphia. He attempted to bring one to Detroit in 1998 but plans dissolved. The Chicago and Oakland Kwanzaa expos are run independently of Ferrer. Also, Dallas, Texas has held a Kwanzaa fest since the early 1990s under the direction of Dallas County Commissioner John Wiley Price.

54 The New York Urban Coalition was a social service organization that arose out of the civil unrest of the 1960s and 1970s. After working five years at a community-based agency called Operation Helping Hand, Ferrer was appointed Director of Community Development at the New York Urban Coalition in 1976. After his appointment, Ferrer hired Malik Ahmed. "Interview with Jose Ferrer," November 4, 1998, 1–3.

55 "A Conversation with Jose Ferrer: Kwanzaa Fest's Founder Talks about the Making of the World's Largest Kwanzaa Celebration," *Kwanzaa Fest '98 (New York Daily News)*, December 1998, 5; "What is Kwanzaa?: Thirty-Two Years After its Creation, The Holiday Remains Misunderstood By Many," *Kwanzaa Fest '98 (Caribbean Life)*, December 1998, 7; "Interview with Jose Ferrer," November 4, 1998, 6–7.

56 "A Conversation With Jose Ferrer," *Kwanzaa Fest '98*, December 1998, 26; "Interview with Jose Ferrer," November 4, 1998, 4, 6–7; *Special Supplements*, December 2000, 5.

57 Malik Ahmed, "Why African-Americans Celebrate Kwanzaa," *St. Louis American*, December 9, 1993, 8A.

58 "Interview with Jose Ferrer," November 4, 1998, 12–14.

59 Ibid., 8, 15–16.

60 During the 1980s and 1990s, the *Daily News*' image had been tarnished in the New York black community for being racist in their coverage of events such as Bernard Getz's shooting of four young black men; Tawana Brawley; its depiction of black leaders like Al Sharpton; and the firings of black columnists. The Committee to Eliminate Media Offensive to African People (CEMOTAP) had been at the forefront of this criticism. Wilbert A. Tatum, "Daily News and Wall Street Journal Aim .357 Magnum at Our Hearts While Black Entertainment Television Holds Us Down," *New York Amsterdam News*, December 30, 1995, 10.

61 "Interview with Jose Ferrer," November 4, 1998, 7; "Good Morning America Returns to Kwanzaa Fest," *Kwanzaa Magazine (Daily News)*, December 1997, 3.

62 "Interview with Jose Ferrer," November 4, 1998, 17.

63 *Special Supplements*, December 2000, 14, 19.

64 Jose Ferrer, "Flexing Our Economic Muscle," *Kwanzaa Magazine (Daily News)*, December 1997, 4.

65 Quote taken from Thomas Frank, "Why Johnny Can't Dissent," in *Commodify Your Dissent*, ed. Frank and Weiland, 36.

66 David Toop, *Rap Attack 3: African Rap to Global Hip Hop* (London: Serpents Tail, 2000 [1984]); S.H. Fernando, Jr., *The New Beats: Exploring the Music, Culture, and Attitudes of Hip Hop* (New York: Anchor Books, 1994); Tricia Rose, *Black Noise: Rap Music and Black Culture in Contemporary America* (Hanover: Wesleyan University Press, 1994).

67 DuCille, *Skin Trade*, 33–34; "Shindana Discovers the 'Together' Dolls," *Black Enterprise*, December 1970, 24–27.

68 Quote taken from DuCille, *Skin Trade*, 34 in Cynthia Roberts, *Barbie: Thirty Years of America's Doll* (Chicago: Contemporary Books, 1989), 44.

69 DuCille, *Skin Trade*, 35–36.

70 Lisa Jones, "Africa-TM," *The Village Voice*, August 24, 1993, 42.

71 "The Chisholm-Mingo Group: Linking Advertisers to Urban Markets," Multicultural Marketing Profiles, November/December 1997, www.inforesources.com/test/news/profiles (accessed 2009).

72 Tobacco and alcohol companies have come under attack for advertising certain products solely to the African-American community. Other corporations have also been attacked for racist comments from employees or, as in the case in the 1970s and 1980s, having commercial investments in Apartheid South Africa.

73 Ken Smikle, "The Image Makers: Black Ad Agencies Use Diversified Services and General Market Accounts to Further Their Growth," *Black Enterprise*, December 1985, 46.

74 Dana Canedy, "Companies View Ethnic Holidays Like Kwanzaa and Three Kings Day as a Way to Reach a Niche," *New York Times*, December 30, 1998, 3.

75 Alfred L. Schreiber, *Multicultural Marketing: Selling to the New America* (Chicago: NTC Business Books, 2001).

76 Dana Canedy, "Companies View Ethnic Holidays Like Kwanzaa and Three Kings Day as a Way to Reach a Niche," *New York Times*, December 30, 1998, 3. Public relations is not new. See David Nye, *Image Worlds: Corporate Identities at General Electric, 1890–1920* (Cambridge, MA: MIT Press, 1985) and Roland Marchand, *Creating the Corporate Soul: The Rise of Public Relations and Corporate Imagery* (Berkeley: University of California Press, 1998). But the phenomenon of multicultural marketing and public relations is specific to the 1980s and 1990s. See Marlene L. Rossman, *Multicultural Marketing: Selling to a Diverse America* (New York: AMACOM, 1994) and Schreiber, *Multicultural Marketing*.

77 Canedy, "Companies View Ethnic Holidays Like Kwanzaa and Three Kings Day as a Way to Reach a Niche," *New York Times*, December 30, 1998, 3.

78 Smikle, "The Image Makers: Black Ad Agencies Use Diversified Services and General Market Accounts to Further Their Growth," *Black Enterprise*, December 1985, 47.

79 John Zeaman, "The Art of the Celebration Black History Month Brings Six Exhibits," *The Record*, February 4, 1990, E1.

80 "The Kwanzaa Connection," *Long Island Monthly*, December 4, 1989, 83.

81 Kevin Moore, *Museums and Popular Culture* (London: Cassell, 1997), 142.

82 MacDonald and Fyfe, eds. *Theorizing Museums*, 2

83 "Charles H. Wright Museum of African-American History's Revised Kwanzaa Programming Schedule," *PR Newswire*, December 22, 1998.

84 Tonya Fox, "Philadelphia Museum of Art Celebrates Kwanzaa on Saturday," *Philadelphia Tribune*, December 24, 1996, 1D; C. Anthony Davis, "Art Museum Fete to Show How Culture Was Preserved," *Philadelphia Tribune*, December 23, 1997, 1D.

85 "Special Events and Exhibition-Related Programs," Education, American Museum of Natural History, Kwanzaa 2000, www.amnh.org (accessed 2009); "Forces of Nature Dance Theatre Company—American Griot," Kwanzaa program, December 30, 2000; Don Thomas, "Kwanzaa Performances At Museum of Natural History," *New York Beacon*, January 7, 1998, 16.

86 "Special Events and Exhibition-Related Programs," Education, American Museum of Natural History, December 2000, www.amnh.org (accessed 2009).

87 The Kwanzaa community in Chicago had long linked education and entertainment, especially during their pre-Kwanzaa celebrations. Also see Hilde S.

Hein, *The Museum in Transition: A Philosophical Perspective* (Washington, DC: Smithsonian Institution Press, 2000), 106–8.

88 Margaret Schmitz Rizzo, "Museum Teaches Kwanzaa Values Through Celebration," *Kansas City Star*, December 24, 1998, 21.

89 "IL First Lady Hosts 'Tree of Lights' Celebration Honoring Traditions from Around the World," *Italian Voice*, January 2, 1997, 1.

90 "A Merry Little Kwanzaa Does Its Share For 'Christmas Creep,'" *The Age*, December 28, 1994, 8.

91 Mary Gillespie, "Spiritual Values to Receive a Special Seasonal Tribute," *Chicago Sun-Times*, December 1, 1989, 11.

92 Susan Eastman, "Museum Offers Children a Cultural Look at Holiday," *St. Petersburg Times*, December 6, 1993, 6.

93 "Celebrate 'Winterfest' at Museum," *Oakland Post*, November 22, 1995, S8.

94 Claudine Rosenbaum, "Smithsonian Takes a Look at Holiday Diversity," *Washington Times*, December 24, 1992, M10.

95 MacDonald and Fyfe, eds. *Theorizing Museums*, 2.

96 Corey Hall, "Black Activists Discuss Experiences of First Karamu Ya Imani Celebration," *Chicago Citizen*, December 26, 1996, 1.

97 Angelo A. Williams, "Cultural Celebration: Over 300 Attend Wo'se Community Church Kwanzaa Event," *Sacramento Observer*, January 7, 1998, B3.

98 Rhonda Bates-Rudd, "Celebrating Heritage and the Holidays: This is a Holy Time of the Year for Many Churches with Celebrations Lasting Well into the New Year," *Detroit News*, December 23, 1998, S6.

99 Kevin Leonard Cater, "A 'Festival of Friends': Black Culture Night Held at Church of Scientology," *Sacramento Observer*, January 6, 1999, A3.

100 "De Profundis—The A Capella Men's Choir of Albuquerque," www.unm.edu/~shapiro/music/deprofundis (accessed 2009).

101 Mark Skertic, "Kwanzaa For People of All Colors," *Chicago Sun-Times*, December 28, 1998, 5.

102 Robert Farley, "Unitarians Host Kwanzaa Festival," *St. Petersburg Times*, December 28, 1998, 1.

103 Paul Baldwin, "Unitarians Join Celebration of Kwanzaa in Spirit of Unity," *Louisville Courier-Journal*, December 7, 1998, 01B.

104 Ervin Dyer, "A Lesson in Kwanzaa, Wilkinsburg Minister Focuses on the Bonds between Religious Concepts and Cultural Norm," *Pittsburgh Post-Gazette*, December 24, 1998, D1.

105 "More Churches Recognizing Cultural Holiday of Kwanzaa," *Washington Post*, December 26, 1998, B7.

106 Zaudie K. Abiade, "Kwanzaa: A Christian Perspective," *Black Child*, December 31, 1996, 26.

107 Ibid., 26; "A Catholic Perspective of Kwanzaa," www.home.att.net (accessed 2009).

108 Abiade, "Kwanzaa: A Christian Perspective," *Black Child*, December 31, 1996, 26; "A Catholic Perspective of Kwanzaa," www.home.att.net (accessed 2009).

109 Chike Akua (Justin Fenwick), *A Kwanzaa Awakening* (Decatur, GA: Imani Enterprises, 2000), 42–48; Rev. Chike Akua, "Kwanzaa in Christ," Victory Baptist Church, audio recording, December 1999; also see, Ndugu T'Ofori-Atta, *ChristKwanza* (Lithonia, GA: SCP/Third World Literature Publishing House, 1990).

110 Denise Wilson-El, "Religion Must Impart a Sense of Self-Worth and Cultural Identity if it's to Have Meaning," *Miami Times*, June 3, 1993, 1C.

111 Rev. Dr. Lynn Collins, "Kwanzaa Celebration: From the Cross to the Crib," *Selected Sermons*, December 2000, www.ecusa.anglican.org (accessed 2009).

112 Gail Forsyth-Vail, "Lessons From the Kwanzaa Candles," North Parish Church, www.uua.org (accessed 2009).

113 Arthur James, "Discrediting Reverend Banks' Theory and Ideas on Kwanzaa," *Philadelphia Tribune*, January 6, 1995, 7A.

114 Dale Koppel, "Kwanzaa and Christmas, Rev. Shepard Finds Way to Link the Two," *Ft. Lauderdale Sun-Sentinel*, January 1, 1999, 5.

115 Barbara DeWitt, "Kwanzaa Celebrates African Heritage," *Los Angeles Daily News*, December 27, 1994, L1.

116 Laura Griffin, "Many Older Blacks New to Kwanzaa, Started in '66, Celebration Observed Mainly by Young," *Dallas Morning News*, December 12, 1998, 41A.

117 Skertic, "Kwanzaa For People of All Colors," *Chicago Sun-Times*, December 28, 1998, 5.

118 Leslie Berestein, "The Traditions Vary, But Still It's Christmas: Holiday Celebrations Have a Decidedly Ethnic Spin Within L.A.'s Neighborhood Enclaves," *Los Angeles Times*, December 18, 1994, 3.

119 Patricia Gaines, "Embracing the New Traditions of Kwanzaa: African-Americans Celebrate the Principles and Symbols of Their Heritage," *Washington Post*, December 31, 1998, D3.

120 Tammerlin Drummond, "Holidays in Harmony, A Joint Celebration of Hanukkah and Kwanzaa Brings More Than 200 African-Americans and Jews Together in Santa Ana," *Los Angeles Times*, December 27, 1993, B1; Liz Harris, "Chanukah-Kwanzaa Party Symbolizes a Step Forward," *Jewish Bulletin*, December 20, 1996, 10; Naomi Geschwind, "From Inside Out: For Jews, Lighting a Candle is Not Just to Dispel Darkness," *Jewish Exponent*, January 2, 1997, 14X; Judy Fruchter Minkove, "Chanzaa? African-American and Jewish Students Gather to Discuss Meanings of Chanukah and Kwanzaa," *Baltimore Jewish Times*, December 20, 1996, 26.

121 "Readers' Letters," *San Diego Union-Tribune*, January 6, 2001, E2.

122 Tobias K. Houpe, "Texaco Settles Suit for $175 Million," *Cleveland Call & Post*, November 21, 1996, 1; Samuel F. Yette, "Nationwide Boycott of Texaco Recommended," *Tennessee Tribune*, November 20, 1996, 6.

123 Paul Mulshine, "The Founder of Kwanzaa Has a Lot of Explaining to Do," *Newark Star-Ledger*, December 20, 1998, 3.

124 Quotes taken from Anna Day Wilde, "Mainstreaming Kwanzaa," *Public Interest*, March 22, 1995, 68.

125 "Kwanzaa Club Puts Gender Spin on Classic with its 'Cinderfella,'" *Pittsburgh Post-Gazette*, February 24, 1998, D1.

126 IBBMEC pronounced I-BA-MEC is an acronym for the International Black Buyers and Manufacturers Expo and Conference. MATAH is not an acronym. A company profile explained, "the letters 'M' and 'A' which dominate the name, MATAH, symbolize the great Pyramids of Giza. Conceptually, the Great Pyramids were built by starting with a broad base, building up gradually by overlapping and interconnecting large stones. The Great Pyramids represent everlasting principles of 'creativity' and 'strength from unity.' The rising sun that is also featured in the MATAH logo symbolizes a new day in our thinking, inspired by greater knowledge of our true African past." See "A New Day," www.matah.com/anewday (accessed 2001).

127 "Kwanzaa Notes," *Ba Papyrus (Soul Papers)* 3, no. 3 (1994), 6; Sherice L. Shields, "IBBMEC Trade Winds: Inspired Marketing for Manufacturers and Retailers," *about . . . time Magazine*, December 31, 1999, 22; "Black Retailers, Manufacturers Say Enough As They Prepare For UDC Conference," *Washington Informer*, October 1, 1997, 10; Sala Damali, telephone interview with author, July 18, 2001. Also see IBBMEC Kwanzaa Position Statement, www.ibbmec.com (accessed 2009).

128 Ken Bridges was one of the victims in the Washington, DC area sniper attacks. He was tragically killed on October 11, 2002.

129 "What is MATAH?" www.matah.com/FAQ (accessed 2001).

130 Dr. Maulana Karenga, "Kwanzaa and Corporate Commercialism," (unpublished paper, n.d.), 2; Karenga, *Kwanzaa* (1998), 118–19; "Keeping Kwanzaa Real," *Essence*, December 1998.

131 Conrad W. Worrill, "Preserve the Sanctity and Integrity of Kwanzaa," *Michigan Citizen*, December 24, 1994, A6.

132 Smikle, "The Image Makers: Black Agencies Use Diversified Services and General Market Accounts to Further Their Growth," *Black Enterprise*, December 1985, 48, 50, 52; Worrill, "Preserve the Sanctity and Integrity of Kwanzaa," *Michigan Citizen*, December 24, 1994, A6.

133 Worrill, "Preserve the Sanctity and Integrity of Kwanzaa," *Michigan Citizen*, December 24, 1994, A6.

134 Conrad Worrill, "Kwanzaa Belongs to Us, Don't Let Them Commercialize It," *Philadelphia Tribune*, January 25, 1994, 7A; Dr. Conrad Worrill, "Selling Kwanzaa to White Corporations," www.itskwanzaatime.com (accessed 2009).

135 Desiree A. Graves, "Colors on Flag of Kwanzaa Stamp Not Wrong Says Post Office," *Washington Afro-American*, November 11, 1997, A1; Karenga, *Kwanzaa* (1998), 88.

136 These items paled in comparison to the explosion of commercial activity in publishing, particularly involving Kwanzaa children's books, recipe books, and how-to-celebrate Kwanzaa manuals. See Deborah M. Newton Chocolate, *Kwanzaa* (Chicago: Children's Press, 1990); Copage, *Kwanzaa: An African-American Celebration of Culture and Cooking*; Jessica B. Harris, *A Kwanzaa Keepsake: Celebrating the Holiday with New Traditions and Feasts* (New York: Fireside, 1995); Cedric McClester, *Kwanzaa: Everything You Always Wanted to Know But Didn't Know Where to Ask* (New York: Gumbs & Thomas, 1985).

137 "Kwanzaa Symbol Added to Collection," *Michigan Chronicle*, November 29, 1994, 4C; "The Advent of Kwanzaa: Will Success Spoil an African-American Fest?"

*Newsweek*, December 11, 1995; "Kwanzaa Teddy," www.kwanzaateddy.com (accessed 2009); Marc A. Cummings, "The Commercialization of Our Soul," *New Pittsburgh Courier*, January 24, 1996, A7.

138 "Interview with David Hall," January 5, 2001.

139 Ibid.

140 Ibid.; "Historic Upstate Kings Lodge Renamed Betty Shabazz Wholistic Retreat Center," *New York Amsterdam News*, July 15, 1998, 28. When the black resort fell on hard times in the mid-1990s, Grady and Judy Owens, whose family had owned the twenty-acre resort since 1937, solicited the help of the NBWS. The NBWS raised money from its members and received investments from black personalities like Susan Taylor and Iyanla Vanzant who gave $160,000. With this additional help, the NBWS prevented the foreclosure of Kings Lodge and bought it from the Owens family, keeping them on the Board of Directors. In 1998, the NBWS renamed the site the Betty Shabazz Wholistic Retreat Center after Shabazz's untimely death.

141 Angela Kinamore, "Heritage Getaways, A Wealth of Retreats and Conferences Celebrate the African diaspora," *Essence*, December 1991, 92; "Interview with David Hall," January 5, 2001.

142 "Interview with David Hall," January 5, 2001; Kinamore, "Heritage Getaways, A Wealth of Retreats and Conferences Celebrate the African diaspora," *Essence*, December 1991, 92.

143 The book does not answer how many Kwanzaa celebrants exist. There is indeed no reliable data on the number of Kwanzaa celebrants. One reason is the difficulty in defining a Kwanzaa "celebrant." What distinguishes a committed celebrant as opposed to a casual observer—seven days, three days, one day? What about people who put on a Kwanzaa celebration in their homes vis-a-vis those who attend a public Kwanzaa? These problems have produced a plethora of numbers, some publicized by the holiday's creator. In 1979, Karenga reported that over 10 million people celebrated Kwanzaa ("Interview with Dr. M. R. Karenga, Creator of Kwanzaa," *Black News,* December 1979, 5). By 1998, he reported that over 20 million blacks worldwide celebrated the holiday, both times without attribution (Maulana Karenga, *Kwanzaa: A Celebration of Family, Community, and Culture*, Los Angeles: University of Sankore Press, 1998, xv). *U.S. News & World Report* and *Newsweek* provided a more conservative number: five million in 1992. The Maritz Marketing Research in *American Demographics* said in 1997 that two percent of American adults celebrate Kwanzaa (Tibbett L. Speer, "Stretching the Holiday Season," *American Demographics*, November 19, 1997, 42–49). The reported number of Kwanzaa celebrants often includes blacks in the diaspora. This book only examines Kwanzaa in the United States. Beyond its scope are Kwanzaa celebrants in places like London, Paris, Toronto, and in the Caribbean.

## 5 BLACK HOLIDAYS AND AMERICAN CALENDAR LEGITIMACY

1 Although the Clinton presidency signaled an end to conservative Republican rule, his centrist Democratic policies, particularly on welfare and crime reform, did

not restore government largesse to pre-Reagan levels. Also, the Clinton administration left sentencing disparities unchecked and helped facilitate the privatization of new prisons.

2 Quotes taken from H. Carl McCall, "Blacks and the Bicentennial," *New York Amsterdam News*, December 3, 1975, A5.

3 Due to the criticism of the Bicentennial and the pressure from groups, including the Association for the Study of Negro Life, President Gerald Ford began calling on Americans in 1976 to celebrate the entire month of February as Black History Month. "Black History Month is Supported by Ford," *New York Times*, February 11, 1976, 33. Black History Month was given proclamation recognition by President Jimmy Carter beginning in 1977. Carter wrote, "This month gives Black Americans a wonderful opportunity to review their roots, their achievements and their projections; and it provides for all Americans a chance to rejoice and take pride in a heritage that adds so much to our way of life. I commend the Association for the Study of Afro-American Life and History on its sponsorship of this traditional observance." Jimmy Carter, "National Afro-American (Black) History Month, February 1978, Message of the President," January 27, 1978, www.presidency.ucsb.edu/ws/index (accessed 2009).

4 In the immediate post-Bicentennial climate of the Bakke decision rendered by the Supreme Court in 1978, Black History Month was couched in the language of affirmative action. "When you think about the idea of a week (or a month) devoted to black history, you have to wonder whether we are not rapidly approaching a time when such 'set-asides' will be irrelevant." *Washington Post*, February 19, 1977, A12.

5 Critics of Black History Month, especially members of the Universal Negro Improvement Association (UNIA) splinter groups, felt that the February observance was too short and too mainstream. In an attempt to centralize Marcus Garvey Day (August 17) and to capitalize off Black History Month's expansion, the King Holiday Movement, and Kwanzaa's growing popularity, Marcus Garvey Day promoters created African Heritage Month in 1980. Black holiday promoter Ron Daniels went a step further advocating not only a national Marcus Garvey Day, but rather a national day in recognition of the flag Garvey created, writing, "I am proposing that we as Africans in America declare August 17 the birthday of Marcus Garvey, National American Flag Day. Garvey's birthday should become a major focal point for the dissemination of information about our flag and the massive display of the Flag by millions of black people in parades, Garvey Day events, and on our homes." Ron Daniels, "Garvey's Birthday Should be a National Holiday," *Journal & Guide*, August 7, 1991, 2.

6 Michael Brown, "How Dr. King's Birthday Became a National Holiday," *Chicago Defender*, January 13, 1990, 46.

7 Paul Hodge, "Fairfax School Unit Votes Holiday for Dr. King's Birthday," *Washington Post*, April 10, 1981.

8 Helen Dewar, "Battle to Block King Holiday May Have Hurt Helms at Home," *Washington Post*, October 23, 1983, A2; Richard Severo, "Dr. King and Communism: No Link Ever Proved," *New York Times*, October 22, 1983. Some cities and states were more comfortable designating bridges with King's name than a holiday. See "Big Change in Thinking," *Washington Post*, August 10, 1983. But naming streets for King

mirrored similar black grassroots struggles in achieving a King Holiday. See Derek H. Alderman, "Naming Streets for Martin Luther King Jr.: No Easy Road," in *Landscape and Race in the United States*, ed. Richard H. Schein (New York: Routledge, 2006), 213–36.

9 "Congressman Conyers Predicts Passage of King Holiday Bill," *Jet*, January 29, 1981, 13.

10 Mariene Rodriques Andrade, "Martin Luther King, Jr.," *Cape Verdean News*, February 28, 1981, 1.

11 Republican nominee Ronald Reagan launched his general election campaign in Philadelphia, Mississippi on August 3, 1980, the murder site of civil rights workers, James Chaney, Andrew Goodman, and Michael Schwerner during SNCC's Freedom Summer initiative in 1964.

12 Stevie Wonder, "Happy Birthday," *Hotter Than July* (Motown 1980).

13 The National King Day rallies had other components to them, such as lobbying efforts inside the Capitol. "After the Friday march, the demonstrators will visit congressional offices to demand that their representatives support the bills and afterwards will prepare a 'report card' on how these lawmakers stand. The results will be forwarded to groups in the lawmaker's home district so grassroots pressure can be applied to strengthen support for the bills." "March For King to Flood D.C.: 'National Holiday' Drive Set," *Daily World*, January 14, 1982, 18.

14 Laura Williams, "Thousands Honor King's Birthday," *Washington Star*, January 16, 1981, B1; Herbert H. Denton, "Wonder's Chord Touches Crowd: Rally Reflects a Crisis of Leadership in Movement," *Washington Post*, January (?), 1981.

15 Mary Ellen Perry, "A Yearning for a Symbolic Figure Like King," *Washington Star*, January 15, 1978, E1.

16 Williams, "Thousands Honor King's Birthday," *Washington Star*, January 16, 1981, B2.

17 Ibid.

18 "13 Years Later They Gather in King's Honor," *Washington Star*, April 5, 1981.

19 Denton, "Wonder's Chord Touches Crowd," *Washington Post*, January (?) 1981. The connection between black holidays and the black condition was not lost on the *Daily World*: "The march to make King's birthday the national property of us all is also a struggle to make the criminal plight of our youth the property and responsibility of us all, but especially the federal government." *Daily World*, January 14, 1982.

20 Steven V. Roberts, "Senate, 78–22, Votes Holiday to Honor Dr. King," *New York Times*, October 20, 1983, B9; David Hoffman, "King is Saluted as President Signs Holiday Into Law," *Washington Post*, November 3, 1983, A1.

21 "Paying for a King Holiday," *Washington Post*, October 24, 1983; George Lardner, Jr., "Martin Luther King, Jr. Day Voted," *Washington Post*, August 3, 1983, A15.

22 Hoffman, "King is Saluted As President Signs Holiday Into Law," *Washington Post*, November 3, 1983, A18; Clayborne Carson, "Martin Luther King, Jr.'s Birthday," in *Encyclopedia of American Holidays and National Days*, ed. Len Travers (Westport: Greenwood Press, 2006), vol. 1, 4–5.

23 "Only Two States Remain to Name King's Holiday," *New York Amsterdam News*, April 13, 1991, 22. Many believed that Arizona capitulated because of the overwhelming criticism coming from outside of the state triggering "convention and tourism boycotts . . . that cost it an estimated $200 million in business" as well as the potential loss of the 1993 Super Bowl. See "King Holiday Foes File Petition to Force Vote," *Los Angles Chronicle*, October 5, 1989. Matthew Dennis, *Red, White, and Blue Letter Days: An American Calendar* (Ithaca: Cornell University Press, 2002), 263–64.

24 Fifteen years later similar efforts were made in Boston when local blacks approached the Boston Landmarks Commission to designate the boyhood home of Malcolm X a historic landmark. Pamela Ferdinand, "Tea Party, Bunker Hill, Minuteman, Malcolm X Vertical File: Commemorating Revolutionaries," *Washington Post*, May 2, 1998, A3.

25 "Why Remember Malcolm in the 1980s?" Cooperative Research Network in Black Studies, brochure, 1985, Malcolm X Vertical File; Manning Marable, "Remember Malcolm X," *Chicago Defender* [?], 1985.

26 Public Enemy, "Party for Your Right to Fight," *It Takes A Nation of Millions to Hold Us Back* (Public Enemy 1989).

27 Public Enemy, "Fight the Power," *Do the Right Thing* (1989).

28 Malcolm X was assassinated in the Audubon Ballroom in New York City. Columbia University bought the property and wanted to use it as a biomedical research site. The struggle in the 1990s between black grassroots activists and the university resulted in both a memorial for Malcolm X and a campus facility.

29 David Mills, "The Resurrection of Malcolm X: 25 Years After His Assassination, Rekindled Interest in the Slain Activist," *Washington Post*, February 20, 1990, F1.

30 "Is Malcolm X The New Jesus Christ?" *The Truth*, May 1992.

31 Henry Louis Gates, "Generation X—Interview with Spike Lee," *Black Film Review* 7, no. 3 (1992).

32 Kiburi Lee, "The Real Meaning of Malcolm X Day," *Pittsburgh Courier*, May 7, 1994, A7.

33 Harold E. Charles, "National Malcolm X Day," *Chicago Defender*, February 23, 1991, 16 and May 4, 1991, 18; Lee, "The Real Meaning of Malcolm X Day," *Pittsburgh Courier*, May 7, 1994, A7; Herman Ferguson, "Letter to Howard University Moorland-Spingarn Research Center," June 16, 1993.

34 "Juneteenth," House Congress Resolution, 107th Congress, 1st Session, June 21, 2001; Lula Briggs Galloway, *Juneteenth: Ring the Bell of Freedom* (Saginaw, MI: National Association of Juneteenth Lineage, 1998).

35 "Black on Black Love vs. Black Crime," *Chicago Defender*, February 21, 1984, 10; "Valentine's Day and Black on Black Love," *Chicago Defender*, February 14, 1985, 16.

36 Many people in the Black Power Movement were converted vegetarians.

37 Kevin Wilson, "Learning from Set-Backs Helps Her Rise to the Top," *Washington Afro-American*, August 13, 1999, B1; "Biographical Sketch of Ayo Handy-Clary," n.d.; "Profile of Ayo Handy-Clary," n.d.; both in personal papers of Ayo Handy-Kendi.

38 DeNeen L. Brown, "Heart and Soul: D.C. Woman Who Started Black Love Day Asks Community to Be Its Own Valentine," *Washington Post*, February 13, 1995, B1.

39 Ibid.

40 Dorothy Gilliam, "Building a Love to Help Us Heal," *Washington Post*, February 13, 1993, B1.

41 "Black Love Day—A Solution to Stop Violence?" *Capital Spotlight*, February 10, 1994, 11.

42 Ayo Handy-Kendi, *The Black Love Book* (Washington, DC, 2000); "Feel the Love," *Journey: Florida A&M University's Campus Magazine*, February 2004, 6–7.

43 "Chase Calendar of Events 2004," African American Holiday Association, personal papers of Ayo Handy-Kendi; Ward 1 representative Wilma R. Harvey wrote, "Throughout the past four years Black Love Day has addressed many special needs in the community. . . . During my nearly 10 years of service to the Board of Education, I have witnessed an escalation of violence in our schools. I believe that together we can make a difference and that Black Love Day . . . will encourage the necessary healing of mental pain, conflicts, stress and frustration associated with the violence in our schools." Wilma R. Harvey, Ward 1 Representative, District of Columbia Board of Education, February 13, 1996, personal papers of Ayo Handy-Kendi; Harry L. Thomas, Sr. "In Celebration of the Fourth Annual Black Love Day Relationship Ceremony," Council of the District of Columbia, Washington, DC, February 13, 1996, personal papers of Ayo Handy-Kendi.

44 "Call for Membership Development in the African American Holiday Association (AAHA)," May 2004; "The History of the Organization," n.d., personal papers of Ayo Handy-Kendi. The Free D.C. Movement is a struggle that advocates for making the District of Columbia a state.

45 Claude Lewis, "Blacks Should 'Seize' King Day," *The National Leader*, February 3, 1983, 15.

46 Ibid.

47 Ibid.; Karenga quoted in Ovetta Wiggins, "A Holiday about US Feting Black Culture: Kwanzaa Celebration Begins," *The Record*, December 26, 1996, A1. By the 1990s, Kwanzaa began receiving annual public recognition from Presidents Clinton and Bush.

48 Mary Ellen Perry, "A Yearning for a Symbolic Figure Like King," *Washington Star*, January 15, 1978, E1.

49 Ron Dellums, "In Celebration of Black History Month," *Congressional Records – Extensions*, 105th Congress, 1st Session, February 12, 1997.

50 Black holidays as a form of teaching and pedagogy inside classrooms has been identified as conservative multiculturalism. See Paul Gorski, "The Unintentional Undermining of Multicultural Education: Educators at the Equity Crossroads," in *White Teachers/Diverse Classrooms*, eds. Julie Landsman and Chance W. Lewis (Sterling, VA: Stylus, 2006).

# Bibliography

## Interviews by Author

Aboagye, Julius, conversation with author, 22 September 2001.

Adams, Bruce, conversation with author, 23 September 2001.

Ali, Ngoma, conversation with author, 9 May 2001.

Ali, Ngoma, conversation with author, 15 May 2001.

Ali, Ngoma, conversation with author, 23 September 2001.

Aminifu, Buddy Rose, conversation with author, 23 May 2001.

Chavunduka, conversation with author, 14 December 2000.

Crowe, Larry, conversation with author, 27 November 2000.

Damali, Sala, conversation with author, 18 July 2001.

Davis, Troy, conversation with author, 22 September 2001.

Ferrer, Jose, conversation with author, 4 November 1998.

Gellineau, Victor, conversation with author, 22 September 2001.

Halisi, Clyde Daniels, conversation with author, 30 April 2001.

Hall, David, conversation with author, 5 January 2001.

Hekima, Karl Key, conversation with author, 24 April 2001.

Heshimu, Oliver, conversation with author, 16 Feburary 2004.

Hoyes, Bernard, conversation with author, 29 July 2001.

Jadi, Tulivu, conversation with author, 14 September 2000.

Jones, Carolyn, conversation with author, 14 April 2001.

Karenga, Maulana, conversation with author, 9 February 1999.

Karenga, Maulana, conversation with author, 15 September 1999.

Karenga, Maulana, conversation with author, 12 May 2000.

Kulubally, Mansong, conversation with author, 10 October 2000.

Kulubally, Mansong, conversation with author, 27 November 2000.

Mesmaji, Fabunmi Webb, conversation with author, 23 April 2001.

Mtume, Faida, conversation with author, 3 February 2004.

Ongoza, Maisha Sullivan, and Ongoza, Kauli, conversation with author, 15 October 2000.
Sasha, Diarra, conversation with author, 23 September 2001.
Shabaka, Segun, conversation with author, 21 October 2000.
Sibeko-Kouate, Makinya, conversation with author, 26 June 2000.
Sibeko-Kouate, Makinya, conversation with author, 29 December 2000.
Sibeko-Kouate, Makinya, conversation with author, 2 April 2001.
Sibeko-Kouate, Makinya, conversation with author, 24 April 2001.
Spencer, Rod, conversation with author, 23 September 2001.
Sukumu, Vernon, conversation with author, 12 May 2001.
Whitaker, Sylvester, conversation with author, 6 November 2000.
Worrill, Conrad, conversation with author, 13 December 2000.
Worrill, Conrad, conversation with author, 16 December 2000.
Zulu, Huruma, conversation with author, 12 April 2000.
Zulu, Itibari, conversation with author, 10 February 1999.
Zulu, Itibari, conversation with author, 12 May 2000.

## ARCHIVAL MATERIALS AND PRIVATE COLLECTIONS

Amiri Baraka Papers, Moorland-Spingarn Research Center, Howard University, Washington, DC, 2001.
Carter G. Woodson Papers, Moorland-Spingarn Research Center, Howard University, Washington, DC, 2004.
Kwanzaa, Vertical File, UCLA Center for African-American Studies Library, Los Angeles, CA, 1999.
Kwanzaa Collection, Library of Congress, Washington, DC, 2001.
Kwanzaa Collection, Schomburg Center for Research in Black Culture, New York City, 2000.
Malcolm X Vertical File, Moorland-Spingarn Research Center, Howard University, Washington, DC, 2005.
Martin Luther King, Jr. Vertical File, Moorland-Spingarn Research Center, Howard University, Washington, DC, 2005.
McCone Commission Papers, Princeton University, Firestone Library, Princeton University, Princeton, NJ, 1999.
Personal Papers of Ayo Handy-Kendi, in the hands of Ayo Handy-Kendi, 2004.
Personal Papers of Clyde Daniels-Halisi, in the hands of Clyde Daniels-Halisi, 2001.
Personal Papers of Conrad Worrill, in the hands of Conrad Worrill, 2000.
Personal Papers of Maisha Ongoza, in the hands of Maisha Ongoza, 2000.
Personal Papers of Makinya Sibeko-Kouate, in the hands of Makinya Sibeko-Kouate, 2001.
Personal Papers of Mansong Kulubally, in the hands of Mansong Kulubally, 2000.
Personal Papers of Ngoma Ali, in the hands of Ngoma Ali, 2001.
Personal Papers of Segun Shabaka, in the hands of Segun Shabaka, 2000.

## AUDIOVISUAL SOURCES

Akua, Rev. Chike. *Kwanzaa in Christ*. Imani Interprises, 1999. Audio recording.

Asante, M.K. *The Black Candle: A Kwanzaa Celebration*. Asante Filmworx, 2008. DVD.

Cobb, Steve and Chavunduka. *Seven Principles*, 1993. Compact disc.

Karenga, Dr. Maulana. *The African-American Holiday of Kwanzaa*. Interview with Dr. Maulana Karenga, the Creator of Kwanzaa, Los Angeles: University of Sankore Press, 1995. Videocassette.

Karenga, Dr. Maulana. *The Black Man as a Cultural Representative: Practicing the Seven Principles (The Nguzo Saba)*. 12th Annual Black Man Think Tank, African American Cultural and Research Center, University of Cincinnati, Cincinnati, January 1997. Videocassette.

*Kwanzaa Kwest*. Konscious Kommunications, 1994. Videocassette.

*Kwanzaa Kwest*. Original soundtrack to the video, Konscious Kommunications, 1993. Audio recording.

*The Nguzo Saba*. Konscious Kassettes, n.d. Audio recording.

## UNPUBLISHED SOURCES

Austin, Regina. "Kwanzaa and the Commodification of Black Culture." Unpublished paper, 10 April 2001.

Halisi, Imamu Clyde, ed. *Kwanzaa: May Your Holiday Be with Much Happiness*. Los Angeles: US Organization, 1968?

Karenga, Maulana. "Kwanzaa and Corporate Commercialism." Unpublished paper, n.d.

US Organization. "1969 Kwanzaa Program." US Organization, School of Afroamerican Culture, Education Committe, n.d.

## UNPUBLISHED INTERVIEWS

"Black Leadership in Los Angeles: Robert Singleton," *UCLA Center for African-American Studies*, Oral History Program, 1999.

"Black Leadership in Los Angeles: Virgil P. Roberts," *UCLA Center for African-American Studies*, Oral History Program, 1998.

"Black Leadership in Los Angeles: Marnesba Tackett," *UCLA Center for African-American Studies*, Oral History Program, 1988.

"Black Leadership in Los Angeles: Mary Jane Hewitt," *UCLA Center for African-American Studies*, Oral History Program, 2001.

"Black Power Conference Reports—Philadelphia and Bermuda." *Afram Associates*, 1970.

"Statement by Wesley Brazier, Executive Director of the Los Angeles Urban League to the McCone Commission." 14 October 1965, *McCone Papers*, vol. 4.

"Testimony of H. Hartford Brookins, Pastor, First African Methodist Episcopal Church to the McCone Commission." 29 September 1965, *McCone Papers*, vol. 4.

"Testimony of Norman B. Houston, President of the Los Angeles Branch of the NAACP to the McCone Commission." 12 October 1965, *McCone Papers*, vol. 8.

"Testimony of Wendell Collins, Vice-Chairman of the Los Angeles Branch of CORE to the McCone Commission." 4 November 1965, *McCone Papers*, vol. 5.

## DISSERTATIONS

Brown, Scot. "The US Organization: African-American Cultural Nationalism in the Era of Black Power, 1965 to the 1970s." PhD dissertation, Cornell University, 1999.

Glasgow, Douglas Graham. "The Sons of Watts Improvement Association: The Sons of Watts – Analysis of Mobility Aspirations and Life-Styles in the Aftermath of the Watts Riot, 1965." PhD dissertation, University of Southern California, 1968.

Karenga, Maulana. "MAAT – The Moral Ideal in Ancient Egypt: A Study in Classical African Ethics." PhD dissertation, University of Southern California, 1994.

Tyler, Bruce. "Black Radicalism in Southern California, 1950–1982." PhD dissertation, University of California—Los Angeles, 1983.

## GOVERNMENT DOCUMENTS

Carter, Jimmy. "National Afro-American (Black) History Month," www.presidency.ucsb.edu/ws/index, 27 January 1978.

Clinton, William J. "Message on the Observance of Kwanzaa, 1997," *Weekly Compilation of Presidential documents,* 29 December 1997.

Report by the Governor's Commission on the Los Angeles Riots. *Violence in the City – An End or a Beginning?* 2 December 1965.

U.S. Congress, Senate. *Requesting the President to Proclaim February 1 as National Freedom Day.* 80th Congress, 1st Session, 25 July 1947.

U.S. Congress, House of Representatives, Committee on the Judiciary. *Requesting the President to Proclaim February 1 as National Freedom Day.* 80th Congress, 2nd Session, 17 June 1948.

U.S. Congress, Senate, Congressional Record. Senate Joint Resolution 159. *Introduction of Joint Resolution Designating January 15 of Each Year as Martin Luther King Day.* 8 April 1968.

U.S. Congress, House of Representatives, Congressional Record. *Monday Holidays.* 90th Congress, 2nd Session, 8 May 1968–15 May 1968, vol. 114, part 10.

U.S. Congress, House of Representatives, Congressional Record. *School Holiday Urged on Birthday of Malcolm X.* 90th Congress, 2nd Session, 16 May 1968–24 May 1968, vol. 114, part 11.

U.S. Congress, House of Representatives, Subcommittee on Census and Population of the Committee on Post Office and Civil Service. *Designate the Birthday of Martin Luther King, Jr. as a Legal Pubic Holiday.* 94th Congress, 1st Session, Washington, DC, 1975.

U.S. Congress, House of Representatives, Congressional Records – Extensions. *The 26th Anniversary of Kwanzaa.* 102nd Congress, 2nd Session, 3 January 1992.

U.S. Congress, House of Representatives, Congressional Records. Ron Dellums, *In Celebration of Black History Month.* 105th Congress, 1st Session, 12 February 1997.

U.S. Congress. House of Representatives, Congressional Record Extensions. *The Occasion of the 30th Anniversary of the S.H.A.P.E. Community Center.* 106th Congress, 2nd Session, 11 May 2000.

U.S. Congress, House of Representatives, House Congress Resolution. *Juneteenth.* 107th Congress, 1st Session, 21 June 2001.

## Newspapers, Magazines, Journals

about . . . time Magazine

Afro-Americans in New York Life and History

American Anthropologist

American Studies

Atlanta Inquirer

Atlanta Journal-Constitution

Atlantic Monthly

Avon Boutique

Baltimore Afro-American

Baltimore Jewish Times

Ba Papyrus (Soul Papers)

Bay State Banner

Black Books Bulletin

Black Child

Black Collegian

Black Enterprise

Black Film Review

Black Journal Strike Bulletin

Black Lines

Black News

Black Scholar

Black World

Business Wire

California Voice

Cape Verdean News

Capital Spotlight

Chicago Citizen

Chicago Defender

Chicago Sun-Times

Chicago Weekend

Christian Science Monitor

Cleveland Call & Post

Daily World

Dallas Morning News
Detroit News
Diversity Folio
Ebony
Encore
Essence
Evening Star
Ft. Lauderdale Sun-Sentinel
Ghana Notes and Queries
Group Notes
Heart & Soul
Herald-Dispatch
Hilltop
Hyde Park Citizen
Italian Voice
Jacksonville Free Press
Jet
Jewish Bulletin
Jewish Exponent
Journal & Guide
Journal of American Ethnic History
Journal of American History
Journal of Black Psychology
Journal of Blacks in Higher Education
Journal of Community Advocacy and Activism
Journal of Negro History
Journal of Women's History
Journey: Florida A&M University's Campus Magazine
Kansas City Star
Kuumba Report
Kwanzaa Fest '98 (Caribbean Life)
Kwanzaa Fest '98 (New York Daily News)
Kwanzaa Magazine (Daily News)
LA Community Coupon Clipper
Life
Long Beach Free Press
Long Island Monthly
Look Magazine
Los Angeles Chronicle
Los Angeles Collegian
Los Angeles Daily News
Los Angeles Free Press
Los Angeles Sentinel
Los Angeles Times

Louisville Courier-Journal
Merritt College Reporter
Miami Times
Michigan Chronicle
Michigan Citizen
Muhammad Speaks
Negro Digest
Negro History Bulletin
Newark Star-Ledger
New Moon Network
New Orleans Times-Picayune
New Pittsburgh Courier
Newsweek
New York Amsterdam News
New York Beacon
New York Daily News
New York Times
New York Voice
Nommo
Oakland Post
Oakland Tribune
Omaha World-Herald
Pamoja
Philadelphia Tribune
Pittsburgh Courier
Pittsburgh Post-Gazette
Portland Oregonian
PR Newswire
Public Interest
Public Relations Journal
Radical History Review
Reunion
Sacramento Observer
San Diego Union-Tribune
Soul
Special Supplements
St. Louis American
St. Petersburg Times
Sun Reporter
Sunday Star
Sunday Tribune
Tennessee Tribune
The Age
The Black Panther

The Crisis
The Movement
The National Leader
The Record
The Truth
The Village Voice
Time
Tri-State Defender
UCLA Daily Bruin
U.S. News & World Report
Wall Street Journal
Washington Afro-American
Washington Informer
Washington Post
Washington Star
Washington Times

## BOOKS

Afin, Iya, and Ayobunmi Sangode. *Rites of Passage: Psychology of Female Power.* Brooklyn, NY: Athelia Henrietta Press, Inc., 1999.

Akua, Chike (Justin Fenwick). *A Kwanzaa Awakening.* Decautur, GA: Imani Enterprises, 2000.

Allen, James de Vere. *Swahili Origins: Swahili Culture & The Shungwaya Phenomenon.* Athens: Ohio University Press, 1993.

Allen, Robert L. *Black Awakening in Capitalist America.* New York: Anchor Books, 1969.

Amadi, Elechi. *Ethics In Nigerian Culture.* Ibadan: Heinemann Education Books, 1982.

American Assembly. *The United States and Africa.* New York: Columbia University, 1958.

——, ed. *Black Economic Development.* Englewood Cliffs: Prentice Hall, 1969.

Anderson, Benedict. *Imagined Communities: Reflections on the Origin and Spread of Nationalism.* London: Verso, 1991 [1983].

Anderson, Frederick E. *The Development of Leadership and Organization Building in the Black Community of Los Angeles from 1900 Through World War I.* Saratoga: Century Twenty One Publishing, 1980.

Anthony, Earl. *The Time of the Furnaces: A Case Study of Black Student Revolt.* New York: The Dial Press, 1971.

Anyike, James C. *African American Holidays: A Historical Research and Resource Guide to Cultural Celebrations.* Chicago: Popular Truth Inc., 1991.

Appelbaum, Diana Karter. *Thanksgiving: An American Holiday, An American History.* New York: Facts On File Publications, 1984.

Appiah, Kwame Anthony. *In My Father's House: Africa in the Philosophy of Culture.* New York: Oxford University Press, 1992.

Appiah, Kwame Anthony, and Henry Louis Gates, Jr., eds. *Identities.* Chicago: University of Chicago Press, 1995.

Aptheker, Herbert, ed. *The Correspondence of W.E.B. Du Bois: Volume 1 – Selections, 1877–1934*. Amherst: University of Massachusetts Press, 1973.

Austin, Algernon. *Achieving Blackness: Race, Black Nationalism and Afrocentrism in the Twentieth Century*. New York: NYU Press, 2006.

Averitt, Robert T. *The Duel Economy: The Dynamics of American Industry Structure*. New York: W.W. Norton, 1968.

Awolalu, Omosade F. *Yoruba Beliefs and Sacrificial Rites*. London: Longmans Group Ltd., 1979.

Baraka, Amiri. *Raise, Race, Rays, Raze: Essays Since 1965*. New York: Random House, 1969.

—, ed. *African Congress: A Documentary of the First Modern Pan-African Congress*. New York: William Morrow & Company Inc., 1972.

—. *Kawaida Studies: The New Nationalism*. Chicago: Third World Press, 1972.

—. *Kawaida National Liberation and Socialism*. Newark: Jihad, 1974.

—. *Daggers and Javelins: Essays, 1974–1979*. New York: Quill, 1984.

—. *The Autobiography of Leroi Jones*. Chicago: Lawrence Hill Books, 1997 [1984].

—. *The LeRoi Jones/Amiri Baraka Reader*. New York: Thunder's Mouth Press, 1989.

Barashango, Rev. Ishakamusa. *Afrikan People and European Holidays: A Mental Genocide, Book I*. Silver Spring, MD: Fourth Dynasty Publishing Company, 1980.

—. *Afrikan People and European Holidays: A Mental Genocide, Book II*. Silver Spring, MD: Fourth Dynasty Publishing Company, 1983.

Barbour, Floyd B., ed. *The Black Seventies*. Boston: Extending Horizons Books, 1968.

—, ed. *The Black Power Revolt: A Collection of Essays*. Boston: Extending Horizons Books, 1968.

Barker, Anthony J. *The African Link: British Attitudes to the Negro in the Era of the Atlantic Slave Trade, 1550–1807*. London: Frank Cass and Company, Ltd., 1978.

Barrett, Sr., Leonard E. *The Rastafarians: Sounds of Cultural Dissonance*. Boston: Beacon Press, 1988 [1977].

Bass, Amy. *Not the Struggle But the Triumph: The 1968 Olympics and the Making of the Black Athlete*. Minneapolis: University of Minnesota Press, 2002.

Bauer, Raymond A., and Scott M. Cunningham. *Studies in the Negro Market*. Cambridge: Marketing Science Institute, Harvard Graduate School of Business Administration, 1970.

Bell, Bernard W., Emily R. Grosholz, and James B. Stewart, eds. *W.E.B. Du Bois on Race and Culture: Philosophy, Politics, and Poetics*. New York: Routledge, 1996.

Bell, Catherine. *Ritual Theory, Ritual Practice*. New York: Oxford University Press, 1992.

—. *Ritual: Perspectives and Dimensions*. New York: Oxford University Press, 1997.

Benhabib, Seyla, ed. *Democracy and Difference: Contesting the Boundaries of the Political*. Princeton: Princeton University Press, 1996.

Benko, Georges, and Ulf Strohmayer, eds. *Space & Social Theory: Interpreting Modernity and Postmodernity*. Oxford: Blackwell Publishers Ltd., 1997.

Benson Henderson, Alexa, and Janice Sumler-Edmond. *Freedom's Odyssey: African American History Essays from Phylon*. Atlanta: Clark Atlanta University Press, 1999.

Berghahn, Marion. *Images of Africa In Black American Literature*. London: The Macmillan Press Ltd., 1977.

Berube, Maurice R., and Marilyn Gittell, eds. *Confrontation At Ocean Hill-Brownsville: The New York School Strikes of 1968*. New York: Frederick A. Praeger, 1969.

Bethel, Elizabeth Rauh. *The Roots of African-American Identity: Memory and History in Free Antebellum Communities*. New York: St. Martin's Press, 1997.

Black Public Sphere Collective, eds. *The Black Public Sphere: A Public Culture Book*. Chicago: University of Chicago Press, 1995.

Blight, David W. *Race and Reunion: The Civil War in American Memory*. Cambridge: The Belknap Press of Harvard University Press, 2001.

Bollins, John C., and Grant B. Geyer. *Yorty: Politics of a Constant Candidate*. Pacific Palisades: Palisades Publishers, 1973.

Boorstin, Daniel J. *The Americans: The Democratic Experience*. New York: Vintage Books, 1973.

Boswell, David, and Jessica Evans, eds. *Representing the Nation: A Reader: Histories, Heritage and Museums*. London: Routledge, 1999.

Bourgault, Louise. *Playing for Life: Performance in Africa in the Age of AIDS*. Durham, NC: Carolina Academic Press, 2003.

Boyarin, Jonathan. *Remapping Memory: The Politics of TimeSpace*. Minneapolis: University of Minnesota Press, 1994.

Brackman, Barbara. *Facts and Fabrications: Unraveling the History of Quilts and Slavery*. Concord, CA: C&T Publishing, 2006.

Bracy, Jr., John H., August Meier, and Elliott Rudwick, eds. *Black Nationalism in America*. Indianapolis: The Bobbs-Merrill Company, Inc., 1970.

Briggs Galloway, Lula. *Juneteenth: Ring the Bell of Freedom*. Saginaw, MI: National Association of Juneteenth Lineage, 1998.

Brown, Elaine. *A Taste of Power: A Black Woman's Story*. New York: Doubleday, 1992.

Brown, Scot. *Fighting for US: Maulana Karenga, the US Organization, and Black Cultural Nationalism*. New York: New York University Press, 2003.

Brundage, Fitzhugh W. *Where These Memories Grow: History, Memory, and Southern Identity*. Chapel Hill: University of North Carolina Press, 2000.

Bulpin, T.V. *Natal and the Zulu Country*. Cape Town: Books of Africa, 1966.

Bush, Rod. *We Are Not What We Seem: Black Nationalism and Class Struggle in the American Century*. New York: New York University Press, 1999.

Butler, John Sibley. *Entrepreneurship and Self-Help Among Black Americans: A Reconsideration of Race and Economics*. Albany: State University of New York Press, 1991.

Carmichael, Stokely. *Stokely Speaks: Black Power Back to Pan Africanism*. New York: Random House, 1971 [1965].

——, and Charles Hamilton. *Black Power: The Politics of Liberation in America*. New York: Vintage, 1967.

Carson, Clayborne. *In Struggle: SNCC and the Black Awakening of the 1960s*. Cambridge: Harvard University Press, 1981.

——, ed. *The Movement, 1964–1970*. Westport: Greenwood Press, 1993.

Carter, Erica, James Donald, and Judith Squires, eds. *Cultural Remix: Theories of Politics and the Popular*. London: Lawrence & Wishart, 1995.

Cashmore, Ellis. *The Black Culture Industry*. London: Routledge, 1997.

Chester, Edward W. *Clash of Titans: Africa and U.S. Foreign Policy*. New York: Orbis Books, 1974.

Chocolate, Deborah M. Newton. *Kwanzaa*. Chicago: Children's Press, 1990.

Clark, Kathleen Ann. *Defining Moments: African American Commemoration and Political Culture in the South, 1863–1913*. Chapel Hill: University of North Carolina Press, 2005.

Cleaver, Kathleen, and Geroge Katsiaficas, eds. *Liberation, Imagination, and the Black Panther Party: A New Look At the Panthers and Their Legacy*. New York: Routledge, 2001.

Clifford, James. *The Predicament of Culture: Twentieth-Century Ethnography, Literature, and Art*. Cambridge, MA: Harvard University Press, 1988.

Cohen, Abner. *Masquerade Politics: Explorations in the Structure of Urban Cultural Movements*. Providence: Berg Publishers Limited, 1993.

Coles, Robert. *Doing Documentary Work*. New York: Oxford University Press, 1997.

Collins, Keith E. *Black Los Angeles: The Maturing Of The Ghetto, 1940–1950*. Saratoga: Century Twenty One Publishing, 1980.

Comaroff, John, and Jean Comaroff. *Ethnography and the Historical Imagination*. Boulder: Westview Press, 1992.

Connelly, Mark. *Christmas: A Social History*. London: I.B. Tauris Publishers, 1999.

Cook, Debrorah. *The Culture Industry Revisited: Theodor W. Adorno on Mass Culture*. London: Rowman and Littlefield Publishers Inc., 1996.

Coombe, Rosemary J. *The Cultural Life of Intellectual Properties: Authorship, Appropriation, and the Law*. Durham, NC: Duke University Press, 1998.

Copage, Eric V. *Kwanzaa: An African-American Celebration of Culture and Cooking*. New York: Quill/William Morrow, 1991.

Cowley, John. *Carnival, Canboulay and Calypso: Traditions In The Making*. Cambridge: Cambridge University Press, 1996.

Cressy, David. *Bonfires and Bells: National Memory and the Protestant Calendar in Elizabethan and Stuart England*. London: Weidenfeld and Nicolson, 1989.

Cromwell Hill, Adelaide, and Martin Kilson, eds. *Apropos of Africa: Sentiments of Negro American Leaders on Africa from the 1800s to the 1950s*. London: Frank Cass and Company Limited, 1969.

Crummell, Alex. *Africa and America: Addresses and Discourses*. Miami: Mnemosyne Publishing Inc., 1969.

Cruse, Harold. *The Crisis of the Negro Intellectual*. New York: Quill, 1984.

Dávila, Arlene. *Latinos, Inc.: The Marketing and Making of a People*. Berkeley: University of California Press, 2001.

Davis, Angela. *Angela Davis: An Autobiography*. New York: International Publishers, 1988 [1974].

Davis, Benjamin J. *Communist Councilman From Harlem: Autobiographical Notes Written In A Federal Penitentiary*. New York: International Publishers, 1969.

Davis, James F. *Who Is Black: One Nation's Definition*. University Park: The Pennsylvania State University Press, 1991.

Davis, Mike. *City Of Quartz: Excavating The Future In Los Angeles*. New York: Vintage Books, 1990.

Davis, Natalie Zemon. *Society and Culture in Early Modern France*. Stanford: Stanford University Press, 1965.

Davis, Richard A. *The Myth of Black Ethnicity: Monophylety, Diversity, and the Dilemma of Identity*. Greenwich: Ablex Publishing Corporation, 1997.

Davis, Susan G. *Parades and Power: Street Theatre in Nineteenth-Century Philadelphia*. Philadelphia: Temple University Press, 1986.

Davis Pickney, Andrea. *Seven Candles for Kwanzaa*. New York: Dial Books for Young Readers, 1993.

DeLeon, David, ed. *Leaders from the 1960s: A Biographical Sourcebook of American Activism*. Westport: Greenwood Press, 1994.

Dennis, Matthew. *Red, White, and Blue Letter Days: An American Calendar*. Ithaca: Cornell University Press, 2002.

Derrida, Jacques. *Writing and Difference*. Chicago: University of Chicago Press, 1978.

Ding, Francis Mading. *The Dinka of the Sudan*. New York: Holt, Rinehart, and Winston, 1972.

Dirks, Robert. *The Black Saturnalia: Conflict and Its Ritual Expression On British West Indian Slave Plantations*. Gainesville: University of Florida Press, 1987.

Drake, St. Clair. *The Redemption of Africa and Black Religion*. Chicago: Third World Press, 1970.

Draper, Theodore. *The Rediscovery of Black Nationalism*. New York: The Viking Press, 1970 [1969].

Du Bois, W.E.B. *The Negro in Business*. New York: Arno Press, 1968 [1899].

——. *The Negro*. New York: Holt, 1915.

DuCille, Ann. *Skin Trade*. Cambridge: Harvard University Press, 1996.

du Gay, Paul. *Production of Culture / Cultures of Production*. London: Sage Publications, 1997.

Edwards, Paul K. *The Southern Urban Negro As a Consumer*. New York: Prentice Hall Inc., 1932.

Eklof, Barbara. *For Every Season: The Complete Guide to African American Celebrations Traditional to Contemporary*. New York: HarperCollins, 1997.

Esedebe, Olisanwuche P. *Pan-Africanism: The Idea and Movement, 1776–1991*. Washington: Howard University Press, 1994.

Etzioni, Amitai, and Jared Bloom. *We Are What We Celebrate: Understanding Holidays and Rituals*. New York: New York University Press, 2004.

Fabre, Geneviève, and Robert O'Meally, eds. *History & Memory in African-American Culture*. New York: Oxford University Press, 1994.

Falola, Toyin. *Culture and Customs of Nigeria*. Westport: Greenwood Press, 2001.

Fanon, Frantz. *Toward the African Revolution*. New York: Grove Press, 1964.

——. *Black Skin, White Masks*. New York: Grove Press, 1967.

——. *The Wretched of the Earth*. New York: Grove Press, 1968.

Fernando, Jr., S.H. *The New Beats: Exploring the Music, Culture, and Attitudes of Hip Hop*. New York: Anchor Books, 1994.

Finn, Julio. *Voices of Negritude*. London: Quartet Books, 1988.

Flowers, Sandra Hollin. *African American Nationalist Literature of the 1960s: Pens of Fire*. New York: Garland Publishing, Inc., 1996.

Foner, Philip S., ed. *The Life and Writings of Frederick Douglass,* vol. 2. New York: International Publishers, 1950.

—., ed. *The Black Panthers Speak*. New York: Da Capo Press, 1995 [1970].

Ford, Juwanda G., and Ken Wilson-Max. *K is for Kwanzaa: A Kwanzaa Alphabet Book*. New York: Scholastic, Inc., 1997.

Forde, Daryll. *African Worlds: Studies in the Cosmological Ideas and Social Values of African Peoples*. London: Oxford University Press, 1954.

Foster, Julian, and Durward Long, eds. *Protest! Student Activism in America*. New York: William Morrow & Company, Inc., 1970.

Foucault, Michel. *Power/Knowledge: Selected Interviews and Other Writings, 1972–1977*, ed. Colin Gordon. New York: Pantheon Books, 1980.

Frank, Thomas, and Matt Weiland, eds. *Commodify Your Dissent: Salvos from The Baffler*. New York: W.W. Norton and Company, Inc., 1997.

Fried, Richard M. *The Russians Are Coming! The Russians Are Coming!: Pageantry and Patriotism in Cold-War America*. New York: Oxford University Press, 1998.

Fry, Gladys Marie. *Stitched from the Soul: Slave Quilts from the Antebellum South*. New York: Dutton Studio Books, 1990.

Fulop, Timothy E., and Albert Rabateau, eds. *African-American Religion: Interpretive Essays in History and Culture*. New York: Routledge, 1997.

Geertz, Clifford. *The Interpretation of Cultures*. New York: Basic Books, 1973.

Genovese, Eugene. *Roll Jordan Roll: The World the Slaves Made*. New York: Pantheon, 1972.

Gibson, Parke D. *The $30 Billion Negro*. London: Collier-Macmillan Ltd., 1969.

Gillis, John R., ed. *Commemorations: The Politics of National Identity*. New Jersey: Princeton University Press, 1994.

Gilroy, Paul. *The Black Atlantic: Modernity and Double Consciousness*. Cambridge: Harvard University Press, 1993.

Glassberg, David. *American Historical Pageantry: The Uses of Tradition in the Early Twentieth Century*. Chapel Hill: The University of North Carolina Press, 1990.

Glazer, Nathan. *We Are All Multiculturalists Now*. Cambridge: Harvard University Press, 1997.

Goldberg, David Theo., ed. *Multiculturalism: A Critical Reader*. Oxford: Blackwell Publishers Inc., 1994.

Goldschmidt, Walter, ed. *The United States and Africa*. New York: Frederick A. Praeger, Inc., 1963.

Green, Stephanie. *The Rugrats' First Kwanzaa*. New York: Simon Spotlight/Nickelodeon, 2001.

Greenberg, Cheryl. *Or Does It Explode?: Black Harlem in the Great Depression*. New York: Oxford University Press, 1991.

Greene, Lorenzo J. *Working with Carter G. Woodson, The Father of Black History: A Diary, 1928–1930*. Baton Rouge: Louisiana State University Press, 1989.

——. *Selling Black History For Carter G. Woodson: A Diary, 1930–1933*. Columbia: University of Missouri Press, 1996.

Greenstone, David J., and Paul E. Peterson. *Race and Authority in Urban Politics: Community Participation and the War on Poverty*. New York: Russell Sage Foundation, 1973.

Gregory, Ruth W. *Anniversaries and Holidays: Third Edition*. Chicago: American Library Association, 1975.

Grele, Ronald J. *Envelopes of Sound: The Art of Oral History*. Chicago: Precedent Publishing Inc., 1985.

Griaule, Marcel. *Conversations with Ogotemmeli: An Introduction to Dogon Religious Ideas*. London: Oxford University Press, 1965.

Guillory, Monique, and Richard C. Green, eds. *Soul: Black Power, Politics, and Pleasure*. New York: New York University Press, 1998.

Gutierrez, Ramon, and Geneviève Fabre, eds. *Feasts and Celebrations: In North American Ethnic Communities*. Albuquerque: University of New Mexico Press, 1995.

Gyekeye, Kwame. *Tradition and Modernity: Philosophical Reflections on the African Experience*. New York: Oxford University Press, 1997.

Haddad, William F., and G. Douglas Pugh, eds. *Black Economic Development*. Englewood Cliffs: Prentice Hall, Inc., 1969.

Hailey, Alex. *Roots*. New York: Doubleday & Company, Inc., 1976.

Halbwachs, Maurice. *On Collective Memory*. Chicago: University of Chicago Press, 1992.

Halisi, Clyde, ed. *Kitabu: Beginning Concepts in Kawaida*. Los Angeles: Temple of Kawaida, 1971.

——, and James Mtume, eds. *The Quotable Karenga*. Los Angeles: US Organization, 1967.

Hall, Stuart, and Martin Jacques, eds. *New Times: The Changing Face of Politics in the 1990s*. London: Lawrence & Wishart, 1989.

Halter, Marilyn. *Shopping for Identity: The Marketing of Ethnicity*. New York: Schocken Books, 2000.

Handy-Kendi, Ayo. *The Black Love Book*. Washington, DC, 2000.

Harris, Jessica B. *A Kwanzaa Keepsake: Celebrating the Holiday with New Traditions and Feasts*. New York: Fireside, 1995.

Harris, Leonard. *Philosophy Born of Struggle: Anthology of Afro-American Philosophy from 1917*. Dubuque: Kendall/Hunt Publishing Company, 1983.

Harris, Neil. *Cultural Excursions: Marketing Appetites and Cultural Tastes in Modern America*. Chicago: University of Chicago Press, 1990.

Harris, Norman. *The Sixties: A Black Chronology*. Georgia: The Black Resource Center, 1990.

Hartmann, Douglas. *Race, Culture, and the Revolt of the Black Athlete: The 1968 Olympic Protests and Their Aftermath*. Chicago: University of Chicago Press, 2003.

Harvey, David. *Justice, Nature & the Geography of Difference*. Oxford: Blackwell, 1996.

Haskins, James. *Profiles in Black Power*. New York: Doubleday, 1971.

Hatch, Jane M. *The American Book of Days*, 3rd edn. New York: H. W. Wilson, 1978.

Haven, Kendall. *New Year's to Kwanzaa: Original Stories of Celebration*. Golden: Fulcrum Resources, 1999.

Hebdige, Dick. *Subculture: The Meaning of Style*. London: Routledge, 1979.

Hein, Hilde S. *The Museum in Transition: A Philosophical Perspective*. Washington, DC: Smithsonian Institution Press, 2000.

Heinze, Andrew R. *Adapting to Abundance: Jewish Immigrants, Mass Consumption, and the Search for American Identity*. New York: Columbia University Press, 1990.

Herskovits, Melville J. *The Myth of the Negro Past*. Boston: Beacon Press, 1958 [1941].

Hobsbawm, Eric, and Terence Ranger, eds. *The Invention of Tradition*. Cambridge: Cambridge University Press, 1983.

Hollinger, David A. *Postethnic America: Beyond Multiculturalism*. New York: Basic Books, 1995.

Holloway, Joseph E., ed. *Africanisms In American Culture*. Bloomington: Indiana University Press, 1990.

Hooper-Greenhill, ed. *Cultural Diversity: Developing Museum Audiences in Britain*. London: University Press, 1997.

Horde, Fred Lee, and Jonathan Scott Lee, eds. *I Am Because We Are: Readings in Black Philosophy*. Amherst: University of Massachusetts Press, 1995.

Horne, Donald. *The Public Culture: The Triumph of Industrialism*. London: Pluto Press, 1986.

Horne, Gerald. *Black Liberation / Red Scare: Ben Davis and the Communist Party*. Newark: University of Delaware Press, 1994.

Horne, Gerald. *Fire This Time: The Watts Uprising and the 1960s*. New York: Da Capo Press, 1997.

Horsley, Richard, and James Tracy, eds. *Christmas Unwrapped: Consumerism, Christ, and Culture*. Harrisburg: Trinity Press International, 2001.

Howe, Stephen. *Afrocentrism: Mythical Pasts and Imagined Homes*. London: Verso, 1998.

Humphrey, Imani A. *First Fruits: The Family Guide to Celebrating Kwanzaa*. Chicago: Third World Press, 1993.

Humphrey, Theodore C., and Lin T. Humphrey, eds. *We Gather Together: Food and Festival in American Life*. Ann Arbor: UMI Research Press, 1988.

Hutchinson, John. *The Dynamics of Cultural Nationalism: The Gaelic Revival and the Creation of the Irish Nation State*. London: Allen and Unwin, 1987.

Hutchinson, John, and Anthony D. Smith, eds. *Ethnicity*. Oxford: Oxford University Press, 1996.

Hutton, Patrick H. *History as an Art of Memory*. Hanover: University Press of New England, 1993.

Isaacs, Harold R. *The New World of Negro Americans*. New York: The Viking Press, 1963.

——. *Idols of the Tribe: Group Identity and Political Change*. New York: Harper and Row Publishers, 1975.

Jacques Garvey, Amy, ed. *The Philosophy & Opinions of Marcus Garvey*. Dover: The Majority Press, 1986.

James, E.O. *Seasonal Feasts and Festivals*. New York: Barnes and Noble Inc., 1961.

Jenkins, David. *Black Zion: Africa, Imagined and Real, as Seen By Today's Blacks*. New York: Harcourt Brace Jovanovich, 1975.

Johnson, Charles. *Being & Race: Black Writing Since 1970*. Bloomington: Indiana University Press, 1990.

Jones, Charles E., ed. *The Black Panther Party: Reconsidered*. Baltimore: Black Classic Press, 1978.

Jones, LeRoi. *Home: Social Essays*. New York: William Morrow & Co., Inc., 1966.

Jordan, Winthrop D. *White Over Black: American Attitudes Toward the Negro, 1550–1812*. New York: W.W. Norton & Company, 1968.

Joseph, Peniel, ed. *Black Power: Rethinking the Civil Rights and Black Power Era*. New York: Routledge, 2006.

——. *Waiting 'Til the Midnight Hour: A Narrative History of Black Power in America*. New York: Henry Holt, 2006.

Joyce, George. *The Black Consumer: Dimensions of Behavior and Strategy*. New York: Random House, Inc., 1971.

Junod, Henri A. *The Life of a South African Tribe*, 2. vols. New Hyde Park, NY University Books, 1966.

Kachun, Mitchell. *Festivals of Freedom: Memory and Meaning in African American Emancipation Celebrations, 1808–1915*. Amherst: University of Massachusetts Press, 2003.

Kammen, Michael. *Mystic Chords of Memory: The Transformation of Tradition in American Culture*. New York: Vintage Books, 1991.

Kanneh, Kadiatu. *Race, Nation, and Culture In Ethnography, Pan Africanism and Black Literatures*. London: Routledge, 1998.

Karagueuzian, Dikran. *Blow It Up! The Black Student Revolt At San Francisco State College and the Emergence of Dr. Hayakawa*. Boston: Gambit, Inc., 1971.

Karenga, Maulana. *Kawaida Theory: An Introductory Outline*. Inglewood: Kawaida Publications, 1980.

——. *Introduction to Black Studies*. Los Angeles: Kawaida Publications, 1982.

——. *Selections from the Husia: Sacred Wisdom of Ancient Egypt*. Los Angeles: University of Sankore Press, 1984.

——. *The African American Holiday of Kwanzaa: A Celebration of Family, Community, and Culture*. Los Angeles: University of Sankore Press, 1988.

——. *Kwanzaa: A Celebration of Family, Community, and Culture*. Los Angeles: University of Sankore Press, 1998.

——. *Odu Ifa: The Ethical Teachings*. Los Angeles: University of Sankore Press, 1999.

Karenga, Maulana Ron. *Kwanzaa: May Your Holiday Be with Much Happiness*. San Diego: Kawaida Publications, 1975.

——. *Kwanzaa: Origins, Concepts, Practice*. Inglewood: Kawaida Publications, 1977.

——. *Essays on Struggle: Position and Analysis*. San Diego: Kawaida Publications, 1978.

Kavanagh, Gaynor, ed. *Making Histories in Museums*. London: Leicester University Press, 1996.

Kenyatta, Jomo. *Facing Mount Kenya: The Tribal Life of the Gikuyu*. New York: Vintage Books, 1962.

Kijakazi, Kilolo. *African-American Economic Development and Small Business Ownership*. New York: Garland Publishing, 1997.

King, Woodie, and Earl Anthony, eds. *Black Poets and Prophets*. New York: New American Library, 1972.

Konadu, Kwasi. *Truth Crushed to the Earth Will Rise Again: The EAST Organization and the Principles and Practice of Black Nationalist Development.* Trenton: Africa World Press, 2005.

Krige, Eileen Jensen. *The Social System of the Zulus.* Pietermaritzburg: Shuter & Shooter, 1965 [1936].

Kulubally, Mansong, ed. *We Must Come Together*, vol. 4. Jacksonville, FL: Some Positive People, 1992.

Kunjufu, Jawanza. *Black Economics: Solutions for Economic and Community Empowerment.* Chicago: African American Images, 1991.

Kusimba, Chapurukha M. *The Rise and Fall of Swahili States.* Walnut Creek: AltaMira Press, 1999.

Kymlicka, Will. *Multicultural Citizenship: A Liberal Theory of Minority Rights.* New York: Oxford University Press, 1995.

Landsman, Julie, and Chance W. Lewis, eds. *White Teachers/Diverse Classrooms.* Sterling, VA: Stylus, 2006.

Lemelle, Sidney, and Robin D. G. Kelley, eds. *Imagining Home: Class, Culture, and Nationalism in the African diaspora.* London: Verso, 1994.

Levine, Naomi, and Richard Cohen. *Ocean Hill-Brownsville: Schools In Crisis – A Case History.* New York: Popular Library, 1969.

Litwicki, Ellen M. *America's Public Holidays, 1865–1920.* Washington: Smithsonian Institution Press, 2000.

Lorini, Alessandra. *Rituals of Race: American Public Culture and the Search For Racial Democracy.* Charlottesville: University of Virginia Press, 1999.

Lowenthal, David. *The Past is a Foreign Country.* Cambridge: Cambridge University Press, 1985.

——. *The Heritage Crusade and the Spoils of History.* Cambridge: Cambridge University Press, 1998.

MacAloon, John J., ed. *Rite, Drama, Festival, Spectacle: Rehearsals Toward A Theory of Cultural Performance.* Philadelphia: The Institute for the Study of Human Issues, 1984.

Macdonald, Sharon, and Gordon Fyfe, eds. *Theorizing Museums: Representing Identity and Diversity in a Changing World.* Oxford: Blackwell Publishers, 1996.

Madhubuti, Haki R. *Kwanzaa: A Progressive and Uplifting African American Holiday.* Chicago: Third World Press, 1972.

——. *Enemies: The Clash of Races.* Chicago: Third World Press, 1978.

——. *Groundwork: New and Selected Poems of Don Lee / Haki R. Madhubuti from 1966–1996.* Chicago: Third World Press, 1996.

Magubane, Bernard Makhosezwe. *The Ties that Bind: African-American Consciousness of Africa.* Trenton: Africa World Press, Inc., 1987.

Makinya, Sister (H. Smith). *Kwanza.* Berkeley: Educational Services Associates, 1971.

Marable, Manning. *Race, Reform, and Rebellion: The Second Reconstruction In Black America, 1945–1982.* Jackson: The University Press of Mississippi, 1984.

Marchand, Roland. *Creating the Corporate Soul: The Rise of Public Relations and Corporate Imagery.* Berkeley: University of California Press, 1998.

Masotti, Louis H., and Don R. Bowen, eds. *Riots and Rebellion: Civil Violence in the Urban Community*. Beverly Hills: Sage Publications, 1968.

Massey, Doreen. *Space, Place, and Gender*. Minneapolis: University of Minnesota Press, 1994.

Matustik, Martin J. *Postnational Identity: Critical Theory and Existential Philosophy in Habermas, Kierkegaard, and Havel*. New York: The Guilford Press, 1993.

Mazloomi, Carolyn. *Textural Rhythms: Quilting the Jazz Tradition*. West Chester, OH: Paper Moon Publishing, 2007.

Mazrui, Alamin. *Swahili Beyond the Boundaries: Literature, Language, and Identity*. Athens: Ohio University Press, 2007.

McClester, Cedric. *Kwanzaa: Everything You Always Wanted to Know But Didn't Know Where to Ask*. New York: Gumbs & Thomas, 1985.

McEvoy, James, and Abraham Miller, eds. *Black Power and Student Rebellion*. Belmont: Wadsworth Publishing Company, Inc., 1969.

McInerney, Peter K. *Time and Experience*. Philadelphia: Temple University Press, 1991.

McSpadden, J. Walker. *The Book of Holidays*. New York: Thomas Crowell, 1958.

Meier, August. *Negro Thought in America: Racial Ideologies in the Age of Booker T. Washington, 1880–1915*. Ann Arbor: University of Michigan Press, 1988 [1963].

Melzer, Arthur M., Jerry Weinberger, and M. Richard Zinman, eds. *Multiculturalism and American Democracy*. Kansas: University Press of Kansas, 1998.

Merelman, Richard M. *Representing Black Culture: Racial Conflict and Cultural Politics in the United States*. New York: Routledge, 1995.

Miller, Daniel, ed. *Unwrapping Christmas*. Oxford: Clarendon Press, 1993.

Mintz, Sidney, and Richard Price. *The Birth of African-American Culture – An Anthropological Perspective*. Boston: Beacon Press, 1976.

Moore, Kevin. *Museums and Popular Culture*. London: Cassell, 1997.

Moore, Richard B. *The Name "Negro": Its Origin and Evil Use*. Baltimore: Black Classic Press, 1992.

Morgan, Edmund S. *American Slavery American Freedom: The Ordeal of Colonial Virginia*. New York: W.W. Norton Company, 1975.

Morgan, Philip D. *Slave Counterpoint: Black Culture in the Eighteenth Century Chesapeake & Lowcountry*. Chapel Hill: University of North Carolina Press, 1998.

Morris, Aldon D., and Carol McClurg Mueller, eds. *Frontiers in Social Movement Theory*. New Haven: Yale University Press, 1992.

Moses, Wilson Jeremiah. *The Golden Age of Black Nationalism, 1850–1925*. New York: Oxford University Press, 1978.

——. *The Wings of Ethiopia: Studies in African-American Life and Letters*. Ames: Iowa University Press, 1990.

——, ed. *Classical Black Nationalism from the American Revolution to Marcus Garvey*. New York: New York University Press, 1996.

——. *Afrotopia: The Roots of African American Popular History*. Cambridge, UK: Cambridge University Press, 1998.

Mudimbe, V.Y. *The Invention of Africa: Gnosis, Philosophy, and the Order of Knowledge*. Bloomington: Indiana University Press, 1988.

——. *The Idea of Africa*. Bloomington: Indiana University Press, 1994.

Murdoch, Jonathan. *Post-Structuralist Geography: A Guide to Relational Space*. Thousand Oaks, CA: Sage, 2006.

Murray, Albert. *The Omni Americans: Some Alternatives to the Folklore of White Supremacy*. New York: Da Capo Press, Inc., 1970.

Myers, Robert J. *Celebrations: The Complete Book of American Holidays*. New York: Doubleday, 1972.

Napper, George. *Blacker Than Thou: The Struggle For Campus Unity*. Michigan: William B. Eerdmans Publishing Company, 1973.

Newton, Huey P. *To Die For The People: The Writings of Huey P. Newton*. New York: Random House, 1972.

——. *Revolutionary Suicide*. New York: Harcourt Brace Jovanovich, 1973.

Newton, Michael. *Bitter Grain: Huey Newton and the Black Panther Party*. Los Angeles: Holloway House Publishing, 1991 [1980].

Nkrumah, Kwame. *Ghana: The Autobiography of Kwame Nkrumah*. New York: International Publishers, 1957.

Nurse, Derek, and Thomas Spear. *The Swahili: Reconstructing the History and Language of an African Society, 800–1500*. Philadelphia: University of Pennsylvania Press, 1985.

Nye, David. *Image Worlds: Corporate Identities at General Electric, 1890–1920*. Cambridge, MA: MIT Press, 1985.

Nyerere, Julius K. *Freedom and Unity / Uhuru Na Umoja: A Selection from Writings and Speeches 1952–1965*. London: Oxford University Press, 1967.

——. *Freedom and Socialism / Uhuru Na Ujamaa: A Selection from Writings and Speeches 1965–1967*. London: Oxford University Press, 1968.

——. *Ujamaa: Essays on Socialism*. New York: Oxford University Press, 1968.

——. *Freedom and Development / Uhuru Na Maendeleo: A Selection Of Writings and Speeches 1968–1973*. London: Oxford University Press, 1973.

Ohmann, Richard. *Selling Culture: Magazines, Markets, and Class at the Turn Of the Century*. London: Verso, 1996.

Okoye, Felix N. *The American Image: Myth and Reality*. Buffalo: Black Academy Press, Inc., 1971.

O'Reilly, Kenneth. *Racial Matters: The FBI's Secret File On Black America, 1960–1972*. New York: The Free Press, 1989.

——. *Black Americans: The FBI Files*. New York: Carroll & Graf Publishers, Inc., 1994.

Orsi, Robert A. *Thank You, St. Jude: Women's Devotion to the Patron Saint of Hopeless Causes*. New Haven: Yale University Press, 1996.

O'Toole, James. *Watts and Woodstock: Identity and Culture in the United States and South Africa*. New York: Holt, Rinehart, and Winston Inc., 1973.

Ottaway, Marina, and David. *Afrocommunism*. New York: Africana Publishing Company, 1986.

Paris, Peter J. *The Spirituality of African Peoples: The Search For a Common Moral Discourse*. Minneapolis: Fortress Press, 1995.

Paschal, Andrew G., ed. *A W.E.B. Du Bois Reader*. New York: Macmillan Publishing Company, 1971.

Pickney, Alphonso. *Red, Black, and Green: Black Nationalism in the United States.* Cambridge: Cambridge University Press, 1976.

Piersen, William D. *Black Legacy: America's Hidden Heritage.* Amherst: The University Of Massachusetts Press, 1993.

Porter, Dorothy, ed. *Negro Protest Pamphlets.* New York: Arno Press, 1969.

——, ed. *Early Negro Writing, 1760–1837.* Boston: Beacon Press, 1971.

Quaynor, Thomas Addo. *A Documented History of Black Consciousness.* New York: Vantage Press, 1986.

Rahier, Jean Muteba. *Representations of Blackness and the Performance of Identities.* Westport: Bergin and Garvey, 1999.

Rajchman, John. *The Identity in Question.* New York: Routledge, 1995.

Raleigh Yow, Valerie. *Recording Oral History: A Practical Guide For Social Scientists.* California: Sage Publications Inc., 1994.

Rattray, Capt. R.S. *Ashanti.* Oxford: Oxford University Press, 1923.

——. *Religion & Art in Ashanti.* Oxford: Oxford University Press, 1927.

——. *The Tribes of the Ashanti Hinterland.* Oxford: Oxford University Press, 1932.

——. *The Tribes of the Ashanti Hinterland: Volume II.* Oxford: Oxford University Press, 1932.

Restad, Penne L. *Christmas in America: A History.* New York: Oxford University Press, 1995.

Robinson, Armstead L., Craig C. Foster, and Donald H. Ogilvie, eds. *Black Studies in the University: A Symposium.* New Haven: Yale University Press, 1969.

Root, Deborah. *Cannibal Culture: Art, Appropriation, & the Commodification of Difference.* Boulder: Westview Press, 1996.

Rose, Peter I., ed. *Americans from Africa: Old Memories, New Moods.* New York: Atherton Press Inc., 1970.

——, ed. *Americans from Africa: Slavery and Its Aftermath.* New York: Atherton Press Inc., 1970.

Rose, Tricia. *Black Noise: Rap Music and Black Culture in Contemporary America.* Hanover: Wesleyan University Press, 1994.

Rosenzweig, Roy, and David Thelen. *The Presence of the Past: Popular Uses of History in American Life.* New York: Columbia University Press, 1998.

Ross Barnett, Marguerite. *The Politics of Cultural Nationalism in South India.* Princeton: Princeton University Press, 1976.

Rossman, Marlene L. *Multicultural Marketing: Selling to a Diverse America.* New York: AMACOM, 1994.

Rutherford, Jonathan. *Identity: Community, Culture, Difference.* London: Lawrence & Wishart, 1990.

Ryan, Bill. *Making Capital from Culture: The Corporate Form of Capitalist Cultural Production.* Berlin: Walter de Gruyter, 1992.

Ryan, Mary P. *Civic Wars: Democracy and Public Life in the American City During the Nineteenth Century.* Berkeley: University of California Press, 1997.

Salaam, Kalamu Ya. *What is Life?: Reclaiming The Black Blues Self.* Chicago: Third World Press, 1994.

Sales, Jr., William W. *From Civil Rights to Black Liberation: Malcolm X and the Organization of Afro American Unity.* Boston: South End Press, 1994.

Santino, Jack. *All Around the Year: Holidays and Celebrations in American Life*. Urbana: University of Illinois Press, 1994.

——, ed. *Halloween and other Festivals of Death and Life*. Knoxville: The University of Tennessee Press, 1994.

——. *New Old Fashioned Ways: Holidays and Popular Culture*. Knoxville: The University of Tennessee Press, 1996.

Sarpong, Peter. *The Sacred Stools of the Akan*. Ghana: Ghana Publishing Corporation, 1971.

Sarup, Madan. *Identity, Culture, and the Postmodern World*. Athens: The University of Georgia Press, 1996.

Senghor, Leopold Sedar. *On African Socialism*. New York: Frederick A. Praeger, 1968.

Schaefer, Lola M. *Kwanzaa*. Mankato, MN: Pebble Books, 2001.

Schein, Richard H., ed. *Landscape and Race in the United States*. New York: Routledge, 2006.

Schiller, Herbert I. *Culture Inc: The Corporate Takeover of Public Expression*. New York: Oxford University Press, 1989.

Schmidt, Leigh Eric. *Consumer Rites: The Buying and Selling of American Holidays*. Princeton: Princeton University Press, 1995.

Schreiber, Alfred L. *Multicultural Marketing: Selling to the New America*. Chicago: NTC Business Books, 2001.

Schulberg, Budd, ed. *From the Ashes: Voices of Watts*. New York: New American Library, 1967.

Seale, Bobby. *A Lonely Rage: The Autobiography of Bobby Seale*. New York: New York Times Press, 1978.

Searle, John. *Speech Acts*. Cambridge: Cambridge University Press, 1969.

Servon, Lisa J. *Bootstrap Capital: Microenterprises and the American Poor*. Washington, DC: Brookings Institution Press, 1999.

Sheehy, Gail. *Panthermania: The Clash of Black Against Black in One American City*. New York: Harper & Row Publishers, 1971.

Sims, Edward. *Umoja Karamu: A Ritual for the Black Family*. Philadelphia, 1971.

Skinner, Elliott P. *African American and U.S. Policy Toward Africa 1850–1924: In Defense of Black Nationality*. Washington: Howard University Press, 1995.

Slater, Don. *Consumer Culture & Modernity*. Cambridge, UK: Polity Press, 1997.

Smelser, Neil J., and Jeffrey C. Alexander, eds. *Diversity and Its Discontents: Cultural Conflict and Common Ground in Contemporary American Society*. Princeton: Princeton University Press, 1999.

Smethurst, James Edward. *The Black Arts Movement: Literary Nationalism in the 1960s and 1970s*. Chapel Hill: University of North Carolina Press, 2005.

Smith, Anthony D. *The Ethnic Origins of Nations*. Oxford: Blackwell Publishers Ltd., 1986.

Smith, Robert C. *Racism in the Post-Civil Rights Era: Now You See It, Now You Don't*. Albany: State University of New York Press, 1995.

——. *We Have No Leaders: African Americans in the Post-Civil Rights Era*. New York: State University of New York Press, 1996.

Smock, Raymond W., ed. *Booker T. Washington in Perspective: Essays of Louis Harlan*. Jackson: University of Mississippi Press, 1988.

Soja, Edward. *Postmodern Geographies: The Reassertion of Space in Critical Social Theory*. London: Verso, 1989.

——. *Thirdspace: Journeys to Los Angeles and Other Real-and-Imagined Places*. Cambridge, MA: Blackwell, 1996.

Sonenshein, Raphael F. *Politics in Black and White: Race and Power in Los Angeles*. Princeton: Princeton University Press, 1993.

Spencer, Jon Michael. *The Rhythms of Black Folk: Race, Religion and Pan-Africanism*. Trenton: Africa World Press, Inc., 1995.

Spruill Redford, Dorothy. *Somerset Homecoming: Recovering a Lost Heritage*. New York: Doubleday, 1988.

Staniland, Martin. *American Intellectuals and African Nationalists, 1955–1970*. New Haven: Yale University Press, 1991.

Stewart, Charles, and Rosalind Shaw, eds. *Syncretism/Anti-Syncretism: The Politics of Religious Synthesis*. New York: Routledge, 1994.

St. Julien, Mtumishi. *Upon the Shoulders of Elephants We Reach the Sky*. New Orleans: Runagate Press, 1995.

Stuckey, Sterling, ed. *The Ideological Origins of Black Nationalism*. Boston: Beacon Press, 1972.

——. *Slave Culture: Nationalist Theory & The Foundations of Black America*. New York: Oxford University Press, 1987.

——. *Going Through the Storm: The Influence of African American Art in History*. New York: Oxford University Press, 1994.

Sundquist, Eric J. *To Wake the Nations: Race in the Making of American Literature*. London: Harvard University Press, 1993.

Sutherland, Marcia. *Black Authenticity: A Psychology for Liberating People of African Decent*. Chicago: Third World Press, 1997.

Tackwood, Louis. *The Glass House Tapes*. New York: Avon Books, 1973.

Taylor, Charles. *Multiculturalism: Examining the Politics of Recognition*. Princeton: Princeton University Press, 1994.

Taylor, Quintard. *In Search of the Racial Frontier: African Americans In the American West, 1528–1990*. New York: W.W. Norton, 1998.

Thomas, Bert J., ed. *The Struggle For Liberation: From DuBois to Nyerere*. Brooklyn: Theo Gaus, Ltd., 1982.

Thomas, Garen Eileen. *Santa's Kwanzaa*. New York: Hyperion Books for Children, 2004.

Tomlinson, John. *Cultural Imperialism*. Baltimore: The Johns Hopkins University Press, 1991.

Toop, David. *Rap Attack 3: African Rap to Global Hip Hop*. London: Serpents Tail, 2000 [1984].

Toure, Ahmed Sekou. *Revolution, Culture, and Panafricanism*. Conakry, Republic of Guinea: The Press Office At State House, 1978.

Toure, Sekou. *Toward Full Re-Africanization*. Paris: Presence Africaine, 1959.

Travers, Len. *Celebrating the Fourth: Independence Day and the Rites of Nationalism in the Early Republic*. Amherst: University of Massachusetts Press, 1997.

—, ed. *Encyclopedia of American Holidays and National Days*, vols. 1 & 2. Westport: Greenwood Press, 2006.

Ture, Kwame, and Charles V. Hamilton. *Black Power: The Politics of Liberation*. New York: Vintage Books, 1992.

Turner, Victor, ed. *Celebration: Studies in Festivity and Ritual*. Washington: Smithsonian Institution Press, 1982.

Van Deburg, William L. *New Day in Babylon: The Black Power Movement and American Culture, 1965–1975*. Chicago: University of Chicago Press, 1992.

—, ed. *Modern Black Nationalism: From Marcus Garvey to Louis Farrakhan*. New York: New York University Press, 1997.

Verge, Arthur C. *Paradise Transformed: Los Angeles During the Second World War*. Dubuque: Kendall Hunt Publishing Company, 1993.

Von Eschen, Penny M. *Race Against Empire: Black Americans and Anticolonialism 1937–1957*. Ithaca: Cornell University Press, 1997.

Wahlman, Maude Southwell. *Signs and Symbols: African Images in American Quilts*. New York: Studio Books, 1993.

Waits, William B. *The Modern Christmas in America: A Cultural History of Gift Giving*. New York: New York University Press, 1994 [1993].

Walker, Susannah. *Style & Status: Selling Beauty to African American Women, 1920–1975*. Lexington: The University Press of Kentucky, 2007.

Ward, Douglas Turner. *Happy Ending and Day of Absence: Two Plays by Douglas Turner Ward*. New York: The Third Press, 1966.

Washington, Booker T. *The Negro in Business*. New York: AMS Press, 1971 [1907].

Weems, Robert. *Desegregating the Dollar: African American Consumerism in the Twentieth Century*. New York: New York University Press, 1998.

Weil, Stephen E. *Rethinking the Museum and other Meditations*. Washington: Smithsonian Institution Press, 1990.

Weisbord, Robert G. *Ebony Kinship: Africa, Africans, and the Afro-American*. Westport: Greenwood Press Inc., 1973.

Wertheimer, Jack. *The Uses of Tradition: Jewish Continuity in the Modern Era*. New York: The Jewish Theological Seminary of America, 1992.

West, Cornell. *Keeping Faith: Philosophy and Race in America*. New York: Routledge, 1993.

Wheeler, B. Gordon. *Black California: The History of African Americans in the Golden State*. New York: Hippocrene Books Inc., 1993.

Whiteley, Wilfred. *Swahili: The Rise of a National Language*. London: Methuen & Co., 1974 [1969].

Wiggins, William H. *O Freedom!: Afro-American Emancipation Celebrations*. Knoxville: The University of Tennessee Press, 1987.

Willett, Cynthia. *Theorizing Multiculturalism: A Guide to Current Debate*. Oxford: Blackwell Publishers Ltd., 1998.

Williams, Evelyn. *Inadmissible Evidence: The Story of the Afro-American Trial Lawyer Who Defended the Liberation Army*. New York: Lawrence Hill Books, 1993.

Williams, Nancy. *A Kwanzaa Celebration Pop-Up Book*. New York: Little Simon, 1995.

Williams, Jr., Vernon J. *Rethinking Race: Franz Boas and His Contemporaries*. Lexington: The University Press of Kentucky, 1996.

Willoughby, W.C. *The Soul of the Bantu: A Sympathetic Study of the Magico-Religious Practices and Beliefs of the Bantu Tribes of Africa.* London: Student Christian Movement, 1928.

Winbush Riley, Dorothy. *The Complete Kwanzaa: Celebrating Our Cultural Harvest.* New York: HarperCollins, 1995.

Woodard, Komozi. *A Nation Within a Nation: Amiri Baraka (LeRoi Jones) & Black Power Politics.* Chapel Hill: University of North Carolina Press, 1999.

Wright, Jr., Nathan. *Black Power and Urban Unrest.* New York: Hawthorne Books, 1967.

Wright, Richard. *Black Power: A Record of Reactions in a Land of Pathos.* New York: Harper and Brothers, 1954.

Ziff, Bruce, and Pratima V. Rao, eds. *Borrowed Power: Essays on Cultural Appropriation.* New Brunswick: Rutgers University Press, 1997.

# Appendix

| HOLIDAY/CELEBRATION (COMMENCED) | OBSERVED (DATE) |
| --- | --- |
| Martin Luther King Jr.'s Birthday (1969) (1983)[1] | 3RD MONDAY IN JANUARY |
| Negro History Week (1926) /Black History Month (1976) | MONTH OF FEBRUARY |
| Abraham Lincoln's Birthday | FEBRUARY 12 |
| Black Love Day (1993) | FEBRUARY 13 |
| Valentine's Day | FEBRUARY 14 |
| Frederick Douglass' Birthday | FEBRUARY 14 |
| Presidents' Day (Uniform Monday Holiday Act – 1971)[2] | 3RD MONDAY IN FEBRUARY |
| Malcolm X Day (Assassination – 1966) | FEBRUARY 21 |
| A Day of Praise (1998) | SATURDAY BEFORE EASTER |
| Easter | MARCH 23 (2008) |
| Ancestor Honor Day (1998) | 3RD MONDAY IN MAY |
| Malcolm X's Birthday (1965) | MAY 19 |
| African Freedom Day (1958) / African Liberation Day (1963) | MAY 25 |
| Memorial Day | 4TH MONDAY IN MAY |
| Juneteenth (1865) | JUNE 19 |
| Independence Day | JULY 4 |
| African American Heritage Month (1980) | MONTH OF AUGUST |
| Marcus Garvey's Birthday | AUGUST 17 |
| Labor Day | 1ST MONDAY IN SEPTEMBER |
| Indigenous People Day / African Holocaust Day (1992) | SUNDAY BEFORE COLUMBUS |
| Columbus Day | 2ND MONDAY IN OCTOBER |
| Black Solidarity Day (1969) | 1ST MONDAY IN NOVEMBER |
| Election Day | 1ST TUESDAY IN NOVEMBER |
| Umoja Karamu (1969) | 4TH SUNDAY IN NOVEMBER |
| Thanksgiving Day | 4TH THURSDAY IN NOVEMBER |
| Christmas Day | DECEMBER 25 |
| Kwanzaa (1966) | DECEMBER 26 – JANUARY 1 |

(2008)

### January

| S | M | T | W | TH | F | S |
|---|---|---|---|---|---|---|
|  |  | 1 | 2 | 3 | 4 | 5 |
| 6 | 7 | 8 | 9 | 10 | 11 | 12 |
| 13 | 14 | 15 | 16 | 17 | 18 | 19 |
| 20 | 21 | 22 | 23 | 24 | 25 | 26 |
| 27 | 28 | 29 | 30 | 31 |  |  |

### February

| S | M | T | W | TH | F | S |
|---|---|---|---|---|---|---|
|  |  |  |  |  | 1 | 2 |
| 3 | 4 | 5 | 6 | 7 | 8 | 9 |
| 10 | 11 | 12 | 13 | 14 | 15 | 16 |
| 17 | 18 | 19 | 20 | 21 | 22 | 23 |
| 24 | 25 | 26 | 27 | 28 | 29 |  |

### March

| S | M | T | W | TH | F | S |
|---|---|---|---|---|---|---|
|  |  |  |  |  |  | 1 |
| 2 | 3 | 4 | 5 | 6 | 7 | 8 |
| 9 | 10 | 11 | 12 | 13 | 14 | 15 |
| 16 | 17 | 18 | 19 | 20 | 21 | 22 |
| 23 | 24 | 25 | 26 | 27 | 28 | 29 |
| 30 | 31 |  |  |  |  |  |

### April

| S | M | T | W | TH | F | S |
|---|---|---|---|---|---|---|
|  |  | 1 | 2 | 3 | 4 | 5 |
| 6 | 7 | 8 | 9 | 10 | 11 | 12 |
| 13 | 14 | 15 | 16 | 17 | 18 | 19 |
| 20 | 21 | 22 | 23 | 24 | 25 | 26 |
| 27 | 28 | 29 | 30 |  |  |  |

### May

| S | M | T | W | TH | F | S |
|---|---|---|---|---|---|---|
|  |  |  |  | 1 | 2 | 3 |
| 4 | 5 | 6 | 7 | 8 | 9 | 10 |
| 11 | 12 | 13 | 14 | 15 | 16 | 17 |
| 18 | 19 | 20 | 21 | 22 | 23 | 24 |
| 25 | 26 | 27 | 28 | 29 | 30 | 31 |

### June

| S | M | T | W | TH | F | S |
|---|---|---|---|---|---|---|
| 1 | 2 | 3 | 4 | 5 | 6 | 7 |
| 8 | 9 | 10 | 11 | 12 | 13 | 14 |
| 15 | 16 | 17 | 18 | 19 | 20 | 21 |
| 22 | 23 | 24 | 25 | 26 | 27 | 28 |
| 29 | 30 |  |  |  |  |  |

### July

| S | M | T | W | TH | F | S |
|---|---|---|---|---|---|---|
|  |  | 1 | 2 | 3 | 4 | 5 |
| 6 | 7 | 8 | 9 | 10 | 11 | 12 |
| 13 | 14 | 15 | 16 | 17 | 18 | 19 |
| 20 | 21 | 22 | 23 | 24 | 25 | 26 |
| 27 | 28 | 29 | 30 |  |  |  |

### August

| S | M | T | W | TH | F | S |
|---|---|---|---|---|---|---|
|  |  |  |  |  | 1 | 2 |
| 3 | 4 | 5 | 6 | 7 | 8 | 9 |
| 10 | 11 | 12 | 13 | 14 | 15 | 16 |
| 17 | 18 | 19 | 20 | 21 | 22 | 23 |
| 24 | 25 | 26 | 27 | 28 | 29 | 30 |
| 31 |  |  |  |  |  |  |

### September

| S | M | T | W | TH | F | S |
|---|---|---|---|---|---|---|
|  | 1 | 2 | 3 | 4 | 5 | 6 |
| 7 | 8 | 9 | 10 | 11 | 12 | 13 |
| 14 | 15 | 16 | 17 | 18 | 19 | 20 |
| 21 | 22 | 23 | 24 | 25 | 26 | 27 |
| 28 | 29 | 30 |  |  |  |  |

### October

| S | M | T | W | TH | F | S |
|---|---|---|---|---|---|---|
|  |  |  | 1 | 2 | 3 | 4 |
| 5 | 6 | 7 | 8 | 9 | 10 | 11 |
| 12 | 13 | 14 | 15 | 16 | 17 | 18 |
| 19 | 20 | 21 | 22 | 23 | 24 | 25 |
| 26 | 27 | 28 | 29 | 30 | 31 |  |

### November

| S | M | T | W | TH | F | S |
|---|---|---|---|---|---|---|
|  |  |  |  |  |  | 1 |
| 2 | 3 | 4 | 5 | 6 | 7 | 8 |
| 9 | 10 | 11 | 12 | 13 | 14 | 15 |
| 16 | 17 | 18 | 19 | 20 | 21 | 22 |
| 23 | 24 | 25 | 26 | 27 | 28 | 29 |
| 30 |  |  |  |  |  |  |

### December

| S | M | T | W | TH | F | S |
|---|---|---|---|---|---|---|
|  | 1 | 2 | 3 | 4 | 5 | 6 |
| 7 | 8 | 9 | 10 | 11 | 12 | 13 |
| 14 | 15 | 16 | 17 | 18 | 19 | 20 |
| 21 | 22 | 23 | 24 | 25 | 26 | 27 |
| 28 | 29 | 30 | 31 |  |  |  |

[1] Grassroots observance on January 15 beginning 1969; Congressional Act (1983).

[2] George Washington's birthday observed on February 22 until Uniform Monday Holiday Act (1971) moved it to the third Monday in February, Presidents' Day. Abraham Lincoln's birthday also merged under Presidents' Day.

# Index